Soul of the Age

Soul of the Age

The Life, Mind and World of William Shakespeare

JONATHAN BATE

VIKING

an imprint of

PENGUIN BOOKS

VIKING

Published by the Penguin Group
Penguin Books Ltd, 80 Strand, London WC2R ORL, England
Penguin Group (USA) Inc., 375 Hudson Street, New York, New York 10014, USA
Penguin Group (Canada), 90 Eglinton Avenue East, Suite 700, Toronto, Ontario, Canada M4P 2Y3
(a division of Pearson Penguin Canada Inc.)
Penguin Ireland, 25 St Stephen's Green, Dublin 2, Ireland
(a division of Penguin Books Ltd)
Penguin Group (Australia), 250 Camberwell Road, Camberwell, Victoria 3124, Australia
(a division of Pearson Australia Group Pty Ltd)
Penguin Books India Pvt Ltd, 11 Community Centre, Panchsheel Park, New Delhi – 110 017, India
Penguin Group (NZ), 67 Apollo Drive, Rosedale, North Shore 0632, New Zealand
(a division of Pearson New Zealand Ltd)
Penguin Books (South Africa) (Pty) Ltd, 24 Sturdee Avenue, Rosebank, Johannesburg 2196, South Africa

Penguin Books Ltd, Registered Offices: 80 Strand, London WC2R ORL, England

www.penguin.com

First published 2008
1

Copyright © Jonathan Bate, 2008

The moral right of the author has been asserted

Set in 12/14.75pt Monotype Bembo
Typeset by Rowland Phototypesetting Ltd, Bury St Edmunds, Suffolk
Printed in Great Britain by Clays Ltd, St Ives plc

A CIP catalogue record for this book is available from the British Library

ISBN: 978-0-670-91482-1

www.greenpenguin.co.uk

for Harry (if not England and St George)

Contents

List of Illustrations

The Seven Ages of Man: fourteenth-century German woodcut (BPK Images)

Portrait of a child aged 4 years, 1572, English School (private collection / The Bridgeman Art Library)

Engraving after Marcus Gheeraerts the younger, the 'Ditchley' portrait of Queen Elizabeth I (private collection)

Map of England and Wales, 1579, by Christopher Saxton (© Royal Geographical Society, London / The Bridgeman Art Library)

Close-up of Shakespeare country from Saxton's Map of Warwickshire and Leicestershire, 1576, (private collection)

Frontispiece to Michael Drayton's *Poly-olbion*, 1612 (private collection)

Thomas Digges, 'A Perfect Description of the Celestial Orbs', 1576 (The Wellcome Library, London)

Frontispiece to John Case's *Sphaera Civitatis*, 1588 (private collection)

Engraving of a schoolroom scene in Tudor times (private collection / The Bridgeman Art Library)

A page from the Geneva Bible, 1560 (private collection)

'A Young Man Leaning Against a Tree Among Roses' (bodycolour on vellum), by Nicholas Hilliard (Victoria and Albert Museum, London / The Bridgeman Art Library)

Frontispiece of Thomas Randolph's *Cornelianum dolium*, 1638 (The Wellcome Library, London)

The teenage sons of the fourth Earl of Pembroke: detail from *Philip Herbert (1584–1650), 4th Earl of Pembroke and his family* (oil on canvas), by Sir Anthony van Dyck (© Collection of the Earl of Pembroke, Wilton House, Wiltshire / The Bridgeman Art Library)

John Davies of Hereford: portrait frontispiece from his *Writing Schoolmaster*, 1633 (private collection)

'Shakespeare is the only biographer of Shakespeare'

'Every true man is a cause, a country, and an age'

Ralph Waldo Emerson, from 'Shakespeare' (1850)
and 'Self-Reliance' (1841)

'HIDE THY LIFE'

Motto of Epicurus, quoted in Michel de Montaigne,
'Of Glory', translated by John Florio (1603)

The Seven Ages of Man: fourteenth-century German woodcut, with the 'wheel of fortune' in the centre

Introduction

All the world's a stage,
And all the men and women merely players;
They have their exits and their entrances,
And one man in his time plays many parts,
His acts being seven ages. At first the infant,
Mewling and puking in the nurse's arms.
Then the whining schoolboy, with his satchel
And shining morning face, creeping like snail
Unwillingly to school. And then the lover,
Sighing like furnace, with a woeful ballad
Made to his mistress' eyebrow. Then a soldier,
Full of strange oaths and bearded like the pard,
Jealous in honour, sudden and quick in quarrel,
Seeking the bubble reputation
Even in the cannon's mouth. And then the justice,
In fair round belly with good capon lined,
With eyes severe and beard of formal cut,
Full of wise saws and modern instances.
And so he plays his part. The sixth age shifts
Into the lean and slippered pantaloon,
With spectacles on nose and pouch on side,
His youthful hose, well saved, a world too wide
For his shrunk shank, and his big manly voice,
Turning again toward childish treble, pipes
And whistles in his sound. Last scene of all,
That ends this strange eventful history,
Is second childishness and mere oblivion,
Sans teeth, sans eyes, sans taste, sans everything.

'*He was not of an age, but for all time!*' So wrote Ben Jonson in the poem of praise published in the First Folio of his friend and rival William Shakespeare's collected plays. My earlier book *The Genius of Shakespeare* took that claim seriously and suggested that what we mean by 'Shakespeare' is not just a life that lasted from 1564 to 1616. We also mean a body of words, characters, ideas and stage-images that have remained alive for four centuries because of their endless capacity for renewal and adaptation through the work of succeeding generations of actors and spectators, appreciative readers, and creative artists in every conceivable medium.

In the same poem Jonson also described Shakespeare as '*Soul of the Age*'. In this book, I turn to that claim, taking it equally seriously. The Elizabethans regarded the soul as 'the principle of life': through his works, Shakespeare gives life to his age. In trying to imagine what Jonson meant by his claim, we need to ask both 'what was it like *being Shakespeare*?' and 'what are the most telling ways in which Shakespeare's works embody – or rather *ensoul* – the world-picture of his age?' We have to shuttle back and forth between the Shakespearean mind and what has been usefully called 'the Shakespearean moment'. Shakespeare's uniqueness must be held in balance with his typicality.

Both '*not of an age*' and '*Soul of the Age*'. For Ralph Waldo Emerson, writing in nineteenth-century New England, Shakespeare was 'inconceivably wise', possessed of a brain so uniquely vast that no one can penetrate it. But at the same time, he was the incarnation of 'a cause, a country, and an age'. It is this double quality that makes Shakespeare, in Emerson's fine phrase, the *representative* poet.

The soul was considered to be the seat of both thought and feeling. Through his characters and dramatic situations, Shakespeare not only represented the essentials of what it is to be human:

he also gave immediate emotional life to the ideas of his age. My aim is to track him in that process, to observe the interplay of his mind and his world. The book is intended as an intellectual biography of the man in the context of the mind-set into which he was born and out of which his works were created.

In giving structure to the task, I have followed his own example and divided the life into seven ages. I like to think that Shakespeare would have adopted a similar procedure if he had been commissioned to write his own biography. Each of the seven ages invites us to consider a cultural moment and a broad theme: survival and environment for the infant, book-learning for the schoolboy, the nature of sexual desire for the lover, war and social unrest for the soldier, law and politics for the justice, wisdom and folly for the old man, the art of facing death for the age of 'oblivion'. What the approach cannot offer is an exact mapping whereby we see the Bard in swaddling clothes in the first age and in a particular lover's bed in the third – we do not have the evidence for such fancies and, even if we did, they would not take us very far into the *mind* of Shakespeare.

There is, though, a unifying image: that of the player. Each of humankind's ages, says Jaques in his famous speech in *As You Like It*, is a *part*, a dramatic role. That we are all actors is, of course, Shakespeare's leading metaphor throughout his career. That he was himself an actor as well as a play-maker is what sets him apart from his greatest theatrical contemporary, Christopher Marlowe.

Following the tracks that led from rural Stratford-upon-Avon to urban London and back again, Shakespeare's life feels cyclical, not sequential. For Prospero, time is a 'dark backward and abysm'. For Hamlet, the process of 'looking before and after' defines the 'large discourse' – the power of reason and speech – that makes man something more than a 'beast'. Shakespeare licenses us to loop backwards and forwards through his life as we try to read his mind and discover the senses in which he was soul of the age.

Because of the power of memory and imagination – two of Shakespeare's greatest gifts – the mind does not obey the same rule of time as the entropic human body. In writing a life of Shakespeare's mind that looks 'before and after', we might just be able to escape not only the deadening march of chronological sequence that is biography's besetting vice, but also the depressingly reductive narrative that George Bernard Shaw discerned in the life when it is told in the traditional way:

Everything we know about Shakespeare can be got into a half-hour sketch. He was a very civil gentleman who got round men of all classes; he was extremely susceptible to word-music and to graces of speech; he picked up all sorts of odds and ends from books and from the street talk of his day and welded them into his work . . . Add to this that he was, like all highly intelligent and conscientious people, business-like about money and appreciative of the value of respectability and the discomfort and discredit of Bohemianism; also that he stood on his social position and desired to have it affirmed by the grant of a coat of arms, and you have all we know of Shakespeare beyond what we gather from his plays.

Gathering what we can from his plays and poems: that is how we will write a biography that is true to him. But the process has immense perils. As the critic Barbara Everett writes in an acute essay on the problem of Shakespearean life-writing, 'if his biography is to be found it has to be here, in the plays and poems, *but never literally and never provably*'. That Shakespeare wrote in sonnet 37 of being 'made lame by Fortune's dearest spite' does not necessarily mean that he had a limp, as more than one biographer has supposed. An accurate triangulation of the life, the work and the world must be more subtle. It must look for traces of cultural DNA − little details such as a reference to Warwickshire or the knowledge of a particular school textbook − and must be prepared to make surprising connections in the style of Shakespeare's own inventive metaphorical imagination. We must by indirections find directions out.

FIRST AGE

Infant

At first the infant,
Mewling and puking in the nurse's arms.

Portrait of a child aged 4 years (painted in 1572)

1. Stratford 1564

Here begins the plague

Exit pursued by a bear: Antigonus is torn to pieces. A clownish young shepherd witnesses his death on the land and many more at sea as a tempest-tossed ship is swallowed by the waves. 'A sad tale's best for winter,' little Prince Mamillius has said, before being struck by death himself. But Shakespeare's *Winter's Tale* veers from tragedy to comedy. Young Shepherd's breathless description of heavy matters is counterpointed against Old Shepherd's amazed discovery of new life in the form of the abandoned baby Perdita. 'Thou met'st with things dying,' he serenely remarks to his son, 'I with things new born.'

In Shakespeare's England, birth and death went cheek by jowl. Each entry in the parish register of Holy Trinity Church, Stratford-upon-Avon, is encoded with a single letter: 'C' for christened, 'M' for married and 'B' for buried. A ceaseless procession of birth, copulation and death: human life stripped to its essentials. Shortly after the entry that reads '1564, Apr. 26. C. Gulielmus filius Johannes Shakspere' – 26 April 1564, christened, William, son of John Shakespeare – the entries marked 'B' begin to thicken on the page. There were no more than twenty deaths in the first half of 1564, well over 200 in the second. The population of this small but prosperous market town in the English midland county of Warwickshire was about 1,500, so more than one in seven were taken in those few months of devastation. The cause is duly noted in a marginal annotation opposite the burial entry for Oliver Gunne, apprentice: *hic incepit pestis*. Here begins the plague.

In August, the town council met in emergency session in the garden of the Gild Chapel, hoping that the outdoor air would be less contagious than that of the Gild Hall. They discussed relief for the plague victims. 'Burgess' (councillor) John Shakespeare gave a generous sum of money. The horror faced by the townspeople may be glimpsed from a contemporary account of a plague outbreak in London. If just one member of a family was struck down, the rest would have been closed up in the house to prevent the spread of infection:

What an unmatchable torment were it for a man to be barred up every night in a vast silent charnel-house! Hung (to make it more hideous) with lamps dimly and slowly burning, in hollow and glimmering corners: where all the pavement should, instead of green rushes, be strewed with blasted rosemary, withered hyacinths, fatal cypress and yew, thickly mingled with heaps of dead men's bones: the bare ribs of a father that begat him, lying there: here the chapless hollow skull of a mother that bore him.

The previous year, John and Mary Shakespeare had lost their infant Margaret at four months, and some time before that, another girl, Joan. Cause of deaths unknown. But the loss not uncommon – everyone knew infant mortality.

They were doubly lucky this time. William was what every respectable couple wanted: a son to maintain the family name and estate. His sex was their first stroke of good fortune. Second was his survival of the plague. What John and Mary could never know was that he would not merely survive, but make the Shakespeare name live as long as humankind has books and stories.

Plague was the single most powerful force shaping his life and those of his contemporaries. John Stow's annals of English history summarized the key events of the year of Shakespeare's birth. The previous autumn, Londoners had suffered terribly:

Forsomuch as the plague of pestilence was so hot in the city of London, there was no term kept at Michaelmas: to be short, the poor citizens of London were this year plagued with a threefold plague, pestilence, scarcity of money, and dearth of victuals: the misery whereof, were too long here to write, no doubt the poor remember it, the rich by flight into the countries made shift for themselves.

John Stow, denominated 'Citizen of London' on his title page, would not have bothered to record an outbreak of plague in a small town in the midlands. There is London and there is the rest of England. London is far bigger than every other conurbation. It is more densely populated, so the spread of plague is more rapid. And it is the location of the institutions that govern the nation: the royal court, the houses of parliament and the law courts, Lambeth Palace (London residence of the Archbishop of Canterbury and administrative headquarters of the Church of England). In bad times, the rich and their institutions could take flight to the country, leaving the London poor to shift for themselves. The royal court was supremely mobile, with the queen moving on a whim or a plague-warning from Whitehall in central London to one of her other palaces – Greenwich downstream, Hampton Court upstream, Richmond or Windsor secluded in their deer parks, or Nonsuch deep in rural Surrey.

It was a litigious age. Stow measures the seasons by the four terms of the legal year, when the courts were in session. During times of plague, as in Michaelmas term (October to December) 1563 and Hilary term (January to March) 1564, the judges and lawyers met out of town. Throughout Shakespeare's professional career, there were close links between the worlds of law and theatre. Many of his fellow-dramatists trained at the Inns of Court. Law students were a key element of the theatre audience. Hack writer Tom Nashe railed against the 'tedious dead vacation' when there were no lawyers to see his plays or buy his pamphlets. And, like the law courts, the acting companies travelled out of town when plague was severe.

So it was that plague determined several turning-points in Shakespeare's career. In January 1593, just as he was making his name as an actor turned playwright, an order went out from the Privy Council: 'Forasmuch as by the certificate of the last week it appeareth the infection doth increase . . . we think it fit that all manner of concourse and public meetings of the people at plays, bear-baitings, bowlings and other like assemblies for sports be forbidden.' Save for a few weeks' remission the following winter, the theatres remained closed for a year and a half. The actors toured, while a different Shakespeare emerged. The rewrite man, the patcher of old plays from the existing repertoire, turned himself into an original poet. In April 1593, he published 'the first heir' of his 'invention', *Venus and Adonis*. Its stylistic brilliance and risqué content made his name among the smart set. It became the best-selling long poem of the age, the favoured reading of under-graduates and Inns of Court men. Dedicated to Henry Wriothesley, the third Earl of Southampton, it was also a bid for the receipt of patronage.

The dedicatory epistle that begins the more serious and rhetori-cally elaborate follow-up poem, *The Rape of Lucrece*, published the next year, suggests that the bid was successful. Where Shakespeare's letter prefacing *Venus and Adonis* dwells on his 'hopeful expec-tation', the one attached to *Lucrece* speaks repeatedly of 'duty' and devoted service: 'What I have done is yours, what I have to do is yours, being part in all I have, devoted yours.' There is a strong possibility that Shakespeare spent part of the plague year in some form of service in Southampton's household at Titchfield in Hampshire.

The association with Southampton had three key consequences. It transformed Shakespeare from jobbing playwright to courtly poet, marked him out as the crossover man who could appeal equally to penny-paying groundlings and powerful courtiers or even the queen herself. Politically, it brought him into the orbit of the Earl of Essex, to whom young Southampton was devoted. This would have potentially dangerous consequences a few years later. And intellectually, it introduced him to the work of the Anglo-Italian man of letters John Florio, Southampton's tutor, through whom he was exposed to Italianate culture and, later, the essays of Michel de Montaigne, whose subtle, sympathetic mind was perfectly attuned to his own.

The plague of 1593–94 provided an enforced sabbatical after which Shakespeare returned to the theatre with a new-minted verbal art. In the next couple of years, he wrote the plays in which his literary style truly matures: the dazzlingly intellectual (Florioesque) *Love's Labour's Lost*, the miraculously imaginative *Midsummer Night's Dream* and the quicksilver *Romeo and Juliet*, with its growth from love's artifice to the heart's authenticity. When Mercutio dies with the words 'A plague o' both your houses', it is no idle oath: the play was written in the aftermath of a period when the households of many members of Shakespeare's London audience would have been struck by plague. And plague is indeed subtly woven into the plot: the reason Romeo does not get Friar Laurence's crucial letter is that Friar John is detained for fear that he might have been infected. Parents are supposed to die before their children, the old before the young. With plague, it is not always like that. The tragic irony of *Romeo and Juliet* is that the houses of both Capulet and Montague escape the plague, yet still the children die first. The final scene takes place in an ancestral tomb, but those who lie dead are the flower of a city's youth — Mercutio, Tybalt, Paris, Juliet and her Romeo.

Plague also shapes the deep structure of Shakespeare's imaginative world. As Queen Elizabeth secluded herself from infection at Richmond and Nonsuch, so Ferdinand King of Navarre and his courtiers in *Love's Labour's Lost* enclose themselves in a garden world. As *A Midsummer Night's Dream* counterpoints city and court (Athens) against green world and fairy lore (the wood), so Shakespeare always moved between two worlds: London for business and busy-ness, Stratford for home and rest. The classical poet Horace made a distinction between *negotium* (social, mercantile, legal and political transactions, the pursuit of wealth and power), always associated with the great city of Rome, and *otium* (peace, pastoral idleness), found on his country farm. Whenever asked 'Business or Pleasure?' we are inheritors of that Horatian choice. Pleasure is *otium*, business its opposite (the word *negotium* is derived from *otium* and the prefix *nec*, not). Like a second Rome, London was synonymous with *negotium*, while the quiet town on the edge of Arden Forest represented *otium*. Shakespeare knew all about the dialectic of Horace's two worlds from his reading in generations of pastoral literature, but he also lived the difference every time he walked or rode from his rented lodgings in London to his own home in Stratford. Plague was a key factor in determining the frequency of those journeys.

Mewling and puking

Even if you grow up to become the greatest writer the world has ever seen, you begin like every other baby. Mewling and puking. When William Shakespeare was born in April 1564, he doubtless mewled because he had come into the world that he would one day call 'this great stage of fools'. But in whose arms? Jaques addresses his 'seven ages' speech to a group of courtiers. In their world, a baby would have been passed straight to a wet-nurse, so it is dramatically appropriate that the infant is imagined mewling and puking in the *nurse's* arms, not a mother's. Shakespeare's mother Mary claimed kinship with the illustrious Warwickshire family of Arden, but is unlikely to have been in the position to hire a wet-nurse. Twenty years later, Shakespeare's wife Anne would breast-feed her own daughter.

But perhaps we should not attach too much significance to the choice of nurse as opposed to mother. Nurse could simply mean 'nourisher'. Shakespeare may have been the first person to take the word out of the nursery and use it in its modern sense, to apply it to general healthcare as opposed to the specific context of rearing an infant. In *The Comedy of Errors*, when the confusion created by the unrecognized presence of two sets of identical twins becomes so intense that Antipholus of Ephesus is supposed to have gone mad, his wife Adriana says:

> I will attend my husband, be his nurse,
> Diet his sickness, for it is my office,
> And will have no attorney but myself,
> And therefore let me have him home with me.

The juxtaposition of 'nurse', usually associated with mothers and infants, to 'attorney', a word belonging to the grown-up male world of the legal profession ('And then the justice . . .'), is typical of Shakespeare's mingling of not only 'the ages of man' but also the customary roles of men and women.

There aren't many babies in the plays. In tragedy and history, we hear whispers of sterility and infanticide. Richard III has no compunction in ordering the murder of the princes in the tower, King Lear curses the womb of his eldest daughter Goneril, Macbeth is tormented by the fact that he has no children to inherit his crown, while his wife talks of plucking her nipple from a baby's boneless gums and dashing the brains out. Given that she is a Lady and a future Queen of Scotland, the image of her doing her own breastfeeding, rather than relying on a wet-nurse, is an additional startling detail to set beside the violence.

The few babies that do appear – stage-dolls, one assumes – are given a hard time. When Paulina in *The Winter's Tale* brings Leontes his new-born daughter, she describes in beautiful detail how a baby appears to be a miniaturized 'print' of its parent:

> Behold, my lords,
> Although the print be little, the whole matter
> And copy of the father: eye, nose, lip,
> The trick of 's frown, his forehead, nay, the valley,
> The pretty dimples of his chin and cheek, his smiles,
> The very mould and frame of hand, nail, finger.

But Leontes is convinced his wife has been unfaithful to him:

> This brat is none of mine.
> It is the issue of Polixenes.
> Hence with it, and together with the dam
> Commit them to the fire!

Paulina's husband, Antigonus, saves the baby and takes her to the wilds of Polixenes' own kingdom of Bohemia. For his pains, he exits where we began – pursued by a bear, leaving the baby, named Perdita, the lost one, to be found by the shepherds, raised as a shepherdess and theatrically transformed back to the princess as which she was born.

In the bloody Roman play *Titus Andronicus*, it looks for a moment as though the black baby born of the clandestine affair between villainous Aaron the Moor and Tamora, Queen of Goths and Empress of Rome, will also be dispatched at birth. 'The empress sends it thee, thy stamp, thy seal, / And bids thee christen it with thy dagger's point.' But Aaron turns on the Nurse: 'Zounds, you whore! Is black so base a hue?' The baby's half-brother says he'll 'broach the tadpole on my rapier's point', but Aaron stabs the Nurse instead: 'Go to the empress, tell her this I said: [*He kills her*] / Weke, weke! So cries a pig preparèd to th'spit.' He saves his baby and leaves the city of Rome.

A little while later, an army of Goths is marching towards Rome. Being cast as the Second Goth Soldier in *Titus Andronicus* is probably not the summit of any actor's ambition, but Shakespeare has a way of giving life even to his bit-part characters. This chap seems to have a taste for architectural ruins. One imagines him touring the shires with bicycle clips and a battered copy of Pevsner's *Buildings of England*.

> Renownèd Lucius, from our troops I strayed
> To gaze upon a ruinous monastery.
> And as I earnestly did fix mine eye
> Upon the wasted building, suddenly
> I heard a child cry underneath a wall.

It is Aaron's baby. But what is a ruined monastery doing in a play set in ancient Rome? And why is it that a few lines later Aaron himself speaks of 'popish tricks and ceremonies'? Shakespeare is full of purposeful anachronisms whereby the past illuminates the present and vice versa. In the blink of an eye we have been transported from the ancient Roman empire to the modern Roman Catholic church, from an imagined Italy to the landscape of Shakespeare's own time, an England of 'bare ruined choirs where late the sweet birds sang'.

For defacing images

Winter 1563. Mary Shakespeare, born Mary Arden in the village of Wilmcote on the fringes of the forest of Arden, is pregnant for the third time. John Shakespeare, her husband, is a busy man. His father had farmed in the village of Snitterfield, but he has moved into the town of Stratford-upon-Avon. His glove business is going well. He deals in wool on the side. And he is making an impression in local government. First he was the town's ale-taster or 'conner', assisting at the leet court where people went to complain about false measures and watered ale. He weighed the bread and tasted the beer, ensuring the brew was good and wholesome. Then he became Constable. Then 'affeeror', whose business it was to levy fines in the local court. And then burgess, borough councillor. Now that Mary is pregnant with William, he is chamberlain, keeping the town's accounts.

That winter, he and his fellow-chamberlain John Taylor, shearman of Sheep Street, add a new entry: 'Item, payd for defasyng ymages in ye chappell – ij^s.' Two shillings, worth a dozen loaves of bread or a bottle of French wine or forty-eight tankards of ale (or, a generation later, twenty-four standing spaces to watch a play at the Globe), paid for the defacing of images in the chapel next door to the school on the corner of Church Street and Dead Lane.

The Gild of the Holy Cross had been at the heart of Stratford life for 300 years. Its members, both men and women, pledged to keep fraternal relations, to attend each other's funerals in Augustinian hoods and to make payments for the souls of the dead, whose masses were sung by priests in the chapel. The gild had maintained the free-school and almshouses for the poor.

Following the Protestant revolution, purgatory was abolished and prayers for the dead became redundant. The dead were either blessed and safe in heaven or damned and burning in hell, and that was that. And did not the Bible condemn graven images as idolatrous? The walls of the Gild Chapel had been covered in frescoes – there you could see St George and the dragon, the murder of Thomas Becket, local saints and English heroes, and, above the arch of the nave, a great cross, the risen Christ and the Last Judgement, showing the souls of the saved on their way to heaven, the devil and the seven deadly sins taking the damned to the other place, being marched via the primrose path of dalliance to the everlasting bonfire.

With lime and wash, and a two-shilling bill to follow, workmen covered over all these images, obliterating the signs of a shared faith and a folk memory. A few months later, Chamberlain Shakespeare's first son would be born into a new world, a new dispensation. But the wash of lime blanking out the old world was a thin layer. Scratch away at the surface and the old ways are still visible. Always between two worlds he would be, this poet of double vision.

William Shakespeare grew up to become the father of twins and in his work to be a mingler of comedy and tragedy, low life and high, prose and verse. He was a countryman who worked in the city, a teller of English folktales who was equally versed in the mythology of ancient Greece and Rome. His mind and world were poised between Catholicism and Protestantism, old feudal ways and new bourgeois ambitions, rational thinking and visceral instinct, faith and scepticism.

After the plague, the Reformation is the second great shadow cast across the moment of Shakespeare's infancy. He lived between the two great cataclysms in English history: the break from the universal Roman Catholic church and the execution of King Charles I. His plays were made possible by the first and helped to create the conditions that made possible the second.

For centuries, the staple of English drama had been the cycles of 'miracle' or 'mystery' plays, dramatizations of biblical stories organized by the gilds of tradesmen in the major towns and cities around the country. They were destroyed by the Protestant Reformation. In 1532, within months of King Henry VIII's defiance of the Vatican over his divorce from Catherine of Aragon, references to loyalty to the Pope were removed from the proclamation of the Chester cycle. In the 1540s, during the reign of the boy king, Edward VI, when hard-line Protestantism was established in England for the first time, the Mary plays were omitted from the

York cycle and the Feast of Corpus Christi, traditional occasion for the performances of the cycles, was suppressed. Protestant theology not only abhorred Catholic veneration of the Virgin Mary and the saints, but regarded the very act of representing God as a form of idolatry. As the frescoes were whitewashed in the Stratford Gild Chapel and the heads knocked off statues in churches across the land, so the Chester plays were performed for the last time in 1575. The following year the Diocesan Court of York banned the 'counterfeit or representation' of any part of the Trinity or the sacraments of baptism or Lord's Supper or anything tending to 'maintenance of superstition or idolatry'. Young Shakespeare might have caught a glimpse of ranting Herod in one of the last performances of the Coventry plays, which annually until 1579 brought thousands of spectators from across the region into Coventry on the feast of Corpus Christi. But by the time he began writing plays himself, the old religious drama was dead and buried.

2. The Discovery of England

A new theatre for a new state

Public playing had been banned altogether during the brief reign of Edward VI, but in 1559 Queen Elizabeth I personally drafted a document allowing travelling players to perform, provided that their plays were pre-licensed by the local Mayor or Justices of the Peace. 'Matters of religion or of the governance of the estate of the common weal' were not to be handled, save before audiences of 'grave and discreet persons', an exception that allowed more serious political matter to be touched upon in academic drama at Oxford and Cambridge and in plays performed before the lawyers of the Inns of Court, who were always hungry for intellectually stimulating entertainment.

There are many parallels between the Elizabethan drama and the contemporaneous 'Golden Age' theatre of Calderón and Lope de Vega in Spain. The big difference was that many Spanish plays were explicitly religious, based on the Bible or the lives of the saints, and profoundly shaped by Catholic sensibilities. The proscription of the cycle plays meant that Shakespeare's theatre, by contrast, was altogether secular. The old religious drama had offered its audiences a constant reminder that they were under the watchful eye of God. The new Elizabethan drama concentrated instead on people in relationship with each other and with society. When travelling players visited Stratford in Shakespeare's childhood, offering him his first glimpse of indoor theatre, the repertoire was moral but secular.

One of the effects of the break from the Roman church was a perceived need to buttress the English nation by proving the dignity of the English language and the native culture. Until the mid-sixteenth century, England had been part of Catholic Europe, of a united Christendom. The language of diplomacy and the law was also that of the Roman church: Latin. The reading of ancient Roman culture had long been at the centre of the educational system.

When Shakespeare was born in 1564, everything was changing. In a delicate balancing act called the Act of Settlement, Queen Elizabeth and her closest courtiers had established the Anglican church on a middle ground between the sacramental traditions of Catholicism, to which the majority of the people remained loyal, and the Protestant doctrines of grace and election that were being urged by the reformers. A semblance of stability was returning after the chaotic decade from 1547–58 during which the state had lurched from the radical Protestantism of Edward's reign to the Catholic revival of Mary's. Elizabeth's most brilliant political decision was to use her unmarried status as a political device. Her half-sister Mary had been hated because she had married Philip of Spain – not so much because he was a Roman Catholic as because the union effectively placed a foreign king on the English throne.

Elizabeth learned the lesson. To marry a French duke or a princeling from the Holy Roman Empire was not the solution. Instead, she preserved her virginity and proclaimed her marriage to the English nation itself. She set about unifying her people, encouraging a rhetoric in which she was empress of a new international power of independence and future greatness. She continued the work of her father, Henry VIII, in consolidating the power of the monarchy through bureaucracy and surveillance. Her naval entrepreneurs helped in the task, but so did a concerted campaign to create a national *culture*. The initial phase of this latter endeavour was entrusted in the 1560s to her favourite, Robert Dudley.

Five months after Shakespeare's birth, Dudley, Knight of the Garter and Master of the Horse to the Queen's Majesty, was created Earl of Leicester. The ceremony took place at Saint James's Palace in Whitehall on Michaelmas Day (the Feast of St Michael and All Angels, 29 September). Stow described the proceedings in detail far surpassing that of his other observations on the year 1564. His account offers a glimpse into the elaborate ceremonial world of the Elizabethan court:

First, the said Lord attended on the Queen's Highness, to the Chapel, and from the Chapel to service, and when he was returned to the Chamber of Presence, the said Lord with other[s] departed to the Lord Chamberlain's Chamber, and shifted them [i.e. put on their costumes], the said Lord Robert in his Sur-coat with the hood, his mantle borne before him by the Lord Hunsdon, and led by the Lord Clinton Lord Admiral by the right hand, and the Lord Strange on the left hand, in their Parliament robes, Garter bearing the Patent, and before him the Officers of Arms, and so proceeded into the Chamber of Presence, where the Queen's Highness sat under the cloth of Estate with the Noble men on each side of her, the Ambassador of France was also present with another stranger an Italian, and when the fair Lord with the other came in the Queen's sight, they made their obeisance three times, the said Lord kneeled down, after the which Garter presented the Letters patents to the Lord Chamberlain, and he presented the same to the Queen's Highness, who gave it to Sir William Cecil Secretary, who read the same with a loud voice, and at the words of *Creduimus*, the Lord of Hunsdon presented the Mantle to the Queen's Majesty.

And that is just the first sentence of an account that proceeds for several pages.

Here courtiership is a kind of theatre, which the drama of Shakespeare and his contemporaries will seek to replicate – a task in which they were assisted by the fact that more money was spent on the purchase of costumes than the commissioning of scripts. The kings, dukes and ladies in the plays would have looked impressively courtly not least because their wardrobe consisted in part of the second-hand clothes of courtiers: often when aristocrats died, they would bequeath items of clothing to their servants, who would sell them to the players. From his reading and his first-hand experience of submitting his work for the approval of the Master of the Revels, then of performing at court, Shakespeare learned the language and manners of courtiership. So his characters came to speak and to gesture, as well as to be dressed, in the manner of monarchs and their entourage. A Duke of Buckingham or an Earl of Pembroke in the audience might have seen himself mirrored in one of his ancestors in the chronicle plays.

Robert Dudley, Earl of Leicester, was a patron with a political purpose: he commissioned an array of publications, including history books and translations of the Latin classics as a way of flying the flag for English traditions and the English language. He saw that the drama could help in this work, so he also sponsored a small troupe of players. They toured the country – in Shakespeare's childhood, Stratford-upon-Avon was on their itinerary – and in 1574 they were given a royal patent to perform in London. By this time their leader was a man named James Burbage. He realized the potential offered by the massive expansion in the population of London that had occurred over the previous two generations: build a permanent playhouse and you have full control of your box-office and your programming. You also have the potential to establish an audience-base of repeat attendees in a way that was not possible when you were perpetually on the road.

In 1576 James Burbage took a twenty-one-year lease on a site in Shoreditch and set about building a theatre, working in partnership with his brother-in-law John Brayne, who some years before had embarked on a similar project, building the Red Lion on the Mile End road. By 1578, Burbage's theatre – simply called The Theatre – had become a landmark. A preacher at St Paul's Cross spoke of the 'gorgeous Playing-place erected in the fields', adding that it resembled 'the old heathenish Theatre at Rome' in being 'a showplace of all beastly and filthy matters'. The city of London was dominated by Puritan-leaning figures who for generations would habitually associate plays with 'unchastity', 'sedition' and 'uncomely matter'. That is why the public playhouses were always built in the 'liberties' on the margins of London to the north-east or south of the river Thames, outside the jurisdiction of the city fathers. It is also why Shakespeare took pleasure in teasing or exposing such puritanical figures as Malvolio in *Twelfth Night* and Angelo in *Measure for Measure*.

The establishment of a public theatre analogous to that of ancient Rome helped to do the work of making England seem like a new Rome. Besides, there was much politic wisdom and civic virtue to be found in the imitation of Seneca's tragedies. And, more important than this, the court needed entertainment for festivals, holidays and diplomatic visits. In 1581, the powers of Edmund Tilney, Master of the Revels, an official in the Lord Chamberlain's office at court, were expanded. Previously he had been responsible only for choosing court entertainment. Now, all plays – 'tragedies, comedies or shows' – were to be recited before him and he was given authority to 'order and reform, authorise and put [them] down'. This sounds like state censorship but was intended as an opportunity for him to familiarize himself with the repertoire in order to get the best shows to court. The licensing recitation was effectively an audition. The principle remained the same during Shakespeare's career, even though by that time the Master of Revels was given a script rather than a recitation. Technically speaking, all public performances were merely rehearsals in readiness for the summons to play at court. Whereas the Puritans of the city were enemies to the players, the court was where Shakespeare and his colleagues would find powerful friends.

In 1583, the twelve best actors from the existing companies were formed into the Queen's Men. They travelled the land – again, Stratford-upon-Avon was on the itinerary – with their markedly patriotic and Protestant repertoire. It has even been suggested that they were spies, reporting back to their masters at court on the mood of the nation.

Four years later, a new theatre, the Rose, opened in Southwark, in an area known for prostitution and gambling. Under the management of Philip Henslowe, it was used by several of the acting companies who over the next few years broke the monopoly of the Queen's Men. Among those who played there were Lord Strange's Men. Their patron, Ferdinando Stanley, Lord Strange (later Earl of Derby), had taken over some of Leicester's Men, just as he followed in Leicester's footsteps in supporting the publication of translations and other literary works. James Burbage's son Richard was a leading figure in the troupe. Several others from Strange's Men were to join Burbage in forming the core of a new company, the Lord Chamberlain's Men, in 1594, after the mysterious sudden death of their patron. Shakespeare's plays first emerge in the repertoire of Strange's at the Rose. It may be inferred that Burbage, who became his closest colleague, was someone he met very soon after making his way into the theatre world.

The licensing of the secular drama let the genie out of the bottle. Plays were supposed to inculcate virtue and civic obedience: to show the folly of rebellion, whether domestic or public, and to reveal the downfall of tyrants and the triumph of rightful monarchs. Inventive dramatists, good actors and quick-witted audience members did not, however, submit themselves to a didactic agenda. Their comedies played havoc with time-honoured customs of sexual restraint, law-abiding passivity, filial and wifely obedience. According to an altogether typical 'Puritan' anti-stage polemic by Stephen Gosson,

The argument of Tragedies is wrath, cruelty, incest, injury, murder either violent by sword, or voluntary by poison. The persons, Gods, Goddesses, juries, friends, kings, queens, and mighty men. The ground work of comedies is love, cozenage, flattery, bawdry, sly conveyance of whoredom; the persons, cooks, knaves, bawds, parasites, courtesans, lecherous old men, amorous young men.

With that sort of line-up, both tragedies and comedies had the potential to turn the world upside-down, especially as much of this unseemly matter was performed by cross-dressed young apprentices. No wonder those of a moral disposition and a value-system shaped by the biblical commandments were disturbed:

In stage plays for a boy to put on the attire, the gesture, the passions of a woman; for a mean person to take upon him the title of a prince with counterfeit port and train, is by outward signs to show themselves otherwise than they are, and so within the compass of a lie, which by Aristotle's judgement is naught of itself and to be fled.

When the Puritans took power in 1642, they closed the theatres. But, quite intangibly, those same theatres had prepared the way for the moment seven years later when the axe came down on the king's head in Whitehall. Where was it that Londoners had previously confronted the image of monarchs being removed from

their thrones? Where was it that they had seen ordinary people –
actors, who were still regarded as little better than rogues and
vagabonds – daring to look into the minds of princes, and in so
doing showing that kings and queens are not so much God's
vice-regents on earth as ordinary mortals like all the rest of us? In
the theatre.

Give me the map there

Early in *Henry IV Part 1*, the rebels bring out a map and discuss
how they will carve up the land when they win power. Their
respective territories will be bordered by rivers, 'sandy-bottomed
Severn' and 'smug and silver Trent'. The Trent flows across the
middle of England from west to east. It was traditionally regarded
as the boundary between the south and the north. This matters in
the play because the rebel Percy family are barons of the north. It
mattered to the Elizabethans because it was the northern earls with
their Catholic sympathies who were regarded as the greatest threat
to the unity of the state.

If you cross the Trent at Newark on the great road to York, it
still looks 'smug and silver'. Shakespeare must have made that
journey to have noticed this detail, but we do not know when he
did so. Early in his career, he may have acted with Pembroke's
Men, who toured to York. Both Pembroke's and Lord Strange's
Men, the other company with which he might have spent his early
career, played the western circuit, so he would have had ample
opportunity to observe the sandy bottom of the Severn at Shrewsbury, Worcester or Gloucester. In *Henry IV*, 'Wales beyond the
Severn shore' is earmarked for Owen Glendower, the north above
Trent for Hotspur and the 'south and east' for Mortimer. Like her
father Henry VIII, Queen Elizabeth took pride in holding England
and Wales together as one nation. A threefold division such as this
would have been abhorrent to her.

In 1592 the queen visited the estate of Sir Henry Lee at Ditchley
Park in Oxfordshire, a location that Shakespeare would have
skirted on the first leg of his journey every time he walked or

rode from Stratford to London. Lee commemorated the visit by commissioning the young Dutch artist Marcus Gheeraerts to paint a magnificent portrait of Elizabeth. She looks like the fairy queen with her dazzling white dress, embroidered in gold, her hair encrusted with jewels, pearls hanging from her neck down to her tiny nipped-in waist, a fan like a wand in her right hand. She is standing on a map of England and Wales, with the point of her left foot on Ditchley. England and Wales are sheltered beneath her ample skirts. One queen, one nation, storm-clouds banished by her presence. The map, with its coloured counties, its rivers and towns (Oxford just below that left foot), is clearly identifiable.

The Ditchley portrait of Queen Elizabeth I

Maps were instruments of power. In the year of Shakespeare's birth, Gerard Mercator engraved the contours of the British Isles in eight sheets. Pieced together, the sheets created a large wall map, which was particularly accurate in its representation of the coastline. The representation of inland is patchier in quality, with the kingdom of Scotland standing out as an improvement on all previous maps. On one of the information panels at the margins, Mercator attributes the map's origin to an anonymous friend. Scholars have long argued over the latter's identity, but the likeliest candidate is John Elder, a Scotsman with strong associations with Mary Queen of Scots. In ideological terms, it is striking that the Mercator map did not mark the Protestant diocese into which Henry VIII had divided England under the ecclesiastical jurisdiction of his bishops. In practical terms, its well-represented coastline, with ports and havens, would have been of great value to a potential Catholic invading force from the Continent.

If England's enemies had such a map, the English state needed one too. Imagine the palace of Whitehall, deep in the reign of Queen Elizabeth. The office of William Cecil, Lord Burghley. First minister of state, eyes and ears of Her Majesty. A table piled high with state papers; a steady stream of officials coming in with reports, requesting signatures on letters for dispatch out into the regions. Burghley is the man who holds Elizabethan England together. Hanging on the wall of his office is a picture. It is a newly minted image, the work of a man called Christopher Saxton. An image that was prized throughout the land. You might expect it to have been a portrait of Queen Elizabeth herself. But it is not the queen: it is the map on which she is standing in the Ditchley portrait. Offering a far more detailed representation of towns and rivers across England than that provided by Mercator, it was the first ever accurate map of the whole country. It was one of the keys to the Elizabethans' discovery of their own land.

To have in their hands a picture of every corner of England, revealing the exact location of each town and village, charting the course of each river and road: this was the dream of the men of power who set Saxton to work on his monumental surveying expedition. The map offered such a new way of seeing England that Saxton's atlas grew into one of the most powerful icons of the age. The reign of Elizabeth was the first time anyone had ever seen the precise outline that is so familiar to us from school geography lessons and nightly television weather charts: Devon and Cornwall extending out like a foot, the inlets of Humber and Severn. Saxton's atlas or *Survey*, published in 1579, included not only 'Anglia', showing the whole of England and Wales (with Ireland on the margin and the independent kingdom of Scotland cut off the top), but also detailed regional maps. Each one reveals the lie of the land

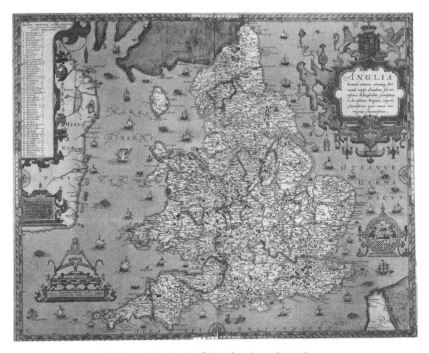

Saxton's map of England and Wales

with little images that look like molehills representing the high
ground. Even in the Ditchley painting, one can see the tentacles of
rivers as they join and part. Thanks to Saxton, the Elizabethans were
the first English people to have a clear sense of the physical shape of
their own nation. And that gave them a new sense of belonging.

Country and county

When we imagine Elizabethan England, we think first of the
glorious court of the Virgin Queen herself or of the bustle of
London, with its theatres and crowds gathered to hear open-air
sermons or witness public executions. But London is no more than
a blot on Saxton's map. He is more interested in the rivers, hills
and woods, where the names of villages nestle among the natural
features of the landscape. He gives us another image: that of rural
England, of the country which in the writing of the period is so
often set in opposition to the city and the court. The dream of

getting out of London and finding some peace and quiet in the countryside was very much alive in the sixteenth century.

The tension between court and country, the centre and the provinces, the active life of London politics and the contemplative ease of the rural estate, was crucial to the Elizabethans' sense of who they were. The commonwealth of England was like a set of Chinese boxes: the biggest box was the nation itself; the smallest was the parish. The crucial middle-sized box was the county. Christopher Saxton's thirty-four maps of the different parts of England are organized county by county. And on some copies of his map of the whole nation, each county is in a different colour. Elizabethans were as loyal to their county as they were to their country. William Shakespeare was renowned as a Warwickshire man, Sir Walter Ralegh and Francis Drake proud of their Devonshire heritage.

Tudor intellectuals were so intrigued by this idea of Englishness as a mixture of county and national identity that they invented a new art form to express it: 'chorography' or the geographical and historical description of a particular region. The pioneer of the genre was a Kentish gentleman called William Lambarde, whose *Perambulation* of his native shire was the first ever county history. Lambarde imagines Kent as the garden of England, reminiscent not only of biblical Eden but also of the garden of the Hesperides in classical mythology, where Hercules found apples of gold:

This Tenham with thirty other parishes (lying on each side this port way, and extending from Rainham to Blean Wood) be the cherry garden and apple orchard of Kent . . . In which respect you may fantasy that you now see *Hesperidum Hortos*, if not where Hercules found the golden apples, (which is reckoned for one of his heroical labours) yet where our honest patriot Richard Harris (fruiterer to King Henry the 8) planted by his great cost and rare industry the sweet cherry, the temperate pippin and the golden rennet.

Lambarde explains that the orchards of Kent were planted for reasons of national security, so as to save the nation from dependence on imported fruit. At the same time, he extols the beauty of the ordered rural landscape and introduces the classical allusion to Hercules as a way of fashioning a new myth of England. The vogue for chorography soon caught on. From Cornwall to Hertfordshire, from Middlesex to Cheshire, other counties received similar treatment. To put your own place on the map was regarded as a patriotic duty.

Shakespeare would participate in this work. He was interested in Lambarde's Kent. A key scene in *Henry VI Part 2* shows the Kentish rebel Jack Cade being killed by the Kentish squire Alexander Iden, whose name suggests Eden. Iden is discovered in his garden, in the tradition of genteel Horatian *otium*:

> Lord, who would live turmoiled in the court,
> And may enjoy such quiet walks as these?
> This small inheritance my father left me
> Contenteth me, and worth a monarchy.

Kent was praised by Julius Caesar in his commentaries on the Gallic Wars. The county was famous for its distinctive form of land tenure, 'gavelkind', whereby land was shared between brothers, as opposed to 'primogeniture', where the estate passed to the eldest son. And Kentishmen were traditionally freedom fighters: they had supposedly resisted the Norman yoke, never being conquered like their neighbours in Sussex. Shakespeare's Lord Saye has these traditions in mind when he describes Kent as the most civil place in all the isle, where the people are 'liberal, valiant, active, wealthy'.

Closer to home, Shakespeare was unique among the dramatists of his age in locating scenes in Warwickshire and Gloucestershire. This little-observed fact is something of a problem for those conspiracy theorists who do not believe that the plays were written by a grammar-school boy from Warwickshire. 'What a devil dost thou in Warwickshire?' Prince Hal asks Falstaff in a scene set on the road between Coventry and Sutton Coldfield, a town in the same county. 'In Warwickshire I have true-hearted friends', says the Earl of Warwick, king-maker, in *Henry VI Part 3*.

One of Warwick's loyal friends is a character called Somerville who in the following scene arrives at Coventry from Southam,

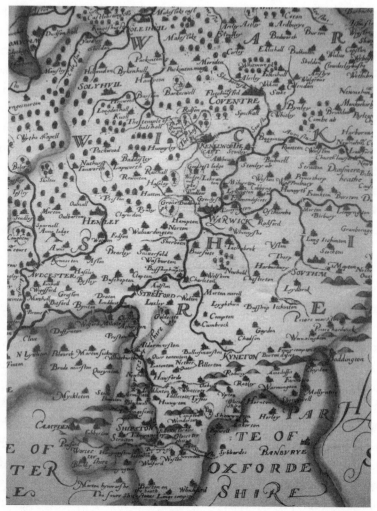

Shakespeare country: Warwickshire and neighbouring counties from
Saxton's map. To the south, Oxfordshire, through which Shakespeare
would have travelled on the road to London. To the south-west,
Gloucestershire, where he would imagine Justice Shallow in his richest
representation of rural England. To the east of Stratford, Southam from
where 'Somerville' arrives in Henry VI Part 3. *To the north-east,*
Warwick, fiefdom of the Grevilles, and beyond, Coventry, the largest
city in the midlands, where as a boy Shakespeare may have seen one of
the last performances of the old mystery plays. To the north-west,
Henley and the forest of Arden.

just east of Stratford. Somerville is an invented character, not a name taken from the chronicle histories that Shakespeare was dramatizing. To an Elizabethan audience, or at least to anyone from the west midlands, the name would immediately have evoked a Warwickshire man who had been portrayed as anything but a 'true-hearted friend' to the queen: John Somerville of Edstone, a village four miles north of Stratford. In 1583, the year when Shakespeare had his first child, Somerville was arrested at an inn near Banbury on the road to London where – allegedly – he was boasting that he intended to assassinate the queen. His father-in-law was Edward Arden of Park Hall. These Ardens were a prominent Warwickshire Catholic family, in all probability kin to Shakespeare's mother.

The Earl of Leicester had old scores to settle with the Ardens and the alleged Somerville plot gave him his opportunity. Edward Arden, his wife Mary and his priest Hugh Hall – who was arrested just outside Stratford at a house belonging to the recusant family from whom Shakespeare later bought his home, New Place – were taken to the Tower of London. The men were tortured on the rack. Somerville was found strangled in prison. Arden was hanged by the neck, his body cut down while he was still alive, his privy members cut off and his bowels removed and burned in front of his eyes. He protested his innocence, claiming that his only crime was adherence to the old faith. Mary Arden, namesake and probable kinswoman of Shakespeare's mother, was reprieved. The tiny role of Somerville in *Henry VI Part 3* may have been Shakespeare's way of saying that it was possible to be both a Warwickshire Catholic and a 'true-hearted friend' of queen and country.

An Elizabethan armed with a full set of county histories in the tradition of Lambarde, together with Christopher Saxton's atlas of England, could claim to have a complete picture – historical, geographical and chorographical – of the parts that made up the whole of the nation. But something more was needed. Michael Drayton, a Warwickshire man like Shakespeare, turned chorography into poetry. His vast poem *Poly-olbion* devoted one section to Cornwall, one to Devon, one to Dorset, and so on. And each was preceded by a fold-out county map, based on Saxton. On its frontispiece, Drayton's book has an evocative image: a figure of Britannia is dressed in a robe that is patterned like Saxton's map, with its hills and rivers and woods and churches. It is as if she is wearing the land itself. The image prepares us for a poem in which the history and legends of the nation are retold by the very features of the landscape.

Britannia wrapped in the map: frontispiece to Drayton's Poly-olbion

The map beneath the queen's feet on the Ditchley portrait was meant as a sign that her power extended to every corner of England. But Saxton's maps took on a life of their own. Together with the new sense of county identity explored by chorographers such as Lambarde and Drayton, and along with the image, which was pervasive in both prose romance and pastoral poetry, of rural England as an Arcadian idyll, they helped to shape a new sense that Englishness was not just a matter of loyalty to the crown. They helped to establish the new idea – which seems so obvious to us today – that the essence of the nation lay not only in the monarchy but above all in the land itself.

If the land was a body, as Drayton's frontispiece suggests, then where was its heart? Not in Westminster, but somewhere in the midlands, deep in the shires. Civil war – a battle between Lancastrians and Yorkists fought at Coventry, say, as in *Henry VI Part 3* – can make 'the very heart of England bleed'. In a dedicatory poem to Sir William Dugdale's volume of antiquarian researches in which an engraving of Shakespeare's tomb was published for the first time, Sir Aston Cokaine wrote

> Now *Stratford* upon *Avon*, we would choose
> Thy gentle and ingenuous *Shakespeare's* Muse,
> (Were he among the living yet) to raise
> T'our Antiquaries' merit some just praise.

Having added Drayton's name, Cokaine concludes

> Our *Warwickshire* the Heart of *England* is,
> As you most evidently have proved by this;
> Having it with more spirit dignified,
> Than all our *English* Counties are beside.

It was in no small measure because of Shakespeare (and Drayton) that Warwickshire became the heart of England. That identity perhaps becomes tangible at the moment in *Henry IV Part 1* when Falstaff breaks his journey from London to Shrewsbury along the old Roman road of Watling Street near Coventry, the capital of the midlands, the place where the boy Shakespeare would have gained his first smell of city life. And in *Part 2*, when Falstaff goes recruiting in Justice Shallow's parish in the neighbouring shire of Gloucester, Shakespeare begins the invention of deep England.

3. The Boy from the Greenwood

Arden's grandson

Pre-school, we are shaped by family and environment. Father: the alderman with his civic business, his trade as a glover. Mother: from a little further up the social ladder, with a network of associations in the local gentry of the old faith. Paternal grandfather: Richard Shakespeare, yeoman farmer from the village of Snitterfield on the fringes of the forest of Arden. Maternal grandfather: owner of the land that Richard farmed, Robert Arden of nearby Wilmcote.

And what of the environment? A glimpse of Shakespeare country is provided by a seventeenth-century gazetteer:

Warwickshire, Varvicensis Comitatus, is bounded on the North by Stafford-shire, on the East by Leicester and Northamptonshires, on the South by Oxford and Gloucester, and on the West by the County of Worcester. In length from North to South thirty three Miles, in breadth twenty five; the whole Circumference one hundred and thirty five; containing one hundred and fifty eight Parishes, and fifteen Market Towns. As it is seated well near in the heart of England, so the Air and Soil are of the best; the River Avon divides it in the middle. What lies South of that River is divided between fruitful Corn-Fields and lovely Meadows; which from Edge-hill present the Viewer with a Plain equal to that of Jordan. That which lies North is Wood Land.

The market town of Stratford lay in a borderland ecological niche: the forest of Arden to the north, farmland stretching towards Oxfordshire to the south. Shakespeare kept an eye in each direction, at once drawn to the road that led to the city of learning and thence to London, yet at the same time pulled back to the forest of Arden. The village of Wilmcote, home to his mother, herself an Arden, is that little bit closer to the forest, the place of origin and refuge. Like Corin in *As You Like It*, the Arden family farmed on the edge of the forest.

Thomas Lodge's elegant prose romance *Rosalynd* is located in the Ardennes forest in France. When Shakespeare dramatized the tale and called it *As You Like It*, he domesticated the setting. The first we hear of the exiled duke is that, 'like the old Robin Hood of England', he is in the forest with a group of 'merry men'. Ostensibly, the qualifier 'of England' is an indication that the action is supposed to take place in France, but the deeper effect is to identify Arden with Sherwood. About a year before the play was written, rival acting company the Admiral's Men had played a two-part drama on the subject of Robin Hood called *Robert Earl of Huntingdon* – the first work in the long history of the legend to turn Robin into a disguised aristocrat as opposed to a genuinely subversive outlaw. The Arden scenes of *As You Like It* begin with the exiled duke contrasting the natural order of the forest to the flattery and envy of the court. As in the Robin Hood story, the wished-for conclusion is the restoration of the right ruler.

Yet the play ironizes as well as idealizes. The most prominent figure in the duke's forest circle is not a merry man but a melancholy man, the satirical Jaques. Often wrongly described as one of the duke's courtiers, he is a gentleman who has sold his lands in order to become a 'traveller', a wry detached observer of manners and morals. The forest order is dependent on hunting, leading Jaques to sympathize with the wounded stag and suggest that the good duke usurps the place of the deer every bit as much as the bad duke has usurped power back at court. Jaques and Touchstone the jester – the two key characters invented by Shakespeare without precedent in Lodge – spar with each other because the satire of the former and the witty foolery of the latter are rival modes of mocking courtly pretensions such as Orlando's highly romanticized language of love-service.

Arden is also compared to the mythological 'golden age' and the play duly has its complement of classically named shepherds, signalling the influence of the ancient tradition of pastoral verse. The golden age was the imagined infancy of humankind, another Eden, a playground in which Nature offered up her fruits and the winter wind never blew. But Shakespeare complicates the picture. The duke's very first speech sees Arden as a place less to 'fleet the time carelessly as they did in the golden world' than to draw moral lessons from the natural world. This is no Arcadia of perpetual summer: the seasons do change, it is just that 'the penalty of Adam' – being forced to labour for subsistence – seems less harsh than the vicissitudes of the court. The myth of the golden age made Utopia into the state that society had fallen from instead of that which it aspired to: a place where everybody was happy and there was no such thing as property. But the Arden of *As You Like It* is not quite a return to the golden age. The old shepherd Corin is a voice of happiness, yet he has no illusions about the need for labour and his dependence on property that he does not own. He is shepherd to another man's flock and only keeps his job because Celia buys the farm.

Many of Shakespeare's plays keep up a constant shuttle between symbolically opposed locations – Venice and Belmont, Rome and Egypt, Sicilian court and Bohemian country – but *As You Like It* moves all the major players to Arden as swiftly as possible. Once there, the scenes run together fluently. There is no clock ticking in the forest, no sense of time being marked by the scene breaks. Initially, however, there are two discernible imaginary locations: the farm and the cave, Corin's world of agricultural labour and the deep forest where the duke and his men play at being Robin Hood. Orlando and Jaques drift between the two, whereas Rosalind/ Ganymede and Celia/Aliena are not allowed to penetrate too far into the deep forest. Their reunion with the duke must be withheld for the climax.

The merging of Ardennes and Arden is only the most extreme example of Shakespeare's tendency to swerve back to his point of origin. The Athenian wood in *A Midsummer Night's Dream* is peopled by very English fairies and artisans. In *All's Well That Ends Well*, Helen is travelling between Italy and France. She disguises herself as a pilgrim on the way to 'Saint Jaques le Grand'. Assuming that this was a reference to the famous shrine of St Iago at Compostella in Spain, Dr Johnson remarked that she appeared to have gone somewhat out of her road. The diversion may have been even more circuitous than he imagined, because the choice of saint is also a nod to the parish church of St James the Great at Snitterfield, the village just east of Stratford where Shakespeare's father was born.

Again, in imagining the national past in the *Henry* plays, Shakespeare could not resist echoing his own past: Peto was the name of a commissioner in a 1581 Stratford law case involving John Shakespeare, while a Bardolph and a Fluellen appear alongside Shakespeare's father in a 1592 list of those absent from church for fear of process for debt. The country justice scenes in *Henry IV Part 2* have an unprecedented degree of local specificity, with references to Hinckley Fair near Coventry and a legal dispute between 'William Visor of Woncot' (the Visor or Vizard family of Woodmancote) and 'Clement Perkes o'th'Hill' (the Purchase or Perkis family on nearby Stinchcombe Hill), together with one of the earliest recorded usages of the term 'Cotswold' ('Will Squele, a Cotsole man' – the spelling indicative of Shakespeare's regional dialect).

Perhaps what is most distinctive about Shakespeare's representation of his own land is this sense of the local, the regionally specific, the provincial. The social and natural ecology of rural Warwickshire plays a key part in his vision. This preoccupation was shaped by his own origin and suggestive of his insecurity in the capital. He did not accumulate property and influence near London, in the manner of the great actor and entrepreneur Edward Alleyn. His own family life made him acutely conscious of his distance from the cultural centre. He was a provincial outsider, and that may go some way to explaining why he was so fascinated by outsiders such as Shylock the Jew and Othello the Moor in Venice.

The earliest clear record of Shakespeare in the London theatre world, dating from the autumn of 1592, sees a rival playwright, Cambridge-educated Robert Greene, insulting him precisely because of his origins, associating him with the *country*, a word often used to suggest the 'county' as opposed to court and city interest:

There is an upstart crow beautified with our feathers that, with his *Tiger's heart wrapped in a player's hide*, supposes he is as well able to bombast out a blank verse as the best of you: and being an absolute *Johannes fac totum*, is in his own conceit the only Shake-scene in a country.

There can be no doubt that this refers to Shakespeare, the player turned 'maker' who is here accused of borrowing the stylistic plumage of university-educated playwrights such as Greene himself. Shakespeare made his theatrical name with the barnstorming *Henry VI* plays, in one of which Queen Margaret places a paper crown on the head of Richard Duke of York and is rewarded with a diatribe describing her as an 'Amazonian trull' with a 'tiger's heart wrapt in a woman's hide'. The quotation, with *woman* altered to *player*, is unmistakable. A *Johannes fac totum* was a Jack of all trades – English culture has a long history of men from the professions, armed with degrees from the universities of Oxford and Cambridge, looking down their noses at hard-working men from a *trade* background who lack a degree (which in the Elizabethan age allowed you to call yourself a gentleman). *Greene's Groatsworth of Wit* goes on to call Shake-scene a 'rude groom' and a 'peasant'. This is the snobbery of the town sophisticate towards the country bumpkin as well as the professional towards the trader. We do not know whether the insult '*in his own conceit* the only Shake-scene' indicates that Shakespeare played on his own name in a pun in one of his early plays or as a backstage or bar-room joke. He certainly had a predilection for phrases such as 'shake my sword', 'shake his weapon', 'shake your shaking', 'shake his tail' and 'shake off these names'.

There is little doubt that Shakespeare was provoked by *Greene's Groatsworth of Wit*, though the evidence for his reaction is not that which is usually adduced. Henry Chettle, who saw the book through the press and probably wrote most of it himself, admitted that two 'play-makers' had taken offence at the pamphlet. He claimed that he was not acquainted with either of them and that 'with one of them I care not if I never be'. He then apologized to the other, saying that he had subsequently met him and found 'his demeanour no less civil than he excellent in the quality he professes'. Besides, 'divers of worship have reported his uprightness of dealing, which argues his honesty, and his facetious grace in writing, that approves his art'. Greene, as ventriloquized by Chettle, had warned his fellow university men, Christopher Marlowe, Tom Nashe and George Peele, against the players for whom they wrote. Any of these three might have taken offence at his tone, even though Shakespeare and his fellow-players were the real object of the rebuke.

Scholars usually assume that the man Chettle cares not ever to be acquainted with is Marlowe – a way of dissociating himself from the latter's notorious atheism – but the remark could be a continuation of his lofty disdain for Shakespeare (who would want the acquaintance of that peasant?). If Shakespeare was the other man, whom Chettle has now seen, then the references to his civility, 'quality', professing (as opposed to trading), uprightness, honesty, grace and the esteem of 'divers of worship' all suggest that the apology was a clear retraction of the class insult. On balance, though, it is most likely that the first man was Marlowe and the apology was to Peele: Chettle says that those who have taken offence are one or two of the play-makers *to whom Greene's remarks were addressed*, and Shakespeare was not one of those. The upstart crow does not get a look in.

The evidence that Shakespeare was insulted – or amused, or both – by the 'upstart crow' quip is, rather, apparent from the way that 'Greene's' terms lodged themselves in his memory. Some years later, he has Hamlet writing a love-letter 'to the celestial and my soul's idol, the most beautified Ophelia'. Polonius interjects 'That's an ill phrase, a vile phrase: "beautified" is a vile phrase.' This sounds very like a memory of 'beautified with our feathers'. The repeated 'vile' is a telling parry because the word was associated with social inferiority, which was exactly what Shakespeare had been accused of in the original 'upstart crow' insult.

In *The Comedy of Errors*, a play written soon after the publication of *Greene's Groatsworth*, Shakespeare includes the following witty banter on the subject of a crowbar:

ANTIPHOLUS OF EPHESUS: Well, I'll break in. Go borrow me a crow.
DROMIO OF EPHESUS: A crow without feather? Master, mean you so?

For a fish without a fin, there's a fowl without a feather,

If a crow help us in, sirrah, we'll pluck a crow together.

ANTIPHOLUS OF EPHESUS: Go get thee gone, fetch me an iron crow.

BALTHAZAR: Have patience, sir, O, let it not be so!

Herein you war against your reputation.

The juxtaposition of 'a crow without feather' and talk of 'reputation' is unlikely to be coincidental. *Greene's Groatsworth* accused Shake-scene the upstart crow of the conceit of playing on his own name, so he duly obliges with 'pluck a crow' and 'iron crow': 'pluck' suggests *Shake* and 'iron' a weapon such as a *spear*.

Again, in several of *Shakespeare's Sonnets* there are references to being 'vile esteemed' and to 'vulgar scandal' that 'o'er-green[s] my bad'. *Vile* and *vulgar* are both terms with strong class connotations. 'O'er-green' might even be a nudge at Greene's name. It was William Shakespeare, not his father John, who devoted time and money in the late 1590s to the process of obtaining a coat of arms for the family that would allow him to describe himself as a gentleman. He was mocked for this by contemporaries such as Ben Jonson.

In Elizabethan England it was very hard to escape the stigma of birth. Terms such as 'gentle' and 'base' ensured that moral judgements were linked to class origin. Shakespeare never forgot that he was the grandson of a yeoman farmer and the son of a provincial shopkeeper whose business collapsed (perhaps partly because he was too busy devoting himself to gaining positions on the local council that made him seem a man of importance). Nor did he ever forget that he belonged to the country, not the city: the one dramatic genre he never attempted was the 'city comedy' at which playwrights such as Thomas Dekker, Thomas Middleton and Philip Massinger excelled. His most English comedy, *The Merry Wives*, is signally located not in London but in bourgeois small-town Windsor, a place far more like Stratford (albeit with a royal castle on its doorstep).

When someone insults your origin, you ignore it or you retreat into your shell or you fight back. Shakespeare took the bold course. He penned his *Venus and Adonis* soon after the 'upstart crow' jibe was published, as if to show that you didn't need an Oxford or Cambridge degree to turn out elegant poetry in imitation of the classics of ancient Rome. He adorned its title page with a Latin quotation pointedly setting himself apart from the 'vile' and the 'vulgar' (*vilia . . . vulgus*). But the poem is also a proud reaffirmation of his 'greenwood' credentials. It rejoices in a lushly realized pastoral setting. Only a country boy could write with such precision and empathy of the hunted hare:

> By this, poor Wat, far off upon a hill,
> Stands on his hinder legs with list'ning ear
> To harken if his foes pursue him still.
> Anon their loud alarums he doth hear,
>   And now his grief may be comparèd well
>   To one sore sick that hears the passing-bell.
>
> Then shalt thou see the dew-bedabbled wretch
> Turn and return, indenting with the way.
> Each envious briar his weary legs do scratch,
> Each shadow makes him stop, each murmur stay:
>   For misery is trodden on by many
>   And, being low, never relieved by any.

There can be little doubt that Poor Wat is a Shakespearean memory of a pursuit through the warrens of his native Warwickshire.

One of Shakespeare's earliest plays is *The Taming of the Shrew*. It seems to be a reworking of an anonymous comedy, *The Taming of a Shrew*. Each work begins with the framing device of an 'induction'. That in *A Shrew* is completely without local realization, whereas Shakespeare's version of the Christopher Sly business is full of detail, ranging from questions of the proper pedigree of rural gentry families to specific Warwickshire place names. Suppose that *The Shrew* was Shakespeare's first play and that he started by writing the induction. His career would then have begun thus:

I'll pheeze you, in faith.
A pair of stocks, you rogue!
You're a baggage, the Slys are no rogues. Look in the chronicles, we
    came in with Richard Conqueror.

The exchange both proclaims and mocks the idea of English lineage. Sly becomes Shakespeare's calling card, both assertion and parody of his own country bumpkin origins. It is not outrageous to imagine Shakespeare the actor speaking his own lines:

Am not I Christopher Sly, old Sly's son of Burtonheath, by birth a pedlar, by education a cardmaker, by transmutation a bear-herd, and now by present profession a tinker? Ask Marian Hacket, the fat ale-wife of Wincot, if she know me not.

Wincot is a tiny hamlet south of Stratford; there was a Hacket family there in 1591. Burtonheath is Barton on the Heath, where Shakespeare had relatives who, as will be seen, played a key role in drawing him into the world of the law. Sly's self-portrait is at once a proclamation of Shakespearean origins and an exemplification of the process of metamorphosis through role-playing that is the essence of theatre. Shakespeare the actor was by association a bear-herd, because the players shared their theatre space with bear-keepers and their baitings. Sly's sub-text might just be this: 'Am not I William Shakespeare – old Shakespeare's son of Stratford-upon-Avon, by birth a glover, by education a reader, by transmutation an actor and now by present profession a tinkerer with other men's plays?'

About ten years later, when *As You Like It* was written, he was confident enough in his success to use his own name when teasing himself for his humble origins in Arden:

TOUCHSTONE: Is thy name William?
WILLIAM: William, sir.
TOUCHSTONE: A fair name. Wast born i'th'forest here?
WILLIAM: Ay, sir, I thank God.
TOUCHSTONE: 'Thank God'. A good answer. Art rich?
WILLIAM: Faith, sir, so-so.
TOUCHSTONE: 'So-so' is good, very good, very excellent good. And yet it is not, it is but so-so. Art thou wise?
WILLIAM: Ay, sir, I have a pretty wit.
TOUCHSTONE: Why, thou sayest well. I do now remember a saying:

'The fool doth think he is wise, but the wise man knows himself to be a fool.'

Noting the consonance of sexual word-play between shaking a spear (penis) and touching a stone (testicle), the critic Katherine Duncan-Jones brilliantly suggests that Touchstone as well as William is a version of Shakespeare: 'their dialogue can be read as an exchange between the wealthy and quick-witted playwright and the provincial youth he has left behind him in the Forest of Arden.' William is at the 'ripe age' of twenty-five: could it have been at the same age, in 1589, that his creator left the forest and began his career as a witty player? By the time of *As You Like It* Shakespeare was at the height of his powers, writing on demand for the court. He was bringing to a climax the cycle of history plays in which he staked his claim to be the voice of the nation. But he was still the Shake-scene who kept returning to the country from which he came.

Who speaks for England?

'Speak, citizens, for England,' says the King of France to the townsmen of Angiers as it is besieged by rival armies from opposite sides of the English Channel. Of all Shakespeare's history plays, *King John* is the one that most explicitly asks what it might mean to speak for England. It explores questions about legitimacy and inheritance that were of concern to all propertied families in Tudor England, but of monumental significance to the monarchy – especially at a time when an aged childless queen was sitting on the throne. In the much better-known play of *King Lear*, the legitimate son Edgar is the virtuous one and the illegitimate Edmund is the villain. *King John* imagines a more challenging possibility: suppose that a great king dies and that his bravest, most honest and most intelligent son is an illegitimate one. In such a circumstance, inheritance on the basis of merit is not possible: if a bastard were to ascend the throne, the legitimacy of the entire monarchical system would be called into question. The seamless interdependence of patrilineal state, law, church and family would begin to unravel.

In the first scene, before there is any resolution to all the difficult questions of succession and faith, power and proprietorship, a sheriff enters. His presence signals the jurisdiction of the shires, the 'country' as opposed to the 'court' interest. The question of which of two brothers will inherit a parcel of land in the shires parallels that of which of Richard Coeur de Lion's brothers, John or Geoffrey (through Arthur), will inherit the nation as a whole. For the original audience in the 1590s, an encounter set in the distant thirteenth century would have echoed with debates in their own time, where it was not unknown for a provincial Member of Parliament to give voice in the House of Commons to words that one might have expected to belong to the queen alone: 'I speak for all England.' In many quarters, there was a strongly held view that 'England' was not synonymous with the English queen and her court based in and around London. Though the Tudor monarchs had tried to unify the nation by establishing a network of legal representatives across the shires, the 'country' gentry as well as the great barons of the north and west guarded their autonomy fiercely.

The Bastard announces himself as a gentleman born in Northamptonshire; he is 'a good blunt fellow', which is to say a plain-speaking English countryman. Later, he appeals to St George, the patron saint of England. His, then, is the voice of Shakespeare's own place of origin, the midlands, deep England. He is given a choice: to inherit the Falconbridge estates or take his 'chance' and assume the name, though not the patrimony, of the royal father who sired him out of wedlock.

The norm in the English gentry was for the older son to inherit the land and the younger to become mobile, to go to London and find a career in the law, the clergy, the army, the diplomatic corps, or possibly even the entertainment business. Settled legitimacy was pitched against the life of the adventurer. By accepting his illegitimacy and renouncing the land he is actually entitled to (because it was his mother's adultery, not his father's, he is not forcibly disinherited in the manner of Edmund in *King Lear*), the

Bastard takes the route that was usually that of the younger brother. Shakespeare did the same when he left Stratford-upon-Avon.

The Bastard's origin in middle England is further stressed by the arrival of Lady Falconbridge and James Gurney, wearing riding-robes that signify the journey from country to court. The Bastard then describes his half-brother as 'Colbrand the Giant, that same mighty man'. Colbrand was a Danish invader who was defeated in single combat by Guy of Warwick – a legendary figure who was immensely popular in chapbook, ballad and drama. If Robert Falconbridge is symbolically Colbrand, then Philip the Bastard is symbolically Guy, a Warwickshire folk hero. Perhaps he is even a version of Robin Hood, with the sheriff of Northampton standing in for his colleague from Nottingham. Robin Hood himself, the most famous folk hero from the reign of John, cannot be mentioned because his name would immediately turn the king into a villain, which Shakespeare did not want to do at the beginning of the play, both because he wanted to keep open the question of the relative legitimacy of the claims of John and Arthur and because he was working in that tradition of chronicle and drama in which King John was a proto-Protestant hero because of his refusal to allow the Pope's nominee, Stephen Langton, to become Arch-bishop of Canterbury.

The Bastard stands in for Guy of Warwick, who stands in for Robin Hood of old England. It was Robin who maintained the values of good King Richard at home, whilst the latter was fighting his *jihad* in the Middle East ('Richard that robbed the lion of his heart / And fought the holy wars in Palestine'). As the play progresses, the Bastard's role shifts to that of stand-in for the dead Coeur de Lion himself. He ends up fighting the war on John's behalf and at one point comes within a whisker of ascending the throne. He speaks for England in the closing lines:

> This England never did, nor never shall,
> Lie at the proud foot of a conqueror,
> But when it first did help to wound itself.
>   . . . Nought shall make us rue,
> If England to itself do rest but true.

The world-weary voice is that of a dramatist who in his *Henry VI* plays has shown the bloody consequences of England turning against itself.

The Bastard is the conscience of the nation, the symbolic heir of Lionheart, the voice of the shires. But he is also an adventurer, the embodiment of illegitimacy, a new man, an individualist who foreshadows the more sinister figure of Edmund in *Lear*: 'I am I, howe'er I was begot.' Improviser, player, speaker of soliloquies, both inside and outside history, could he be the voice not only of Guy but also of William of Warwickshire? Who speaks for deep England? A challenger of legitimacy. An entrepreneur. A player. A man who idealizes the shires even as he leaves them to enter the theatre, the market, the emergent empire. Who speaks? A Shakespeare.

Two funerals and a wedding

For William Shakespeare 1607 was the year of two funerals, a wedding and a pregnancy. The funerals were in London, the wedding and pregnancy in Stratford-upon-Avon. That August, Shakespeare's young nephew was buried in St Giles, Cripplegate. A child born out of wedlock, the dead infant was the son of Edmund Shakespeare, player.

Edmund Shakespeare, Will's junior by sixteen years, seems to have been the only family member to follow his big brother to London. Could he have been Shakespeare's apprentice in the acting company? The leading boys among the Lord Chamberlain's men – that is to say, the teenage apprentices for whom Shakespeare wrote such parts as Juliet, Portia, Viola and Rosalind – were Nick Tooley, apprentice to Burbage, and Alexander (known as Sander) Cooke, apprentice to John Hemings. A document that may be dated to 1597 or early 1598 lists another of the apprentices as 'Ned'. Edmund Shakespeare was seventeen at this time. It is unlikely that he could have become a player without being an apprentice first. Where else would he have learned his craft but in his brother's company? Apprentices continued to lodge with their masters even after their indenture was ended. Nick Tooley remained in Burbage's household until the master-actor's death, and Richard Robinson, another of his 'boys', married his master's widow, Winifred Burbage. It is highly probable that Ned Shakespeare lodged with Will and played with the Chamberlain's/King's Men at least until the completion of his apprenticeship, or even until his death. Alas, attractive as it would be, it is far-fetched to suppose that such a junior actor would have been given the role of brother Edmund in *King Lear*.

Just after Christmas, father followed son to his grave. On 31 December 1607 'Edmond Shakespeare, a player' was laid to rest in the church of St Saviour's, Southwark, a short walk from the Globe Theatre. He was buried inside the church, not in the yard. This was usually the preserve of the gentry. It would have cost money – as did the tolling of a forenoon knell of the great bell. The charge for the latter memorial gesture was twenty shillings and Will Shakespeare is usually assumed to have been the man who paid for it. The church contained a superb effigy of the fourteenth-century poet John Gower. It has often been suggested that the sight of it inspired Shakespeare to bring Gower back from the grave as narrator of *Pericles*, which was written and first performed over the next few months. But there is no firm evidence that he attended his brother's funeral: it may have been precisely because he didn't attend that he sent money for the tolling of the bell as a mark of fraternal respect.

It is highly probable that Edmund was a plague victim. For most of the time from the summer of 1606 to the summer of 1608, plague raged and the theatres remained closed. It is a fair inference that Shakespeare spent many months during this two-year period in the cleaner air of Stratford-upon-Avon. We perhaps catch a glimpse of him in a pamphlet of this time by Robert Armin, his company clown, which includes a somewhat laborious joke about a new pair of boots for 'a Gentleman [who was] to ride down into Warwickshire, about payment of an hundred pound upon a bond forfeiture'.

Shakespeare would probably therefore have witnessed the courtship, marriage and pregnancy of his eldest born, Susanna. For a man in his early forties with two grown daughters and the memory of his only son Hamnet having died at the age of eleven, the question of sons-in-law and grandchildren has a degree of urgency. That summer of 1607, Susanna made a good match. In June she married a doctor: just what every father wants for his eldest daughter. The following February she gave birth to a daughter, Elizabeth, Shakespeare's first grandchild – the only grandchild he would know. Some years later, Susanna's younger sister, Judith, dead Hamnet's twin, had a much sorrier time when her fiancé got another woman pregnant, causing Will Shakespeare to alter his will.

The good doctor was John Hall, a mature and learned man – a decade older than Susanna, he was only a decade younger than his father-in-law. He was a staunch Protestant and, though unlicensed, a conscientious practitioner of his craft. Some of his cures were as old as Aristotle, others were new and sometimes improvised. Some, such as a treatment for scurvy that made use of herbs rich in ascorbic acid, were ahead of their time. Other seem to us frankly bizarre: spiders' webs and sliced radishes applied to the extremities in order to draw forth foul humours (though we should not forget that bat dung, another favoured remedy, is notably rich in vitamin A). Hall's casebook, entitled *Select Observations on English Bodies of Eminent Persons in Desperate Diseases,* was published later in the seventeenth century. Observation nineteen describes a treatment for Shakespeare's daughter:

Mrs *Hall* of *Stratford,* my Wife, being miserably tormented with the Colic, was cured as followeth. R. *Diaphaen. Diacatholic.* Ana 3i. *Pul. Holand* 3ii. *Ol. Rute* 3i. *Lact. Q.s.f. Clyt.* This injected gave her two Stools, yet the Pain continued, being but little mitigated; therefore I appointed to inject a Pint of Sack made hot. This presently brought forth a great deal of Wind, and freed her from all Pain. To her Stomach was applied a Plaister *de Labd. Crat. Cum Caran. & Spec. Aromat. Rosat & ol. Macis.* With one of these Clysters I delivered the Earl of *Northampton* from a grievous Colic.

One may gain a glimpse into Hall's world simply by listing the traditional composition of just one of the ingredients of that clyster:

aromaticum rosatum is a powder made of a mixture of red roses, liquorice, aloeswood, yellow sanders, cinnamon, cloves, mace, gum, tragacanth, nutmegs, cardamoms, galangals, spikenard, ambergris and musk. Less exotically, consider the clyster for Mary Wilson, aged twenty-two, afflicted with a hectic fever, noted on the opposite page to the remedy for Susanna Shakespeare. It consisted of chicken broth in which was boiled seed of poppies, flowers of water-lilies, violets, lettuce, mallows; being strained, there was added oil of violets, white sugar, honey of violets, common salt, the yolk of one egg. Admittedly this patient died a year later, but Hall did have many successes:

Mr *Hunt* of *Stock-green*, aged about 46. Labouring of a grievous Scab and Itch, was thus helped: [prescription:] *Fumitory, Borage, Bugloss, Scabious, Wormwood, of each a like quantity, as much as you please; draw out the juices, of which take* 2 pints, *boiling it in whey to the consumption of the whey, always scumming of it; after it is boiled suffer it to settle.* Drink every day a good draught of it cold, with sugar. This is the *syrup of Scabious* by *Johannes Anglici*, and a secret by which he cured many of the Scab, with which I have cured many also.

Fumitory is a member of the poppy family, rich in alkaloids. It has been shown clinically to help regulate the flow of bile, acting as an amphicholeretic agent in cases of gall bladder problems such as biliary colic. Borage, recommended by many sixteenth-century herbalists as a cordial to expel pensiveness and melancholy, has diuretic, demulcent and emollient properties. Its saline constituents assist the kidneys in filtering toxins, while its potassium and calcium content are good for the heart. Bugloss has similar properties. *Scabiosa* is an expectorant that assists both skin problems and the lungs. Wormwood, or mugwort, still prevalent in Chinese medicine, was highly versatile. Girolami Ruscelli's *A verye excellent and profitable booke conteining six hundred foure score and odde experienced medicines apperteyning unto phisick and surgerie*, translated out of Italian into English by Richard Androse in 1569, listed many uses: to take away blueness or blackness of the eyelids, to treat bruises, cure jaundice, remedy the coming out of the matrix; against headaches and sleeplessness, against the falling sickness and weakness of the stomach through cold, to kill worms in children, to heal spots in the eyes and droppings of the eye; for sore breasts, swellings and obstruction of the mesaraical veins, and more.

Where did Hall obtain his poppies, violets, lettuce and mallows for Mary Wilson's poultice, his fumitory, borage, bugloss, scabious and wormwood for Mr Hunt? Some would have been purchased from Philip Rogers, the apothecary on the High Street (whom Shakespeare once sued over an unrestored loan), some gathered by herb women in the fields around Stratford (remember Friar Laurence, going out at dawn to fill his basket with 'baleful weeds and precious-juicèd flowers'). Others could have been grown in his own garden. After Shakespeare's death, John and Susanna moved to New Place, where there was a fine garden. In a letter of 1631 Sir Thomas Temple requested his man Harry Rose to ride to Stratford to desire Mr Hall to give him some shoots of his vine. New Place is gone, but the garden remains, with its famous mulberry tree. Today, however, the garden is purely decorative: the visitor gains no sense of the intimate relationship between plants and medicine in Shakespeare's time.

We must always be wary of attempts to map Shakespeare's life on to his work. But writers cannot avoid drawing on their experience. Is it a coincidence that in Shakespeare's earlier works there are two comic doctors – Pinch in *The Comedy of Errors* and Caius in *The Merry Wives of Windsor* – whereas in the plays written after John Hall's arrival in Stratford-upon-Avon, there are several dignified, sympathetically portrayed medical men? Among them are the physician who has to deal with that difficult patient Lady Macbeth, the doctor who revives the exhausted King Lear in the quarto version of that play, and Dr Cornelius in *Cymbeline* (who tricks the wicked stepmother, giving her a sleeping draught rather than the poison she desires). And, most suggestively, there is Cerimon in *Pericles*, the play about father and daughter, death and rebirth, written in the wake of Edmund Shakespeare's death and during the final months of the pregnancy of Susanna and perhaps the first weeks of the life of Shakespeare's first grandchild, Elizabeth.

The play was begun by the hack writer George Wilkins. Shakespeare took over the script at the beginning of the third act. Gower enters. There is a dumbshow, in which Thaisa is shown pregnant. A baby girl is then born in a storm. The mother dies in childbirth, only to be revived in the following scene by the medical arts of the Lord Cerimon. He voices a doctor's *credo*:

> I hold it ever
> Virtue and cunning were endowments greater
> Than nobleness and riches. Careless heirs
> May the two latter darken and expend,
> But immortality attends the former,
> Making a man a god. 'Tis known I ever
> Have studied physic, through which secret art,
> By turning o'er authorities, I have,
> Together with my practice, made familiar
> To me and to my aid the blest infusions
> That dwells in vegetives, in metals, stones,
> And I can speak of the disturbances
> That nature works and of her cures, which doth give me
> A more content in course of true delight
> Than to be thirsty after tottering honour,
> Or tie my treasure up in silken bags
> To please the fool and death.

Given that Hall had a formidable library of medical 'authorities' as well as a thriving practice and an encyclopaedic knowledge of 'the blest infusions / That dwells in vegetives', it seems more than fortuitous that Shakespeare wrote these lines in this context at this time in his life. This is not to say that Cerimon *is* Hall, that the pregnancy of Thaisa is that of Susanna, or that Marina is Elizabeth. But family circumstances, and in particular the stabilizing figure of Hall, do seem to have been on Shakespeare's mind at this time.

At a deeper level, beyond the biographical, the speech establishes an opposition between the knowledge of nature, on the one hand, and the pursuit of 'tottering honour' and wealth on the other. For Shakespeare, London was the place associated with the pursuit of honour, status, wealth and recognition at court, but also the place of plague and mass death. And of the commercialization of sex: the link between the theatre industry and the sex trade was symbiotic. Not only did prostitutes work the playhouses for trade: George Wilkins, co-writer of *Pericles*, owned a string of brothels.

Stratford-upon-Avon, in contrast to London, was associated with stability, community, garden, field and health. Whether or not Shakespeare did ever take the mercury-bath cure for syphilis, as the final two sonnets in his collection suggest he might have done, he regularly took the nature cure by returning to his home town. Like the Lord Cerimon, Master Shakespeare speaks of the disturbances that nature works and of her cures.

Perhaps the hopes that he had once placed in Hamnet, then in Edmund and his son, now rested in Hall and his daughter. The late plays are full of deep, longing thoughts about fathers and daughters – but they are also thinkings of the return to nature. Thus in *The Winter's Tale*: Sicilia is a court, Bohemia the country. And in *Cymbeline* the court is set against the countryside of Wales. Nature cure is the deep structure of romance.

It is perhaps in *Cymbeline* that Shakespeare's art of natural observation is at its most acute. The supposedly dead Fidele is apostrophized with the phrase 'the azured harebell like thy veins'. The colour and structure of the harebell precisely resemble those of human veins. Then there is Belarius speaking of how his two adopted sons show princely natures even as they are dressed as shepherds:

> O thou goddess,
> Thou divine Nature, thou thyself thou blazon'st
> In these two princely boys! They are as gentle
> As zephyrs blowing below the violet,
> Not wagging his sweet head; and yet as rough,
> Their royal blood enchafed, as the rud'st wind,
> That by the top doth take the mountain pine,
> And make him stoop to th'vale.

The wind has the capacity not to move a violet but to flatten a mountain pine: Shakespeare likes that paradox.

And the mole on Innogen's left breast: 'cinque-spotted, like the crimson drops / I'th'bottom of a cowslip'. Is there any other English poet, save John Clare, who has such an eye as this? Like Clare, Shakespeare knows his botany. Perdita in *The Winter's Tale* speaks of 'The marigold that goes to bed with the sun, / And with him rises weeping'. The point here is that this is a domesticated flower from the cottage garden: the garden marigold closes its petals or florets at sunset and opens at sunrise, whereas the field marigold does not.

It is unlikely to be a coincidence that Shakespeare turned to pastoral romance in the plague years around 1607–10: of all his plays, *Cymbeline* and *The Winter's Tale* are the ones that have the most distinctive air of having been written back home in Stratford.

The herbal economy

The world we have lost, Shakespeare's world, is one where there is folk knowledge of the medicinal uses of plants. Macbeth on the disappearance of the weird sisters: 'Were such things here as we do speak about? / Or have we eaten on the insane root / That takes the reason prisoner?' Henbane is described in Thomas Berthelette's translation of *Bartholomaeus, de proprietatibus rebus* as breeding 'woodness' or 'slow likeness of sleep'. It was known as *insana* because it took away wit or reason.

Ophelia's flowers: it is clear that rosemary is for remembrance and pansies for thoughts, because Ophelia says so (pansies are from French *pensées*). But the signification of her other flowers is left for the audience to supply. Scholars usually assume that rue is for the queen, fennel and columbines for the king, but some commentators propose vice versa on the grounds that fennel signifies flattery and is also associated with wanton and dissembling women, while the horned shape of the columbine suggests cuckoldry (a joke in *Love's Labour's Lost* turns on this association). Rue is for repentance, which is what Claudius has been trying unsuccessfully to engage in.

Turning to *King Lear*, it helps to know that Hill's *Herbal* offers the information that marjoram comforts the brain: the madmen's shared password is 'sweet marjoram'. Shakespearean botany, though, is revelatory not just of medicinal issues. It also creates larger thematic resonances. When Lear's fantastic garland is described, it contains exactly what one would find in an arable field and its margins in England at the end of summer or the beginning of autumn:

> Alack, 'tis he; why, he was met even now
> As mad as the vexed sea, singing aloud,
> Crowned with rank fumiter, and furrow weeds,
> With hardocks, hemlock, nettles, cuckoo-flowers,
> Darnel, and all the idle weeds that grow
> In our sustaining corn.

The verb 'crowned' stands here in a metonymic relationship to Lear's kingship. By synecdoche (the substitution of the part for the whole), the flower-crown makes us see the king anew, bearing a weight not of gold but of weeds. The cornfield, meanwhile, is a metonymy for the commonweal ('sustaining' anticipates 'the gored state sustain' at the end of the play). The image suggests the relationship between food supply, grain chiefly, and politics: a matter that was both the starting point of the political drama of *Coriolanus* and a big issue during Shakespeare's lifetime, what with bad harvests in the 1590s and grain riots in the early Jacobean period. Shakespeare himself was a part-time dealer in, and notorious hoarder of, grain.

Then there are those 'idle weeds': idleness conjures up beggars, vagabonds, masterless men – people on the margins who don't sustain the state. Idleness was a matter of special concern in relation to the nascent Protestant work ethic (200 years later, John Clare was conscious of how he would be condemned for 'soodling' in the fields instead of labouring there). Actors were conscious of their historic links with the idle class. *King Lear*, performed by the King's Men before the majesty of their patron, King James, at Whitehall on St Stephen's Night 1606, boldly portrays a king of idlers, with Tom o'Bedlam and the poor naked wretches as his subjects, his crown of idle weeds the sign of this relationship. But weeds was also a term for clothes: a key image in the play is that of removing clothes – the entropy from the robes and furred gowns that hide all down to the simplicity of 'unbutton'. Botany thus becomes a means of representing and subverting the hierarchies of the social order.

Perdita's disquisition on art and nature in *The Winter's Tale* is another exploration of the relationship between botany and rank, but also of gardening as reconciliation between the human arts and natural wildness. John Parkinson in *A Garden of all sorts of Pleasant Flowers* anticipates Perdita when he accounts 'Carnations and gilly-flowers' to be 'the chiefest flowers of account in all our English gardens . . . the queen of delight and of flowers . . . they flower not until the heat of the year, which is in July, and continue flowering until the colds of the autumn check them, or until they have wholly outspent themselves; and these fair flowers are usually increased by slips.'

The precision of the enumeration of the weeds in Lear's crown demands further pause. Fumitory is *fumaria officinalis*, sometimes known as *fumus terrae*, 'smoke of the earth', because of its tendency to sprawl across the ground. Hardock is perhaps charlock or carlock (*rapistrum aruorum*) or wild mustard (*sinapis arvensis*), which was common in cornfields. In the chapter 'Of Wild turnips' in Gerard's *Herbal*, we find that

There be three sorts of wild turnips; one our common rape which beareth the seed whereof is made rape oil, and feedeth singing birds: the other *the common enemy to corn*, which we call Charlock; whereof there be two kinds, one with a yellow, or else purple flower, the other with a white flower: there is also another of the water and marish grounds.

The name 'Harlock' is mentioned by that other Warwickshire man, Michael Drayton in a poetic flower-catalogue in his *Shepherd's Garland* – Drayton is the one contemporary to match Shakespeare in botanical exactitude. Some scholars, however, suppose that hardocks are actually burdocks (*arctium lappa*), the leaf of which John Hall mentions as an ingredient in a potion for sciatica and the root in an admixture for gout.

Hemlock is *conium maculatum*, darnel *lolium temulentum*, cuckoo-flowers any one of a number of wild flowers that bloom when the cuckoo is heard in high summer. We have lost this biodiversity: I live at the edge of a cornfield three miles out of Stratford-upon-Avon and its furrow-weeds are now confined to nettle and poppy. But we have also lost the frame of reference: how many students and playgoers today could identify specimens of fumitory, darnel or cuckoo-flower? Shakespeare, brought up in the country, had a field education, in all probability before he even went to school.

The London compositors who set his plays into print struggled with these words: the quarto text of *King Lear* calls fumitory 'femiter' and the Folio 'Fenitar'. The hardocks, charlocks or bur-docks are 'hor-docks' and 'Hardokes'. One wonders to what extent a London theatre audience would have appreciated the minute observation of oxlip on Titania's bank in *A Midsummer Night's Dream* and the knowledge of folk names which recur at many points in the plays, most famously with the 'long purples' that 'liberal shepherds give a grosser name' in Gertrude's account of the flowers garlanding the dead Ophelia.

Shakespeare was born into the herbal economy of rural England. Falstaff in *Henry IV Part 2* says that the wit of Poins is as thick as Tewkesbury mustard – Tewkesbury was known for the best mus-tard in England. Perhaps because he toured Kent with his fellow-actors, Shakespeare observed the thriving samphire-gathering trade on Dover cliff. But he always remained more interested in the domestic rather than the global plant economy. He evinced little interest in the international spice trade. Not even *The Tempest*, with its imperial matter and semi-New World setting, is about the things on which empire was built: trade, spice.

Shortly after the publication of the First Folio, Shakespeare's grand-daughter Elizabeth, now a girl of sixteen, returned from London with a cold, from which she fell into a distemper. Her father John Hall cured it in sixteen days, principally through the expedient of making her eat large quantities of nutmeg. Modern historians associate nutmeg with the race for colonial domination between the Dutch and British East India companies. Nutmeg was indeed very valuable in Elizabethan England because it was thought to guard against plague, but Shakespeare does not conjure up the spice routes from the Indies. He merely gives the clownish young shepherd in *The Winter's Tale* seven nutmegs on his shopping list for a very English sheep-shearing feast, albeit one transposed to Bohemia. The Young Shepherd is also required to purchase 'saffron to colour the warden pies'. One senses that it is the 'warden' more than the saffron that Shakespeare cared about. William Bulleyn's *Book of Simples* (1562) commended the 'red warden' pear as 'of great virtue, roasted or baked, to quench choler'. Provincial Shakespeare, who had been an infant deep in the shires, was always more interested in different species of England pear and apple than the globalized nutmeg and saffron market.

4. Old World, New Man?

I dreamt that I was with the Queen

We now look back on 1564 as the year of the birth of William Shakespeare. And of the deaths of Michelangelo, apogee of the Italian Renaissance, and John Calvin, leader of the Protestant Reformation in Geneva. To judge from Stow's *Annals*, the Elizabethans remembered it not only for plague, but also for extreme weather: floods in September, an *aurora borealis* setting the night sky aflame to the north in October, then just before Christmas a great frost which froze the rivers, so that on New Year's Eve people walked along the Thames on the ice from London Bridge to Westminster, some playing at football 'as boldly there as if it had been on the dry land'. Over the Christmas festival season, courtiers came out from the palace at Westminster and 'shot daily at pricks [archery targets] set upon the Thames'.

It was also the year when 'an honourable and joyful peace was concluded betwixt the Queen's Majesty and the French King, their realms, dominions and subjects, which peace was proclaimed with sound of trumpet at her castle of Windsor, and also at London on the thirteenth day of April'. On signing the peace treaty at Troyes, the English renounced their claim on Calais in return for a payment of more than 200,000 crowns. Later in the year, a solemn obsequy was held in St Paul's Cathedral to mark the death of another peacemaker, Ferdinand I, Holy Roman Emperor and Archduke of Austria, who had (temporarily) ended religious strife in the statelets of what is now Germany, while also converting the elected crowns of Bohemia and Hungary into hereditary Habsburg possessions – though with eastern Hungary remaining subservient to the Ottoman empire. That same year, Ottoman Turks took the island of Malta (Marlowe would set his hugely successful play *The Jew of Malta* at this moment). An unstable France, Roman Catholic dominion in southern Europe, Ottoman might in the Mediterranean: it was against this background that Queen Elizabeth, her courtiers, diplomats and public intellectuals were attempting to establish national security and a strong sense of identity for England. Shakespeare's plays, though rarely propagandistic, would be part of this foundational project, sometimes through their representation of English history, sometimes through their location in political hotspots such as Venice, Cyprus and Bohemia.

Elizabeth was not yet Gloriana, the fairy queen of Edmund Spenser's epic national poem, the figure with her foot on the map. But she was busy establishing her image through procession and visitation, debate and play. Early August 1564 saw her progressing through Cambridge. At the university she was 'honourably and joyfully received' by the students in King's College, where she lay for the duration of her visit: 'The days of her abode were passed in scholastical exercises of philosophy, Physic and Divinity, the nights in Comedies and Tragedies, set forth partly by the whole University, and partly by the Students of the Kings College.' Though the drama might have constituted the after-dinner entertainment, intellectually it was of a piece with the philosophical and theological exercises and debates so beloved of the queen.

While the court calendar was set by the queen's progresses, life in rural England was shaped by the agricultural cycle and the ecclesiastical year, in which ancient days of ritual and rest were yoked to the 'holy days' of the church. There was a time to sow and a time to harvest. Social life revolved around the festive year. May Day and Midsummer Eve were the times when fairies like Puck worked their mischief. In *A Midsummer Night's Dream*, Shakespeare, who always had his cake and ate it too, magically merges his midsummer night with a hunt at dawn on May Day. He creates a glorious mish-mash of popular and aristocratic customs, mingling morris-men and royal spectacle.

In pulpit and classroom, people were taught about the magical correspondences between the order of nature and the structure of society. There was a cosmic hierarchy, with God at the top and then the angels and then humankind and then the beasts. By the same account, there was a social hierarchy, with kings and queens

at the top, then the nobles, gentry, common folk, and lastly vagabonds, whores and masterless men. Actors, naturally, were little
better than vagabonds. The young apprentices, who played the
female parts on stage, were regarded as the adult actors' male
whores.

Some of Shakespeare's characters – those who have a vested
interest in doing so – talk about the importance of maintaining
this structure of 'degree' and 'order'. But it is disorder that makes
good theatre. At the centre of *A Midsummer Night's Dream* is a
fantasy about a man of humble origins, Bottom the weaver. He at
one and the same time slides down the scale of degree, becoming
a hairy ass, and climbs to the very top, making love to the Fairy
Queen.

The queen made much of her image as a virgin. This appears to
have provoked fantastic desires in the minds of her subjects. Simon
Forman was one of the best-known astrologers of the age. In the
year 1597, he took a break from scribbling down horoscopes and
prognostications, and recorded instead a dream of his own:

I dreamt that I was with the Queen, and that she was a little elderly
woman in a coarse white petticoat all unready; and she and I walked up
and down through lanes and closes, talking and reasoning of many
matters. At last we came over a great close where were many people,
and there were two men at hard words. One of them was a weaver, a
tall man with a reddish beard, distract of his wits. She talked to him and
he spoke very merrily unto her, and at last did take her and kiss her. So
I took her by the arm and put her away; and told her the fellow was
frantic. And so we went from him and I led her by the arm still, and
then we went through a dirty lane. She had a long, white smock, very
clean and fair, and it trailed in the dirt and her coat behind. I took her
coat and did carry it up a good way, and then it hung too low before. I
told her she should do me a favour to let me wait on her, and she said
I should.

Then said I, 'I mean to wait *upon* you and not under you, that I might
make this belly a little bigger to carry up this smock and coats out of the
dirt.' And so we talked merrily and then she began to lean upon me,
when we were past the dirt, and to be very familiar with me, and

methought she began to love me. And when we were alone, out of
sight, methought she would have kissed me.

On this brink, Dr Forman awoke. Dr Freud would no doubt have
something to say about all the dirt in that dream. Forman was a
keen playgoer, so there is a strong possibility that his dream was
partly shaped by his witnessing of a performance of *A Midsummer
Night's Dream*: the choice of weaver as profession for the humble
man who kisses the queen and the similarity of his phrasing to
Bottom's would otherwise be an extraordinary coincidence.

In a kind of reverse alchemy, Forman's dream transformed
Shakespearean gold into base metal. Because the miracle of
Bottom's dream, in which he becomes an ass endowed with a very
long pair of ears that are fondled by the fairy queen, is its *innocence*:

When my cue comes, call me, and I will answer. My next is, 'Most fair
Pyramus.' Hey-ho! Peter Quince? Flute, the bellows-mender? Snout,
the tinker? Starveling? God's my life, stolen hence and left me asleep! I
have had a most rare vision. I had a dream, past the wit of man to say
what dream it was. Man is but an ass, if he go about to expound this
dream. Methought I was – there is no man can tell what. Methought I
was – and methought I had – but man is but a patched fool if he will
offer to say what methought I had. The eye of man hath not heard, the
ear of man hath not seen, man's hand is not able to taste, his tongue to
conceive, nor his heart to report, what my dream was. I will get Peter
Quince to write a ballad of this dream: it shall be called 'Bottom's
Dream', because it hath no bottom; and I will sing it in the latter end of
a play, before the duke.

The wit of this comes from its play on a famous biblical phrase
that must have long since lodged itself in Shakespeare's memory.
Many members of the original audience, steeped as they were in
the New Testament, would have recognized Bottom's account of
his dream as an allusion – with the attributes of the different senses
comically garbled – to a famous passage in the first Epistle to the
Corinthians, in which St Paul says that the eye of man has not seen
and the ear of man has not heard the glories that will await us

when we enter the Kingdom of Heaven. In the Geneva translation of the Bible, which Shakespeare knew well, the passage speaks of how the human spirit searches 'the bottom of God's secrets'. Jesus said that in order to enter his kingdom, one had to make oneself as a child. The same may be said of the kingdom of theatre. It is because Bottom has the uncynical, believing spirit of a child that he is vouchsafed his vision. Where does this childlike sense of wonder come from? Perhaps from a country boy remembering how as a child he loved stories of animals and transformations and queens, but how he never dreamed that one day his stories would be played out with all the pomp of court before the very eyes of the Virgin Queen herself.

New star, new man

The village of Alderminster is five miles south of Stratford, on the Oxford road. It was home to Thomas Russell, a prosperous landowner who was a few years younger than Shakespeare. The kind of friend whom Will cultivated in his later years. Together with Stratford attorney Francis Collins, Russell was executor of Shakespeare's will, a mark of the respect and trust in which he was held. Along with the duty came a bequest of five pounds, more money than Shakespeare left to his fellow-actors put together. Not that Russell needed the money: his second marriage had been to an extremely wealthy widow, Ann Digges.

Leonard Digges, her son, was a great fan of Shakespeare. He contributed a dedicatory poem to the First Folio of 1623, where he revealed his own local knowledge by mentioning the monument to the poet in Holy Trinity Church. Some other lines of praise by him were included in a collection of Shakespeare's poems that was published in 1640. He had particular admiration for *Romeo and Juliet*, the Roman plays, Othello and Iago, Falstaff, Malvolio, and Beatrice and Benedick.

Widow Digges' other son, Sir Dudley, was on the council of the Virginia Company that had established the colony at Jamestown in 1607. It may have been through him that Shakespeare obtained information about the wreck of the *Sea Venture* on Bermuda, which furnished him with details for the storm in *The Tempest*.

Shakespeare probably did not know the father of the Digges boys, but may well have known about him. Thomas Digges, who died in 1595, was the greatest English geometrician and astronomer of the age — besides being a Member of Parliament who would put his mathematical brilliance to use in his role as a military technician in the 'war party' associated with the Earl of Leicester. Digges' watching of the skies serves to remind us that Shakespeare lived in a time during which old certainties about the divine order of things were being called into question.

Prospero in *The Tempest* teaches the orphaned Caliban how 'To name the bigger light, and how the less, that burn by day and night'. *Sun* and *moon* are among the first words that our parents teach us. John and Mary Shakespeare would have believed that God created the universe in six days, then rested on the seventh. On the fourth day He made 'two great lights: a greater light to rule the day, and a less light to rule the night'. Caliban unmistakably echoes this verse from the book of Genesis. As a young child, Will Shakespeare would have believed the biblical account of creation without question, and he would have assumed that the earth was the centre of the universe.

Ptolemy's ancient cosmological system had been accepted for centuries: the universe consisted of a concentric series of material but transparent spheres, moving around the earth on a single axle-tree. Above us, the sphere of the air, then those of the moon, the sun and the stars. More highly educated people would have known that the spheres of Mercury and Venus were closer to the earth than that of the sun and that there were, as Marlowe's Mephistopheles reminds Dr Faustus, nine heavens or spheres, 'the seven planets, the firmament and the empyreal heaven'. As the spheres moved on their axle-tree, the friction between them created a kind of heavenly music, which is often alluded to, and sometimes imagined to be heard, in Shakespeare's plays.

The important thing about this system was its stability. Any change was a portent, a sign of divine intervention. Comets imported 'change of times and states', as in the opening lines of

Henry VI Part 1. Sun-spots, eclipses and planetary disturbances were, as in *Hamlet*, 'harbingers preceding still the fates / And prologue to the omen coming on'. Christ's birth, the turning point in history, was signalled by the appearance of a new star over Bethlehem, observed by Persian magi. A marginal explanatory note in the Geneva Bible explained that the star was 'an extraordinary sign to set forth that King's [i.e. Christ's] honour, whom the world did not esteem'.

Late in the year 1572 a bright new star appeared in the sky. Most people would have interpreted this as some kind of divine warning. But a different view was taken by Thomas Digges, who was one of the first to separate astronomy (the empirical observation of the stars) from astrology (the art of divining the influence of the stars on people and events). For him, the appearance of the new star, which he reported in a Latin treatise addressed to fellow intellectuals across Europe, was an opportunity to test out the veracity of Copernicus' recent hypothesis that the earth revolved around the sun and not vice versa.

The new star disappeared before Digges could draw any conclusions, but a few years later he oversaw a new edition of a popular almanac by his father, *A Prognostication Everlasting*, to which he appended a short treatise of his own entitled 'Perfect Description of the Celestial Orbs'. Old Digges' astrological prognostications bumped up against young Digges' astronomical science. His 'Perfect Description' was a loose translation of the key cosmological sections of Copernicus' *De revolutionibus orbium coelestium* (1543). It was primarily through young Digges, then, that the new Copernican cosmology reached an English audience. He included a diagram showing an infinite universe in which the stars extended outwards from the solar system. Like all educated men of the period, he looked to the classics for intellectual authority: the system is accordingly called 'Pythagorean' as opposed to 'Copernican': though Ptolemy's geocentrism had held sway for centuries, in ancient Greece a few of the followers of Pythagoras, most notably Aristarchus of Samos, had posited the heliocentric model.

Copernicus had decentred man by putting the sun instead of the earth at the centre of his cosmos. Digges' vision of infinity had

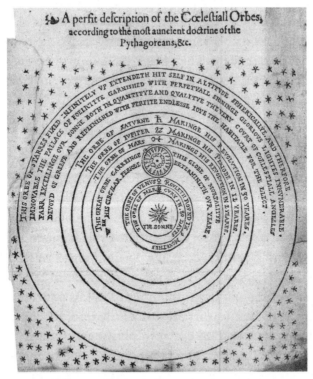

Thomas Digges' Copernican universe

the potential to strike a further blow at the traditional idea of humankind's special status as God's last and best creation. John Donne's famous lines in his 'Anatomy of the World' register the shock-waves:

> And new philosophy calls all in doubt,
> The element of fire is quite put out;
> The sun is lost, and th'earth, and no man's wit
> Can well direct him where to look for it.
> And freely men confess that this world's spent,
> When in the planets, and the firmament
> They seek so many new; they see that this
> Is crumbled out again to his atomies.
> 'Tis all in pieces, all coherence gone;
> All just supply, and all relation:

> Prince, subject, father, son, are things forgot,
> For every man alone thinks he hath got
> To be a phoenix, and that then can be
> None of that kind, of which he is, but he.
> This is the world's condition now.

The element of 'fire', which in the Ptolemaic model circles above and around us, is put quite out of place by the Pythagorean/ Copernican/Diggesian theory of a heliocentric universe. According to Donne's ranging, associative frame of mind, the fact that people such as Galileo Galilei – like Shakespeare, a child of the year 1564 – have started looking for new worlds through their telescopes proves that our world has had its day and is in a state of decay. Furthermore, according to the long-established theory of the correspondence between the macrocosm of the cosmic order and the microcosm of the state, the loss of fixed hierarchy and stability in the heavens presages similar upheaval in the social order. Stable relationships between prince and subject, father and son, are seen to be subject to the same stress as the cosmic hierarchy, the 'great chain of being'.

Shakespeare's Ulysses, in *Troilus and Cressida*, is the archetypal politician, a master of the art of rhetorical manipulation. He argues that there is a correspondence between the order of the cosmos and that of the state.

> The heavens themselves, the planets and this centre
> Observe degree, priority and place,
> Insisture, course, proportion, season, form,
> Office and custom, in all line of order:
> And therefore is the glorious planet Sol
> In noble eminence enthroned and sphered
> Amidst the others.

As the sun ('Sol') is throned in eminence above the other planets, so the king is throned in eminence as the head of state. But even in this articulation of the traditional image of the hierarchy of 'degree', there is potential for instability. Ulysses' model is essentially geocentric – the earth is 'this centre' and the sun is in its sphere 'amidst the others' – but the emphasis on the particular eminence of the sun may hint towards the new heliocentric astronomy.

Ulysses' speech about the need for society to maintain a strict hierarchical order or 'degree' is a political strategy. He argues that one of the causes of the untuning of degree in the Greek camp is the fact that their exemplary warrior Achilles is sulking in his tent when he should be in the appropriate place for an exemplary warrior, namely on the battlefield. But the method he proposes by which Achilles is to be restored to his proper place is itself a disruption of degree. Hector has issued a challenge to single combat. Degree should dictate that Hector's equal on the Greek side, Achilles, is put forward, but Ulysses proposes Ajax instead, thus snubbing Achilles and provoking him into rejoining the army. Ulysses then achieves his end by rigging an election.

In the midst of a rhetorically powerful vision of the chaos that ensues when the moral and social order are not upheld, Ulysses lets slip his knowledge of the relativity of value. 'Take but degree away', and the music of the spheres will be untuned. God's division of the sea and land will be undone, the 'solid globe' will become a mere 'sop',

> Strength should be lord of imbecility,
> And the rude son should strike his father dead:
> Force should be right, or rather, right and wrong,
> Between whose endless jar justice resides,
> Should lose their names, and so should justice too.
> Then everything includes itself in power,
> Power into will, will into appetite,
> And appetite, an universal wolf,
> So doubly seconded with will and power,
> Must make perforce an universal prey,
> And last eat up himself.

In the very act of warning that 'right and wrong' will 'lose their names' if 'degree' is not observed, Ulysses adds parenthetically that justice resides not inherently on the side of right, as one would expect it to, but rather in the middle of the 'endless jar' between right and wrong. The play *Troilus and Cressida* as a whole is a demonstration that order, moral and social, is not a pre-determined value system answerable to a harmonious cosmic design, but rather a process, an endless debate and negotiation of terms, in which reason and judgement cannot be separated from appetite and will.

An orthodox thinker such as Richard Hooker, apologist for the established Anglican church, held fast to his belief in the correspondence between the cosmic and the political order: 'If celestial spheres should forget their wonted motions . . . what would become of man himself, whom these things now do all serve?' As a child, Shakespeare would have heard weekly homilies read from the pulpit in Holy Trinity Church. Sometimes they concerned 'Order, and Obedience to Ruler and Magistrates' or thundered 'Against Disobedience and Wilful Rebellion'. The original book of *Homilies* for use in church was published the year before Shakespeare's birth. The homily against rebellion was added after the failure of the uprising of the northern earls when he was five. 'Take away kings, princes, rulers, magistrates, judges and such estates of God's order,' the vicar would have proclaimed, and 'there must needs follow all mischief and utter destruction both of soul, bodies, goods and commonwealths'.

But in Shakespeare's plays, *Troilus and Cressida* especially, 'moral philosophy' is not a fixed point of reference. It is itself interrogated and found wanting. Hector attempts to distinguish between the dangers of actions based on emotion ('the hot passion of distempered blood') and the propriety of those based on reason ('a free determination / 'Twixt right and wrong'). In the case of the Trojan war, right and wrong cannot be judged objectively: 'What's aught but as 'tis valued?' asks Troilus. Hector tries to maintain the case that value exists above 'particular will', but the play as a whole – with its counterpoint of Trojan and Greek, battlefield and bedroom, high rhetoric and low bawdy – proposes that all moral judgements are relative. It is Ulysses who makes this point most eloquently: a man or an action can only be judged

by reflection,
As when his virtues shining upon others
Heat them and they retort that heat again
To the first giver.

The real threat to degree was not the shift from Ptolemy's universe to that of Copernicus and Digges. Having the sun, symbolic of the monarch, at the centre of the universe did not undo the queen's pre-eminence. The frontispiece to *Sphaera Civitatis* ('The Spheres of Government'), John Case's 1588 commentary on Aristotle's *Politics*, equates the revolving planets with Elizabeth's moral and political virtues. She presides over the whole scheme in such a way that it wouldn't matter if the diagram, which is Ptolemaic, had actually been Diggesian.

Frontispiece to Sphaera Civitatis

In a system depending on stability, irregular motions such as that of the planet Mars presented some difficulty. 'Mars his true moving, even as in the heavens / So in the earth, to this day is not known,' says the French king early in *Henry VI Part 1*. But the most dangerous threat came from the act of breaking the correspondence

between macrocosm and microcosm, the order of the heavens and
the order of society. For Digges, it was not a contradiction in terms
to append his astronomical innovations to his father's 'almanac',
a form of writing that presupposes the divine influence of the
heavens on the earthly history of states and individuals. But for
Shakespeare's Edmund in *King Lear*, the whole notion of astral
influences is merely an excuse for the failure of individuals to
take responsibility for their own destinies. Gloucester voices the
orthodox view that 'these late eclipses in the sun and moon portend
no good to us', in response to which Edmund scornfully decon-
structs the whole edifice of correspondences:

This is the excellent foppery of the world, that when we are sick in
fortune – often the surfeits of our own behaviour – we make guilty of
our disasters the sun, the moon and stars, as if we were villains on
necessity, fools by heavenly compulsion, knaves, thieves and treachers
by spherical predominance, drunkards, liars and adulterers by an enforced
obedience of planetary influence, and all that we are evil in, by a divine
thrusting on: an admirable evasion of whoremaster man, to lay his goatish
disposition on the charge of a star! My father compounded with my
mother under the dragon's tail and my nativity was under Ursa Major,
so that it follows I am rough and lecherous. I should have been that I am
had the maidenliest star in the firmament twinkled on my bastardizing.

Edmund is embodiment of the 'new man' who emerged in tandem
with the 'new philosophy'. The man who, following Machiavelli,
defines himself as first and foremost himself, in contrast to the 'old
man' who would have defined himself in terms of the old hierarchies as a dutiful subject to his prince and son to his father. In
Donne's metaphor in his 'Anatomy of the World', the new man
claims that he can reinvent himself like the legendary – and traditionally unique – phoenix which rebegets itself out of its own ashes.
The great, and closely related, intellectual and spiritual revolutions
of the sixteenth century stoked the fire in which the new man begot
himself: the intellectual claim of humanism was that individual and
social life could be bettered through pursuit of the ideals embodied
in the pagan culture of ancient Greece and classical Rome, while the

spiritual claim of the Reformation was that Heaven could be reached only through the inner contract of the individual, not through the traditional intermediaries of priestly intercession and ecclesiastically ordained duties, works and observances.

Some of the greatness of Donne's own poetry comes from the tension between that part of him which is an energetic, thrusting new man and that other part – bequeathed by his Catholic pedigree – which yearns for the security of the old order. Perhaps the same may be said of Shakespeare. Let us imagine for a moment the young dramatist's ambitions, and the dilemma brought with them, at the beginning of his career.

Once again, the place of his infancy is paramount. It is a universal phenomenon that rural communities, regulated by the rhythm of the seasons, are conservative. The ideals of the French Revolution throve in Paris, but the attempt to impose them on the provinces failed disastrously. Anti-royalism and anti-clericism did not take root among the peasantry. So too with the English Reformation of the sixteenth century. As the historian Eamon Duffy has documented so fully and powerfully, centuries of Roman Catholic belief and observance in the English provinces could not be wiped out overnight by the fiat of the Tudor governmental machinery. Though the corporation of Stratford-upon-Avon embraced Protestantism with a vengeance, there is ample evidence of recusancy in the environment of Shakespeare's youth. Many scholars have contended that John Shakespeare held fast to the old faith, though the matter is still fiercely debated. Inconclusively so, principally because of the uncertainty regarding a Catholic testament of faith apparently signed by John, found in his Henley Street house in the eighteenth century. The first page of it was a forgery, and the rest is likely to have been, but some still argue for its authenticity.

Whether the Shakespeares were recusants, Protestants or 'church papists' who conformed outwardly with the Anglican church whilst remaining Catholics in their hearts, the balance of probability is that William Shakespeare's own instincts and inheritance were cautious, traditional, respectable, suspicious of change. We may as well say conservative.

But then he got the acting bug. Ben Jonson more than once

imagined a scene that has been played out again and again down the
ages – and that we can easily imagine being played out in the Shakespeare household. Father insists that Son should follow a respectable
profession like the law, but Son wants to go his own bohemian way.
Thus in *Every Man in his Humour*, the father objects to his son's

> Dreaming on naught but idle poetry,
> That fruitless and unprofitable art,
> Good unto none, but least to the professors.

The name of William Shakespeare is in the cast list of the original
production of *Every Man in his Humour*. There would have been a
special piquancy to this exchange if, as is eminently plausible, he
played the part of the father. Given that Shakespeare was known
as the modern Ovid, a similar sequence in Jonson's *Poetaster* is also
apposite. Ovid Senior upbraids Ovid Junior:

Are these the fruits of all my travails and expenses? Is this the scope and
aim of all thy studies? Are these the hopeful courses wherewith I have
so long flattered my expectation from thee? Verses? *Poetry*? Ovid, who
I thought to see the pleader, become Ovid the play-maker?

John Shakespeare, coming from a class where 'idleness' was a
sin, would have subscribed to the common view that actors were
little better than vagabonds. His successors on the Stratford town
council banned them from playing in the town. When John heard
that his son had become employed in the theatre, he would have
been flabbergasted. The dramatic profession was a completely
unknown quantity. Playhouses functioning as businesses by charg-
ing an entrance fee, a repertoire of secular drama performed all the
year round, not just at ecclesiastical festivals and as aristocratic
entertainments: these were innovations in late sixteenth-century
England, and were exclusively London phenomena. By whatever
route William Shakespeare reached the London theatre world in
the late 1580s or early 1590s, he was going against the grain of his
background and taking a very considerable financial risk.

As for the content of the plays that dominated the theatre world which Shakespeare entered, the example of Christopher Marlowe, born in the same year as Shakespeare, scandalized the traditional world-view. Marlowe had transformed the London stage with a string of brilliant and constantly revived plays: the two parts of *Tamburlaine the Great*, *The Jew of Malta*, *Dr Faustus*. Dazzling in their verse, audacious in their intellectual reach, with central roles that provided leading actor Edward Alleyn with his most powerful vehicles, they must have mesmerized Shakespeare in his early London years. The theatre-world was still a small one, so he would probably have known Marlowe personally, but even if he did not he would surely have discovered a little of his background – born in 1564, provincial rather than London, a father in trade, an education at a local grammar school (King's, Canterbury: King's, Stratford-upon-Avon). But there the resemblance ended: Marlowe had gone on to Cambridge and become an archetypal 'new man', associated with the 'new philosophy' in its most radical inflection – 'atheism' and Machiavellianism. What is more, he made the autonomous self the very basis of his drama: what are Tamburlaine, Faustus and Barabas if not new men incarnate?

This, in a nutshell, was Shakespeare's dilemma: to make his way as a new dramatist while remaining true to his conservative herit-age, to outdo Marlowe without doing away with traditional values. But perhaps it was an opportunity more than a dilemma. Shake-speare was very canny. He read Marlowe's plays better than Marlowe did himself: what happens to the unrestrained new man in those plays? Tamburlaine, Faustus and Barabas die and are damned. What happened to Marlowe? Less than a year after the dire admonition of *Greene's Groatsworth*, he too was dead. What happened to Shake-speare? He was the great survivor. He was the one dramatist of his generation never to be imprisoned or censured in connection with his work. He was the one dramatist who eventually ended his career out of choice, not by force of circumstance. He became a wealthy man and bought a large house called New Place. He abhorred and yet he was fascinated by the new men, of whom his great examples were Edmund in *Lear* and his forerunners, Richard III, Aaron in *Titus Andronicus*, the Bastard in *King John* and Iago in *Othello*. Perhaps that was because he was the true new man himself.

SECOND AGE
Schoolboy

Then the whining schoolboy, with his satchel
And shining morning face, creeping like snail
Unwillingly to school.

*A Tudor schoolroom: boys only, with different classes in the same room,
and frequent resort to the birch*

5. Stratford Grammar

To school

The hour at which he crept, willingly or unwillingly, would have been a few minutes before six o'clock on summer mornings. Seven o'clock in winter darkness. Turning left out of the family home and glove-making workshop on Henley Street, right at the market cross, past the pillory at the top of Sheep Street, along Chapel Street and in behind the half-timbered almshouses that still stand on Church Street. Educated for free in the King's New Grammar School, by courtesy of his father's position on the town council. Up a stone staircase behind the Gild Chapel, where the images had been washed with lime. Into the big schoolroom. The carved bosses on its chamfered oak beams show painted roses and hearts – the red rose of Lancaster with a white heart of York, symbolizing the Tudor reconciliation of the ancient grudge of two royal households.

Grammar meant Latin grammar. From dawn to dusk, six days a week, all the year round (though Thursdays and Saturdays were half days). Shakespeare's masters were Simon Hunt and then Thomas Jenkins – perhaps a Welshman, like Hugh Evans the schoolmaster in *The Merry Wives of Windsor*, who gives a Latin lesson to a clever but cheeky boy called William. Latin was a language for boys only (unless you were a princess or a very well-born lady), so the presence of Mistress Quickly leads to some glorious linguistic misapprehensions:

EVANS: William, how many numbers is in nouns?

WILLIAM: Two.

MISTRESS QUICKLY: Truly, I thought there had been one number more, because they say, 'Od's nouns'.

EVANS: Peace your tattlings! What is 'fair', William?

WILLIAM: *Pulcher.*

MISTRESS QUICKLY: Polecats? There are fairer things than polecats, sure.

EVANS: You are a very simplicity 'oman. I pray you peace.
What is *lapis*, William?

WILLIAM: A stone.

EVANS: And what is 'a stone', William?

WILLIAM: A pebble.

EVANS: No, it is *lapis.* I pray you, remember in your prain.

WILLIAM: *Lapis.*

EVANS: That is a good William. What is he, William, that does lend articles?

WILLIAM: Articles are borrowed of the pronoun, and be thus declined: *Singulariter, nominativo, hic, haec, hoc.*

EVANS: *Nominativo, hig, hag, hog,* pray you mark: *genitivo, huius.* Well, what is your accusative case?

WILLIAM: *Accusativo, hinc* – [*Faltering*]

EVANS: I pray you, have your remembrance, child, *accusativo, hing, hang, hog.*

MISTRESS QUICKLY: 'Hang-hog' is Latin for bacon, I warrant you.

EVANS: Leave your prabbles, 'oman. What is the focative case, William?

WILLIAM: O, – *vocativo*, O.

EVANS: Remember, William, focative is *caret.*

MISTRESS QUICKLY: And that's a good root.

EVANS: 'Oman, forbear.

MISTRESS PAGE: Peace!

EVANS: What is your genitive case plural, William?

WILLIAM: Genitive case?

EVANS: Ay.

WILLIAM: Genitive: *horum, harum, horum.*

MISTRESS QUICKLY: Vengeance of Ginny's case, fie on her!
Never name her, child, if she be a whore.

EVANS: For shame, 'oman.

MISTRESS QUICKLY: You do ill to teach the child such words: he teaches him to hick and to hack, which they'll do fast enough of themselves, and to call 'horum' – fie upon you!

EVANS: 'Oman, art thou lunatics? Hast thou no understandings for thy cases and the numbers of the genders? Thou art as foolish Christian creatures as I would desires.

The cases, the numbers, the genders, the articles. This is how Shakespeare learned his Latin. Rote learning in the style of the catechism. What is *lapis*? A stone. And what is 'a stone'? No, not 'a pebble' – you are not required to think – 'a stone' is *lapis*. Double translation, backwards and forwards between English and Latin, day in, day out. A clever boy survives such a regime by sniggering: *hog* for *hoc*, *fuck-ative* for *vocative*, *whore* for *horum*, *root* and *case* as not only technical terms in grammar but also slang for, respectively, the male and female parts.

Ben Jonson, who went to a more famous school (Westminster), sneered at Shakespeare's 'small Latin'. Jonson had all the intellectual snobbery to be expected of one of the very few middle-ranking Englishmen of the age to have possessed a substantial library of Greek and Latin historical and philosophical texts. For a bright boy like Will, a few years in an Elizabethan grammar school would have yielded enough Latin to last a lifetime. He would have achieved a level of proficiency above that of many a modern undergraduate student of the classics.

During the brief reign of Edward the boy king in the mid-sixteenth century, some of the revenue from the suppressed chantries and monastic colleges had been put towards the foundation of the network of grammar schools that still bear the king's name. The aim was that 'good literature and discipline might be diffused and propagated throughout all parts of our Kingdom, as wherein the best government and administration of affairs consists'. Literacy and moral education were regarded as the very foundation of the state or 'commonwealth'. According to Desiderius Erasmus in the standard textbook on the art of verbal and written copiousness, the study and imitation of the Latin classics were of inestimable value:

In this kind of thing it is best that youth be exercised variously and diligently, because besides the fruit of style, by this means they imbibe the old and memorable stories as if doing something else, and fix them deep in memory; they become accustomed to the names of men and places; moreover they learn especially the power of honesty and the nature of probity, the especial virtues of eloquence.

There is, however, a tension here. To be trained in 'the power of honesty and the nature of probity' is one thing; to learn style and the art of eloquence potentially quite another. After all, many of the oldest and most memorable stories from the poems and histories of the ancients turned on duplicity rather than probity.

The enrolment registers of King Edward's in Stratford-upon-Avon are lost, but there can be no doubt that Shakespeare attended, as was his entitlement. Evidence enough for that is provided by the exact knowledge of Elizabethan grammar-school methods of education revealed in the exchange between William and teacher Evans, together with the pattern of allusions to grammar-school texts scattered across the plays. These run from Holofernes' reference to 'old Mantuan' in *Love's Labour's Lost* to Prospero's quotation from Ovid's *Metamorphoses* in *The Tempest*. Whereas the infant's 'nurse' suggests that the seven ages speech begins in the specific context of courtly customs, by the time Jaques reaches the second age he is imagining the life of the commoner, not the courtier. Aristocrats such as the Earls of Oxford and Southampton had private tutors and did not attend grammar school.

The syllabus of the Stratford school does not survive, but all the English schools of the reformed Tudor age covered similar ground with similar methods, so the statutes of a comparable establishment open a window on to the expectations that would have been placed upon Shakespeare the schoolboy:

And to the intent the scholars of the said school may be placed in a seemly order whereby they may more quietly apply their learning, the said school shall be divided in four several forms.

And in the first shall be placed young beginners commonly called *Petitts* until they can read perfectly, pronounce also and sound their words plainly and distinctly . . .

In the second form, the master shall teach the scholars the *Introduction of Grammar*, commonly called the eight parts of speech as they be set forth and generally used in this realm . . .

In the third form, the master shall teach Terence, Aesop's *Fables*, Virgil, Tully's *Epistles* (or so many of them as he shall think fit for the capacity and profit of his scholars in the same), and, as he shall perceive them profit in Learning, so shall he place them in the fourth form – where every day he shall give them an English to be made in Latin and teach unto them there placed Sallust, Ovid, Tully's *Offices*, the *Commentaries* of Caesar, *Copia Verborum et Rerum Erasmi*, and also he shall teach the art and rules of versifying (if he himself be expert therein).

And the practice of the scholars in this fourth form must be daily to turn and translate sentences from English into Latin and so contrary from Latin into English and at certain times to write Epistles one of them to another and the Master to peruse the same over and amend the faults that he findeth therein.

The scholars of the third and fourth forms shall speak nothing in the schoolhouse but Latin, save in their teaching of the lower forms.

Before being admitted to big school, there was 'petit' or 'petty' school, where boys learned to read and were drilled in the catechism of the established church. Then they would proceed to Latin grammar, beginning by learning their entire textbook by heart.

The standard text was prescribed by law. Early in the sixteenth century, William Lily of St Paul's School in London had produced both an *Introduction of the Eight Parts of Speech*, otherwise known as the 'English accidence', and a Latin grammar that later came to be entitled *Brevissima Institutio*. By a royal proclamation of Edward VI, these two works, printed jointly as the *Short Introduction of Grammar*, became the set text for Latin teaching in grammar schools throughout England for generations to come.

Though the second form was synonymous with grammar, grammar, grammar, Shakespeare was exposed to both literary composition and rhetorical flourish from the start. Lily's language exercises were frequently worked upon 'sentences' – pithy statements of proverbial wisdom or exhortations to moral virtue –

taken from classical authors. In the early tragedy *Titus Andronicus*, in which Shakespeare frequently showed off his literariness, a bundle of weapons wrapped in an inscribed scroll is brought to Chiron and Demetrius, sons of Tamora queen of the Goths:

DEMETRIUS: What's here? A scroll, and written round about?
  Let's see:
  '*Integer vitae, scelerisque purus,*
  Non eget Mauri jaculis, nec arcu.'
CHIRON: O, 'tis a verse in Horace, I know it well:
  I read it in the grammar long ago.

Shakespeare himself would also have read it in the grammar, for these lines from one of Horace's odes were twice quoted by Lily in the *Short Introduction*. The words are ironically apposite to the dramatic context: 'The man of upright life and free from crime does not need the javelins or bows of the Moor.' Chiron and Demetrius, egged on by Aaron the Moor, have murdered, raped and mutilated. Titus sends them javelins and bows precisely in order to indicate that he knows they are anything but men of upright life and free from crime. He has method in his madness: he knows that even if they recognize Horace's lines, they will not see the application to themselves. Chiron and Demetrius are good pupils when instructed by Aaron in the art of villainy, but they offer a salutary reminder that not all grammar school boys will fulfil the Tudor educational ideal of a smooth path from reading about integrity of life in the classics to practising it in civil society.

The way in which Shakespeare learned Latin shaped his subsequent life of writing as decisively as did the content of the books he went on to read in later years. Lily proceeded from grounding in syntax to exercises in the art of *elocutio*, eloquent composition. As the boy William is reminded in *The Merry Wives of Windsor*, Latin has complicated rules of declensions, cases and numbers, whereby different parts of speech have to agree with each other. Nouns and pronouns vary according to their place in a sentence: the student has to decline them by rote, singular and plural, through nominative (for the subject), vocative for an address (William remembers that one: 'O, – *vocativo*, O'), accusative for the object, genitive (thus '*hic*' means 'this', while '*horum*', as in the joke about Ginny's case, means 'of these'), dative and the dreaded ablative. At the same time, a noun may be masculine, feminine or neuter and the ending of the adjective that qualifies it must be correspondingly adjusted. It is not sufficient to know that the masculine genitive plural of '*hic*' is '*horum*': you will also have need of feminine '*harum*' and neuter, which (mercifully or confusingly) is another '*horum*'.

In everyday English, grammar relies heavily on word order ('Shakespeare studied Latin': subject, verb, object). In Latin, because you can work out the grammar from the agreement of the word-endings, you can vary the word order. The verb is frequently held back to the end of the sentence. In order to illustrate Latin grammar at work, textbook and master have to keep building word upon word. An adjective is added to a noun and the class is required to make them agree. Then bring together a pair of adjectives or a pair of nouns. Such doublings and amplifications were drilled into Shakespeare in the classroom so thoroughly that they became second nature in his writing, sometimes obsessively so, as in *Hamlet*, where one epithet will never do when two are possible: 'one auspicious and one dropping eye', 'disjoint and out of frame', 'impotent and bedrid', 'the trappings and the suits of woe', 'An understanding simple and unschooled' – all these and more are to be found in the first hundred lines of the first court scene of the play.

Lily's introductory grammar again: two pairs of pronouns and adjectives, the first pair in the first person and the second pair in the second, are placed in apposition to each other, causing the verb to be drawn from the first person to the second. The textbook example is

Ego pauper laboro, I being poor do labour.
Tu dives ludis, Thou being rich dost play.

Because of '*tu*' ('thou'), we have second person '*ludis*' as opposed to first person '*ludo*' in the manner of '*laboro*'. In the act of illustrating this point, Lily has both created a symmetrical pattern and produced a piece of proverbial wisdom regarding the social order.

Grammar has slid into rhetoric: the figurative arrangement of words for the purpose of argument, often of a political, legal or ethical kind. From grammatical modulation to force of argument. Shakespeare remembered the trick and bettered it:

QUEEN MARGARET: I had an Edward, till a Richard killed him:
  I had a husband, till a Richard killed him:
  Thou hadst an Edward, till a Richard killed him:
  Thou hadst a Richard, till a Richard killed him.
DUCHESS OF YORK: I had a Richard too, and thou didst kill him:
  I had a Rutland too, thou holp'st to kill him.

Lily goes on to show how Latin grammar allows a statement of the whole to precede several statements of the parts. He calls this *prolepsis*. The device will be one of the essential building blocks of the Shakespearean sonnet and soliloquy.

Again, the *Short Introduction of Grammar* explains how the rule of agreement should operate when a single verb serves two or more nouns, a figure called zeugma, exemplified by a mighty example from Cicero:

Nihil te nocturnum praesidium palatii? Nihil urbis vigiliae? Nihil timor populi? Nihil concursus bonorum omnium? Nihil hic munitissimus habendi Senatus locus? Nihil horum ora vultusque moverunt?

Imagine young William in the second form at Stratford grammar, Lily's *Brevissima* on his desk and schoolmaster Simon Hunt standing at the front asking him to translate Cicero's extended zeugma. The single verb *moverunt*, held back to the end for effect, serves no fewer than six noun phrases, each introduced by *nihil*, 'nothing'. William's English translation will need repetition at the start of each sentence, though it will not be grammatically possible to replicate Cicero's powerfully prominent placing of *nihil*. And English grammar will require the student to keep repeating the verb in order to make sense. William is bound to pause for breath and thought at the end of each sentence, so his translation will be something like this:

Did the night-guarding of the palace nothing move thee?
Did the watching of the City nothing move thee?
Did the fear of the people nothing move thee?
Did the running together of all good men nothing move thee?
Did this most strong place of holding the Senate nothing move thee?
Did the face and countenance of these nothing move thee?

He is less than ten years old, and yet already he is speaking like a poet, seeking to move an audience through the elaborately patterned manipulation of language. Both the imagery and the structure are highly memorable. The night-guarding of the palace, the watching of the city. The fear of the people, the good men running in the street. The authority of the Roman Senate, the face and countenance that both reveal and conceal. The sound of the words, the rhythm of the sentences – a whisper of the beat of blank verse? The mesmerizing force of repetition at the beginning and end of each line. All are impressed on his ardent young mind.

Around twenty years later, he will be hard at his own repetitions:

> So many hours must I tend my flock,
> So many hours must I take my rest,
> So many hours must I contemplate,
> So many hours must I sport myself.

And another eight years or so after this, in *Julius Caesar*, he will bring Cicero's Roman world alive on stage – complete with a cameo appearance from the man himself, memorably described as having 'silver hairs', 'gravity' and 'judgement' that will purchase 'good opinion', but also a politician's 'ferret eyes'. And in dramatizing the Ciceronian world, Shakespeare will also take to new heights that art of moving a public audience through the force of rhetorical patterning:

> Friends, Romans, countrymen, lend me your ears:
> I come to bury Caesar, not to praise him . . .
> Here, under leave of Brutus, and the rest –

> For Brutus is an honourable man:
> So are they all, all honourable men . . .
> But Brutus says, he was ambitious,
> And Brutus is an honourable man . . .
> I thrice presented him a kingly crown,
> Which he did thrice refuse. Was this ambition?
> Yet Brutus says, he was ambitious,
> And sure he is an honourable man.

Mark Antony is master not only of his rhetorical schemes – the arrangement of words in memorable patterns of repetition and variation – but also of his rhetorical tropes, the shifting of meanings from their surface sense. He says that he is not coming to praise Caesar, but praise him he does. He repeatedly emphasizes Brutus' reputation as an honourable man in order to highlight the dishonour of the assassination of Caesar. Brutus has described his action one way: 'Romans, countrymen, and lovers, hear me for my cause and be silent . . . If then that friend demand why Brutus rose against Caesar, this is my answer: not that I loved Caesar less, but that I loved Rome more.' Antony redescribes the same actions with the opposite interpretation. The art of rhetoric, whereby advanced students were taught to argue both sides of a case, is what makes the dramatic opposition possible.

The key to the process is that word of Cicero's, *moverunt*. The persuasive orator and his kinsman the convincing actor seek to 'move' their listeners in two senses of the word. By shifting the sense of words and lines of thought, they make the audience change their position, come over to the speaker's side of the argument. And they do so by affecting the emotions: the forcefulness, the evocative excess, of their verbal invention stirs the hearts and minds of the auditors. It did not go unnoticed in either classical times or Shakespeare's that persuasive rhetoric involved exaggeration or even downright contradiction of plain truth. Antony's claim that he has not come to praise Caesar is patently false. As the much-cited Roman theorist Quintilian put it in his *Institutio Oratoria*, 'this is an art which relies on moving the emotions by saying that which is false'. And as the wise Shakespearean clown Touchstone put it in *As You Like It*, 'The truest poetry is the most feigning.' That was one of the reasons why Puritans, committed to God's unadulterated truth, distrusted the theatre.

In all, Lily's *Grammar* offers eight 'figures' of grammatical repetition, variation and elaboration, the last and richest of them being *synecdoche*, the substitution of the part for the whole, which is illustrated with the example '*Aethiops albus dentes*'. These three words mean 'Ethiopian', 'white' and 'teeth'. *Aethiops* ('Ethiopian') is nominative singular and *dentes* ('teeth') is accusative plural. The conventional sense – a black man with strikingly contrasting white teeth – would lead one to expect *albus* (white) to agree with *dentes*, but here the adjective is nominative singular rather than accusative plural. *Albus* agrees with *Aethiops*: the figure of synecdoche is a grammatical trick that attributes the whiteness to 'the whole Ethiopian or Black Moor'.

It is unlikely that elaborate handbooks listing dozens of arcane rhetorical figures were on the syllabus at the Stratford-upon-Avon grammar school. They did not need to be: an intelligent reader such as Shakespeare would intuitively have extended Lily's figures such as zeugma and synecdoche from a narrowly grammatical application into a broadly rhetorical one. All he needed to do was follow the examples from Cicero, Horace and the other classical authors that formed the illustrative quotations in the *Introduction of Grammar*.

The trick of synecdoche that whitens the whole Ethiopian, not just his teeth, comes at the very climax of Lily's course of instruction. It may be imagined as an end-of-year party-piece for the enjoyment of boys who have progressed sufficiently to proceed onward and upward to the next form. I suspect that Shakespeare took particular delight in it. Synecdoche became one of his favourite figures of speech because it makes for dramatic solidity and immediacy. 'Uneasy lies the head that wears a crown' is far more tactile and memorable than would be an abstract 'Uneasy sleeps the monarch burdened with the responsibility of sovereignty.'

What he would have especially liked about the example of the Ethiopian is its paradoxical inversion of the normative sense. This is the kind of device that Feste has in mind when – in a figure that smacks of John Shakespeare's glove workshop as well as Simon Hunt's schoolroom three streets away – he compares a 'sentence' (proverbial saying) in the hands of a witty speaker to a 'cheveril' (soft kid-skin) glove: 'How easily the wrong side may be turned outward.' Shakespeare pulled off this trick again and again, both linguistically and in the wider vision of his plays: he shows you one thing, then he turns it inside out before your very eyes and ears. There is, I suspect, a direct line from his discovery of the synecdoche *Aethiops albus dentes* in the second form at school to Aaron the Moor's inversions of the age's racial commonplaces in *Titus Andronicus*: orthodoxy proclaims that mankind is essentially white and the skin of Moors is burned black by their exposure to the African sun, whereas Aaron suggests that mankind is essentially black and the skin of those Goth schoolboys Chiron and Demetrius has been limewashed or painted a superficial white:

> Ye white-limed walls, ye ale-house painted signs!
> Coal-black is better than another hue
> In that it scorns to bear another hue,
> For all the water in the ocean
> Can never turn the swan's black legs to white,
> Although she lave them hourly in the flood.

Rhetorically inventive language *can* turn black to white, apply the Ethiop's bright teeth to his whole self. Having seen that, Shakespeare has taken the first step towards the world of *Othello*, with its cheveril-glove inversion of the age's expectation that a Moor will always be barbarous and a Venetian civilized.

Cicero has a very small part in *Julius Caesar*: his authority is appealed to in his absence more often than he voices his opinions on stage. But one of the speeches that Shakespeare creates for him reveals the profoundly organic relationship between Shakespeare's experience in the classroom and his art as a dramatist:

> Indeed, it is a strange-disposèd time:
> But men may construe things after their fashion
> Clean from the purpose of the things themselves.

The context is Casca's account of the prodigies attending the times: a fiery tempest, the hand of a common slave ablaze and yet unscorched. The stage Cicero's response, 'it is a strange-disposèd time', is an allusion to one of the most frequently quoted phrases of the real Cicero, '*O tempora, O mores!*' – 'O times, O morals!' or, to translate more colloquially but without the rhetorical structure of repetition, 'The country is going to the dogs.'

But it is Cicero's qualifying statement that is really interesting. For all the differences between paganism and Christianity, the orthodox religious world-view of both Roman and Tudor times regarded freak occurrences of weather and bizarre disruptions to the natural order as signs of divine disapproval, portents of disaster, indications that the state is out of joint. Cicero, though, points out that the power to manipulate language, for which another word is rhetoric, allows men to 'construe' such things in any way they want, wrest them 'clean from the purpose' proposed by orthodox thinking. 'Construe' is a technical term from the classroom. When schoolmaster Hunt told young William to translate or interpret a passage of Latin, he would have said 'Construe, William, construe.' The implication is that there is a *correct* meaning. There usually will be, at the level of basic grammar. But what happens when *figurative* speech is introduced? Figurative language ranges from structural turnings-inside-out like that of the cheveril glove through to semantic twists, most notably *metaphor*, where one thing is carried across and applied to another, with which it does not have a natural relationship. So, for example, Cleopatra's elision of a death-bringing poisonous snake and a life-sucking infant at the breast: 'Dost thou not see my baby at my breast / That sucks the nurse asleep?' Whenever figures are present, the relationship between words and things is liable to be destabilized.

Then interpretation becomes a battle of wills. Each man and woman on stage construes things after his or her own fashion and the audience remembers not what is most true but what is spoken most memorably. In *Macbeth*, Lennox and Ross speak piously of the portents of a strange-disposed time, but what we remember are the paradoxes and equivocations of the weird or 'weyard' sisters and the Macbeths themselves: 'Cannot be ill, cannot be good . . . And nothing is, but what is not . . . palter with us in a double sense.'

Reading the classics

With Lily's grammar mastered, William could proceed to the third form. From comprehension to composition: once the boys had learned to read Latin fluently, they were taught to write it.

They would begin with simple collections of sayings – there was one entitled *Sententiae pueriles* ('sentences for boys') and another colloquially known as *Cato's Distichs* ('most elegant sayings attributed to Cato'). The *Sententiae* provided a series of building blocks for composition. First there were sentences of two words such as '*Amicis opitulare*' ('help your friends') and '*Cognosce teipsum*' ('know yourself'). Then of more: '*Assidua exercitatio omnia potest*' ('assiduous practice makes everything possible'), '*Amicitia omnibus rebus anteponenda*' ('friendship before everything else'), '*Mendacem memorem esse oportet*' ('a liar needs a good memory'). Pupils would be required to play around with such phrases. We can again imagine the Stratford schoolmaster in the room with the carved bosses on the roof beams. Addressing Richard Field, a slightly older boy: 'Turn it into a question and put it into the future tense, Richard, *Will you help your friends?*' Addressing William Shakespeare: 'Construe in the plural, William, *Liars need to have good memories.*' He will remember this: if you are going to make up a story, whether you are writing a play or plotting to destroy a rival in the manner of Richard III or Iago, you will need to have a good memory so that your plot is consistent with itself.

The next step was some basic conversation and letter-writing classes. Erasmus' *Colloquies* was widely used. It proposed that conversation begins with greeting. The Latin term was *salve*. Though often translated simply as *hail* or *greetings*, the literal meaning was *save you*, analogous to the English greeting 'God give you good morrow', which was customarily abbreviated to 'good morrow' (and now 'good morning' or just 'morning'). *Salve pater*: 'greetings, father'. *Salve mi frater*: 'greetings, my brother'. But Erasmus wants learning to be fun, so he quickly moves on to some more colourful combinations. *Salve vini pernicies*: 'greetings, consumer of quart-sized pots of wine'. And in response: *Salve et tu, gurges helluoque placentarum*, 'greetings to you too, you who devours cakes into the bottomless pit of your stomach'. The flyting of Hal and Falstaff, the wit-combats of Beatrice and Benedick, have their origins here.

Letter-writing usually began with some of the simpler epistles in Cicero's *Ad Familiares* (inculcations of friendship again), but then relied on Erasmus' handbook *De conscribendis epistolis*. This exemplified not only such technicalities as the appropriate forms for beginning and ending letters, but a whole range of literary techniques from the use of historical examples to the appropriate stylistic register for lamenting sorrows or offering praise. Pupils would be required to imagine they were a particular character, perhaps from classical mythology or history, writing a letter in a particular situation.

Write a letter as if you were Antenor persuading Priam that he should return the stolen Helen to her Menelaus, either because it was just in itself, or because it would be a very foolish ruler who caused many brave men to enter battle on account of the most shameful love of such an effeminate youth as Paris.

Write that, Master William, and you're on the road to inventing dramatic character, to composing *Troilus and Cressida*.

The composition of Latin epistles was intended to make the boys skilled in rhetoric, the persuasive use of words for the purposes of argument. Rhetoric meant learning how to order your speeches: exordium, narration, arguments in favour, arguments against, refutation, exemplification, testimony, conclusion. It meant honing your metaphors and developing elaborate figures of verbal symmetry – syllepsis, antimetabole, zeugma, threefold *amplificatio* (otherwise known as *tricolon*). Even today, when politicians are making speeches they still have a way of making three points when one would do. Shakespeare never lost his taste for the intellectual gymnastics whereby rhetoric was put into the service of political argument:

> Paris and Troilus, you have both said well,
> And on the cause and question now in hand
> Have glozed, but superficially, not much
> Unlike young men, whom Aristotle thought
> Unfit to hear moral philosophy:
> The reasons you allege do more conduce
> To the hot passion of distempered blood
> Than to make up a free determination
> 'Twixt right and wrong.

He also loved sending up intellectual gymnastics. Holofernes, the pedantic schoolmaster in *Love's Labour's Lost*, describes 'a companion of the king's, who is intituled, nominated, or called Don Adriano de Armado':

Novi hominem tanquam te: his humour is lofty, his discourse peremptory, his tongue filed, his eye ambitious, his gait majestical, and his general behaviour vain, ridiculous, and thrasonical. He is too picked, too spruce, too affected, too odd, as it were, too peregrinate, as I may call it . . . He draweth out the thread of his verbosity finer than the staple of his argument. I abhor such fanatical phantasimes, such insociable and point-device companions, such rackers of orthography, as to speak 'dout', fine, when he should say 'doubt', 'det', when he should pronounce 'debt': d, e, b, t, not d, e, t. He clepeth a calf 'cauf', half 'hauf', neighbour *vocatur* 'nebour', neigh abbreviated 'ne'. This is abhominable, which he would call 'abominable'. It insinuateth me of insanie. *Ne intelligis, domine?* To make frantic, lunatic.

As with Parson Evans' 'lunatics', there is a distinct suggestion on Shakespeare's part that there is something insane about the verbosity of so-called learning. One senses from exchanges such as this that young William would have found something fundamentally comic in the exercise in another of Erasmus' textbooks, *De copia rerum et verborum* ('on copiousness of things and words'), whereby the sentence 'your letter pleased me greatly' is expressed in 195 different ways.

After much more in the Holofernes vein of schoolroom construal, the teacher turns to Dull the Constable and says '*Via*, goodman Dull! Thou hast spoken no word all this while.' To which Dull replies, in a line that guarantees a huge laugh in the theatre, 'Nor understood none neither, sir.' There is more warmth than scorn in Shakespeare's remembrance of both the school-masters and the dullards of his Stratford boyhood. The key to his theatrical magnanimity was his capacity to imagine Holofernes and Dull with equal affection.

Classical literature was introduced in the third form, usually beginning with extracts from the Roman dramatist Terence – Shakespeare's first exposure to comedy, though since the study was of choice passages rather than full plays, there would have been little sense of drama. There would also have been simple animal fables in the Aesop tradition and a first taste of the real master, Virgil: some of his pastoral *Eclogues* and some highlights from his epic *Aeneid*. It was perhaps because Shakespeare was first introduced to Virgil in this way that his sense of the *Aeneid* seems to have been of a series of great set-pieces – Dido's farewell, the retrospective narrative of the sack of Troy and the death of Priam, Aeneas' descent into the underworld – rather than a sustained narrative.

This tendency to read literature selectively was a function not only of the grammar-school syllabus, but also of one of the prevail-ing theories of good reading in the period. Lily's *Brevissima* had included some advice from Erasmus on how to read: first go through a text to gain the general sense, then parse it word by word with close attention to vocabulary and grammar, then undertake a rhetorical or stylistic analysis (look for figures, elegant turns of phrase, aphorisms and proverbial wisdom, histories and fables, extended similitudes), and finally attend to ethical matters, taking particular note of morally improving passages and narrative examples. The logical consequence of this latter procedure was to read for highlights, marking them in the margin or copying them out for oneself into a 'commonplace book', otherwise known as a 'table', in order to have a ready record of examples of general truths about life and behaviour. This is the procedure to which Hamlet alludes when he says that he will erase all the observations he has learned from books and replace them with the dark knowledge he has derived from his father's ghost:

> Yea, from the table of my memory
> I'll wipe away all trivial fond records,
> All saws of books, all forms, all pressures past
> That youth and observation copied there;
> And thy commandment all alone shall live
> Within the book and volume of my brain . . .
> O villain, villain, smiling damnèd villain!
> My tables,
> My tables: meet it is I set it down:
> That one may smile and smile and be a villain.

This last sentence, to be written in Hamlet's tables, is expressed in the aphoristic form which Shakespeare had been taught to recognize ever since he was exposed to the *Brevissima* and the *Sententiae pueriles* in the classroom.

Many commonplace books from the period survive, including a selection from those of Ben Jonson, which was published under the title *Timber: or, Discoveries made upon Men and Matter*. A marginal note indicates each topic discussed. The matter ranges from extended quotation from classical authors to aphorisms such as 'language most shows a man' to autobiographical reminiscence, including a justly famous discussion *De Shakespeare nostrati* ('concerning our Shakespeare'):

I remember the players have often mentioned it as an honour to Shakespeare that in his writing, whatsoever he penned, he never blotted out line. My answer hath been, would he had blotted a thousand. Which they thought a malevolent speech. I had not told posterity this, but for their ignorance, who choose that circumstance to commend their friend by, wherein he most faulted. And to justify mine own candour: for I loved the man and do honour his memory, on this side idolatry, as much as any. He was indeed honest and of an open and free nature, had an excellent fancy, brave notions and gentle expressions, wherein he flowed with that facility that sometime it was necessary he should be stopped.

Sufflaminandus erat, as Augustus said of Haterius. His wit was in his own power; would the rule of it had been so too. Many times he fell into those things [that] could not escape laughter: as when he said in the person of Caesar, one speaking to him, *Caesar thou dost me wrong*. He replied: *Caesar did never wrong, but with just cause* and such like, which were ridiculous. But he redeemed his vices with his virtues.

There was ever more in him to be praised than to be pardoned. In passing, it is worth wondering how anybody who has ever meditated upon this passage could ever again doubt that the author of the plays was William Shakespeare of Stratford, friendly rival of Jonson and colleague of the players. But let that be. What is interesting for our purposes here is the attention paid by Jonson to rhetorical skill and to particular phrases. He regards Shakespeare as an over-intelligent schoolboy who has gone too far with the advice of Erasmus' fourth-form handbook concerning the art of copiousness in composition: he just does not know when to stop.

Furthermore, Jonson suggests that Shakespeare's linguistic facility sometimes got in the way of his logical sense. 'Caesar did never wrong, but with just cause' is, rhetorically speaking, a clever riposte to the accusation 'Caesar thou dost me wrong.' It turns the original phrase back on the first speaker, turning its sense inside out by means of a qualifying amplification. To Jonson's more logical mind, the reply is ridiculous: if the cause is just, the action cannot be wrong. Shakespeare nearly always preferred the doubleness of rhetoric to the singularity of logic, but if Jonson pointed out the fault to him, he may on this occasion have been stung into revision – into the very act of 'blotting' his line that Jonson said he always resisted – for in the only surviving text of the play, Caesar's quick response to the man who says he has been wronged is conspicuous by its absence.

Jonson had a way of picking out phrases in Shakespeare and other authors for either praise or ridicule, testing them against the truth of experience. This method of reading for highlights and low spots was complemented in the period by an alternative form of critical analysis that paid close attention to dramatic context. A teacher's handbook includes a salutary reminder that even as pupils construed the sense of their texts word by word and line by line, they were also encouraged to 'keep in fresh memory the argument, matter and drift of the place which they are to construe'. They were required to consider the *quis*, the *quid*, the *cui*, the *causa*, the *locus*, the *quo tempore*, the *prima sequela*: 'That is, who speaks in that place, what he speaks, to whom he speaks, upon what occasion he speaks, or to what end, where he spake, at what time it was, what went before in the sentences next, what followeth next after.' Though Shakespeare studded his works with adages and *sententiae*, classical allusions and occasional Latin tags of the sort that Jonson so loved, one suspects that it was this latter mode of reading that really attracted him. Always attend to the speaker, the context, the motivation for the speech. Do not assume that there is a disinterested truth, that the words of the speaker are those of the author. This is the dramatist's way of working. Dramatically, it is perfectly appropriate for a character as powerful as Julius Caesar to assume that he can do wrong with just cause. Dramatically, the exchange with the man claiming that he has been wronged could have been one more piece of ammunition for Brutus and the conspirators.

In the fourth form

If Shakespeare proceeded to the fourth form at King Edward's, he would have started reading more extended works, as opposed to the extracts that dominated the early years' syllabus. Julius Caesar's own *Commentaries* on his Gallic wars, to which he makes a couple of passing allusions, would have got him interested in military campaigns and terminology, battles between Romans and so-called barbarians, and the status of ancient Britain as a Roman colony, all themes which he explored in his tragedies and history plays. He would probably also have read Cicero's *De Officiis* ('of duties'), which was studied both for the eloquence of its prose and as a handbook of civic humanism, laying out the obligations of the good citizen and distinguishing between wise counsel and false flattery.

As indicated in the statutes for another small-town grammar

school, quoted above, the fourth form was also the place where the schoolmaster began 'to teach the art and rules of versifying (if he himself be expert therein)'. Stratford had a good pedigree in this regard: John Brownsword, who became master soon after Shakespeare's birth, was a published author of Latin verses. The art of Latin verse composition, with its complex rules of prosody, was often taught by means of the relatively undemanding example of the pastoral *Eclogues* of the Italian neo-Latin poet, Giovanni Baptista Spagnuoli, known (from his birthplace) as Mantuan. Holofernes supplies something that sounds very like a memory of William's schooldays:

Fauste, precor gelida quando pecus omne sub umbra ruminat, – and so forth. Ah, good old Mantuan, I may speak of thee as the traveller doth of Venice:

> *Venetia, Venetia,*
> *Chi non te vede non ti pretia.*

Old Mantuan, old Mantuan! Who understandeth thee not, loves thee not? Ut, re, sol, la, mi, fa.

Holofernes begins by quoting the opening of Mantuan's first *Eclogue*, a traditional starting-point for the teaching of poetry ('Faustus, while all the cattle are chewing the cud in the cool shade, I pray thee . . .'). He proceeds to an Italian proverb ('Venice, Venice, he that does not see thee does not esteem thee'), makes a claim for the easy comprehensibility and the lovable quality of Mantuan, and then hums the notes of the musical scale. He is warming himself up for a verse composition class.

He then asks his sidekick, the curate Nathaniel, to read 'a staff, a stanza, a verse'. '*Lege, domine*' ('read, master'), he says and then settles back to listen to Berowne's composition, a sonnet beginning 'If love make me forsworn, how shall I swear to love?' He complains about Nathaniel's misreading of the metre ('You find not the apostrophus, and so miss the accent') and is equally unimpressed by the young man's compositional effort: 'Here are only numbers ratified.' That is to say, the lines are metrically correct but lacking in 'the flowers' of poetic 'fancy' and 'the jerks' of rhetorical 'invention'.

Though Holofernes would never admit as much, the same was sometimes said of the somewhat laboured verses of Mantuan. Many of the most respected educational commentators would, however, have agreed with his advice as to the best model for truly inventive poetic composition: 'for the elegancy, facility, and golden cadence of poesy, *caret*, Ovidius Naso was the man'. Shakespeare would have agreed too. We do not know exactly how much Ovid he read in school, but it is demonstrable from his work that of all the writers on the syllabus Ovid was the one who appealed to him most strongly, and whom he sought out – albeit mostly in English translation – after he left school.

In the upper forms, it was probable that Shakespeare would have been expected to speak Latin even to his schoolmates. And, being a bright pupil, he would have been expected to set an example in helping to teach the basics to boys in the lower forms. Once those basics were mastered, the essence of the system was translation, translation, translation: from Latin into English, English into Latin and back again. All his career, Shakespeare went on translating source materials into his own language. Fragments of his school-room knowledge stud his work: allusions to Ovid, phrases from Cicero, tags out of Horace.

He may well have acted in his first play while still a schoolboy. In most grammar schools, the boys in the schoolroom didn't only read about Julius Caesar and Roman history. They also performed Latin plays. Stratford's own Peter Quince, a certain Davy Jones, staged a Whitsun pageant for the town (production budget: thirteen shillings and fourpence). When Shakespeare was writing *The Two Gentlemen of Verona*, he remembered a lovely cross-dressed boy in a pageant of just this kind, playing the part of Ariadne, deserted by her lover:

> at Pentecost,
> When all our pageants of delight were played,
> Our youth got me to play the woman's part,
> And I was trimmed in Madam Julia's gown,

Which served me as fit, by all men's judgements,
As if the garment had been made for me:
Therefore I know she is about my height.
And at that time I made her weep a-good,
For I did play a lamentable part.
Madam, 'twas Ariadne, passioning
For Theseus' perjury and unjust flight,
Which I so lively acted with my tears
That my poor mistress, movèd therewithal,
Wept bitterly: and would I might be dead
If I in thought felt not her very sorrow.

That key word 'moved' again, but this time the emotional response is achieved not by rhetoric alone, but by the combination of eloquent speech and 'lively' (lifelike) acting. The recollection is a miniature dramatization of the moment when the two dimensions of the poetic words on the page are transformed into life by the third dimension of performance on the stage.

Davy Jones's Stratford Whitsun show was played in 1583, by which time Shakespeare had left school, his father had run into financial problems and young Will had got an older woman pregnant, then married her. But there is no reason to suppose that a pageant of the deserted Ariadne, probably based on the poem written in her voice in Ovid's *Heroides*, might not have been staged in Stratford in an earlier year, with one of Shakespeare's school-fellows in the title role. Or even Shakespeare himself.

6. After Palingenius

All the world's a stage

In 1558, the bones of Piero Angelo Manzolli of La Stellata, near Ferrara in Italy, were exhumed and burned by order of the Sacred Congregation of the Roman and Universal Inquisition. The reason? His poem, *Zodiacus Vitae*, the zodiac of life, a collection of astronomical and philosophical reflections divided into twelve books. The title was promptly catalogued in the *Index Librorum Prohibitorum*, the list of forbidden books that was published by the Vatican for the first time the following year. Whether the inquisitors were provoked by the book's incidental ecclesiastical and papal satire, or its pagan view of cosmology and the science of human happiness, we do not know. Probably both. Manzolli must have known he was wrestling with dangerous matter when he published his work a quarter of a century earlier: he disguised his identity by rearranging the letters of his name into a Latin anagram, Marcellus Palingenius.

The book's combination of anti-Catholicism with an accessible introduction to ancient astronomical and astrological ideas was such that, having been banned across much of Continental Europe, *Zodiacus Vitae* became a third-form set text in many an Elizabethan grammar school. What Catholic Europe abhorred, Protestant England devoured. And just in case pupils (or even schoolmasters) needed a crib, a young and ardently Protestant poet called Barnaby Googe undertook an English translation in the early 1560s.

William Shakespeare may have become acquainted with Palingenius in the third form of the King's New School in Stratford-upon-Avon. Or he may have picked up the English translation some time later and found his eye falling on one of the explanatory annotations that Googe obligingly provided in the margin: 'The world a stage play.' Palingenius had compared life to a fable or pageant, all the world to a stage and human beings to actors ('*vita haec est fabula quaedam scena autem mundus versatilis histrio et actor*'). Googe's English version is written in the clunking poetic metre of 'eight and six' that Peter Quince recommends for the prologue to his play of 'Pyramus and Thisbe' in *A Midsummer Night's Dream*. This is how he renders the relevant passage:

> Wherefore if thou dost well discern
>   thou shalt behold and see
> This mortal life that here you lead
>   a Pageant for to be.
> The divers parts therein declared
>   the changing world doth show
> The maskers are each one of them
>   with lively breath that blow.
> For almost every man now is
>   disguised from his kind
> And underneath a false pretence
>   they silly souls do blind.
> So move they Gods above to laugh
>   with toys and trifles vain,
> Which here in Pageants fond they pass
>   while they do life retain.

Life is a theatrical spectacle in which we are all actors playing a series of parts. Disguise, deception and pretence are woven into the very fabric of human life. The gods above laugh at the foolish presumption of mortals; they are like a theatre audience looking down from the gallery upon the stage. Every one of these ideas is found in a wealth of sources both classical and medieval.

Every one is also a recurring motif in Shakespeare, where Richard III is too ugly to play the lover so he plays the villain, where Bottom plays the ass, Viola plays the boy and Hamlet plays the madman, Iago is not what he is, Cleopatra plays a part of infinite variety and Rosalind is a boy-actor pretending to be a girl pretending to be a boy pretending to be a girl. And where the 'Pageants fond' of the mortals are a source of divine amusement in both comedy and tragedy. Robin the Puck: 'Shall we their fond pageant see? / Lord, what fools these mortals be!' Caius Martius Coriolanus: 'Behold, the heavens do ope, / The gods look down, and this unnatural scene / They laugh at.'

The seven ages of man

Palingenius did something new with the commonplace idea of the great theatre of the world. He combined it with another ancient commonplace, the division of human life into a series of ages. In ancient Greece, Aristotle had divided life into youth, middle age and old age. In ancient Rome, Ovid's *Metamorphoses* had included a sustained comparison between the four seasons and the passage of human life under the auspices of Time, the devourer of all things (*Tempus edax rerum*). In early Christianity, St Chrysostom had developed a sixfold division – infant, child, adolescent, young man, man of *gravitas*, old man – and suggested that each age had its own particular earthly miseries.

Palingenius also concentrated on the misery of the flesh: his infant cries on being brought into this 'wretched life', his schoolboy is perpetually beaten, his lusty youth runs mad with rage and riot ('No counsel will he take therein, / but witty saws despise'), his man of 'graver age and wiser' faces nothing but the toil of earning bread for his family, and finally there comes 'wrinkled age' when

> The body fades, the strength abates,
> 　　the beauty of his face
> And colour goes, his senses fail,
> 　　his ears and eyes decay,
> His taste is gone, some sickness sore
> 　　frequenteth him alway,
> Scarce chaws his meat his toothless chaps
> 　　scarce walks with staff in hand
> His crooked old unwieldy limbs,
> 　　whereon he scarce may stand.

The mind likewise doth feel decay,
  now dotes he like a childe,
And through his weak and aged years
  is wisdom quite exiled.

The imagery of toothlessness and loss of taste, together with the analogy between dotage and childhood, will sound very familiar to anyone who knows Jaques' famous 'All the world's a stage' speech in *As You Like It*.

Palingenius, then, enumerates five ages of man. Three, four and six ages also had their supporters, but there was a particularly strong case for seven. In a compendium of the age's thought called *The French Academy*, Peter de la Primaudaye explained that whereas many authorities plump for six ages (nicely corresponding with the number of days it took God to create heaven and earth), 'Some have made 7 parts, adding decrepitude or bedrid-age after old age: and they would ground their principal reason of this division upon this, that the number of 7 is an universal and absolute number.'

The elegance of the seven ages was their correspondence to the quasi-magical properties of the number seven. God may have created everything in six days, but there was also the seventh day on which he rested. Both biblical and classical writers often ordered things in sevens, as with Jacob's prediction to Pharaoh of seven fat years, then seven lean ones. It was therefore widely believed that human life went in seven-year cycles.

La Primaudaye proposed the following pattern: the first age is infancy (from Latin *infans*, meaning unable to speak), then comes childhood, which lasts to the age of seven, then youth, which lasts till fourteen, then adolescence, from fourteen to twenty-eight (the reign of 'concupiscence', bodily and especially sexual appetite), then virility or 'man's estate', which continues until the completion of the forty-ninth year. Old age sets in at fifty and lasts until death, if you are a believer in the six ages, or decrepitude, if you prefer seven. The 'climacterical year' of 63 (7 x 9, another number by which cycles or 'climates' were measured) was a likely candidate for either death or decrepitude, as was 81 (9 x 9).

Different authorities placed the divisions in different places, but nearly always using sevens and sometimes nines. Shakespeare's awareness of the pattern of ages and climacterical years can perhaps be discerned from certain details in the plays. Consider the Old Shepherd's entrance line in *The Winter's Tale*: 'I would there were no age between ten and three-and-twenty, or that youth would sleep out the rest, for there is nothing in the between but getting wenches with child, wronging the ancientry, stealing, fighting.' This suggests that Shakespeare, like many of his contemporaries, lumped together 'youth' and 'adolescence' into a single age of sexual indulgence, riot and high spirits, lasting fourteen years. But youth's a stuff will not endure. Now turn to *King Lear*. Shakespeare took care to inform his audience that Lear is in his eighty-first year and thus on the border of senility, as the Earl of Kent is in his forty-ninth, on the cusp between virility and old age. Each is in a climacterical year, living in a time of crisis.

Shakespeare's originality

Often when we think Shakespeare is being original, he is actually voicing the commonplace thoughts of his age. Where he was unique was in the vigour and invention with which he turned traditional 'themes' into living drama. He took Palingenius' hint of linking the succession of ages to the metaphor of life as a play. But he was the first to prove the truth of the metaphor by including the discourse within a play as opposed to a treatise or sermon. He was also the first to assign particular dramatic parts to each age. In all versions, the infant cries. Only in Shakespeare's does it do anything so theatrical as puke – indeed, no writer had ever used the word 'puke' as a verb before. There is a specificity to the schoolboy, with his satchel and 'shining morning face', that is lacking in the generic children of previous versions of the *topos*. Instinctively, Shakespeare dramatizes, individualizes, converts archetype into image, idea into action.

Jaques' seven ages are different from everyone else's because their embodiment is all around him in the stage-play world of *As You Like It*. Orlando has been a boy kept away from school. Named after a famous soldier in Italian epic romance, he has just entered wielding a sword. As Jaques is describing the sixth and seventh ages, Orlando returns carrying their embodiment on his back in the form of his servant Adam (named after our first father and perhaps played by Will Shakespeare). Jaques is constantly meeting – and being rude to – lovers. And the play is full of disquisitions on political (in)justice. Only the infant is absent, but with the multiple marriages at the end of *As You Like It*, it will not be long before several of those enter the play's imaginary afterlife.

Although Jaques begins and ends his oration with the customary figures – infant, schoolboy, old man, very old man – he represents the three ages in the middle not as generic youth and manhood or *adolescens* and *virilitas*, but as three very specific parts: the lover, the soldier and the justice. The awakening of sexual desire, then the life of adventure and action, then the settled middle age of responsibility and public service. It is at once the journey of everyman, of Shakespeare himself and of the succession of his plays as they were ordered by his fellow-actors in the First Folio: from comedy, the realm of lovers, to history, that of soldiers, to tragedy, that of justices and men grappling with old age and death.

At the same time, the images parody the excesses of human role-playing. There are no half-measures. The lover sighs 'like a furnace' and composes a 'woeful' (i.e. full of woe but also woefully bad) poem to his mistress' 'eyebrow'. The soldier swears like the trooper he is, combines bravery and foolhardiness, exhibits extreme symptoms of the humour of choler, all in the name of 'reputation' that, like Falstaff's 'honour' in *Henry IV Part 1*, is an empty bubble liable to be pricked in an instant. The justice who embodies legal and political authority may have at his disposal 'wise saws and modern instances' of the kind that were neglected by Palingenius' youth, but he takes care to line his own belly first. 'And so he plays his part': the figure of the actor is explicitly invoked here, as if to remind us that the ancient Greek word for actor was 'hypocrite'. There is a particular frisson when this is applied to a figure of authority, whether a Polonius who fails to practise what he preaches or the 'rascal beadle' and 'scurvy politician' in Lear's denunciations of the dog obeyed in office.

Uniquely too in Shakespeare, who made his living from his actors' powers of articulation, each age is a *voice*: the infant mewling, the schoolboy whining, the lover sighing, the soldier swearing, the justice preaching, the old man piping and whistling, his voice turning again toward childish treble. And only at the last oblivion comes the rest that is silence.

7. Continuing Education: the Art of Translation

The politics of translation

When it came to the choice of his favourite books, the French essayist Michel de Montaigne, though exceptional in his self-awareness, was representative of the educated taste of his age in both France and England. Among poets, it was Virgil whom he most admired, Ovid whom he most enjoyed. Prose he read in order 'somewhat more' to mix 'profit with pleasure': the great works of classical prose enable us 'to range [our] opinions, and address [our] conditions'. 'The books that serve me thereunto,' Montaigne continues in his essay 'Of books', 'are *Plutarch* (since he spake French,) and *Seneca*; both have this excellent commodity for my humour, that the knowledge I seek in them, is there so scatteringly and loosely handled, that whosoever readeth them is not tied to plod along upon them, whereof I am uncapable.' Montaigne is among the first of the moderns not least because he acknowledges the undisciplined quality of his own temperament. Historical and moral books – the *Lives* of Plutarch and the *Epistles* of Seneca – are read the better to understand and reflect upon the human condition, but wisdom is won from them 'scatteringly', eclectically, almost incidentally, not systematically or ploddingly. The profit does not have to be worked for: it comes as a free gift along with the pleasure.

Montaigne was as fluent in Latin as he was in French, so he could read Seneca with ease in the original tongue. But Greek was a much harder matter: Plutarch, a Greek author, has only become a favourite for Montaigne 'since he spake French', that is to say since the appearance of translations of his *Lives* (1559) and *Moralia* (1572) by Jacques Amyot, bishop of Auxerre. Scholars criticized Amyot for his philological inaccuracies, but Montaigne knew by instinct that Father Jacques had caught the spirit of his original:

I have no skill of the Greek, but I see throughout all his translation a sense so closely-jointed, and so pithily-continued, that either he hath assuredly understood and inned the very imagination, and the true conceit of the author, or having through a long and continual conversation, lively planted in his mind a general idea of that of *Plutarch*, he hath at least lent him nothing that doth belie him, or mis-seem him.

True translation, Montaigne implies, is an art less of philological exactitude than of creative conversation. The true translator 'ins' or enters the imagination of the foreign author in order to convey the 'idea' of him (in the Platonic sense of the word), while at the same time he produces 'closely-jointed' sense and pithy phraseology that is worthy of his own language. Amyot is to be thanked for presenting to his country the invaluable gift of Plutarch. In 1579, Sir Thomas North passed the gift on to the English nation by translating Amyot, and in so doing made possible the Roman plays of Shakespeare. And in 1603, English men and women with small or no French had John Florio to thank, for in that year Montaigne spake English.

In Elizabethan England only those who advanced to the universities had more than the most rudimentary Greek. Shakespeare's provincial grammar-school education gave him sufficient Latin to base his *Rape of Lucrece* on a story in Ovid's *Fasti* that was not translated into English in his lifetime. The translation of Greek texts was much more of a necessity, so it is fitting that the most enduring names among the Elizabethan translators are North for his Plutarch and George Chapman for his Homer. But since gentleman readers – and even relatively humble aspiring gentlemen such as Shakespeare – could comfortably read Latin texts in the original, why was such a high proportion of the literary canon of the ancient Romans translated into the vernacular in the Elizabethan period?

A census of printed translations from the time of Caxton to the end of the sixteenth century reveals a definite shift in interest around the time of Queen Elizabeth's accession to the throne. Caxton printed a version of Ovid's *Metamorphoses* in 1480 and one of Virgil's *Aeneid* in 1490, but his Ovid was adapted from a French version that altered and expanded the text in the medieval tradition of 'Ovide moralisé', the reinterpretation of Ovid's risqué tales by the light of Christian allegory. Caxton's Virgil, meanwhile, was based on a French prose romance that covered the ground of the original without actually being a translation of it. For Caxton, Ovid and Virgil were *auctores* in the old sense of the word: 'authorities' or sources, not authors in the modern sense of individuals the integrity of whose literary art is to be respected. The translations were in prose; their purpose was to convey the narratives of the ancient myths, not the style of the canonical poets. The most characteristic and influential of Caxton's translations was his *Recuyell of the Histories of Troy*, a 'recoil' or 'gathering' that offered a version of a French compendium which stitched together the Troy story from many different sources, not just Homer's original *Iliad*. Shakespeare used it, alongside his Chaucer and his Chapman, in the composition of *Troilus and Cressida*: that play's love-story comes entirely from the medieval sources, whereas its military plot looks back to the Homeric original.

During the reign of Henry VIII, the translations that predominated were those of moral works. Again and again, humanist scholars under the influence of Erasmus commended their Englishings to readers on the basis of the 'counsel' and 'sentences', the moral and civic wisdom couched in the form of pithy sayings, that could be derived from them. Sir Thomas Wyatt translated Plutarch's *De Tranquillitate Animi* ('Quiet of Mind') as a New Year's gift for Queen Catherine in 1528, while Sir Thomas Elyot undertook versions of Plutarch's discourse on *The Education or bringing up of Children* (from a Latin rendering by the Italian humanist, Guarino) and of the Athenian orator Isocrates' *Doctrinal of Princes* (directly from the Greek). Elyot's Isocrates lays out in English the ideals of behaviour associated with the 'Prince', the 'Magistrate' and the 'Gentleman'. It is a companion-piece to his *Book named the Governor* (1531), the classic manual of behaviour for the English ruling class. Translation thus served the early Tudor programme of knitting together an emergent nation-state on the basis of secular hierarchy and entrenched order.

The translation for a wide readership of the major *literary* works of Rome was, then, a new phenomenon in the 1550s. It began with the publication of two older renderings of Virgil which had previously only been available to elite readers in manuscript: Gawin Douglas' complete *Aeneid*, originally undertaken at the Scottish court in 1513, and the Earl of Surrey's translation of the second and fourth books of the same poem, done in manuscript some time before Surrey's execution in 1547. In the year of Queen Elizabeth's accession to the throne, there appeared seven books of a new translation of *The Aeneid* by Thomas Phaer. It was completed by Thomas Twyne a decade and a half later. Jasper Heywood's *Troas*, *Thyestes* and *Hercules Furens*, published in successive years from 1559 to 1561, brought into being the English Seneca whose *Ten Tragedies* were collected in 1581. Arthur Golding undertook the first four books of Ovid's *Metamorphoses* in 1564 and the whole fifteen books three years later. He also produced versions of Caesar's *Gallic Wars* (1565) and several Roman historical works. Ovid's shorter works were also translated, as were Horace's poems, and, among prose works, *The Golden Ass* of Apuleius and selections from Livy's *History of Rome* and Pliny's *Natural History*. A variety of Greek authors, too, were Englished, by way of Latin: not only moralists and historians such as Xenophon and Polybius, but also the novelistic romancer Heliodorus – Thomas Underdowne's rendering of his *Aethiopica* of 1569 was popular enough to be reprinted four times in less than forty years.

To judge from the authorial prefaces to these and the many other works from the classics undertaken in the 1560s and 1570s, the translation movement formed a concerted effort to demonstrate that the English tongue was dignified enough to express the wisdom of the ancients. In a postscript to his first seven books of *The Aeneid*, Thomas Phaer remarks that his native language has often been regarded as 'barbarous': that will no longer be the case, he proposed, once Virgil, the most civilized of poets, is heard to speak English. Golding dedicated his Ovid to Robert Dudley, Earl of Leicester, thanking his lordship for his encouragement of the translators 'in their painful exercises attempted of a zeal and desire to enrich their native language with things not heretofore published in the same'.

Leicester was dedicatee of more than a hundred books in the

thirty years between the queen's accession and his own death. His patronage was an important part of his attempt to further his own vigorously patriotic and Protestant beliefs: he was especially active in his support of chroniclers who furthered the providentialist Tudor reading of English history, of writers on the 'puritan' wing of the Anglican church, and of anti-Catholic propaganda. Golding's allusion to Leicester's encouragement of those who are zealous to 'enrich their native language' lends support to the view that the translation movement was motivated by nationalism and the ideology of aggressive Protestantism.

The translators, especially of histories, wrote in their prefaces of their patriotic intent. They pointed to history for proof of the dangers of faction and the evil of rebellion against a lawful prince. The nobility encouraged the translations, nearly all of which were dedicated to members of the Privy Council or their near relatives, prominent supporters of the Protestant cause and the new government of Queen Elizabeth. But, as so often with literary publication, the law of unintended consequences came into force: though the translation movement was by and large aimed at the courtly elite and dedicated to Protestant nationalism, it provided literate middle-ranking figures such as Shakespeare with a wealth of material that could be pressed into the service of other intentions – such as the composition of entertaining, thought-provoking plays.

Parallel Lives

Where did Shakespeare learn the Roman history that he so memorably dramatized in *Julius Caesar*, *Antony and Cleopatra* and *Coriolanus*? Minor variants and improvisations apart, the answer is simple. While most of his plays involved him in the cutting and pasting of a whole range of literary and theatrical sources, in the Roman tragedies he kept his eye squarely on the pages of a single great book.

That book was Plutarch's *Parallel Lives*. Plutarch was a Greek, born in Boeotia in the first century AD. His book included forty-six biographies of the great figures of ancient history, arranged in pairs, half Greek and half Roman, with a brief 'comparison' between each pair. The purpose of the parallel was to ask such questions as: 'Who was the greater general – the Greek Alexander or the Roman Julius Caesar?' Shakespeare affectionately mocked the device of parallelism in *Henry V*, when Fluellen argues that Harry of Monmouth is like Alexander of Macedon because their respective birthplaces begin with an 'M' and there's a river in each and 'there is salmons in both'. But the comedy here is at Fluellen's expense, not Plutarch's – and, like all of Shakespeare's richest jokes, it has a serious point. As Alexander the Great killed his bosom-friend Cleitus in a drunken brawl, so King Harry in all sobriety caused his old chum Falstaff to die of a broken heart.

For Shakespeare, the historical 'parallel' was a device of great power. The censorship of the stage exercised by court officialdom meant that it was exceedingly risky to dramatize contemporary affairs, so the best way of writing political drama was to take subjects from the past and leave it to the audience to see the parallel in the present. The uncertainty over the succession to the Virgin Queen meant that there were frequent whispers of conspiracy in the final years of Elizabeth's reign. It would hardly have been appropriate to write a play about a group of highly placed courtiers – the Earl of Essex and his circle, say – plotting to overthrow the monarchy. But a play about a group of highly placed Roman patricians – Brutus, Cassius and company – plotting to assassinate Julius Caesar had the capacity to raise some awkward questions by means of the implicit parallel.

Plutarch's greatest importance for Shakespeare was his way of writing history through biography. He taught the playwright that the little human touch often says more than the large impersonal historical force. Plutarch explained his method in the *Life of Alexander*:

My intent is not to write histories, but only lives. For the noblest deeds do not always show men's virtues and vices; but oftentimes a light occasion, a word, or some sport, makes men's natural dispositions and manners appear more plain than the famous battles won wherein are slain ten thousand men, or the great armies, or cities won by siege or assault.

So too in Shakespeare's Roman plays. It is the particular occasion, the single word, the moment of tenderness or jest, that humanizes the superpower politicians. One thinks of Brutus and Cassius making up after their quarrel, the defeated Cleopatra remembering it is her birthday, or Caius Martius exhausted from battle forgetting the name of the man who has helped him in Corioles.

The version in which Shakespeare read Plutarch was Sir Thomas North's English translation of 1579, based on Amyot's French version. Shakespeare must have had the big folio of North's *The Lives of the Noble Grecians and Romans* open on his desk as he wrote. Read the *Life of Marcus Brutus* and you see the raw materials on which the dramatist's imagination set to work:

Now Brutus (who knew very well that for his sake all the noblest, valiantest, and most courageous men of Rome did venture their lives) weighing with himself the greatness of the danger, when he was out of his house he did so frame and fashion his countenance and looks that no man could discern he had anything to trouble his mind. But when night came that he was in his own house, then he was clean changed. For, either care did wake him against his will when he would have slept, or else oftentimes of himself he fell into such deep thoughts of this enterprise, casting in his mind all the dangers that might happen, that his wife, lying by him, found that there was some marvellous great matter that troubled his mind, not being wont to be in that taking, and that he could not well determine with himself.

The glory of the theatre is that it can bring the interior character to life. In act one, we see the public face of an apparently untroubled Brutus, but at the beginning of act two Shakespeare conjures up the atmosphere of night, takes Brutus from his bed and places him alone on the bare boards of the Globe. The art of soliloquy then allows us to enter into that troubled mind, to weigh the greatness of the danger, to share the deep thoughts of the enterprise:

It must be by his death. And for my part,
I know no personal cause to spurn at him
But for the general. He would be crowned:
How that might change his nature, there's the question.

There's the question. Anton Chekhov, perhaps the greatest drama-tist since Shakespeare, said that the business of the dramatist is not to provide solutions but to pose problems in the correct way. The Roman plays don't give us easy answers about the relationship of public duty to private will. Shakespeare was content to dramatize the problem and leave the rest to his audience. It was Plutarch who taught him how to pose the questions.

Humanist theorists would not have been entirely happy with that conclusion, but they had an even greater problem with the poet so admired by Holofernes – and Shakespeare.

P. Ovidius Naso was the man

Ovid was without question Shakespeare's favourite classical poet. The first encounter between the English dramatist and the Roman poet would have occurred in the classroom of the grammar school at Stratford-upon-Avon. The boy William would have been drilled in extracts from Ovid's works in their original Latin – first brief passages in those textbooks for the teaching of grammar and rhetoric, then more substantial sections of the poems themselves.

Ovid's love lyrics, the *Amores*, are among the key precedents for Shakespeare's sonnets: each poetic sequence is a set of variations on the moods of love in which the narrative voice shifts rapidly between different poses and tones. His *Fasti*, which linked major events in Roman history and mythology to the calendrical year, was the principal source for Shakespeare's second narrative poem, *The Rape of Lucrece*. Though Shakespeare could have read the *Amores* in a translation by Christopher Marlowe, the *Fasti* were only available in Latin. This goes to show that when Ben Jonson wrote of Shakespeare's 'small Latin' he was measuring with the yardstick of his own prodigious learning – as should by now be fully apparent, by our modern standards Shakespeare had perfectly adequate Latin.

One of the most popular texts in the Elizabethan classroom was the *Heroides*, Ovid's verse-epistles written from the point of view of women in mythology who are deserted by their lovers – Ariadne on Naxos, Dido after the departure of Aeneas from Carthage, and so on. A frequent exercise was to imitate them – 'write a letter in the style of X or from the point of view of someone who has suffered Y' – and in this sense they, like the letters of Cicero and Erasmus, would have helped the student Shakespeare to take his first steps in the art of dramatic impersonation. John Lyly and Christopher Marlowe, the two dramatists who most influenced him when he began writing plays himself, both made extensive use of the *Heroides* as models for the art of a character's self-examination at moments of emotional crisis. The art, that is to say, of soliloquy.

But the influence of all these works pales beside that of Ovid's *magnum opus*, the *Metamorphoses*. Scholars have calculated that about 90 per cent of Shakespeare's allusions to classical mythology refer to stories included in that epic compendium of tales. Shakespeare knew the book in both the original Latin and in Arthur Golding's translation. We can demonstrate this by considering his most sustained passage of Ovidian imitation, Prospero's renunciation of his rough magic near the end of *The Tempest*. That Shakespeare borrowed in detail from the *Metamorphoses* so late in his career shows that his Ovidianism was no mere young man's affectation, as is sometimes supposed.

Ovid's enchantress Medea begins '*auraeque et venti montesque amnesque lacusque, / dique omnes nemorum, dique omnes noctis adeste*', of which a literal translation might be 'ye breezes and winds and mountains and rivers and lakes, and all ye gods of groves and of night, draw near'. Golding translated this as 'Ye Ayres and windes: ye Elves of Hilles, of Brookes, of Woods alone, / Of standing Lakes, and of the Night approche ye everychone.' Shakespeare's Prospero begins his speech, 'Ye elves of hills, brooks, standing lakes, and groves'. Shakespeare got from Golding the notion of including those very English elves at this point (in Ovid they are 'gods' and are not associated with the hills) and he also followed the translator in amplifying '*lacus*' into '*standing* lakes'. But later in the speech, where Ovid had '*convulsaque robores*' ('and rooted up oaks'), Golding did not specify the kind of tree ('and trees doe drawe'), so Shakespeare must have remembered or looked at the Latin for his 'and rifted Jove's stout oak'. Again, Golding lacks an equivalent for the ghosts actually coming out of their tombs: Prospero's 'Graves at my command / Have waked their sleepers, oped, and let 'em forth' is a version of Ovid's '*manesque exire sepulcris*'. Medea in Ovid says that she has made the sun go pale by means of her 'song'. Golding has 'Our Sorcerie dimmes the Morning faire.' Shakespeare neatly combines the song and the sorcery with Prospero's 'By my so potent art', the art being that of both sorcerer and poet–singer.

That the black arts of Medea are the source for Prospero's seemingly white magic reminds us of the complexity of the Shakespearean vision, the difficulty of assuming easy distinctions between good and evil in the world of his plays. Like Ovid, Shakespeare is interested in the mingled yarn of our human fabric. Both are writers who probe our humanity with great rigour, but ultimately do so in a spirit of sympathy for our frailties and indulgences, rather than stern judgement upon our faults. As will be seen shortly, Prospero is a little too much the schoolmaster to be an exact analogue for his own creator.

Though Prospero's speech valuably demonstrates Shakespeare's continuing interest in the minutiae of Ovid's language even to the end of his career, it is exceptional in the detail of its borrowing. Shakespeare's more habitual use of the *Metamorphoses* was less specific. He would refer to the stories there as parallels, or paradigms, for the emotional turmoil of the characters in his plays. Where Ovid told of bodily metamorphoses wrought by extremes of passion, Shakespeare translated these into psychological transformations and vivid metaphors. In particular, he found in Ovid a great store of examples of female feeling – something that was notably lacking in many of his other models, such as the plays of Marlowe and the history books of Plutarch and Holinshed. What mattered to him most was Ovid's storytelling, and for that the

Latin text was not necessary – in rereading Ovid for pleasure after he left school, Shakespeare seems mostly to have relied on Golding's English version.

Golding's cumbersome 'fourteener' metre may be parodied in the lumbering verse of 'Pyramus and Thisbe', but Shakespeare seems to have taken pleasure in the down-to-earth and very English – often rural – vocabulary of the translation. Golding had something of his own vivid eye for the running hare and the flower-filled meadow. Like Autolycus in *The Winter's Tale*, Shakespeare was a snapper-up of unconsidered trifles – from Golding he filched such linguistic jewels as the bristles on the boar in *Venus and Adonis* and the 'babbling' of the nymph Echo to whom Viola compares herself in *Twelfth Night*.

Shakespeare was most Ovidian at the beginning and the end of his career. Both his narrative poems, written during the period in 1593–94 when the theatres were closed due to plague, were based on Ovidian sources. They were calling cards announcing his poetic sophistication, perhaps in response to Chettle and Greene's jibe about Shake-scene, the upstart crow, the jack-of-all-trades from the country. *Venus and Adonis* takes a 100-line story from the third book of the *Metamorphoses* and expands it into more than 1,000 lines of elegant artifice. Ovid provided the narrative framework: the comic idea of the lovely young Adonis's resistance to love, the dark twist of his boar-speared death, and the final release of floral transformation. Into this structure Shakespeare wove elaborate arguments for and against the 'use' of beauty. These were opportunities for him to show off his rhetorical skill, while also engaging with an issue much debated in Elizabethan times, namely the relative value of courtly accomplishments and military ones. The successful courtier would have been equally adept in the arts of praise and chivalry. Shakespeare gives the chivalric skills to the hunter Adonis, then inverts the norm of man praising woman by having a woman – and not just any woman, but Venus the Queen of Love herself – praise a young man. For this, he pulled together different parts of Ovid: the witty persuasions to love are in the manner of the *Amores* and the *Ars Amatoria*, while the figure of the vain youth has something of Narcissus and that of the forward woman more than a little of Salmacis, who in book four of the *Metamorphoses* seduces another gorgeous but self-absorbed boy, Hermaphroditus.

If *Venus and Adonis* and *The Rape of Lucrece* are poetic explorations of, respectively, the light and the dark sides of desire, then *A Midsummer Night's Dream* (1595–96) and *Titus Andronicus* (written or revised in 1594) are their dramatic equivalents. *Titus* is explicitly patterned on the story of the rape of Philomel in book seven of the *Metamorphoses*. The force of this horrid tale's influence upon Shakespeare is demonstrable from the fact that some fifteen years after *Titus*, he returned to it in *Cymbeline*, where Iachimo notices in Innogen's bedchamber that 'She hath been reading late / The tale of Tereus; here the leaf's turned down / Where Philomel gave up.' In perhaps the most self-consciously literary moment in all Shakespeare, a copy of Ovid's book is actually brought on stage in act four of *Titus* and used as a plot-device for the revelation of the nature of the crime that has been committed. By pointing to the story of Philomel, raped in the secluded woods by her brother-in-law Tereus, Lavinia indicates that she too has been violated. Shakespeare then compounds the allusion by deploying one of his sophisticated interweavings of different sources: in Ovid, Tereus cuts out Philomel's tongue so that she cannot reveal his name, but she gets round her disability by sewing a sampler portraying her fate. The rapists in *Titus* forestall this course of action by cutting off Lavinia's hands as well as removing her tongue. She outwits them – and in so doing Shakespeare proves his wit – by going to another part of the *Metamorphoses*, namely the story of Io, in which a girl who has been transformed into a cow writes her name by scraping her hoof in the sand. So Lavinia writes her rapists' names upon the ground, holding a staff in her mouth, guiding it with her stumps. Titus then acts out his revenge in deliberate homage to that of Procne, Philomel's sister: 'For worse than Philomel you used my daughter,' he says to the murderers Chiron and Demetrius, 'So worse than Procne I will be revenged' – Procne tricked Tereus into eating his own son, whereas Titus goes one better and bakes both Tamora's sons in a pie, which he takes pleasure in serving on-stage to her and her husband.

The wood outside Athens in *A Midsummer Night's Dream* is a place of benign transformations in comparison with those of the Roman hunting grounds in *Titus*. But the comedy and the charm of the *Dream* depend on a certain fragility. Good comedy is tragedy narrowly averted, while fairy charm is only safe from sentimentality if attached to some potential for grotesquerie. Of course we laugh when Bottom wears the head of an ass and makes love to a queen, but the image deliberately courts the suggestion of bestiality. In Ovid, people are driven by bestial desires and are rewarded by being transformed into animals. In Shakespeare, the ass's head is worn in play – significantly, it is assumed during the rehearsal of a dramatic performance – but it remains the closest thing in the drama of the age to an actual animal metamorphosis on stage.

As for the idea of near-tragedy, that is evoked by the staging on the part of Bottom and his friends of a comically bad dramatization of one of Ovid's most tragic stories of doomed love, the tale in book four of the ill-timed misadventures of Pyramus and Thisbe. Ovid's great theme is transformation, the inevitability of change. Book fifteen of the *Metamorphoses* offers a philosophical discourse on the subject, mediated via the philosophy of Pythagoras. From here Shakespeare got many of those images of transience that roll through the sonnets, but in *A Midsummer Night's Dream* he celebrates how something positive and potentially enduring may grow from change. The words are given to the very Ovidian figure of the Amazonian outsider Hippolyta:

> But all the story of the night told over,
> And all their minds transfigured so together,
> More witnesseth than fancy's images
> And grows to something of great constancy;
> But howsoever, strange and admirable.

Though no subsequent comedy has transformation woven so fully into its texture as this, Ovid was of continued importance in Shakespeare's later assays in the genre. At the climax of *The Merchant of Venice* (1597), Lorenzo and Jessica duet upon a sequence of Ovidian characters – Pyramus and Thisbe, Dido, Medea. All these

lovers are associated with the night. Shakespeare thus establishes
the final act of the play as a night of love. But the night-deeds
evoked are dark and bloody, another gesture towards the ease
with which comedy can tumble over the precipice into tragedy
(something that Jessica's father Shylock maybe knows all too well).

Comedy, as Ovid repeatedly shows, can be as cruel as it is funny.
Sometimes it goes a little too far, as with the gulling of Malvolio
into near-madness. Ovid provided Shakespeare with many a
reminder that sexual desire can lead men not only to foolishness,
but to outright destruction. Most famously, there was Actaeon,
transformed into a hart and torn to pieces by his own hounds as
punishment for his lascivious gaze upon the naked goddess Diana
as she bathed in a pool. The horns of Herne the Hunter, which
Falstaff is made to wear at the end of *The Merry Wives of Windsor*
(late 1590s or early 1600s), render him a heavyweight but light-
hearted Actaeon. Malvolio, cursing the pack of knaves who have
undone him, is a little closer to the real thing. His undoing ensures
that the end of *Twelfth Night* (1601) is not all celebration. Malvolio
takes to an extreme the tendency of nearly all the natives of Illyria
to over-indulge their passions – a motif suggested by the languorous
Orsino's allusion to Actaeon in the very first scene of the play:

> That instant was I turned into a hart,
> And my desires like fell and cruel hounds
> E'er since pursue me.

To interpret Actaeon's hounds as an image of his own desires is to
offer a psychological reading of Ovid that is a development of the
long medieval tradition of 'moralizing' his erotic tales.

In book five of the *Metamorphoses*, Ovid presented an archetypal
romance: the story of Proserpina, daughter of Ceres, goddess of
the harvest. While out gathering flowers, she is abducted by Pluto
(or Dis), god of the underworld, where she is forced to reside for
half of each year. Her departure into the earth signifies the onset of
winter, her recovery the return of spring. Another young woman,
flowers in hand, compares herself to Proserpina in Shakespeare's
Winter's Tale (1610). Her name, Perdita, 'the lost one', evokes the

mythic romance structure whereby we know that what is lost will eventually be found in a glad reunion. So, too, the play's title surely indicates that the drama will eventually move from Leontes' winter court, ruled by intrigue and jealousy, to the sunnier clime of the pastoral world, where a prince disguises himself in order to woo a shepherdess (who, it turns out, is really a princess herself). Florizel compares his mock-transformation of dress and rank to the disguises of the gods in the *Metamorphoses*:

> The gods themselves,
> Humbling their deities to love, have taken
> The shapes of beasts upon them: Jupiter
> Became a bull, and bellowed: the green Neptune
> A ram, and bleated: and the fire-robed god,
> Golden Apollo, a poor humble swain,
> As I seem now. Their transformations
> Were never for a piece of beauty rarer.

There is something highly Ovidian about this simultaneous extolling of implicitly chaste 'beauty' and gesturing towards sexual satisfaction − the gods in the stories cited here are really high-class rapists, while Florizel's word 'piece' suggests a slang term for woman as sexual meat.

The play's move from dark indoor court to the restorative air of the country follows the path of Shakespeare's principal source, Robert Greene's novella *Pandosto*. But in the source the wronged queen does not return to life. The reanimation of what Leontes takes to be Hermione's statue is Shakespeare's invention. The wonder-filled final scene puts a seemingly life-giving art into the hands of Paulina. That art dramatizes the magical power of theatre itself so that we in the audience, like the characters on stage, awaken our faith. The many-layered quality of the illusion − a boy-actor pretending to be a female character, Hermione, who is herself pretending to be a statue − takes Shakespeare's art to an extreme level of self-consciousness. Fittingly, then, the scene is also an allusion to Ovid, the most self-conscious artist among Shakespeare's models.

In book ten of the *Metamorphoses*, the artist Pygmalion carves an ivory statue so realistic that it seems to be a real girl, so beautiful that he falls in love with it. He desperately wants to believe it is real and there are moments when the perfection of the art is such that the statue does seem to be struggling into life. With a little assistance from the goddess Venus, a kiss then animates the statue in a striking reversal of the usual Ovidian metamorphic pattern in which people turn into things or animals. As Golding has it, 'She felt the kiss, and blushed thereat: and lifting fearfully / Her eyelids up, her lover and the light at once did spy.' At a profound level, Pygmalion is a figure of Ovid himself: the artist who transforms mere words into living forms.

Shakespeare learned from Ovid's Pygmalion both an idea and a style. If you want something badly enough and you believe in it hard enough, you will eventually get it: though tragedy denies this possibility, comedy affirms it. This is the illusion that theatre can foster. Ovid showed Shakespeare that the way to evoke this leap of faith is through pinpricks of sensation. The progression in the animation of Pygmalion's statue is both precise and sensuous: blood pulses through the veins, the lips respond, the ivory face flushes. Correspondingly, Leontes contrasts the warm life his queen once had with the coldness of the statue, but then he seems to see blood in the veins and warmth upon the lips. And when she descends and embraces him, she *is* warm.

Throughout his career Shakespeare metamorphosed Ovid's mythical metamorphoses into verbal and visual metaphors. Malvolio speaks and dresses like a Narcissus without actually becoming a flower. It is Othello's language and actions, not his body, that are reduced to bestiality. Lear's metaphor 'O, you are men of stones' replaces the literal metamorphosis of Niobe into stone. Now near the end of his career, Shakespeare reverses the process, something he had previously only done in comedy (Bottom as ass, Falstaff as Actaeon). In act one, Leontes freezes Hermione out of his life. Her body-contact with Polixenes is, he says, 'Too hot, too hot' – he wants her to be frigidly chaste (even though she is pregnant!). His jealous look is like that of the basilisk or the gorgon Medusa: he turns his wife to stone. In the final act, this metaphor becomes a metamorphosis as Paulina conjures up the illusion of Hermione's depetrification. The transformation is triumphantly realized on stage both linguistically and visually. 'Does not the stone rebuke me / For being more stone than it?' asks Leontes, when confronted with the statue. The hardened image of his wife forces him to turn his gaze inward upon his own hard heart. The play ends with the melting of that heart and the rekindling of love, with its concordant release of Hermione back into softness, warmth and life.

We know in our heads that we are not really watching a statue coming to life. Yet in a good production, at the moment of awakening we feel in our hearts that we are. The magic of the drama occurs in a strange but deeply satisfying space between the two poles of reality and illusion. Metamorphosis is a kind of translation that occurs in the passage from one state to another. Ovid's world shuttles between human passions and natural phenomena. Shakespeare, with the assistance of Arthur Golding, carried the magic of that world across into the medium of theatre, where everything is illusion, but somehow – as he put it in the alternative title of another of his last plays, *Henry VIII* – 'All is True.'

8. The School of Prospero

Shakespeare thought deeply about the value and limitations of reading and education throughout his career. When Prospero is packed off into exile in *The Tempest*, his most precious possessions apart from his three-year-old daughter Miranda are the volumes from his own library with which good Gonzalo has furnished him. Shakespeare's final solo-authored play offers an extended meditation on the 'Renaissance humanist' project that, because of his grammar-school education, made him what he was.

According to Desiderius Erasmus, chief architect of Renaissance humanist educational theory, the main hope of a state lies in the proper education of its youth ('*praecipuam reipublicae spem sitam esse in recta educatione puerorum*'). It was on the basis of this belief that the Tudors endowed their grammar schools. Boys would learn about virtue from books and the wisdom they found in the ancients would be translated into civic action when they grew up. That was the basis of humanist theory.

Prospero is a humanist prince: he imagines that the contemplative study of books in his library will make him into an enlightened leader of his people. Shakespeare, though, is more practically minded than Prospero. His dramatic art translates a theme of ancient books from the *vita contemplativa* to the *vita activa* by virtue of his very medium of production: unlike the private contemplative space of the library, the public sphere of the theatre belongs to the active social life of the citizen. The humanist defence of theatre against Puritanism was its capacity to bring to a wider public the kind of moral edification that was available privately and selectively to elite humanist readers by means of their book learning.

The Tempest asks a central humanist question: what do we have to learn from books? The answer is potentially nothing, potentially everything. That is to say, at one level the play is a melancholy critique of humanist ideals: it begins with a man 'for the liberal arts / Without a parallel', but ends with a drowning of the books, a renunciation of humanism's secular wisdom and a heavy epilogic hint that the only true book is the Bible. But at the same time, the play is itself an embodiment of the regenerative possibilities provided by humanist learning: it simply could not have been written without the education that made Shakespeare what he was. The action of the play is a testing of the power of the book against experience; one of the purposes of the play is a similar testing of the power of the theatre.

Thomas More's classic humanist fable *Utopia* is a meditation on the nature of society, government and the good life. It asks questions of the polity for which it was written by imagining an island characterized by strangeness and difference from that polity. It is beside the point whether or not More's attitude to Utopian communism was ironic: the point was that the description of Utopia forced English and European readers to reflect upon the values and practices of the societies that they inhabited. This was also the technique of Montaigne's essay 'Of the cannibals', which Shakespeare read while he was writing *The Tempest*. Whether or not Shakespeare had direct knowledge of More's *Utopia* (he probably didn't), the book's way of examining the known world by describing an imaginary alternative world is central to the tradition in which he was writing.

An equally important humanist tradition behind *The Tempest* is that of the discourse on education. The governor who reads, the power of the book, the textbook behaviour of courtiers, the relationship between nature and nurture, the importance of good schoolroom practice, the knowledge that comes from the classics: all are key issues in such humanist guides as Erasmus' *Institutio Principis Christiani* (1516, the same year as *Utopia*) and *De Pueris statim ac liberaliter Instituendis* (1529) and Sir Thomas Elyot's *The Book named The Governor* (1531). These are also all key issues in *The Tempest*. Beyond the schoolroom textbooks such as the *Colloquia Familiaria*, *De conscribendis epistolis* and *De copia*, Shakespeare was not widely or deeply read in Erasmus, but he did not need to be: Erasmus' ideas became so influential and widespread in the century

between his work and the play that they permeated the intellectual
and social air breathed by Shakespeare and his original audiences.

The very idea of education was the essence of northern European humanism. What is it that makes a human *humanitas* as
opposed to *feritas*, civilized as opposed to wild? Prospero as opposed
to Caliban? The name of man, according to Scipio as recorded
by Cicero, should be given only to those accomplished in the
arts appropriate to humanity, '*politi propriis humanitatis artibus*'.
Humanitas, wrote Aulus Gellius in the second century AD, is synonymous not with philanthropic kindness but with *paideia*, *studia
humanitatis*, 'education and training in the liberal arts'. This is the
highest achievement of the human; it is what separates us from
the animals. The acquisition of language is the essential civilizing
prerequisite for the effecting of that separation. So it is that eloquence and wisdom are coterminous and that the linguistic study
of classic texts can lead to moral edification and wholeness of life
(*integer vitae*). Exemplars of virtue, piety and good government in
those classic texts, especially in works of history, can be applied in
such a way as to facilitate good government in the present.

In *The Tempest*, the discourse on education emphatically enters
the play in the second scene. The opening scene suggests a different
strand of humanism, the tradition not of handbooks for the courtier
(Elyot, Puttenham) but of critique of courtship (*Utopia*, the Erasmus of *Praise of Folly*). Generally speaking, northern European
humanism was more politically conservative than its Italian avatar.
This is immediately apparent from the reception of Machiavelli:
the defender of liberty and apologist for republicanism as the ideal
form of government was in many quarters (on the Elizabethan
stage, for instance) demonized as an atheist who threatened the
theory of degree and the rights of kings. Northern humanists
tended to argue 'that virtue must be regarded as the only true
nobility, but then neutralised the radicalism of this contention by
adding that the virtues are, as it happens, most fully displayed by
the established members of the ruling classes' (or perhaps, cynically,
that they would be so displayed if the ruling classes had the good
sense to employ humanists to educate their children). Sir Thomas
Elyot in the very first chapter of *The Governor* was eloquent in

defence of degree in the commonweal: 'degrees, whereof proceedeth order . . . take away order from all things, what should then remain?' *The Tempest* shares this conservatism, in that it proposes a reform of the heart, not a revolution in institutional structures or the social order. But there is also a strand of anti-court satire within humanism, as when Erasmus finds folly in those who have power and influence. Our first impression in *The Tempest* is of bad courtiers, of a mismatch between rank and worth. The Boatswain is justified in giving orders to the courtiers: the foul-mouthed Sebastian and Antonio are wrong to insult him for insolence, since they are not working to save the ship. Even Gonzalo (though his language is more moderate) comes off less well than the Boatswain. 'What cares these roarers for the name of king?' The premise of the play is that good kingship cannot be asserted by the name alone, it must be proved through good action.

According to Erasmus' *Education of a Christian Prince*, what makes an effective and virtuous ruler is an education in the liberal arts, a good choice of counsellors and a full acceptance of the responsibilities of power. The difference between a king and a tyrant is that the latter uses his power for himself, the former for the benefit of the commonwealth as a whole. The good ruler will also make himself visible to his people, frequently appearing in public and touring his realm. Consider Prospero, Duke of Milan in the light of these precepts. He is the rightful duke, but is he a right good duke? What is his judgement like in the selection of a deputy? He chooses the perfidious Antonio, 'and to him put / The manage of my state', while he himself, 'for the liberal arts / Without a parallel', gave all his study to those arts, 'And to my state grew stranger, being transported / And rapt in secret studies.' The reference to the 'liberal arts' is a specific, technical allusion to the humanist curriculum: the liberal arts are those worthy of a free man. They are the opposite of the servile or mechanical arts, and were originally divided into the medieval *trivium* of grammar, logic and rhetoric, and *quadrivium* of arithmetic, geometry, music and astronomy. The specifically humanist inflection is the fact that the duke is studying them: the highest reach of the humanist educational revolution was its dissolution of the traditional distinction between the education thought appropriate for rulers and that thought appropriate for clerks. But Prospero has forgotten to make the cardinal move from study to practice. Instead of making his learning the basis of sound government, he pursues it secretly, for his own benefit. This self-centredness brings him closer to the tyrant than the virtuous prince: instead of being visible to his people, he is shut away in his library.

His distance from practical politics, his neglect of *negotium* and the *vita activa*, is signalled by the words 'stranger', 'transported' and 'rapt' – words which also hint that his studies are taking him beyond the approved curriculum into the secret world of magic. The audience is to imagine him as analogous to the Faustus of Marlowe, who in his opening soliloquy shows that he has got bored with – thinks he has exhausted the opportunities of – the applicable arts of logic, law and theology, and is accordingly devoting himself to supra-worldly secrets. But these are only hints. In Milan Prospero did not seem to progress very far beyond the liberal arts into the natural philosophy: if he had, he would surely have had powers of divination regarding the impending *coup d'état*. It is only on the island that he develops his magical arts. Having failed in Milan to use the liberal arts for the benefit of his people and the prosecution of good government, on the island he harnesses a more refined philosophical power so as to rule the forces of nature. But one still wonders if he is ruling well: Erasmus wrote that the Christian prince should abhor slavery, yet Prospero does not hesitate to call both Ariel and Caliban his slaves and to treat them thus.

In Milan, then, Prospero is a bad humanist. Good humanism specifically links sound learning and sound government. Prospero specifically opposes his study to the rule of the realm. His is a life of pure contemplation, where it should be one of practical application. The humanist should create the good ruler, whereas Prospero neglects to be a ruler and in effect creates a bad ruler. He 'Awaked an evil nature' in Antonio: he begets his brother's falsehood. Where good humanism is intended to awake a virtuous nature by means of imaginative empathy (by writing an oration as if you were, say, Cyrus the Great, you become a little like Cyrus the

Great), Prospero's retirement to his library conjures into Antonio's mind the thought that 'He was indeed the duke' and thus opens the way to the usurpation.

When Prospero's library was dukedom enough, when he failed to commit himself to action in the world, he reneged on his 'temporal royalties'. A wide gap of time and a *tempestas* of passion will be necessary before he can return to those royalties and duties. This is where the play begins. Prospero has moved on: where in Milan he educated Antonio into sin by means of his own default, on the island he is a more active educator. His style is that of the schoolmaster. He thus casts himself in the role of Roger Ascham to Miranda's young Queen Elizabeth. In his opening discourse, he uses history – his own past – as a preparation for virtuous action, the restoration of right rule. This sounds promising. His self-description is now as a good humanist tutor, from whom the princess can profit. 'Here in this island', he says, 'here'

> Have I, thy schoolmaster, made thee more profit
> Than other princes can that have more time
> For vainer hours, and tutors not so careful.

But this is not his only tutoring.

Less benign than his training of the princess is his training of his servants for work. With Ariel he relies on a reductive process of rote learning as opposed to a creative application of *exemplum* to action. Once a month, he repeats to his pupil a history lesson about Sycorax and earlier events on the island. He relies on threats as well as the promised reward of freedom. The threat to re-imprison Ariel and the persistent menacing of Caliban with the prospect of corporal punishment make him sound like the bad schoolmaster described in Erasmus' *De Pueris . . . Instituendis*:

Fear is of no real avail in education . . . Love must be the first influence; followed and completed by a trustful and affectionate respect, which compels obedience far more surely than dread can ever do . . . Masters who are conscious of their own incompetence are generally the worst floggers . . . They cannot teach, so they beat.

Act one scene two of *The Tempest* presents three scenes of instruction, in which Prospero's schoolmasterly manner progressively deteriorates. He claims to have used Caliban 'with humane care', but the good humanist does not beat his charges. The claim is therefore belied by 'Whom stripes may move, not kindness'. It is clear that with Caliban the humanist educational project has failed. The aim of education is to tame the passions: good nurture can control a rough nature. The attempted rape shows that it hasn't succeeded in doing so. To what is the failure attributable? Miranda believes that it is due to Caliban's devilish nature, on which nurture will never stick. 'Abhorrèd slave, / Which any print of goodness wilt not take'. The humanist ideal of imprinting virtue through education and example has come unstuck. The placing of these lines in the mouth of Miranda suggests that she has been employed as Prospero's assistant in the island schoolroom of the play's imaginary pre-action, performing the role of usher to his schoolmaster. Worst of all, the 'profit' of teaching language is not eloquence but the ability to curse. The word 'profit', here applied negatively where previously applied positively to the education of Miranda, is a key term in the lexicon of humanists such as Elyot.

But is the lack of profit the result of Caliban's nature or the teaching method? As with Antonio, we need to ask who bears responsibility. Could it be that the problem arises from what Prospero has imprinted on Caliban's memory, not from the latter's nature? Caliban initially welcomes Prospero to the island and offers to share its fruits, every bit in the manner of noble, natural cannibals eulogized in the essay by Montaigne that Shakespeare read as he prepared the play. Caliban acts basely only after Prospero has printed that baseness on him; what makes him 'filth' may be the lessons in which Prospero has taught him that he is 'filth'. In this sense the educational process has worked all too well.

'Where the devil should he learn our language?' asks Stephano in amazement when he first hears Caliban. The learning of language should be what makes man god-like as opposed to beast-like, but since the first effect of Caliban's education is his desire to rape Miranda, one wonders whether there is not in fact something devilish about the way in which Prospero has taught him. Language and learning ought to be paths to right rule, but as Prospero's learning in Milan has led to Antonio's coup, so his teaching on the island leads to Caliban's rebellion. The parallel is made explicit by the way in which Antonio carries out his usurpation in league with high Neapolitans (Alonso and Sebastian) while Caliban carries out his attempt at a usurpation in league with low Neapolitans (Stephano and Trinculo). In the first act, then, the profits of the historical education of the Christian princess and the magical direction of the spirits of the isle are still to be realized, whereas the accounts relating to Prospero's pursuit of the liberal arts and efforts as a language teacher suggest a state of distinctly negative equity.

When Ferdinand enters, he is led by Ariel's song to think that his father is dead and that he will therefore soon have to assume the mantle of kingship. Prospero is thus able to cast himself once again as Ascham preparing a future ruler for the throne or Erasmus writing the *Education of a Christian Prince*. That he wishes to be tutor to both prince and princess is made clear by his annoyance at Miranda's intervention on behalf of Ferdinand: 'My foot my tutor?' Throughout the first act, then, there is persistent recourse to the lexicon of learning and education.

Where act one scene two concerns the education of princes and servants, act two scene one shows the effect of prior education on courtiers. Again, questions are raised as to the efficacy of humanist practice. Gonzalo, for all his virtue, is constrained by his way of thinking in formal themes. His opening speech is a set discourse on the 'theme of woe'. It manifests a certain rhetorical labour in the threefold *amplificatio* of sailor, merchant's master and merchant, a certain lack of nimbleness in its heavy *sententiae* ('when every grief is entertained that's offered, comes to th'entertainer –'). This formality is vulnerable to parody: 'Look, he's winding up the watch of his wit: by and by it will strike.' While Gonzalo speaks conventional humanist wisdom, the interruptions of Sebastian and Antonio suggest the humanist vein of satire, the spirit of dialogue, paradox and multivocality. Morally and politically, they are to be condemned, but the play depends for some of its forward energy on their disruptive voices. The overall pattern is of *temporis filia veritas* ('truth is the daughter of time' – an old humanist adage) in combination with *tempestas* bringing temperance, but for Antonio 'Temperance was a delicate wench.' Drama thrives on such restless wit.

The courtiers' learned dispute on the virtues or vices of Dido is a more formal instance of the spirit of dialogue. It is a humanist dispute not only in its reliance on the citation of a classical exemplar as a way of understanding the present, but also in its demonstration that history is always subject to interpretation. For Gonzalo, 'widow Dido' is an *exemplum* of virtue to whom Claribel may properly be compared. But to the disruptive Antonio and Sebastian she is a negative *exemplum*, associated with infidelity to her late husband and with the straying of Aeneas from his proper imperial course. The debate opens up a series of concerns about the interpretation of history and the relationship between passion and empire. It is because of humanism's method of understanding the present through the authoritative texts of the past that an allusion to the *Aeneid* is able to generate questions about empire, just as it is because of humanism's collapsing of time past, time present and time future that a suggestion of the Utopian possibilities of the Virginian 'new world' is activated by Gonzalo's allusion to the 'golden age' in which Ovid and Montaigne imagined humankind spent its early years.

The play's harmonious resolution allows desire and destiny to coincide. Miranda and Ferdinand are granted the union which Dido and Aeneas are denied. But Claribel's reluctance to wed ('the fair soul herself / Weighed between loathness and obedience') evokes humanist reservations about dynastic liaisons. Erasmus in *The Education of a Christian Prince* wrote, 'I should think that it would be by far most beneficial to the state if the marriage alliances of princes were confined within the limits of their own kingdoms.' Claribel is testimony to Erasmus' argument that

By alliances of this sort the sway of princes is perhaps increased, but the affairs of their people are weakened and shattered. A good prince does not consider his own affairs prosperous unless he looks out for the welfare of the state. I shall not talk about the heartless effect (the result of these

alliances) on the girls themselves, who are sometimes sent away into re-
mote places to [marry] men who have no similarity of language, appearance, character, or habits, just as if they were being abandoned to exile.

The scene thus works through a series of favourite humanist themes
and methods: oration and apophthegm on the subject of woe;
debate on historical exemplum; reflection on dynastic marriage.

Gonzalo then introduces his most fully elaborated theme, the
Utopian discourse: 'Had I plantation of this isle, my lord –.' The
word 'plantation' signals the 'new world' or colonial dimension of
the play, but the structure of the whole sequence subsumes that
dimension within the larger discourse of humanism. The government of a colony is part of the theme, but humanist preoccupations
provide both themes and methods. Gonzalo's method is that of
imitatio: his oration is a free translation, with amplification, of a
passage in Montaigne's essay 'Of the cannibals', which is itself a
free translation, with amplification, of a passage in Ovid's *Metamorphoses*. The 'cannibals' of the new world lived in a state,
Montaigne's interlocutor reports,

that hath no kind of traffic, no knowledge of letters, no intelligence of
numbers, no name of magistrate, nor of politic superiority; no use of
service, of riches or of poverty; no contracts, no successions, no partitions,
no occupation but idle; no respect of kindred, but common, no apparel
but natural, no manuring of lands, no use of wine, corn, or metal. The very
words that import lying, falsehood, treason, dissimulations, covetousness,
envy, detraction, and pardon, were never heard of amongst them.

Gonzalo versifies Montaigne, repeating and expanding upon his
key terms: 'no kind of traffic' (i.e. trade), 'name of magistrate',
'Letters should not be known: riches, poverty, / And use of service,
none: contract, succession . . . all men idle', and so forth. His
theme is the congruence of present and past, the possibility that
the polity of the isle might recreate, even surpass, the 'golden age'
fashioned by classical poets. His purpose is learned from both
classical poets and humanists: Ovid describes the idealized, lost
golden age as part of his critique of empire, city and government

in the present; Montaigne's traveller idealizes the natives of South America as critique of the same.

But the Gonzalo debate as a whole offers not only idealization as critique but also critique of critique. Its theme is the incompatibility of communism and government: 'No sovereignty. / Yet he would be king on't.' Its method is dialogue, highlighted by interruption. As the character of 'More' in the final section of *Utopia* throws the cold water of scepticism on the idealizing discourse of the traveller and narrator Hythlodaeus, so do Sebastian and Antonio upon the idealizing discourse of Gonzalo.

Caliban understands the power of the book: as fashioners of modern *coups d'état* begin by seizing the television station, so he reiterates the need to begin by possessing the books. But Stephano has another book. 'Here is that which will give language to you,' he says to Caliban, replicating Prospero's gaining of control through language – but in a different mode. Textual education is replaced by intoxication: the book that is kissed is the bottle. If Stephano and Trinculo achieve through their alcohol what Prospero achieves through his teaching (in each case Caliban is persuaded to serve and to share the fruits of the isle), is not that teaching exposed as potentially nothing more than a means of social control? Prospero often seems more interested in the power structure that is established by his schoolmastering than in the substance of what he teaches. It is hard to see how making Ferdinand carry logs is intended to inculcate virtue. The purpose of the order is to elicit submission.

Against this – scene by scene the counterpoint shifts from one theme to another – Gonzalo continues in the role of Hythlodaeus or Montaigne's servant, reporting back to Europe on the 'gentlekind' manners of the native inhabitants (the spirits) of the island. In bringing Alonso to repentance, Prospero and his ministers effect the play's first major education into virtue. It is achieved through a striking change of language-register. When Ariel impersonates a harpy, he is mimicking a famous incident in the *Aeneid*. Of all pagan authors, Virgil, thanks to his prophetic-sounding fourth *Eclogue*, predicting the arrival of a Saviour upon the earth, was the most readily translatable into the language of Christianity. So it is that the idiom of the classical precedent is displaced by a very different lexis: sin, heart's sorrow, clear life, trespass. This is the play's first intimation that a choice may have to be made between the secular humanist way to wisdom (via *ratio, oratio, imitatio,* precedent) and the Christian way (via humility and prayer).

The education of Ferdinand and Miranda into virtue, which in their case Prospero makes synonymous with chastity, continues through the masque. This introduces the possibility that theatre can do what humanism traditionally relied on books to do. It also introduces a new humanist political theme, that of the debate on agricultural polity. There was a tradition going back to the mid-sixteenth century of strongly Protestant humanist discourse attacking enclosure and blaming landowners for dearth and popular hunger. This form of protest re-emerged whenever there were bad harvests. Prospero's masque is intended to dramatize the over-coming of this problem. The landscape of Ceres is cultivated, not wild like the nature of the island. It is intended to suggest abund-ance. She is a 'bounteous lady', a generous landowner; 'nibbling sheep' in enclosures are an addition to 'wheat, rye, barley, vetches, oats, and peas', not a substitute for them; a 'donation' is freely given, there is no 'Scarcity and want', the good harvest is shared, and the workers of the land are given a holiday. Prospero seems to be promising that the fears of the radical 'commonwealthmen' are ungrounded.

But can he deliver on his promise? Not when he has forgotten Caliban's conspiracy: the masque is interrupted and he is angrier than Miranda has ever seen him. This commonwealth is still unstable. Prospero is distempered because this is the first moment that his control has slipped. Paradoxically, however, this slippage and the renunciation of power that follows from it effect the final realization of the education into virtue. Prospero's recognition that 'the gorgeous palaces' will dissolve signals another retreat from the *vita activa*. 'Retire' and 'repose' are the climactic verbs in his post-masque oration. But what he is proposing now is neither an easeful *otium* that reneges on *negotium*, nor a return to the library. It is Christian retirement, *contemptus mundi*, religious retreat, prayer and preparation for the grave.

Prospero is upset because the foul conspiracy of Caliban reminds him that his humanist project has not worked. His attempt to nurture the natural man has failed: his 'pains, / Humanely taken' are 'all, all lost, quite lost'. But are they? In recognizing his failure, he begins to realize that all along he has been pursuing power, not wisdom. This has led him into a misreading of Caliban. If Caliban were merely 'a devil, a born devil', as Prospero claims he is, he would not have the capacity to sympathize with other beings which humanism took to be one of the highest capacities of man. He would not enter at this point with the words 'Pray you tread softly, that the blind mole may not hear a footfall.' 'Tread softly' is the voice of the conspirator, but the imagining of 'the blind mole' is a mark of extraordinary sensitivity. It comes not from a language taught by Prospero but from the exquisite natural language in which Caliban speaks with relish of pig-nuts, scammels and marmosets. Caliban is at once the lowest and the highest human, the rebel and the man with music in his soul. The full extent of Prospero's misreading of him is apparent from the oft-remarked fact that, far from only knowing how to curse, he speaks the play's most beautiful verse in the 'isle is full of noises' passage. The attempt to make nurture stick upon him may fail, but there is something within him that leads him finally to seek for grace.

Ariel's key words, leading Prospero to renounce his magic (his power), are 'were I human'. In Milan, Prospero's inward-looking study of the liberal arts had led to the loss of power and the establishment of tyranny. On the island he seeks to make amends by applying what he has learned, by using active magic to bring repentance, restore his kingdom and set up a dynastic marriage. Yet now he sees that to be truly human is a matter not of exercising wisdom for the purposes of rule, but of practising a more strictly Christian version of virtue. For humanism, education in princely virtue means the cultivation for political ends of wisdom, magnanimity, temperance and integrity, the four princely virtues, as listed by Erasmus in *Education of a Christian Prince*. For Prospero what finally matters is kindness. And this is something the master learns from his pupil: it is Ariel who teaches him, not vice versa.

The gap between Christian and classical traditions widens. Prospero's final and most sustained humanist oration is an *imitatio* of a negative *exemplum*: his renunciation of his rough magic is cast in the form of a translation of the incantation of Ovid's witch, Medea. The magic is now revealed to involve a blasphemous transgression of Christian mores, the opening of graves – only God the Father and God the Son are entitled to raise the dead. That Prospero renounces his magic in the form of an *imitatio* suggests that he is also renouncing the very mode he is using, that of reliance on the wisdom of the pagan inheritance. It is an undoing of all the work done by Erasmus in such texts as his *Anti-Barbarians*: the classical and the Christian, which he and his fellow-humanists had so painstakingly held together, are now split apart. The imitation of Medea includes references to Jove and Neptune, but by the end of the speech they will have been drowned along with the pagan books. Prospero's allegiance for the rest of the play is solely to the Christian God. The language of grace replaces that of power. Gonzalo is commended for his holiness, not his facility in imagining the classical golden age. Prospero says 'No' simply and unequivocally to Sebastian's 'The devil speaks in him' exactly because he believes it is now God speaking in him.

But here we have to be careful. It is not God speaking in his own person. There is still something in Prospero that seeks to usurp God's powers and this may be why he is not allowed to succeed in bringing his brother to a statement of repentance. Only God can finally forgive sins. Prospero will not be given the satisfaction of delivering an absolution. Even after he has renounced pagan power, Prospero has a certain arrogance. He only achieves true humility in the epilogue. That achievement is perhaps due to his internalization of evil: his final renunciation is the acknowledgement of Caliban as his own thing of darkness. It is this that frees them both to seek for grace.

That acknowledgement in a certain sense proves Sebastian's 'The devil speaks in him' retrospectively right: Prospero has previously called Caliban a devil, he now calls Caliban his, *ergo*, the devil speaks in Prospero. This suggests that humanist dialogics are still operating, despite the renunciation of the overt educational aims of humanism. The ironic counterpoint of 'O brave new world' and ''Tis new to thee' is a strong instance of the play's

continuing doubleness. This doubleness falls above all upon Caliban, simultaneously most savage (rebel, rapist) and most civilized
(hearer of music). Three times in the play there is an image of
something dropping from the heavens. The third is graceful: it is
Gonzalo's 'Look down, you gods, / And on this couple drop a
blessèd crown.' The first was base: it was the usurped crown
'Dropping upon' the head of Sebastian in the 'strong imagination'
of Antonio. The second is potentially either:

> Be not afeard, the isle is full of noises,
> Sounds and sweet airs, that give delight and hurt not:
> Sometimes a thousand twangling instruments
> Will hum about mine ears; and sometime voices,
> That if I then had waked after long sleep,
> Will make me sleep again, and then in dreaming,
> The clouds methought would open and show riches
> Ready to drop upon me, that when I waked
> I cried to dream again.

If Antonio were imagining these riches they would be earthly; if
Gonzalo, heavenly. With Caliban, one cannot be sure, but the
proximity to heavenly music strongly suggests the latter. His dream
is a preparation for his quest for grace. Prospero's inability to see
this is the play's principal indictment of its principal character's
humanist ideology.

The Tempest is, to borrow a phrase that the intellectual historian
Quentin Skinner applies to the *Utopia*, a 'humanist critique of
humanism'. At the level of narrative development, the critique is
prosecuted through the movement away from secular wisdom and
power towards Christian humility and mortification. At the level
of dramatic technique, it is wrought through persistent dialogic
punctuation and multiple perspective. But at the very end, humanism seems to be recuperated. Prospero's Christian language reaches
its most sustained pitch in the epilogue, but his final request is for
the indulgence not of God but of the audience. At the last moment,
humanist learning is replaced not by Christian but by *theatrical*
faith.

9. Shakespeare's Small Library

Ben Jonson may have been removed from Westminster School before completing his education. He certainly did not go to university. Instead, he was apprenticed into his stepfather's trade as a bricklayer. He always remained loyal to his learned schoolmaster William Camden, describing himself as 'once a pupil, always a friend' ('*Alumnus olim, aeternum Amicus*') and attributing to Camden 'All that I am in arts, all that I know'. But there was a part of him that resented the fact that his family could not afford to send him to Cambridge or Oxford. After abandoning bricklaying, he served as a soldier in the Netherlands. Then he returned to London and immersed himself in independent study. He became an actor and, like Shakespeare, turned himself from performer into play-maker. Unlike Shakespeare, he gave up acting as soon as he could. Whereas Will immersed himself in the life of his theatre company, Ben set himself apart from the actors and cultivated a second career as a poet in pursuit of patronage at court and in the houses of powerful men and women.

He studied methodically, perfected his knowledge of several languages, built up an impressive library, read slowly, underlining key passages and making marginal annotations or copying quotations and observations into his commonplace book. When he bought a book he would inscribe his name on the title page ('*Sui Ben: Jonson liber*', Ben Jonson, his book), together with a motto drawn from his favourite Roman poet, Seneca: '*Tanquam Explorator*', 'as it were a spy'. Books were to be subtly interrogated, privily probed for codes of moral behaviour and hidden wisdom about human nature. The combination of Jonson's prodigious self-inspired learning and his capacity to connect himself with the great eventually brought the reward of honorary degrees from both Oxford and Cambridge, a source of enormous satisfaction in the light of his earlier struggles.

The year 1623 was that in which Jonson did Shakespeare the enormous service of assisting the First Folio into print, complete with dedicatory poems by himself, by his schoolfriend Hugh Holland and another colleague James Mabbe, and by Leonard Digges (stepson of one of Shakespeare's closest friends). It was also the year when disaster struck Jonson: his precious library was destroyed by fire. Stoically, he set about reassembling it, buying and annotating new books, recovering older ones that he had sold when short of money. His library catalogue survives, as do many of his inscribed books. They allow us to reconstruct his habits of reading: noting stylistic eloquence and pithy precepts, weighing the authority of the ancients against the truth of experience ('It is true they opened the gates and made the way that went before us, but as guides, not commanders'). His personal copy of the Shakespeare First Folio probably perished in the fire. If only Jonson's annotations on Shakespeare had survived instead of those on Justus Lipsius' *De Calumnia* or Clement Edmonds' *Observations* on the autobiographical and historical writings of Julius Caesar!

But the truly priceless treasure would be Shakespeare's own notebook, library catalogue or annotated books. Since the cult of his genius emerged in the eighteenth century, over a hundred volumes with his purported signature have turned up, some bearing annotations. Almost all the signatures are demonstrable forgeries. Among the volumes with his supposed signature or initials are a copy of Florio's translation of Montaigne in the British Museum, the Aldine edition of Ovid's *Metamorphoses* in the Bodleian Library in Oxford and Sir Thomas North's translation of Plutarch's *Lives of the Noble Grecians and Romans* in the Greenock Library in Scotland. It is a little suspicious that these books turned up only after it became generally known that Shakespeare was an especially sympathetic reader of Ovid, Plutarch and Montaigne.

Where Jonson was a methodical reader, Shakespeare was an opportune one. He snapped up phrases and ideas from his reading, storing them in his capacious memory. He may not have bothered with underlinings and marginal annotations. As he borrowed words and stories, so he may have borrowed rather than bought some of his books. Schoolfriend Richard Field, two and a half years older, had already walked the road to London, where he had been apprenticed to one of the most distinguished publishers of the age. It was to him, now established in his own business, that Shakespeare turned in 1593–94 for the publication of his poems *Venus and Adonis* and *The Rape of Lucrece*. Field was the printer of the 1595 edition of North's Plutarch and a 1589 Latin edition of Ovid's *Metamorphoses*. He could easily have provided in-house copies to his fellow Stratfordian on long loan – or indeed offered them as gifts or purchases at a discount. Field would probably also have had a copy of the 1587 edition of Holinshed's *Chronicles*, the key source for Shakespeare's English history plays, since the stationer to whom he was apprenticed at the time of its publication was a member of the syndicate who sold the book. He also printed Sir John Harington's translation of Ariosto's *Orlando Furioso*, the source for the main plot of *Much Ado about Nothing*.

Browsing among his old schoolfriend's stock, Shakespeare would also have encountered pamphlets on the recent civil war in France, where he would have learned of the King of Navarre and his followers the dukes of Biron, Dumaine and Longuaville, names he clocked for usage in *Love's Labour's Lost*. Field became an expert at printing foreign language books. On their title pages he would sometimes put his own name in the corresponding language. Thus 'Ricardo del Campo' for several Spanish volumes. It is perhaps in allusion to this habit, as well as being a little gesture of gratitude both for books provided and services rendered (the appearance of *Venus and Adonis* in print was a huge breakthrough), that late in his career Shakespeare paid a jokey compliment to Richard Field. In *Cymbeline* the heroine, disguised as a boy called 'Fidele' ('the faithful one'), invents a name for his master, 'a very valiant Briton' who has fought against the Roman invader: 'Richard du Champ'. Fighting against Rome was something Field knew all about: many of the books that he printed were works of anti-Catholic propaganda.

There would have been other possibilities for book borrowing when Shakespeare moved in the circle of the patron to whom he dedicated his poems, the Earl of Southampton. He certainly got to know both the Italian language manual and the Montaigne translation of Southampton's tutor, John Florio. Later, the Earl of

Pembroke became a notable patron not only of poets but also of Shakespeare's acting company. He gave Jonson an annual New Year's gift of twenty pounds – a considerable sum – to buy books, some of which may have been passed on (or, knowing Jonson, sold second-hand) to Shakespeare.

Jonson's library of more than two hundred volumes consisted mainly of classical works. The poet William Drummond of Hawthornden in Scotland – in conversation with whom Jonson complained that 'Shakespeare wanted [lacked] art' – catalogued his own library in the year 1611. It amounted to 552 books, including poetry by Shakespeare, Sir Philip Sidney, Edmund Spenser, Michael Drayton, Samuel Daniel and Christopher Marlowe (his *Hero and Leander*, a playfully erotic poem in the same Ovidian tradition as *Venus and Adonis*). The quarrelsome Cambridge don and inveterate annotator of books, Gabriel Harvey, owned about a hundred books. The greatest scholar of the age, splendidly named Julius Caesar Scaliger, left 1,382 volumes at the time of his death in 1609. These numbers go to show that even among literary men in the period it was not common to own large numbers of books. Since the eighteenth century there has been a busy scholarly industry in the tracing of Shakespeare's borrowings, the tracking of his sources. But verbal parallels can be coincidental and shared ideas can be derived at second-hand, especially in a culture that encouraged the recycling and amplification of *sententiae* and commonplaces. I suspect that Shakespeare skimmed many a new volume at the bookstalls outside St Paul's, but closely read fewer books than is often imagined by bookish scholars, who (like everyone who writes about Shakespeare) have a subliminal desire to make him more like themselves than he really was.

Books were usually kept in a chest, which would have been heavy to transport. Shakespeare travelled light. He moved between temporary lodgings in London, where he never had a permanent home. He was said to have travelled back to Stratford at least once a year. It is hard to imagine his book chest being carted along with him. He had a restless imagination, not a Jonsonian predilection for mental hoarding. He would gut a book for its nourishment, then cast it aside. Once he finished his cycle of English history plays, he put away his Holinshed for a number of years. The old play scripts that he recycled in his early work probably went back into company stock. Once he had turned Arthur Brooke's laboured narrative poem *The Tragical History of Romeus and Juliet* into an anything but laboured play, he would have had no reason ever to pick it up again.

Let us imagine Shakespeare at the very end of his career, sorting through his book chest. My guess is that it would have contained no more than about forty volumes and possibly as few as twenty (excluding his own).

I have suggested that his most prized books were his copies of Golding's translation of Ovid's *Metamorphoses* and North's translation of Plutarch's *Lives*. Those details in Prospero's borrowing from Medea's incantation that derive from the Latin seem too specific to be attributable to a vague memory of studying the original Latin in school some thirty-five years earlier, so it is a fair assumption that as well as the stout English version of Golding, the book chest would have contained a Latin Ovid. Given that Shakespeare quoted from the *Heroides* in Latin in *The Taming of the Shrew*, based *The Rape of Lucrece* on a story in the untranslated *Fasti* and seems to have known the *Amores* and the *Ars Amatoria*, he may well have possessed several volumes, some with commentaries. So, for example, certain details in *Lucrece* seem at first glance to come not from Ovid's version of the story but from that in Livy's *History of Rome*. On further investigation, however, they appear to be derived from quotations out of Livy in the extensive notes to an edition of the *Fasti*.

He might have owned a Latin text of Horace's *Odes*, but nearly all his Horatian allusions, like his Virgilian ones, can be traced back to extracts studied in the grammar schools. If there was another Latin text in his collection, it was probably dramatic rather than poetic. *The Comedy of Errors* is closely based on the *Menaechmi* of the Roman comic dramatist Plautus, with some cross-borrowing from his *Amphitryon*. The play seems to have been written between the registration and the publication of an English translation of *Menaechmi*. There are verbal resemblances between the two works. Did Shakespeare get to see an early copy of the translation or are the resemblances a coincidence, which is not implausible given that the play is a formal imitation of the Latin original? Plautus, with his character types such as the bragging soldier, the desirable virgin, the old man resisting his daughter's marriage and the clever servant, exercised an enormous influence on Renaissance comedy across Europe. His influence on Shakespeare was both direct and indirect, but on balance the likelihood is that – at least in the early years of his career – the man whom the Elizabethan literary commentator Francis Meres specifically compared to Plautus owned a Latin text of the plays.

Meres wrote that 'As Plautus and Seneca are accounted the best for Comedy and Tragedy among the Latins, so Shakespeare among the English is the most excellent in both kinds for the stage.' In *Hamlet*, Polonius reiterates this standard pairing of Roman examples: 'Seneca cannot be too heavy, nor Plautus too light.' Shakespeare would have read many passages from Seneca's tragedies in Latin at school and it would have been possible for him to purchase them all in English translation (in the old-fashioned 'fourteener' verse style that Golding had used for his Ovid), but, as with Plautus in comedy, the Senecan tragic style exercised such a pervasive influence on the drama of the period that Shakespeare absorbed it as much by osmosis as direct encounter on the page. Whether he owned a Latin Seneca is very much an open question.

The story of the Trojan war fascinated Shakespeare, hardly surprisingly since it is the magnificent foundation of western literature. Allusions to Troy are to be found in the early history plays and *Titus Andronicus*. The description of a picture of Sinon, who insinuated the wooden horse into Troy, is the poetic highpoint of *The Rape of Lucrece*. The player in *Hamlet* recites his great set-piece on the death of Priam and the madness of grief-stricken Hecuba. Achilles, Ajax, Agamemnon, Ulysses, Hector, Paris and the rest are brought to life on stage in *Troilus and Cressida*. The matter of Troy would have been somewhere there in the book chest, but in what form?

It is sometimes forgotten that the latter books of his prized *Metamorphoses* include a version of the Troy story, written in part as a riposte to the Virgilian telling. Aeneas' account to Dido of his escape from the burning city in book two of the *Aeneid* was etched on Shakespeare's memory, with an overlay from Marlowe and Nashe's play *Dido Queen of Carthage*. But that does not mean he owned the books: he could easily have remembered Virgil from the schoolroom and Marlowe from the theatre. The crabbed language of *Troilus and Cressida* may suggest a debt to, or parody of, the convoluted syntax and overblown vocabulary of George Chapman's *Seven Books of the Iliad*, published in 1598. The arguments and insults in the Greek camp may echo the contentions of Achilles and Agamemnon in Chapman's first book, but I rather doubt that Shakespeare would have had the patience to read Chapman all the way through. This is another 'source' that may well boil down to nothing more than a glance at the bookstall and the instant absorption of a style, ripe for unpicking, into that capacious memory. Some scholars have argued for Shakespeare's knowledge of John Lydgate's 26,000-line medieval poetic *Hystorye, Sege and Dystruccyon of Troye*, printed in black letter type long before Shakespeare was born. I find this unlikely. My hunch is that Troy was represented in the Shakespearean chest by just two books in addition to Ovid: William Caxton's prose *Recuyell of the Historyes of Troye* and Geoffrey Chaucer's poetic *Troilus and Criseyde*.

The latter would have been in Thomas Speght's 1598 or 1602 edition of Chaucer's works, which also gave him Robert Henryson's 'continuation' of the Troilus story, 'The Testament of Cressid'. 'The Knight's Tale' was there too: the most admired of *The Canterbury Tales*, in which Arcite and Palamon's knightly friendship is turned to rivalry by their love for Emilia. 'Chaucer – of all admired – the story gives', wrote John Fletcher in the prologue to the dramatization of the tale on which he and Shakespeare collaborated in 1613 or 1614. Around that time, Fletcher and Shakespeare also collaborated on their lost dramatization of the story of Cardenio's love-madness in Cervantes' *Don Quixote*, so it is a fair assumption that Shakespeare also possessed a recently published volume: Thomas Shelton's 1612 translation of Cervantes' hilarious mock-epic novel. Guesswork of course, but I have a hunch that this book would have given Shakespeare more pleasure than any other in the final couple of years of his life.

John Gower, whose effigy Shakespeare would have seen every time he went into the great church near the theatres in Southwark, was almost as highly regarded as Chaucer, his contemporary. Shakespeare definitely knew the (originally Hellenistic) story of Apollonius of Tyre in book eight of Gower's massive compendium of love stories, the *Confessio Amantis*: it was the main source of *Pericles* and the figure of Gower was actually brought on stage as Chorus. In the composition of the play, Gower was supplemented by Lawrence Twine's *The Pattern of Painful Adventures that befell unto Prince Apollonius*, a more down-to-earth prose telling of the same tale, with a racier and more vivid rendition of the brothel sequence. However, Shakespeare only took over the writing of *Pericles* halfway through the play: it was begun by George Wilkins, who could easily have lent Shakespeare his source books and asked for them back afterwards. There is no evidence of Shakespeare having known other parts of Gower's *Confessio Amantis*. The presence of collaborators is a complicating factor in tracking Shakespeare's reading: Archbishop Thomas Cranmer's major role in the final act of *Henry VIII* is strongly shaped by John Foxe's virulently anti-Catholic *Acts and Monuments* (popularly known as *The Book of Martyrs*), but most of that last act was written by Shakespeare's younger co-author John Fletcher, so the copy of Foxe was probably his.

The weightiest volume in Shakespeare's collection would have been Holinshed's 1587 *Chronicles*, which had served him so well through all the history plays. If he was organized in the arrangement of his books, he would have placed it next to Edward Halle's *Union of the Two Noble Illustre Families of Lancaster and York*, to which he had often cross-referred and where he read Thomas More's memorably written but wholly one-sided life of Richard III.

Turning from the classics and the chronicles to the Christian tradition, Shakespeare's chest would have contained a Bible in the Geneva translation, with its printed marginal annotations. The phrasing of Shakespeare's biblical allusions is occasionally closer to the officially sanctioned Bishops' Bible than the Geneva, but that would have come from the memory of listening in church. The phraseology of the Book of Common Prayer and the Homilies

The Geneva Bible: every page had marginal annotations, encouraging an active method of reading that emphasized the arts of interpretation and commentary

also came from church, though it is probable that there would have been a pocket prayer book somewhere among his possessions. However secular his disposition sometimes seems in comparison with many of his pious contemporaries, he would not have disposed of these basic tools of the spiritual life.

Another book that he would almost certainly have taken home to Stratford to reread and meditate upon in his *otium* ('retirement') was Florio's Montaigne translation, which we know from Gonzalo's borrowing was on his mind at the time of *The Tempest* and that was formative of the philosophical vision of *King Lear*. He probably also owned a copy of one or both of Florio's Italian-language manuals, *First Fruits* and *Second Fruits*, and maybe his English–Italian dictionary, *A World of Words*. It is possible that his rudimentary knowledge of Italian came from a combination of Florio's works and a book printed by Thomas Vautrollier during Richard Field's apprenticeship, *La grammatica di M. Scipio Lentulo Napolitano da lui in Latina lingua scritta, & hora nella Italiana, & Inglese tradotta da H.G. = An Italian grammar written in Latin by Scipio Lentulo, a Neapolitan: and turned into English by Henry Granthan*. A teach-yourself-French handbook called *Ortho-epia Gallica*, by a Warwickshire contemporary called John Eliot, may have nestled beside Florio's and Field's Italian materials: from here Shakespeare would have learned enough French to put together the rudimentary language lesson in *Henry V*.

Harington's translation of Ariosto's *Orlando Furioso*, the main source for the Hero plot of *Much Ado*, would perhaps have been returned to Richard Field long ago. Apart from the choice of the hero's name for *As You Like It*, there does not appear to be any interest in Ariosto's epic in Shakespeare's subsequent work.

William Painter's *Palace of Pleasure* (1566, expanded in 1575) was an anthology of 101 'pleasant histories and excellent novels', translated out of a range of Greek, Roman, Italian and French writers. It was there that Shakespeare found an Englishing of more than a dozen stories from Giovanni Boccaccio's *Decameron*, one of which he dramatized in *All's Well that Ends Well*. Possible traces from other stories in the *Palace of Pleasure* can be found elsewhere in Shakespeare – the volume had long been notorious for being 'ransacked to furnish the playhouses in London'.

Matteo Bandello's Italian *Novelle* or possibly the French translation of its stories in François de Belleforest's *Histoires Tragiques* seems to have provided some details for the murder scene in *Othello* and the Hero plot of *Much Ado about Nothing*. The plot of *Twelfth Night* came from Bandello and a related group of Italian plays, but Shakespeare got it from an English version in a collection of novellas by Barnabe Riche called *Riche his Farewell to Military Profession*. Belleforest was also the source through which the Danish saga of Amleth came into English. But since we know that there was an old *Hamlet* play (now lost) in the repertoire, we cannot assume with any certainty that Shakespeare consulted Belleforest as he reworked the action for his own purposes.

He seems at some time to have come across a copy of Giovanni Fiorentino's Italian collection of stories, influenced by Boccaccio, *Il Pecorone*. For it is here, in his tale of Giannetto of Venice and the Lady of Belmont, that we find the principal source of *The Merchant of Venice*. No English translation has been discovered, the plot is a close match and there are a number of verbal parallels, so this connection provides the strongest evidence that Shakespeare had a reading knowledge of Italian. Fiorentino may have been supplemented by Alexandre Sylvain's collection of *Cent Histoires* ('a hundred histories'), which was translated into English in 1596 under the title *The Orator*. Like Bandello and Belleforest, Sylvain took stories and romances from a range of sources, some Roman and others modern. But he did so with the primary purpose of setting up debates on moral questions. The story would be given in relatively perfunctory form, leaving the bulk of each history to be devoted to a speech and a riposte arguing the ethical or legal issue provoked by the narrative. This movement from story to argument explains why the English version was called *The Orator*. Towards the end of the collection we find 'Of a Jew, who would for his debt have a pound of the flesh of a Christian'. The Jew and the Christian put their case to the court, which decides in favour of the Christian. The language of legal argument in the case of *Shylock* v. *Antonio*, with the judgement of Portia, is anticipated here. If Shakespeare flicked through some of the other stories in *The Orator*, he would have discovered several debates on the subject of rape (is death or marriage the appropriate response?), which may have steered him towards the taut ethical debates of *Measure for Measure*. The main source for the latter play was an old drama by George Whetstone called *Promos and Cassandra*, which must once have rested on Shakespeare's desk but is unlikely to have been retained in his book collection.

Certain details in *Measure* seem less close to Whetstone's play than to the story that he was dramatizing, an Italian tale in the *Hecatommithi* ('hundred stories') of Giovanni Baptista Giraldi, known as Cinthio. It was here that Shakespeare found the plot for another play written in close proximity to *Measure for Measure*, around the year 1604: *Othello*. The names Othello and Iago are his invention – Cinthio simply has the Moor and the Ensign – but Desdemona comes directly from the source. Scholars debate whether Shakespeare knew the Italian original or a French translation that was available (or both). I lean towards the Italian: the verbal parallels are a little closer and the language was easy to read if one knew Latin and had Florio's dictionary to hand. Whether Shakespeare ever reread Cinthio for pleasure is doubtful, but his collection of tales was perhaps the principal representative of Italian literature in his chest.

And then there is the question of play books. With a memory trained in school and kept active by the need to learn lines for the plays in which he acted, Shakespeare would have absorbed much of the repertoire through the ear in the theatre. He is unlikely to have bothered to buy and read many plays. Even when he did, would he have kept them? What need would he have had for *The Troublesome Reign of King John*, *The Famous Victories of Henry V* and *The True Chronicle History of King Lear and his Three Daughters* once he had completed his own versions of their stories? He knew Kyd's *Spanish Tragedy* and Marlowe's plays sufficiently well from seeing them. So too with the dramatists who came to prominence in the middle of his career, whose work sometimes echoes his, as he echoes theirs: Ben Jonson, John Marston, Thomas Middleton and Thomas Heywood chief among them.

His early workouts in comedy were shaped by George Gascoigne's *Supposes*, the play that introduced the Italianate comedy of disguise and mistaken identity into English and that provided the prime source for the Bianca and Lucentio plot in *The Taming of the Shrew*. It was an Inns of Court entertainment from the time of Shakespeare's infancy, so it is a work that he would have read rather than seen. He may also have owned printed texts of some of John Lyly's comedies, which, being written for the court and the 'private' boys' companies, were less readily accessible on stage. He certainly knew Lyly's much-reprinted prose romance *Euphues, the Anatomy of Wit* and its sequel *Euphues and his England*, the elaborately symmetrical style of which he parodied, most famously in Falstaff's 'for though the camomile, the more it is trodden the faster it grows, yet youth, the more it is wasted the sooner it wears'. Lyly was the quintessence of high Elizabethan style: if Shakespeare still had his copy of *Euphues* in his later Jacobean years, it was probably gathering dust near the bottom of the trunk.

But he had recently dusted off one of the many Elizabethan prose romances influenced by Lyly's style, Robert Greene's *Pandosto: The Triumph of Time* (1588 and subsequent reprints). It was his primary source for *The Winter's Tale*. Another prose romance in the same vein, Thomas Lodge's *Rosalynde*, very popular and much reprinted, was the story on which he based *As You Like It*. He would unquestionably have owned a copy of this inexpensive little volume.

Turning to the canonical Elizabethan poets represented in Drummond's library, it is hard to pin down the extent (if any) of Shakespeare's knowledge of Edmund Spenser's epic romance *The Faerie Queene*, but he does seem to have admired the work of Samuel Daniel, the best of Spenser's successors. The book chest probably contained copies of the epic poem in eight books, *A History of the Civil Wars between the two Houses of York and Lancaster*, the sonnet sequence *Delia, with the Complaint of Rosamond*, and the 'closet' tragedy (a play written to be read, not performed) *Cleopatra*. There is, however, no firm evidence for a Shakespearean reading of the other most respected neo-Spenserian poet of the age, Michael Drayton, which is mildly surprising, given that he was both a Warwickshire man and a figure who moved between poetry and the theatre.

Marlowe's little poem *Hero and Leander* would have been a prized possession and there should also have been a well-thumbed copy of the volume that Abraham Slender in *The Merry Wives of Windsor* calls 'my Book of Songs and Sonnets', the collection sometimes known as 'Tottel's Miscellany' in which the best lyric poetry of the mid-sixteenth century − by Sir Thomas Wyatt, Henry Howard Earl of Surrey and others − was transmitted to the Elizabethans. Daniel's *Delia* is only one of the dozens of Elizabethan sonnet collections into which Shakespeare may have glanced. Shakespeare's own sonnets both reproduce and parody many of the conventions of the tradition. It is impossible to know whether he owned copies of such and such particular poets. After all, many individual poems by Henry Constable, Richard Barnfield, Bartholomew Griffin, Barnabe Barnes and a host of others circulated in manuscript or were printed in anthologies. In the case of *The Passionate Pilgrim*, the tiny volume of twenty songs and sonnets published by William Jaggard and sold by W. Leake at the sign of the Greyhound in Paul's Churchyard in 1599, sonnets by Barnfield and Griffin were attributed to W. Shakespeare.

Given the posthumous fame of Sir Philip Sidney and the foundational role played by his *Astrophel and Stella* in the Elizabethan vogue for sonnet sequences, it is probable that Shakespeare at least saw the (unauthorized) 1591 printing of those poems. I rather doubt that he owned a copy, but he probably did possess and keep Sidney's much bigger book, the prose romance *Arcadia*, prepared for publication after his death by his sister, Mary Countess of Pembroke. The Gloucester plot in *King Lear* is clearly based on one of the many stories woven into the *Arcadia*.

A very different book, the real curiosity in Shakespeare's collection, was also used for *King Lear*: Samuel Harsnett's aggressively titled *A Declaration of Egregious Popish Impostures, to withdraw the Hearts of her Majesty's Subjects from their Allegiance and from the Truth of Christian Religion professed in England*. The principal 'Popish imposture' in question was the fake exorcism of evil spirits. Shakespeare wasn't generally interested in politico-religious propaganda of this sort, but he may have been drawn to Harsnett's diatribe, published in 1603, because one of the central figures in the exorcism ring it denounced was a Stratford man whom he probably knew, Robert Dibdale (trained as priest at Douai, hanged, drawn and quartered at Tyburn in 1586). The names of the devils conjured up by the Popish priests – Obidicut, Hobbididence, Mahu, Modo and Flibertigibbet – duly reappeared in the ravings of 'Poor Tom' in *Lear*, together with references to '*hysterico passio*' and 'the prince of darkness'.

It is possible that Shakespeare owned one or two miscellanies of commonplace wisdom. Erasmus' *Adagia* ('adages'), perhaps, or at least the selection from them prepared in English by Richard Tavener, where we find a source for a variety of sayings such as

Rosalind's 'good wine needs no bush' and Ulysses' 'wallet of oblivion'. But it is in the nature of commonplaces that they become proverbial, so are hard to trace back to particular sources. So too, as has been suggested, with Erasmus' ideas more generally. It is attractive to suppose, for instance, that Shakespeare read the English translation of *The Praise of Folly*, but such a reading is not necessary for him to have understood and turned to dramatic effect the figure of the wise fool.

There is no certain answer to the question of whether Shakespeare owned a copy of Palingenius, encountered one casually, relied on the memory of school or absorbed the paired themes of 'the seven ages of man' and 'all the world's a stage' indirectly.

As well as the durable works, there would have been casual reading, which is harder to trace. So, for instance, while he was writing *The Tempest* in the year 1611, one of his several acquaintances who were associated with the Virginia Company – the Earl of Pembroke or a member of the Digges family, perhaps – passed him one or more of the 'Bermuda pamphlets' describing the shipwreck of Sir Thomas Gates in the Caribbean. He snapped up a few nautical details, began imagining a tempest, an island and a new world of his own, then in all probability gave the pamphlet back or tossed it aside. Reports of other events that fed into other plays – a grain riot in the midlands for *Coriolanus*, the voyage of a ship called the Tiger for *Macbeth* – may have reached him verbally, in the pub as it were, or through penny broadsheets. Ephemera of this kind drifted on the surface of his world, but was not anchored to the depths of his imagination.

The above list could be divided into big books, such as Holinshed and Plutarch, and small ones, such as the novellas and slim volumes of poetry. Would he have bothered to take the small ones back to Stratford? One could imagine him slipping tales such as *Pandosto* and *Rosalynde* into his luggage with a view to their being gifts for little Elizabeth and any future grandchildren. That would leave the larger ones: Golding's Ovid, North's Plutarch, Florio's Montaigne, the Geneva Bible, Chaucer, Caxton's Trojan history, the chronicles of Holinshed and Hall, Daniel's poetry (especially his Wars of the Roses epic), perhaps Sidney's *Arcadia* (though its style was rather too courtly for his taste), conceivably either or both of Tavener's reduced *Adagia* rendered into English and La Primauday's *The French Academy*, also in translation. And, finally, the recent acquisition of Cervantes in English. These were the books that mattered most deeply to him: maybe a dozen volumes at most, but infinite in their riches.

These speculations are of course a biographical fantasy. But the point is a serious one. Thanks to his undoubted friendship with Richard Field and his very probable acquaintance with John Florio, Shakespeare had easy access to these books. This body of literature offers a deep insight into the mental world in which he lived. If one bears in mind the method of close reading in which he was trained at school, not to mention his prodigious memory both for the plays that he saw or acted in and the other books he devoured and disposed of more casually, then there need be no anxiety about the idea of a middle-class provincial grammar-school boy having the intellectual resources to write the plays.

And what about his own books? Would they have been in the chest as he prepared for his last move back to Stratford? We must set aside modern notions of an author preserving his rough drafts and collecting his own first editions. When Shakespeare completed a play, he handed the script over to the company book-keeper, who would create the master copy for prompt use backstage, then copy out the parts for each actor. The author's script, on a couple of occasions referred to in the period as 'foul papers', would probably have remained with the acting company. Sometimes they formed the basis for a printed text. It is most unlikely that Shakespeare would have retained a sheaf of his own manuscripts.

He would surely have kept copies of the poems that he authorized for the press, *Venus and Adonis*, 'the first heir of my invention', and that 'graver labour', *The Rape of Lucrece*. He would probably have been given a presentation copy of Robert Chester's strange allegorical poem *Love's Martyr* to which he had contributed his verses on 'The Phoenix and Turtle'. The *Sonnets* are an open question: they may or may not have been authorized for publication. If they were not, he might not have wanted a copy. The same goes for *The Passionate Pilgrim*, which was certainly unauthorized, and perhaps the body of half a dozen or more of his plays that were printed in his lifetime in poor-quality versions from unauthorized texts.

That leaves the dozen or so printed plays that do seem to have been authorized by his acting company and thus presumably himself. All had been published in small format, low-cost 'quarto' editions. They didn't occupy much space, so they were probably there in the trunk. He may well have taken a certain pride in the histories and tragedies especially: they represented full versions of plays that on stage must have been cut for reasons of time. But there is no evidence that Shakespeare ever contemplated doing what Samuel Daniel had done a decade before: gathered all his writings into a collected volume called *Works*. That would have to wait for the posthumous labours of his fellow actors, John Hemings and Henry Condell.

THIRD AGE

Lover

And then the lover,
Sighing like furnace, with a woeful ballad
Made to his mistress' eyebrow.

Portrait miniature by Nicholas Hilliard

10. The Married Man

The teenage bridegroom

In the year of Shakespeare's birth, there appeared in print for the first time a treatise on sexually transmitted disease by the great anatomist Gabriele Falloppio. Bubonic fever was not the only plague that ravished sixteenth-century Europe: though less immediate in its effects, syphilis was another mass killer. The ingenious doctor from the renowned Italian university of Padua was known by his Latinized name, Fallopius: the uterine tubes that he discovered are still named after him. In his treatise, he proposed that the best protection against the 'pox', as syphilis was called, was a sheath made of linen, dried bladder or animal intestine, fitted over the penis and secured by the foreskin. Known colloquially as an 'overcoat', the device was eight inches long and tied at the base with a pink ribbon to make it more acceptable to women. Fallopius claimed that it had been tested on over a thousand men with complete success. Not one of them had been infected with the so-called French disease. Nobody seems, however, to have had the idea of marketing the overcoat as a contraceptive device.

One would have expected the absence of contraception from Elizabethan England to have resulted in large numbers of young men impregnating their girlfriends and then being persuaded to marry in order to make them 'honest'. Yet this does not seem to have been the case in rural Warwickshire. An examination of Stratford-upon-Avon parish records for the years 1570 to 1630 throws up a startling result. It was possible to calculate the age at first marriage of just over one hundred men during this period. Three-quarters of them married between the ages of twenty and thirty. The mean age was twenty-six. The most frequently occurring was twenty-four. These figures are consistent with national averages.

The surprise is that of all the men whose ages can be recovered, only three were in their teens when they married. George Davis, a gardener, married one Margaret Batha a month after his seventeenth birthday. William Baylis, a cooper, married Anne Russell when he was eighteen. The Davises never had any children. The Baylises' first child was baptized a year after their wedding. So, unless there was miscarriage or stillbirth, in neither case was the marriage due to the girl's rounding belly. That leaves only one identifiable teenage Stratford husband in the whole sixty-year period whose bride was pregnant on the day of their marriage: the glover's son, eighteen-year-old William Shakespeare.

Furthermore, it was normal for a bride to be rather younger than a groom. In the Stratford records, the mean age of first marriage for women was twenty-four and the most frequently occurring ages seventeen and twenty-one. Again, this is consistent with patterns across the country. Shakespeare's bride, by contrast, was in her twenty-sixth or twenty-seventh year. A young lad, an older woman and pregnant to boot: that was a very unusual combination.

It is, alas, impossible to unearth the significance of this information. Sexual precocity? Passionate ardour? A cunning way with seductive words? Carelessness when it came to the moment? (*Coitus interruptus*, anal and intercrural sex were variously recommended as precautions against pregnancy.) Maybe a calculated forcing of the hand in order to ensure marriage to a wealthier woman, thus redeeming the parlous family fortunes of the Shakespeares? Or conversely, an exceptional sense of honour in making an honest woman of his lover, in an age when fornication and bastardy were stigmatized by the church courts and where many an unmarried mother found herself cast aside by family and decent society? Any, all or none of the above?

All we know is that, according to the register of the diocese of Worcester, on 27 November 1582 a licence was issued for the marriage of William Shaxpere and Anna Whateley of Temple Grafton, a village just west of Stratford-upon-Avon. This was what the church of England now calls a special licence: it was only required in cases where the banns were not going to be read in church on three successive Sundays in advance of the wedding. In the absence of a public proclamation of the banns, there was a greater danger of bigamy, consanguinity, breach of a pre-contract with a third party or some other impediment to the marriage. For this reason, the bishop required a bond of sureties, guaranteeing that the prospective partners were entitled to marry. The Worcester registry has such a bond, dated 28 November 1582, referring to William Shagspere and Anne Hathwey of Stratford.

It is generally assumed that the application for a licence was an indication of hurry: that Anne's pregnancy was discovered and that there was not time for three readings of the banns before the advent and Christmas season, when marriages could not be solemnized without a special licence. The wedding may be assumed to have taken place in early December 1582, possibly in the chapel of the nearby village of Luddington, where a marriage entry for William and Anne is said to have been seen before the register was destroyed. Susanna Shakespeare was baptized on 26 May 1583, so even if she was born somewhat prematurely there can be no doubt that Anne was pregnant on her wedding day.

No satisfactory solution has ever been found to the mystery of the variant surnames in the documents related to the marriage: Whateley on the licence issued one day, Hathwey on the bond dated the next. There is no significance in the variant spellings of Shaxpere and Shagspere. The Shakespeare surname, like many others in the period, is spelt dozens of different ways in the surviving records. Elizabethans were slapdash about names. Miss Hathaway, whom we always call Anne, is actually referred to in her father's will as Agnes, which would have been pronounced 'Annes'. Some biographers have proposed that there were two different women in the case – or perhaps two different men. There were a lot of Shakespeares and Whatelys around Stratford in the late sixteenth century, but what are the chances of one William Shakespeare being named on the request for a special licence to marry a woman called Anne one day and a different William Shakespeare putting in the supporting documentation to marry another woman called Anna the next?

No one has ever found another reference to Anna Whateley of

Temple Grafton, so it is usually supposed that the dozy clerk in Worcester mistranscribed the name of 'Hathwey' when he was copying out his register, perhaps because that same day a William Whateley had been involved in a case before the church court. But that does not explain the presence of Temple Grafton, a village some way to the west of Stratford. The Hathaways were from Shottery, much closer to town. It might be tempting to suppose that the true mistake was the reference in the bond to Anne Hathwey as a 'maiden'. In both the stage comedies of Shakespeare's age and the real world in which he lived, wealthy widows were the most sought-after match for impoverished young men. Could Anne have been born a Hathwey in Stratford and married a Whateley in Temple Grafton? Could she then have been widowed, giving young Will the opportunity to move in swiftly with the offer of sexual solace and the hope of a widow's ample marriage portion? It is not impossible, but the first husband would have had to die very quickly, since we know from the will of old Mr Hathaway that Anne was still unmarried in the autumn of 1581. The probability is that Anne was indeed a 'maiden' and that she was in some form of service, perhaps with a distant relative, in Temple Grafton.

Though it was unusual for a groom to be so young, it was not necessarily scandalous for the bride to be pregnant. Ecclesiastical and legal authorities argued over the matter, but it was generally agreed that a union was legally binding once a solemn spousal promise had been made, so the bedding often preceded the wedding. It is a biographical myth to suppose that Will was marched off to a shotgun wedding by friends of the Hathaways who were incensed at hearing that Miss Anne was in the family way.

Shakespeare's signature work, the poem that made his name and became the favourite reading matter of the bright young things of the Elizabethan age, was *Venus and Adonis*, in which an innocent boy is seduced by a sexually voracious older woman (or rather goddess). Sometimes self-consciously, sometimes not, many biographers have read Shakespeare's marriage through this distorting lens. But the poem was written as a showcase for Shakespeare's art, not a commentary on his life. As for the plays, it has too often been assumed that because Shakespeare wrote *The Taming of the Shrew*, his wife must have been one. There are so many different modes of courtship in the comedies that it is foolish to link any one of them to the dramatist's own experience. I have an instinctive sense that the wooer whom Shakespeare most resembles is Bassanio in *The Merchant of Venice*: clever but cold, an adventurer and a wordsmith who always looks after himself, a man on the lookout for a wealthy woman to help him out of a financial crisis and who has the good fortune to find one who is also beautiful, ultra-intelligent and attracted to him. But there is no more evidence for this fancy than for the idea that William was somehow like Adonis (or Petruchio or Orlando or any of his other characters) or that Anne was like Venus or Kate 'the shrew' or Adriana, the put-upon wife of *The Comedy of Errors*.

Like so much in Shakespeare's life and work, his marriage can be interpreted in diametrically opposed ways. A grand passion prematurely consummated? Perhaps. An arranged union between two families who knew each other well? Quite possibly: Anne's father had just died, leaving her a decent portion to be inherited upon her marriage, while Shakespeare's father was struggling with debt. Only two certainties emerge from the circumstances of Shakespeare's marriage. One is that he was a sexually active young man, who fathered his first child before getting married, with the twins Hamnet and Judith following soon after, putting him in the very unusual situation of being the married father of three children before he came of age on his twenty-first birthday in April 1585. The other certainty is the fact that the first formal record of his life subsequent to his baptism emerges from the diocesan consistory court. We will return to these courts, in which marital and sexual matters were settled.

The breadwinner

There is no evidence of Shakespeare leaving his wife and children in the first few years of his marriage. The oldest and best-attested story concerning his whereabouts prior to his appearance on the

London theatre scene suggests that he was 'a schoolmaster in the country'. He could not have taught at a major grammar school without a degree, but he could have gained a post in a lesser school or as an 'usher', a master's assistant. It would have been perfectly possible to keep his family with him in such circumstances. At some point, however, probably in the late 1580s, he went to London with the hope of making a fortune for himself and his family in a way that would not have been possible out in the sticks. He never set up home alone in the city: he rented lodgings while accumulating land and property back home in Stratford. By the summer of 1597 he was in the position to buy his wife New Place, the second-largest house in town – albeit a property that was in a neglected state of repair, allowing him to obtain it at a knock-down price.

Acting was a surprising path for a glover's son and possible former schoolmaster with a wife and young family to maintain. The only actor who seemed to be making any money was Edward Alleyn, whose star was in the ascendant with his performances as Hieronimo in Thomas Kyd's *Spanish Tragedy* and the lead roles in Christopher Marlowe's storming plays. Shakespeare must have swiftly realized that he was never going to become a stage colossus like Alleyn or Richard Burbage, the leading player in the company he had joined himself, but that he did have a talent for improving the scripts in his company's repertoire – and soon for writing his own. He probably stumbled gradually into his profession of full-time play-maker.

It can hardly have been a consciously planned career move, because when he began there was no precedent for a man making money out of writing for the theatre. Writing was an even more unlikely source of income than playing. A combination of business acumen and powerful acting was making Edward Alleyn a rich and influential man. To judge from his property dealings, Shakespeare had his own measure of the first of Alleyn's talents. Even if he lacked the second, the best prospect of providing for his wife and three children back in Stratford would have been to follow a path similar to Alleyn's or, better still, that of the theatrical entrepreneur Philip Henslowe. In, say, the year 1592, the profession of dramatist would have looked like the worst possible choice. There were no wealthy writers. A quick glance at the pattern of Shakespeare's life in comparison with those of the twelve most highly regarded dramatists among his contemporaries – eight born in the decade before him, four in the decade after – is extremely revealing in this regard.

Brief lives

John Lyly, born 1556, Oxford educated, married a woman of property when he was aged twenty-nine. As a young man he became the most fashionable writer in England, then achieved the position of leading court dramatist in the 1580s. But his plays fell out of fashion and he did not write in the latter part of his life. He died in very modest circumstances, aged fifty-two.

George Peele, born 1556, Oxford educated, married a sixteen-year-old girl with good financial prospects when he was twenty-four. After writing some successful plays in the 1580s and early 1590s, he fell into financial difficulties and died, reputedly of syphilis, aged forty.

Robert Greene, born 1558, Cambridge educated, allegedly married a wealthy gentlewoman named Doll, spent her fortune, and then sent her with a child back to her family in the country while he lived a debauched life as a writer in London. England's first celebrity author, he wrote for money, in every genre available. He allegedly took up with a prostitute, sister to the criminal Cutting Ball, and fathered an illegitimate son named Fortunatus. Soon after, he died of fever in extreme poverty aged thirty-four.

Thomas Kyd, born 1558, educated at grammar school but not university, wrote the highly successful *Spanish Tragedy*, but was imprisoned and tortured during a government investigation into the writing of inflammatory 'libels' against immigrants. He contrived his own release by incriminating his room-mate Christopher Marlowe for holding heretical views, but died in poverty a few months later, aged thirty-five. He never married.

George Chapman, born 1559 or 1560, education unknown, but

with no university degree, seems to have entered the service of a London gentleman, then fought in the Netherlands. During the 1590s he sought patronage by writing poetry and translating Homer. He turned to plays near the end of the decade, but endured continuing financial hardship. He was imprisoned because of his part in the writing of the play *Eastward Ho!*, which satirized Scotsmen in a way displeasing to the new king. Nevertheless, early in the reign of King James, he became sewer-in-ordinary to Henry Prince of Wales, with the promise of £300 a year and a pension, but the latter did not materialize on the prince's death in 1612, causing him to seek other patrons. He lived for a further twenty years, devoting himself to poetry and translation rather than plays. Though he never achieved financial security, he lived to the age of seventy-four. He never married.

Anthony Munday, born 1560, seems to have been educated privately by a London Huguenot, but did not go to university. He was apprenticed to a printer, but left to travel in Europe, spending time at the English (Catholic) college in Rome. He then became an actor. He married by the age of twenty-two and subsequently had five children. He led a double life, serving as a government anti-Catholic spy while establishing himself as a writer of pamphlets, prose works, poetry and plays. Francis Meres regarded him as the 'best plotter' of the age, which seems appropriate for someone in the intelligence service. He wrote, mostly collaboratively, in the team of dramatists employed by Philip Henslowe. After the accession of King James, he seems to have abandoned the public theatre and concentrated on writing civic pageants, which were extremely successful. He died at the age of seventy-three, leaving a second wife (his first had died when he was sixty-one) and an estate valued at the not insignificant sum of £135.

Michael Drayton, born 1563, son of a Warwickshire tanner, education unknown but with no degree, entered the service of a local gentleman. By 1590, he had moved to London in pursuit of patronage through writing in a wide range of genres. He published several widely read poems, then in the late 1590s and early 1600s wrote about twenty plays, mostly collaborative, paid on a piecework basis, for the Lord Admiral's Men (the Alleyn/Henslowe company). In the reign of King James, he went back to poetry alone, dedicating his major work, *Poly-olbion*, to Prince Henry, in return for which he was awarded a £10 annuity, which ceased almost immediately because of the prince's death. He did not include his theatre scripts in the edition of his collected poems that was published in 1619. When he was sixty-four, he appeared before the consistory court in London, charged with incontinence with a married woman. A maidservant claimed that the woman in question raised her skirts to her navel and 'that she clapped her hand on her privy part and said it was a sound and a good one, and that the said Mr Drayton did then also lay his hand upon it and stroke it and said that it was a good one'. Drayton denied the charge and when asked about his finances joked that he had only '20 nobles, debts paid', but that he was 'worth at least £2000 in good parts'. He died at the age of sixty-eight, with an estate valued at just under £25, but with sufficient respectability to have been buried in the north aisle of Westminster Abbey. He seems never to have married and his poetry shows some interest in homoerotic desire.

Christopher Marlowe, born 1564, Cambridge educated, wrote a few dazzlingly successful plays in the late 1580s and early 1590s, but also apparently lived a double life working as a government agent. He was stabbed to death by a twelve-penny dagger inserted just above the eye, in an argument over the 'reckoning' after a day's drinking in the company of spies in Deptford, aged twenty-nine. At the time, he was under investigation for political and religious provocations such as the claim that Jesus Christ had a homosexual relationship with his disciple John. There is no archival record of his ever having had any relationship with a woman.

William Shakespeare, born 1564, son of a Warwickshire glover, educated at grammar school but not university, had a highly successful career as prolific poet and playwright as well as actor and successful sharer in the Chamberlain's/King's Men. He married at age eighteen and had three children. A long-lasting career in the theatre was matched to a long-lasting marriage, after which he died in respectable circumstances in his home town of Stratford-upon-Avon, aged fifty-two, leaving a considerable property portfolio and several hundred pounds of cash.

Thomas Nashe, born 1567, Cambridge educated, was a prolific pamphleteer and collaborative playwright. He was imprisoned several times, sometimes for debt, sometimes because of his writings. He fled London to Great Yarmouth following controversy over his 'lewd, seditious and slanderous' play *The Isle of Dogs* (co-written with the young actor Ben Jonson). He died in obscurity and almost certain poverty, aged about thirty-three. He never married.

Thomas Dekker, born about 1572, probably educated at grammar school, but definitely not university, had no regular patron and no income as an actor or theatre shareholder. He relied on his writing, for which he was remunerated on a piecework basis. His age at first marriage is unknown, but he had several children and his wife died while he was spending a seven-year term in the King's Bench prison for debtors. He died aged about sixty, in debt, leaving his second wife in straitened circumstances.

Ben Jonson, born 1572, attended Westminster School, but not university. He was apprenticed to a bricklayer (his stepfather), became a soldier, then an actor and writer. He married aged twenty-two. He described his wife as 'a shrew yet honest': they had children, but he seems to have lived apart from her for much of his career. 'Five years he had not bedded with her,' he told Drummond of Hawthornden, 'but remained with my Lord Aulbany.' He may also have had children by another woman. Drummond again: 'in his youth, given to venery'. He was imprisoned on various occasions, including for manslaughter and for writing seditious plays. He wrote in many genres, relying on piecework and patronage, never becoming a theatre shareholder. Eventually he found fame and court patronage – and a pension from the king. He became the first writer for the popular stage to publish a complete edition of his literary works, including his plays. He died, impoverished but not in debt, aged sixty-five, and was buried in Westminster Abbey, with his funeral attended by nobility and gentry.

Thomas Heywood, born 1573, Cambridge educated, had a highly successful career as a prolific poet and playwright as well as actor and successful sharer in the Queen Anne's Men. He married in his late twenties and had several children. A long-lasting career in the theatre was matched to a long-lasting marriage, after which he died in respectable circumstances in his home district of Clerkenwell, aged about sixty-eight.

The shareholder

Shakespeare broke the mould in several different ways. His predecessors can be divided into those who married for money and those who were bachelors, either because they preferred to keep the company of men or because they could not afford to marry. No other major writer of the age married before reaching his legal majority, as he did. He was emphatically unlike the university-educated men, who lived from hand to mouth, got into trouble with the authorities and died young. Kyd, the first successful non-university playwright, suffered a similar fate to them.

The contemporaries whom Shakespeare resembled in social and educational origin, and in the manner of their attempt to make money from writing in London, were Chapman, Drayton and Munday. The difference was that none of these three became a shareholder in an acting company and all of them abandoned the commercial theatre early in the reign of King James, when plague dampened the demand for new plays. The sad case of Dekker reveals that there was no money to be made from play-making alone. The financial stability (and longevity) achieved by Munday, and, to a lesser degree, Chapman, Drayton and Jonson, came not from either theatre or publication but from court, aristocratic or civic patronage. It is striking that the men who did best out of their writing were the ones who began as actors: Munday, Shakespeare, Jonson, Heywood.

Jonson's is the most extraordinary story: from bricklayer's apprentice via acting and play-making to unofficial poet laureate, buried with full honours in the Abbey. But he never became wealthy. The career that most closely resembled Shakespeare's was that of Thomas Heywood, and it was clearly modelled on his success: as Shakespeare began as an actor, made his name with the poem *Venus and Adonis*, then became shareholder and in-house playwright with the King's Men, so Heywood began as an actor, made his name with the poem *Oenone and Paris* (closely modelled on *Venus and Adonis*), then became shareholder and in-house playwright with the Queen's Men.

Through becoming a shareholder, Shakespeare was the first to turn play-making into a potentially rewarding profession that could support a marriage and a family. His fortune was made not by a literary innovation but by a business decision. In his early career, Shakespeare would have noted the raw deal suffered by the script-writers, who were paid only a few pounds per play. The serious money was made by manager Henslowe and lead actor Alleyn, who ran the Rose Theatre as an entrepreneurial partnership. Shakespeare and his close associates came up with an alternative arrangement: the Lord Chamberlain's Men was formed in 1594 as a joint stock company, with the profits shared among the players.

Shakespeare's company managers, Augustine Phillips and John Hemings, must have kept account books, similar to those of Hens-lowe that are now preserved at Dulwich College. Had the accounts of the Chamberlain's/King's Men survived, they would have told us the dates of first performance of Shakespeare's plays, the box-office receipts (and hence audience numbers), together with the amount of the profits distributed among the shareholders after the deduction of expenses both capital and recurrent (payments for costumes, carpentry, hired men, scripts by freelancers and so on). In the absence of such documentation, all we know is that Shake-speare's fellow-shareholders did well enough to buy themselves decent properties, often on the outskirts of London. They could afford to get married, unlike so many of the writers, and their wills reveal their prosperity. But their annual income from the theatre business is a matter for conjecture. The best estimate is that, once fully established, Shakespeare may have made between £150 and £200 per year from his shareholding. Modern comparisons are difficult to sustain, but in early twenty-first-century terms that is roughly the equivalent of £30,000–£40,000 per year. We do not know if the company made him extra payments for writing. At the very least, he would have done well out of the 'benefit' system, whereby the box-office profits of the third performance of each new play went to the author. A few people in Elizabethan and Jacobean England were very much richer than Shakespeare, but the vast majority were very much poorer – a high proportion of the residents of Stratford-upon-Avon were indeed on poor relief.

John Shakespeare conspicuously failed to stay solvent for his family. Shakespeare's brothers Richard and Gilbert seem both to have been too poor to marry. Financially speaking, Shakespeare himself did very well by his wife and children, not least through his shrewd investments. In London he always remained in inexpensive lodgings; he was reputedly resistant to spending a lot of time and money out on the town. He saved his money and ploughed it back into property and land at home. So, for instance, in 1602 he invested £320 in the purchase of an estate consisting of 107 acres in the open fields of Old Stratford, together with a farm-house, garden and orchard, twenty acres of pasture and common rights. Then in 1605 he spent another £440 on the outstanding term of a lease of tithes in Stratford parish, which brought in an income of about £60 a year. Making enough money to keep the family going and sustaining a marriage for well over thirty years: these are not the achievements of the romantic lover, but they are manifestations of love.

11. Before the Bawdy Court

Sex and scandal

Lawyers and court officers are better at writing things down than theatre people are. Whether a legal system has a Roman-style code or relies on case law, a paper trail is needed. Theatre, by contrast, is a makeshift, evanescent, oral form. That is why we have more glimpses of Shakespeare in and around the courts than in and around the theatre. His name crops up in various suits for small debt in the Stratford Court of Record. And the only time we hear him speak in his own voice – save perhaps in the dedicatory epistles to *Venus and Adonis* and *The Rape of Lucrece* – is as a witness in the action of Belott v. Mountjoy in the Court of Requests at Westminster.

This too was a matrimonial case: Christopher and Marie Mountjoy were successful Huguenot tiremakers, 'tire' meaning head-tire or attire. They made head-dresses for the royal court and perhaps also for the theatre. Stephen Belott was their apprentice. As was common, a marriage was arranged between the daughter and the apprentice, with a view to sustaining the business in the next generation. A dowry of £60 seems to have been agreed, but was never paid, so Belott eventually took his father-in-law to court. At the time of the marriage arrangement, Shakespeare had been lodging for at least a couple of years in their house in Silver Street in the Cripplegate district of London, close to the residences of several of his fellow-actors and other people with theatrical connections. When the dispute came to the Court of Requests in 1612, nearly a decade after the events in question, Mr William Shakespeare, gentleman of Stratford-upon-Avon in the county of Warwickshire, aged forty-eight, was summoned to appear as a witness. In his deposition, he spoke up for Belott's good character. But he also revealed that Mrs Mountjoy had enlisted his services 'to move and persuade' Belott to go through with the marriage. To move and persuade a young man to marry, somewhat against his will: the very matter of Shakespeare's bestselling poem *Venus and Adonis*, of the first group of his sonnets, and of two plays that he wrote in the Silver Street years, *Measure for Measure* and *All's Well that Ends Well*. Mrs Mountjoy was going to the right man for the job, and Shakespeare duly did the business. We learn from another witness that he actually presided over the handfasting ceremony that sealed the union. In the end, though, instead of resolving the case, the judge referred it to the arbitration of the elders and overseers of the French church in London. They awarded Belott twenty nobles, a lot less than the £60 he was demanding. Mountjoy, damningly, was recorded as being of a 'licentious life'.

Where do we begin a discussion of Shakespeare and love, Shakespeare and sex? Tempting as it is to turn straight to the sonnets or the courtship comedies, it is the law courts that allow us to stand on firmer ground. Linking Shakespeare's love-life to his literary and theatrical works will always be a matter of extreme speculation, whereas it can be said with absolute certainty that Shakespeare's marriage involved the obtaining of a special licence from one court when he was eighteen and that his role in facilitating the Belott marriage led to his appearance in another court when he was forty-eight. It can also be said with absolute certainty that Shakespeare's thinking about the love between men and women was shaped by the knowledge that it could result in children, that once a woman was pregnant it was necessary for the sake of her social status that she should soon marry, and that marriage was a legal bond as much as an affair of the heart, a bond in which questions of portions, dowries and financial settlements played a major part.

The referral of the Mountjoy case to the church fathers is a reminder that Shakespeare's England was a place of multiple, sometimes competing legal jurisdictions. Matrimonial issues could be heard before either a civil or an ecclesiastical court. The church consistory courts, which still exist today, albeit stripped of almost all their powers, were established by a charter of William the Conqueror. They heard many cases involving sex, marriage, adultery and divorce. They were the place where love entered the public arena. The churchwardens reported to the vicar the names of any members of the community who had been guilty of adultery, whoredom, incest, drunkenness, swearing, ribaldry, usury, uncleanness and wickedness of life, absence from church, blasphemy, scandal-mongering or bigamy. Less lurid matters were also addressed. Was the church in a good state of repair? Were all local schoolmasters, physicians and midwives properly licensed?

In a parish such as Stratford, the local consistory court would have been set up inside the church. There was a raised seat for the judge – who was the vicar – and a large table for the notary and the witnesses to sit around. The crier would stand near the notary and the accused stood facing the judge. One might say: as in a play, everyone has his or her appropriate position on the stage. The charge was then read out (in the technical term, 'objected'). If the accused admitted guilt, he or she would be dismissed with a 'monition' or ordered to do penance, which might be either fully public in church before the morning service on a Sunday or semi-public before the minister and local officials. Sunday services were two hours long, with a sermon that many people would have found immensely tedious. Witnessing a local man or woman being made to stand and do penance for some sexual misdemeanour would have livened up proceedings and furnished good material for gossip – the custom might be thought of as the Tudor equivalent of reading the latest scandal in the Sunday papers. In severe cases, the vicar ordered the extreme exposure of public penance, which involved standing clad in a white sheet in the Market Place on Thursday, the busiest day of the week: a rare event, but one to keep tongues wagging in the taverns.

If the accused denied the charge, he or she was ordered to return to the church court on a subsequent occasion and 'purge' him or herself by swearing innocence on oath. Neighbours ('compurgators') could swear their support. Upcoming purgations were announced several days in advance. Those opposing a purge were called three times to come forward. The triple call to state an objection was a customary practice: there is an analogy with the calling of the banns of marriage three times, and indeed with the three calls of the trumpet upon which objectors are summoned to challenge Edmund's right to the title of Duke of Gloucester in *King Lear*.

Contentious cases were known as 'instance' cases. If the accused failed to appear in court having been summonsed to purge themselves (given a 'citation'), they were pronounced 'contumaceous' and excommunicated. Minor excommunication, the more common punishment, meant exclusion from church and the sacraments. Major excommunication meant being cut off from 'the communion of the faithful' to the full extent of exclusion from both commercial activity and the benefit of the law. Some of this legal vocabulary of the consistory court bleeds into Shakespeare's plays. Thus when he uses the word 'purge' and its cognates, the connotations are usually medical, but occasionally suggestive of ecclesiastical law, as with 'You must be purgèd too', with regard to Berowne's breach of his oath in *Love's Labour's Lost*, and 'Here I stand both to impeach and purge / Myself condemnèd and myself excused', with regard to Friar Laurence's role in the events of *Romeo and Juliet*.

Does Petruchio in *The Taming of the Shrew* assault his wife? Does Kate speak slander? Should Proteus be charged with attempted rape of Silvia in *The Two Gentlemen of Verona*? Who got the dairymaid Jacquenetta pregnant in *Love's Labour's Lost* and what should be done about it? In *Much Ado about Nothing*, did Hero sleep with a man other than her husband on the night before her wedding day? Is there any justification in Master Frank Ford's suspicion in *The Merry Wives of Windsor* that his wife has been committing adultery? Did Angelo in *Measure for Measure* break a binding spousal contract when he pulled out of his marriage with Mariana, on discovering that she would not bring him a sufficient dowry? In the same play, should Claudio and Juliet be punished for fornication? Did Bertram commit adultery and otherwise abuse his wife Helen in *All's Well that Ends Well*? Does Hermione's child in *The Winter's Tale* belong to her husband? Is there evidence for Iachimo's accusation in *Cymbeline* that Innogen is wanton? Is the marriage between Romeo and Juliet legal, in the light of her young age and the absence of parental consent? Is Desdemona guilty of adultery or Iago of slander? Such questions drive the plots of Shakespeare's courtship comedies and marriage tragedies. The same questions are often to be found in Shakespeare's sources – the repertoire of older comedies and his reading in English and Italian short stories. Anyone familiar with the *Decameron* of Boccaccio will know that the matter of sex and slander had long been a staple of literature. But before Shakespeare began reading such stories or performing in courtship comedies as an actor, he would have been exposed to questions of a similar kind when as a boy and a young man he witnessed his fellow-townspeople doing penance in the church or the market place, or when – as is bound to have been the case in a small community – he heard the gossip about the latest case to have come before the consistory court. Given the nature of its most interesting business, the people gave that institution a more colloquial name: 'the bawdy court'.

The Stratford bawdy court records for the years before 1590 are lost, so we do not know the details of the cases that might have helped to shape young Shakespeare's imagining of love's entanglements. But we may gain a flavour of the sexual life of Elizabethan Stratford from the surviving act books, which cover the second half of Shakespeare's life. He would certainly have known that in the year 1613 a man named John Lane of Alveston, a nearby village, was accused of slander before the Bishop's higher-level bawdy court at Worcester. Lane had publicly stated that one Susanna Hall, née Shakespeare, 'had the running of the reins and had been naughty with Rafe Smith at John Palmer's'. The plaintiff was Susanna herself and a witness in her support was Robert Whatcott, who just under three years later would be a witness to Shakespeare's will. Lane ignored the citation to appear and defend himself against the charge. He was excommunicated and Susanna's name was cleared – if a name can ever fully be cleared once an alleged scandal has reached the public domain.

On a single day in the Stratford court a certain Alice Clark was presented for saying that Elizabeth Reynolds was Abraham Allway his whore, one Katherine Shingleton failed to appear in answer to the charge that she had called widow Aldern a whore and said that all her children were bastards, and Anne Lane was alleged to have called Katherine Trout a whore and 'that William Bartlett hath publicly confessed before witnesses that Katherine Trout did come to bed with him'. One begins to see why a preacher at Paul's Cross claimed that half the children in the land would be bastards were it not for the church courts.

Shakespeare's brother Richard and his sister Joan were both cited as defendants, in separate cases, in the year 1608, but the act book does not record details of the accusations against them. There are, however, cases among the Stratford bawdy court presentations for fornication or adultery that touch indirectly upon Shakespeare. Katherine Getley, daughter of the man from whom he bought a cottage in Chapel Lane opposite New Place, was excommunicated for begetting a bastard, and Judith, the daughter of Hamlet and Judith Sadler – godparents to Shakespeare's twins – was cited for sexual incontinence. The creator of Angelo in *Measure for Measure* would have taken pleasure in the news that Daniel Baker, Stratford's leading Puritan, who as town bailiff ensured that travelling players were banned from performing in the Gild Hall, was excommunicated for failing to answer the charge that he had got a woman with child and reneged on his promise to marry her.

For Shakespeare, fascinated as he was by the energies of expressive speech, another kind of bawdy court case would have provided rich raw material: the blasphemy suit. In the Stratford court we find the aptly named Joan Taunt accused of leaving church in the middle of the sermon in a highly theatrical manner – 'beckoning with her finger and laughing' and 'swearing by the name of God'. So too was Elizabeth Wheeler called before the court in October 1595 for brawling and abuse. Her response was to say 'God's wounds, a plague of God on you all, a fart of one's arse for you.' For this eloquent outburst, she was excommunicated. But at least her voice was heard. Women, who were habitually encouraged to be silent and submissive, had the opportunity to become active agents in the bawdy court, just as fictional women are active agents – usually wittier and more eloquent than the men – in Shakespeare's comedies.

According to one historian, in the city of London in the early seventeenth century, 80 per cent of sex and marriage cases were brought to the bawdy courts by women. A woman's reputation was her most precious commodity. The bawdy court was the place where she could publicly defend her honour. But it was also the place where quarrels between women could be formalized and played out. To call another woman a whore was not necessarily to accuse her of actual adultery. Elizabeth Stokes, a twenty-year-old servant, heard Phoebe Cartwright call Margery Hipwell an 'impudent quean' in Fleet Street at seven o'clock one April morning. Elizabeth, however, 'did not think that Phoebe Cartwright by calling Margery Hipwell quean did mean that she had committed fornication or adultery or played the whore with any man, but only spoke the same words in her anger' after a quarrel between the two women and Margery's husband.

In this regard, the bawdy court served a similar role to the theatre: as a safety valve where society could release anger and shame in a ritualized fashion that reduced the likelihood of public disorder. Women's cases in the city bawdy courts often did not reach the stage of the plaintiff asking for a definitive sentence. In many cases, women seem to have been more interested in having their complaint heard in court than in obtaining judgement. Men were more likely to want a result. Shakespeare's plays resemble women's cases more than men's: whereas the source stories of, say, *Othello* and *Romeo and Juliet* offer moralizations about the case, the plays want the lovers' stories to be heard and do not press the audience towards condemnation of miscegenation, youthful passion or marriage against parental will.

The bawdy court, like the theatre, was a place of rich linguistic invention in the semantic field of sexual insult. Women did not hesitate to call each other 'maggoty whore', 'mangy carrion', 'shitten whore', 'pocky lousy hedge whore', 'tinker's trull', 'scurvy fart arse quean', 'gouty-legged whore', 'daggletail queen', 'Welsh jade', 'high Dutch whore', 'Hackney whore', 'St Katharine's whore', to accuse one another of being 'as common as a barber's chair' or of having been 'occupied under every hedge over thy milk pail'. That verb 'occupy' frequently occurs in sex cases, as when one Isabel South accused Richard Todd in the following terms: 'thou art a whoremaster and thou didst offer to give me an angel of gold to occupy me and thou didst offer another man's wife the making of an oven to occupy her'.

When Othello laments that his 'occupation' is 'gone', he is referring not only to his military career but also to his sexual possession of Desdemona. In the bawdy court cases, it is usually women who spread gossip, sexual insult and slander. In *Othello* it is Iago who plays this role. The bawdy court was the testing-place of a woman's 'reputation'. In *Othello*, it is Iago who destroys reputations by acting as a malicious bawd.

Shakespeare did not explicitly dramatize the business of women going to the domestic courts, as the legally trained John Webster did in his play *The Devil's Law Case; or, When Women go to Law the Devil is full of Business*, or indeed his great tragedy *The White Devil*, at the centre of which Vittoria Corombona dominates a courtroom. Nor did Shakespeare churn out city comedies on the lines of Henry Porter's *Two Angry Women of Abingdon*, which turns on a 'woman's jar' between neighbours where, in a twist typical of bawdy court cases, blame is shifted from an adulterous husband to his mistress: 'she is a strumpet and thou art no honest man / To stand in her defence against thy wife'. But he did bring to the stage exactly the kind of sexual insults that preoccupied the bawdy courts. In many a bawdy court case, a woman slanders another woman. Strikingly, Shakespeare's noxious gossips and accusers are men, not women: not only Iago, but also Claudio, Don John and his followers in *Much Ado about Nothing*, Bertram in *All's Well that Ends Well*, Posthumus in *Cymbeline*, and for that matter the entire body of the Greek generals slandering Cressida in *Troilus*.

Gossip, bawdy court case and stage comedy share a repertoire of stories and storytelling techniques. Both *Measure for Measure* and *All's Well that Ends Well* turn on a 'bed trick' in which a man thinks that he is committing adultery or fornication but is actually sleeping with his wife or his betrothed. Such tricks abound in the popular literature of the age, but they also found their way into court cases. Elizabeth Trimmell, a London grocer's widow, claimed to have been defamed by a story in which a Herefordshire gentleman was put off from paying court to her by some gossip that he had heard:

I did hear that Mrs Smith, the widow of Wilfred Smith, did make show of going to a sermon unto St Anthonlin's church in London and that her husband mistrusting that she was a dishonest woman of her body, and that she going without a man went to play the whore, followed after her, and observed her to go into a bawdy house in St Swithins Lane in London and her husband went into a barber's shop near unto his wife and caused his beard to be shaved and altered his clothes and then went into the bawdy house after his wife and desired to have a wench brought him, and there was answer made unto him by the bawd that there was none in the house, but such as was very dear, and the husband of the said Elizabeth Trimmell alias Smith asked how dear and the bawd answered that he might have one for five pieces and he told her the bawd that he would give five pieces if he liked the party and gave her a piece in earnest, whereupon the said Elizabeth Smith was brought to her husband Wilfred Smith by the bawd, not knowing he was her husband. But so soon as the said Elizabeth Trimmell alias Smith heard her husband's tongue and perceived that he was her husband she . . . ran away from him and went home and said that she was undone, and her husband followed her home and suddenly fell sick and died with grief.

The interplay of deception, disguise and discovery here is so theatrical that one wonders whether the story was invented as a result of the reading of a story or the witnessing of a play rather than out of any basis in reality. The theatre gave to London's citizens linguistic and narrative models for the telling of sexual stories in the bawdy courts. Just as in any good play all the characters have their own distinctive view of the action, so in the courtroom, plaintiff, defendant and witnesses each offer a different version of the same story.

There is no doubt that the theatre world was particularly associated with sexual licence, which is one of the reasons for Puritan hostility to stage-plays. Prostitutes worked the theatre district and even the auditorium. And women employed in the theatre business were sometimes accused of being no better than sex-workers themselves: 'there are no women that keep playhouse doors but are whores' claimed a plaintiff in a case of 1607.

There is a sense, then, in which the theatre, so often condemned as a place of extreme bawdry, functioned as an alternative bawdy court. Playhouse and consistory court were the two public arenas where questions of sexual behaviour, particularly on the part of women, were explored in graphic and verbally creative detail. A church court case and a staging of *The Taming of the Shrew*: each in its way could be a testing of the limits of domestic violence and the language of sexual combat. An examination of the terms of insult habitually used in the courts throws new light on the play. Reference to a woman's 'tail' was always a sexual insult in court; by contrast, in the dialogue of the play, Kate positively relishes – finds liberation in – her banter with Petruchio concerning his tongue in her tail.

To a Shakespearean audience, the trial of Queen Hermione for adultery in *The Winter's Tale* would at one and the same time have evoked a high-level treason trial and a mundane bawdy court marital case. Every time the bawdy court was set up in a parish church, a place of worship was converted into a place of litigation. Such an instant transformation of church into bawdy court occurs in the wedding ceremony scene of *Much Ado about Nothing* when Claudio accuses Hero of infidelity. The Friar's role switches from that of minister performing the sacrament of marriage to bawdy court judge hearing a case of sexual 'slander'. Again, in *Measure for Measure*, Mariana – like all those real-life women who had the courage to go publicly before the ecclesiastical courts – takes her marital complaint before the Duke, turning the stage into another bawdy court.

Shakespeare's most sustained dramatization of bawdy court matter occurs at the climax of *All's Well that Ends Well*, one of the bitter comedies that he seems to have written around the time that he was being dragged into the marital business of the Mountjoy household on Silver Street in Cripplegate. The closing scene of the play is steeped in the language of court proceedings. Bertram is called before the tribunal. His 'great offence' of infidelity to his wife Helen is cited. He attempts to excuse himself. Witnesses give differing accounts of a ring, the key piece of evidence in the case. A petitioner appears before the court. There is a call for justice to be done. Diana makes her complaint and calls for 'remedy'. Bertram responds to this further 'charge'. The question of 'reputation', and in particular the 'honesty' of a woman, is central to the case: is Diana a chaste maid or 'a common gamester to the camp'? The 'proof' offered by the ring is again invoked: 'Methought you said,' notes the king who is playing the part of judge that the vicar would have played in a bawdy court, 'You saw one here in court could witness it.' Bertram speaks with the casual sexual language that marks many a bawdy court case: 'Certain it is I liked her, / And boarded her i'th'wanton way of youth.' Parolles is then called as a witness. A judgement is reached. There is talk of 'bail' and 'surety'. And then the *coup de théâtre*: Helen, supposedly dead, appears and a happy resolution is achieved. Provisionally, at least: 'All yet *seems* well' says the king, not 'all *is* well'. Helen's response to Bertram's promise that he will 'love her dearly, ever, ever dearly' provided she can explain how she has contrived to make him 'doubly won' implicitly raises the threat of a return to the consistory court, should he not behave better second time around: 'If it appear not plain, and prove untrue, / Deadly divorce step between me and you.'

Not all the language of this scene belongs specifically to the church court: Shakespeare's stage trials use a broad legal lexicon, fusing together the multiple jurisdictions of the age. But it would unquestionably have been the bawdy court that audience members would have held in mind when they witnessed the resolution of a marital dispute of this kind. The difference between the play and a real-life case is that the audience in the theatre are privileged witnesses who know what 'really' happened. The spectators are called not to factual and legal, but to emotional and moral judgement.

The seething bath

The charge against Bertram is that he has slept with a woman other than his wife. Thanks to the bed trick, he has not. One wonders: what would William Shakespeare's response have been if confronted with a similar charge? The evidence is scant, but the plays are so immersed in the experience of love and the language of sex that it is hard to imagine a Shakespeare who had no sexual life during his long residence in London.

Sonnet 129 could have been written only by someone who had experienced, and thought hard about, bodily desire, its fulfilment and the self-disgust that may follow after sexual climax. The poem is premised on the belief that a man's 'vital spirit' — his life-force, if you will — is contained in his semen and that it is of finite quantity, so that each 'expense' diminishes the life that remains, which is why every orgasm was regarded as a little death:

> Th'expense of spirit in a waste of shame
> Is lust in action, and till action, lust
> Is perjured, murd'rous, bloody, full of blame,
> Savage, extreme, rude, cruel, not to trust,
> Enjoyed no sooner but despisèd straight,
> Past reason hunted and, no sooner had,
> Past reason hated as a swallowed bait
> On purpose laid to make the taker mad,
> Mad in pursuit and in possession so,
> Had, having and in quest to have, extreme,
> A bliss in proof and proved a very woe,
> Before, a joy proposed — behind, a dream.
> 　　All this the world well knows, yet none knows well
> 　　To shun the heaven that leads men to this hell.

Most of the poems numbered between 127 and 152 in *Shakespeare's Sonnets* are addressed to a 'dark lady' who is clearly not married to the man in whose voice the poems are written. The relationship described is intensely sexual, in striking contrast to the preceding sonnets addressed to a 'friend', 'lovely boy' or 'man right fair', which idealize rather than sexualize the love-object.

There is no way of knowing whether the 'dark lady' was created out of an imagined relationship or inspired by a real affair. But whatever the biographical origin of the sonnets may or may not have been, Shakespeare seems to have had a reputation for being sexually active outside his marriage:

Upon a time when Burbage played Richard III, there was a citizen grown so far in liking with him that before she went from the play she appointed him to come that night unto her by the name of Richard the Third. Shakespeare overhearing their conclusion went before, was entertained and at his game ere Burbage came. Then message being brought that Richard the Third was at the door, Shakespeare caused return to be made that William the Conqueror was before Richard the Third. Shakespeare's name William.

There is a folk-tale quality to this encounter. Besides, the idea of female spectators throwing themselves at the star is a running motif in the history of the performing arts. So maybe we should not trust the story. It is, however, recorded in two independent sources and it has the feel of emanating from someone 'in the know'. Part of the joke is of course that Burbage shared a Christian name with his most famous stage king, Richard III. There is also a strong possibility that Shakespeare, who became known for playing kingly parts on stage, took the role of William the Conqueror in a comedy called *A Pleasant Comedy of Fair Em, the Miller's Daughter of Manchester, with the Love of William the Conqueror*. This would add a similar layering to the 'William the Conqueror' allusion. If the story has at least a grain of truth in it, then one may say that a casual one-night stand of this sort is unlikely to have been an isolated incident.

Given the prevalence of syphilis in early seventeenth-century London, if Shakespeare was a philanderer he would have exposed himself to the risk of catching the pox. We must tread carefully here, but it is hard not to notice a preoccupation with sexual disease in the plays written early in the reign of King James. *Measure for Measure* begins from an attempt by the authorities to cleanse a city of licentiousness. In the period from May to December 1603, when the theatres were closed due to the worst outbreak of plague for a decade, a royal proclamation ordered a programme of slum clearance in the 'suburbs' such as Southwark, as an attempt simultaneously to prevent the spread of infection between closely packed dwellings and to get rid of brothels and ale-houses full of idle, indigent, dissolute and dangerous people.

POMPEY: You have not heard of the proclamation, have you?

MISTRESS OVERDONE: What proclamation, man?

POMPEY: All houses in the suburbs of Vienna must be plucked down.

MISTRESS OVERDONE: And what shall become of those in the city?

POMPEY: They shall stand for seed: they had gone down too, but that a wise burgher put in for them.

MISTRESS OVERDONE: But shall all our houses of resort in the suburbs be pulled down?

POMPEY: To the ground, mistress.

MISTRESS OVERDONE: Why, here's a change indeed in the commonwealth! What shall become of me?

POMPEY: Come, fear you not: good counsellors lack no clients. Though you change your place, you need not change your trade; I'll be your tapster still. Courage! There will be pity taken on you: you that have worn your eyes almost out in the service, you will be considered.

The closing reference is to the blindness to which syphilis could lead. *Measure for Measure* is filled with references to the purchasing of diseases in brothels, to unwanted pregnancies, to the symptoms of syphilis and purported cures for it. The contemporaneous *All's Well that Ends Well* has many similar references. The language of *Troilus and Cressida*, written in the same phase of Shakespeare's career, oozes with syphilitic sores and references to prostitution. Though set in ancient Troy, the play ends with a pandar telling the 'traders in the flesh' among the London audience that he will be dead from his syphilis within two months. Pandarus refers to 'some gallèd goose of Winchester' and to his intention to 'sweat and seek about for eases'. 'Gallèd' means both 'angrily provoked' and 'inflamed with pox-sores'. A 'Winchester goose' was a slang term for a prostitute, because so many of the brothels, like the theatres, were in Southwark, a district under the jurisdiction of the Bishop of Winchester. 'Sweating' alludes to the most frequently prescribed treatment for syphilis: the sweating-tub.

Not long after composing these plays, Shakespeare wrote the second half of *Pericles*, which had been begun by the dramatist and brothel-keeper George Wilkins, who was a neighbour when he lodged with the Mountjoys in Silver Street. Wilkins was, indeed, another key witness in the Belott case. Given Wilkins' second career, one would have expected him to have been the author of the play's minutely observed brothel scenes, but he was not: Shakespeare wrote them.

Shakespeare's sonnet collection does not end with the poems concerning the sexual relationship with the 'dark lady'. The sequence is rounded off by a distinctive pair of sonnets (numbers 153 and 154). They take the mythological image of Cupid's fountain from classical literature and fuse it with a very different kind of image out of contemporary London life: the sweating-tub.

The 'seething bath', as it is called in sonnet 153, had been strongly advocated by the barber-surgeon William Clowes in his *Brief and Necessary Treatise touching the Cure of the Disease called Morbus Gallicus or Lues Venerea by Unctions and other approved ways of Curing* (1579). Clowes prescribed bloodletting and lancing of the syphilitic sores, dietary measures, the application of unguents, and then, most drastically but also most effectively, the mercury or 'quicksilver' cure. He considered this new procedure to be infallible and little short of miraculous: 'it openeth the body, and provoketh sweat, and emptieth the cause of this disease . . . and the blood thereby is purged from infection, and all the parts of the body is cleansed . . . as we daily see by experience'. The process involved a mercury-based ointment being pasted on the skin several times a day, with the body kept heated to encourage sweating: hence the need to sit in a hot closed room in a tub, which would be kept warm with hot bricks, rather in the manner of a sauna. There is an allusion to the custom in the old nursery rhyme: 'Rub-a-dub-dub, three men in a tub'. The pores would open and

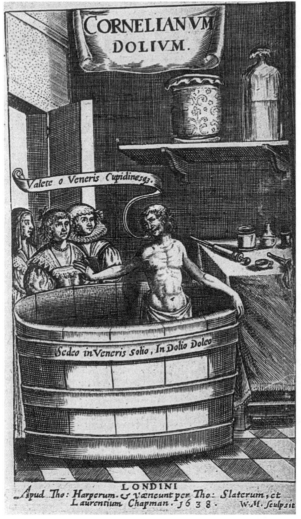

'A seething bath': mercury and sweat as a cure for syphilis

absorb the quicksilver, helping to kill cutaneous infection. As one modern commentator explains, 'Patients would often attain a metallic glow and frequently suffered ill effects of mercury poisoning – their gums would bleed, their teeth would fall out, their mouths and throats would become riddled with ulcers.' But for Clowes, who also believed that stewed prunes were an effective prophylactic against the pox, extreme diseases required extreme remedies, and his methods were widely adopted.

Given the close links between the theatres, the taverns and the sex-trade, Shakespeare would have seen many people suffering the grotesque symptoms of the pox. But we cannot rule out the possibility that he became infected himself. King Lear's disgust at his daughters does seem a little over-fixated on the female genitals as the source of universal corruption and damnation:

> I pardon that man's life. What was thy cause?
> Adultery?
> Thou shalt not die: die for adultery? No.
> The wren goes to't and the small gilded fly
> Does lecher in my sight. Let copulation thrive,
> For Gloucester's bastard son was kinder to his father
> Than were my daughters got 'tween the lawful sheets.
> To't, luxury, pell-mell, for I lack soldiers.
> Behold yond simp'ring dame,
> Whose face between her forks presages snow,
> That minces virtue and does shake the head
> To hear of pleasure's name:
> The fitchew nor the soilèd horse goes to't
> With a more riotous appetite. Down from the waist
> They are centaurs, though women all above:
> But to the girdle do the gods inherit,
> Beneath is all the fiends':
> There's hell, there's darkness, there is the sulphurous pit: burning,
>   scalding, stench, consumption. Fie, fie, fie! Pah, pah!

Lear's disgust is such that in the final lines he cannot maintain the equilibrium of his iambic pentameter verse – the speech collapses into prose.

Around the time he wrote *King Lear*, Shakespeare, in collaboration with the younger dramatist Thomas Middleton, tried an extraordinary experiment: creating a play almost entirely without female parts. The only women in *Timon of Athens* are a pair of prostitutes who put in a brief appearance in order to be abused by Timon in a series of speeches that allude to the symptoms of secondary and tertiary syphilis, including the playwright's own affliction of premature baldness. There is no way of knowing whether Shakespeare's obsession with sexual disease in his early Jacobean plays and the 'seething bath' sonnets grew out of the personal experience of syphilitic symptoms or the mere observation of them.

Suppose that Shakespeare was indeed unfaithful to his wife. Did he then feel remorse as his career came towards its end and he contemplated spending more time back home in Stratford? *The Winter's Tale* was written sixteen years after 1594, the year when he became firmly established as a London-based writer and player with the formation of the Lord Chamberlain's Men. Is it a coincidence that it is a play about a man who asks his wife for a second chance after sixteen years of separation? The problem with making such an inference from one play is that there is then no reason not to start drawing contrary inferences from other plays. The year after *The Winter's Tale*, Shakespeare wrote *The Tempest*, a work which concerns itself deeply with a father's attitude to his daughter's prospective marriage but which has almost no interest in the figure of the wife of a man who lives by 'potent art'. Equally, both *The Winter's Tale* and *Cymbeline*, written around the same time, reveal an obsession with unfaithful wives. The husbands' fears are irrational and groundless, but *Cymbeline* in particular shows that Shakespeare knew how to inhabit the mind of a man imagining his wife in bed with someone else while he is away on business in the great city. The 'dark lady' of the sonnets is also represented as an unfaithful wife. If we are to play the game of inferring Shakespeare's love-life from his plays, then we cannot rule out the possibility that he was – or imagined himself to have been – the victim of marital infidelity as well as the perpetrator of it. Shakespeare the cuckold has not caught the imagination of biographers in the way that Shakespeare the man about town has done, but there is only a little more reason to believe in one than the other.

The only bit of real evidence with regard to Shakespeare's attitude to his wife in the latter end of his life is the notorious bequest to her of his 'second best bed', a last-minute addition to his will, in which she otherwise goes unmentioned. The unusual, though not unique, decision to leave Anne just this one item of furniture has, in typically Shakespearean fashion, been interpreted in diametrically opposed ways. The best bed, which would have been reserved for visitors, would have remained in New Place in the possession of daughter and son-in-law Susanna and John Hall. Did Will bequeath second-best to Anne because it was the old marital bed and he wanted to leave a fond memory of the times they had spent in it? Or was it a calculated insult to palm her off with nothing more than a wormy old piece of furniture? Or did a legacy of a 'second-best' household item have some other meaning now lost to us, perhaps connected to the ancient custom of 'mortuary' whereby the local vicar was entitled to the 'second-best' item of furniture belonging to tithe-holders of the church upon their demise?

The exclusion of Anne Shakespeare from the original draft of the will is a related puzzle. It was not necessarily the case, as scholars once thought, that this was because she was automatically entitled to a 'widow's dower' of one-third of her husband's estate. That would have been so in London, but not in Warwickshire. Maybe there is an answer in some missing document that might also explain the absence from the will of any reference to the Blackfriars gatehouse and Shakespeare's shares in both the Globe Theatre and his acting company.

In the final months of his life, Shakespeare was much more concerned about his younger daughter than his wife. Just four weeks before his death, the Acts of the consistory court before John Rogers, vicar, in the parish church of Stratford on Thursday 26 March 1616, in the presence of Richard Wright, deputy of Thomas Fisher, notary public, include the following indictment:

Thomas Quiney: for incontinence with a certain Margaret Wheeler: cited by Greene: he appeared: admitted that he had had carnal copulation with Wheeler: submitted himself to the correction of the Judge: ordered public penance in a white sheet on three Sundays in the church of Stratford: thereafter he proffered 5s. for the use of the poor of the parish and petitioned the penance to be remitted: ordered to acknowledge the fault in his own attire before the minister of Bishopton according to the schedule: to certify before the next court: dismissed.

Margaret Wheeler and her illegitimate child had been buried the previous week, presumably having died as a result of complications at the time of birth. But there was another woman in the case: Quiney was betrothed to Shakespeare's daughter Judith at the time. His incontinence and the shame it brought to Shakespeare's family, together with the anxiety that he might not prove a reliable husband, caused Shakespeare to change his will in such a way as to protect Judith's interests while at the same time limiting the amount of money that Quiney could get his hands on in the event of marital problems. It was a further blow that the Quiney family had been extremely close to the Shakespeares all his life: the only surviving letter addressed to Master William Shakespeare was written by Quiney senior. As Shakespeare's first appearance in the archive subsequent to his baptism was in relation to his own marriage-case before the Worcester consistory court, so his last appearance prior to his death was this alteration of testamentary arrangements, made as a direct result of Quiney's appearance in the Stratford consistory court.

Though Shakespeare would have been both sad and angry to hear of Quiney's transgression, as the inventor of Angelo in *Measure for Measure* and Bertram in *All's Well that Ends Well*, he would hardly have been surprised. And his lack of optimism about the future course of Judith's marriage is characteristic: his courtship comedies fizz with the joy of being young and in love, but his stage marriages are often marked by distance, alienation or false accusation. Where are the truly happy marriages in Shakespeare? Petruchio and Kate are a match for each other, but theirs is hardly a tranquil household. Hotspur and his Kate in *Henry IV Part 1* have terrific gusto, but their relationship is tempered by the sense that he is happier astride his horse than his wife. It is somehow symptomatic of Shakespeare's particular interest in male bonding that Aufidius in *Coriolanus* speaks of his love for his wife and his happiness on his wedding night, but suggests that he takes more pleasure in seeing his military adversary arrive on his doorstep and in reminiscing about a dream of wrestling Coriolanus to the ground on the battlefield:

> Let me twine
> Mine arms about that body, where against
> My grainèd ash an hundred times hath broke,
> And scarred the moon with splinters: here I clip
> The anvil of my sword, and do contest
> As hotly and as nobly with thy love
> As ever in ambitious strength I did
> Contend against thy valour. Know thou first,
> I loved the maid I married: never man
> Sighed truer breath. But that I see thee here,
> Thou noble thing, more dances my rapt heart
> Than when I first my wedded mistress saw
> Bestride my threshold . . . thou hast beat me out
> Twelve several times, and I have nightly since
> Dreamt of encounters 'twixt thyself and me:
> We have been down together in my sleep,
> Unbuckling helms, fisting each other's throat,
> And waked half dead with nothing.

The imagery here is, to say the least, suggestive.

Of all Shakespeare's married couples, the pair who seem most intimate, whom the audience senses are as in love as man and wife as they were when first they wooed, are the Macbeths. That is a fact that may give pause for thought.

Love's Labour

Only one surviving Shakespeare play has love in its title: *Love's Labour's Lost*. It was such a success, or such a pleasure to write, that he wrote a sequel (alas, lost) called *Love's Labour's Won*. Given that there is so little evidence about Shakespeare's actual experience of love, in asking what he thought about the place of love in the life of the mind, the play with the word in its title is a good place to start.

At the beginning of a long book called *The French Academy*, *wherein is discoursed the institution of manners, and whatsoever else concerneth the good and happy life of all estates and callings, by precepts of doctrine, and examples of the lives of ancient Sages and famous men,* by Peter de la Primaudaye, published in French in 1577 and translated into English by one T. B. C. in 1586, the reader is introduced to four (fictional) young gentlemen of Anjou. Their encounter is set at the time of the religious civil war that tore France apart in the second half of the sixteenth century. The young men withdraw from the stress of war and sectarian dissension, retreating to the country house of an elderly nobleman who puts them under the educational care of a learned man. 'He propounded for the chief part and portion of their studies the moral philosophy of ancient Sages and wise men, together with the understanding, and searching out of histories, which are the light of life.' La Primaudaye's long book purports to be a record of the young gentlemen's discussions concerning the nature of 'the good and happy life'. Each chapter begins with a dialogue between the four and then turns into a little essay on moral philosophy. There is much talk of the necessity of controlling the emotions and culti-vating a Stoical detachment of mind. At the end of 'the first day's work' in their little 'academy', the student called Aser, who embodies happiness or 'felicity', comes up with the proposition that 'philosophy', by which he means the Stoic philosophy of self-restraint in particular, 'purgeth pride, presumption, ambition, choler, revenge, covetousness, injustice'. Philosophy also teaches us 'not to be carried away by lust'.

The cultivation of temperance, with a particular emphasis on sexual restraint, becomes a major theme of subsequent discussion, with the invocation of numerous positive and negative examples, mostly out of classical history and literature. So, for example, Tarquin's rape of Lucrece, with its disastrous political consequences for the early Roman monarchy, is invoked as a classic example of intemperance and submission to the desires of the flesh. The emphasis on sexual sin is an indication that La Primaudaye is propounding a typically sixteenth-century combination of classical Stoicism and Christian, specifically Pauline, theology. He was a product of what intellectual historians call the 'neo-Stoic revival' of the period.

La Primaudaye's compendium of commonplace philosophical and moral thought was widely read in France and, following its translation, in England. But there was a flaw in its premise. The device for dispensing large doses of neo-Stoic exhortations to prudence, temperance, fortitude and justice was to sequester the young men in the academy of the title. But, as is pointed out in the preface to the English translation of 1586, true virtue must be practised '*in life*'. As Aristotle had reminded the ancient Greeks, 'bare knowledge and contemplation thereof in brain' is insufficient. The theory was that, having studied history and philosophy and contemplated the nature of virtue in the academy for, say, three years, one would emerge into the world ready to practise what one had learned. Yet the inevitable consequence of the structural device was to create an image of leisured ease, in which the good life could be cultivated without any awkward intrusions from the day-to-day realities of politics, social inequality, religious contention – or women.

Whether or not Shakespeare specifically knew La Primaudaye's book, his starting-point for *Love's Labour's Lost* was the same: a French academy set up as a retreat from historical, political and sexual engagement. The names of Shakespeare's four young men were all well known from the French wars. The play seems to have been written not long after the King of Navarre converted to Catholicism and took the French throne. 'Paris is worth a mass,' he was reputed to have said. Biron, or Berowne, was the name of Navarre's marshal, who had fought in the siege of Rouen alongside the Earl of Essex and a contingent of English troops. Longuaville was a supporter of Navarre and the Duke de Mayenne (Dumaine) a former opponent who became an ally following a truce in 1595.

Shakespeare imagines a group of courtly men of Navarre who share these names. He removes them from the world of politics and religious faction, and places them in a 'little academe'. The king's first speech is peppered with military language – 'brave conquerors', 'war', 'huge army' – as if to say 'Now that we have won the war, let us win the peace by devoting ourselves to learning and Stoic detachment.' The premise of the exercise is that there is no place for love in intellectual life. Shakespeare, who did not of course spend three years in the all-male environment of an Oxford or Cambridge college, clearly thought that this was nonsense and set about mocking the idea. Love, he proposes instead, is at the centre of intellectual life. The really interesting task is not to reject it, but to find the appropriate language to express it.

Dumaine is happy to sign up to the King of Navarre's contract: he will mortify the flesh and die 'To love, to wealth, to pomp', live only 'in philosophy'. But Berowne immediately expresses a reservation: he agrees to sign up to the three years' programme of academic study, but has grave doubts about the additional 'strict observances': to fast, to sleep but three hours a night and 'not to see a woman' for the entire three-year term. For Berowne, these are 'barren tasks', devoid of life. The essence of Berowne's criticism of the king's project is that the needs of the body – for food, for sleep, for sexual fulfilment – should not be denied. By his account, the pursuit of learning and fame are all very well, but not at the expense of natural instincts, 'For every man with his affects is born, / Not by might mastered but by special grace.' The Stoic ambition of keeping the passions fully under control is an illusion. Only the 'special grace' of divine intervention can prevent us from being the embodied, desiring humans that we are. Divine intervention does not occur in the real world: as Shakespeare put it in another of his most thought-filled comedies, *All's Well that Ends Well*, 'miracles are past'.

In the absence of miracles, the 'affects', the passions, intrude into the academe. The unfolding action proves Berowne right. Wisdom, as so often in Shakespeare, comes from the mouth of a fool: the clownish Costard's irrefutable statement that 'It is the manner of a man to speak to a woman' comes to the core of the play. The presence of Jaquenetta the dairy-maid is a reminder of the inescapable human body. The question of her pregnancy dominates the sub-plot and her very name – a female version of 'Jaques', which was pronounced 'jakes' – conjures up a bodily function that is alluded to in the pageant of the Nine Worthies acted out by the comic characters in the final act: Alexander the Great is imagined sitting not on a royal throne but on a 'close-stool'. Ingesting and expelling are among the actions that make us human, whatever the Stoic philosopher may say about the primacy of 'reason'.

Shakespeare was a supreme realist in matters of love. At the climax of the play, just before the entrance of Monsieur Marcadé darkens the tone and brings death into the academe, Don Armado is described wearing no undershirt save 'a dishclout of Jaquenetta's', which he keeps 'next his heart for a favour'. Since 'dish' – or, as in *Measure for Measure*, 'clack-dish' – was a slang term for the vagina, the 'clout' or cloth in question would appear to suggest not just the dairy-maid's dishcloth but a rag that has been placed between her legs to absorb the discharge of menstrual blood (presumably retained from the time before she became pregnant). The idea of such a thing being worn next to the heart, replacing the traditional lover's token of a handkerchief or silken favour, speaks volumes about Shakespeare's attitude to the fancies of idealizing love-poetry of the kind that the king and his courtiers are found writing when, as happens so swiftly and inevitably, they break their vows on the arrival of the beautiful Princess of France and her three accompanying ladies.

Love's Labour's Lost is a play packed with wit, elegance, philosophical reflection and filthy jokes. For Shakespeare, love meant immersing oneself in each of these four dimensions. The king turns his court into a little academe in the hope of finding philosophical wisdom. It comes in the very form that he has renounced: women, who prove themselves a great deal more intelligent and sensible than the men. The philosophical lesson that has to be learned is that 'women's eyes' have it in them to be 'the books, the arts, the academes, / That show, contain, and nourish all the world'. But the male courtly lovers make a double mistake. Having foolishly renounced love, they then foolishly embrace a false idea of love: they begin praising their ladies' eyes (and other parts) in the affected language of the courtly poetic tradition that goes back to Petrarch in high Renaissance Italy. They write formulaic sonnets and love-songs, they dance a ridiculous masque. The ladies have to teach them a further lesson, namely that 'Taffeta phrases, silken terms precise, / Three-piled hyperboles, spruce affectation, / Figures pedantical' may also be an impediment to love. They have to learn a plainer language that can cope with the harsh realities of life, including death. The men are accordingly not granted the customary ending of comedy: instead of the play concluding with multiple marriages, the courtiers are sentenced to a year's community service, after which the ladies will review the situation. Their assessment presumably occurred in the lost sequel, *Love's Labour's Won*.

As Shakespeare plays at love-poetry, sonneteering in particular, in *Love's Labour's Lost*, one can sense him limbering up for a new project: taking the sonnet form and developing it in a style that is truer to the reality than the romance of love. A style responsive to the reality of bodily desire that is summarized so concisely by Costard: 'Such is the simplicity of man to hearken after the flesh.'

12. The Perplexities of Love

'a man may write of love and not be in love'

(Giles Fletcher, preface to his sonnet sequence *Licia*, published 1593)

Sugared sonnets

In 1598 Francis Meres, Cambridge-educated and with his finger on the literary pulse of the age, wrote that the 'mellifluous and honey-tongued Shakespeare' was circulating 'his sugared sonnets among his private friends'. He also included Shakespeare in a list of poets who were 'the most passionate among us to bewail and bemoan the perplexities of love'. For educated Elizabethans, sonnets were the place where you went for an immersion in the doubts, intricacies, uncertainties, troubles and 'anguish of mind' associated with love. For Meres, Shakespeare was not an isolated genius but one among many. What was the point of writing sonnets? To circulate them among your private friends, whom you could be sure would know enough other sonnets to admire yours for being the sweetest.

Meres' list of the most passionate English love poets begins with two courtiers from the reign of Henry VIII: Sir Thomas Wyatt the elder, who was imprisoned for a time on suspicion of being the lover of Anne Boleyn, and Henry Howard, Earl of Surrey, who was executed for treason shortly before his thirtieth birthday. Their work was known to Shakespeare and his contemporaries through the little book that Master Abraham Slender wishes he had with him as an aid to the wooing of Anne Page in *The Merry Wives of Windsor*: 'I had rather than forty shillings I had my book of *Songs and Sonnets* here.' *Songs and Sonnets*, published by Richard Tottel in 1557, was by far the most frequently reprinted poetic miscellany of the age. It began with substantial selections from Surrey and Wyatt, then proceeded to the lyrics of various lesser poets.

A number of the poems in Tottel were translations or imitations of Italian sonnets by Petrarch and his successors, though in a distinctively English style, pioneered by Surrey, whereby the sonnet was divided into three quatrains and a concluding rhyming couplet instead of the octave and sestet of the Italian model. That is to say, a 4:4:4:2 formation replaced the Italians' 8:6 line-up. Whereas the Italian style favoured a single thought with a turn in the middle, the English encouraged more playful variation: three thrusts and a twist in the tail. The very form offered an incentive to multiplication and digression that encouraged sonnets to be expressions of their authors' wit and ingenuity as much as – perhaps more than – outpourings of their real feelings. Sonnets were conventionally but not exclusively fourteen lines long and conventionally but not exclusively rhymed: for the Elizabethan reader of Tottel, pleasure came from the poets' ability to weave formal and thematic variations.

Tottel added editorial titles to Wyatt's and Surrey's sonnets, connecting one to another in such a way as to make them into sets of variations on the theme of love. A sonnet is a crystallization of the emotion of a moment, but by creating a sequence and giving titles to each poem, Tottel hinted at an implicit narrative behind the succession of moments. Thus for Wyatt: 'The lover for shamefastness hideth his desire within his faithful heart', 'The lover describeth his being stricken with sight of his love', 'The wavering lover willeth and dreadeth to love his desire', 'The lover, having dreamed enjoying of his love, complaineth that the dream is not either longer or truer', 'The lover confesseth him in love with Phillis', 'The lover compareth his state to a ship in perilous storm tossed on the sea', 'Of the jealous man that loved the same woman and espied this other sitting with her'. Out of such titles, the reader can construct the story of an unfolding love-affair. But Wyatt did not in fact write these poems in sequence and address them to a single lover. This provides a cautionary warning for biographers seeking to reconstruct the story that Shakespeare's sonnets supposedly tell.

'Phillis' is a name out of classical pastoral: Wyatt was writing in a self-consciously literary tradition. The essence of his poems is the art of finding an expressive language for the contradictory nature of love. The emotions are intended to echo in the mind of his listener or reader. Our reaction is supposed to be, 'yes, that is how it is, but I've never heard it expressed so elegantly and concisely'. Not: 'who is Phillis, what is she?' The sonnet by Wyatt that Tottel entitles 'Description of the contrarious passions in a lover' may be regarded as a template for the love-poetry of the age:

> I find no peace, and all my war is done:
> I fear and hope: I burn and freeze like ice:
> I fly aloft, yet can I not arise:
> And naught I have, and all the world I seize on.
> That locks nor loseth, holdeth me in prison,
> And holds me not, yet can I scape no wise:
> Nor lets me live nor die at my devise,
> And yet of death it giveth me occasion.
> Without eye I see, without tongue I plain:
> I wish to perish, yet I ask for health:
> I love another and thus I hate myself.
> I feed me in sorrow, and laugh at all my pain.
>   Lo, thus displeaseth me both death and life,
>   And my delight is causer of this strife.

The second half of each line undoes the first; the quatrains build to a couplet that pulls together 'death and life' and 'delight' that causes 'strife'. The rhetorical trope that conveys this contrariness is oxymoron: the paradox of simultaneous burning and freezing, sickness and health. The sonnet looks into the mind of the lover. The poet-lover himself is always the subject. In a key pun, the focus is on the relationship between what is seen by the 'eye' (someone lovely) and what is felt by the 'I' – desire, but also a paradoxical self-disgust. The beloved is an object, sometimes absent, usually frosty and aloof, rarely possessed. As in the long medieval tradition of courtly romance, not to mention Petrarch's hugely influential sonnets to his beloved but unobtainable 'Laura', the poetry thrives on longing. If the lady were to yield, there would be nothing left to write about. All the thrill is in the chase, nearly all the emotion in the delicious pain of yearning.

One other feature of the original *Songs and Sonnets* should be noted: not all the poems are about love. Tottel's miscellany also includes a number of poems 'Of the courtier's life', the finest among them being Wyatt's verse epistle to his friend John Poins, contrasting the febrile world of court ambition with the easefulness of a life of friendship and reading on a country estate in Kent. The name Poins may have stuck in Shakespeare's mind when he read this poem: he gives it to the friend with whom Prince Hal in *Henry IV* shares his life away from the court, though in the city rather than the country. Of more general importance is the way that Wyatt and Surrey created an intimate relationship between the arts of courtship and courtiership. This made it possible to read apparent love poems as coded bids for patronage and preferment at court.

By the time Shakespeare began his literary career, *Songs and Sonnets* had been through eight editions and several other anthologies of love poetry had been published with titles such as *The Paradise of Dainty Devices*, *A Gorgeous Gallery of Gallant Inventions* and *A Handful of Pleasant Delights*. The 1590s was England's greatest decade of lyric poetry. An anthology published in 1600 with the proud title *England's Helicon* – the ancient Greek Muses' spring of invention transposed to the sceptred isle – is the most gorgeous of all the galleries, with most of its songs and sonnets written in the pastoral mode.

Here we find Christopher Marlowe's 'Come live with me, and be my love, / And we will all the pleasures prove' and Sir Walter Ralegh's wry reply to the same ('Thy gowns, thy shoes, thy beds of roses, / Thy cap, thy kirtle, and thy poesies, / Soon break, soon wither, soon forgotten: / In folly ripe, in reason rotten'), not to mention Shakespeare's 'On a day, alack the day / Love whose month was ever May' and numerous lyrics in the genre of the 'blazon', whereby the beauties of a fair mistress are enumerated body-part by body-part from top to toe. One of them is attributed by the compiler of *England's Helicon* to a certain 'W. H.':

First her brow a beauteous globe I deem,
                And golden hair;
And her cheek Aurora's robe doth seem,
                But far more fair.
        Her eyes like stars are right
        And dazzle with their light,
        Rubies her lips to see,
        But to taste, they nectar be.

Orient pearls her teeth, her smile doth link
                The Graces three.
Her white neck doth eyes beguile to think
                It ivory.
        Alas, her lily hand,
        How it doth me command!
        Softer silk none can be,
        And whiter milk none can see.

How shall I her pretty tread express
                When she doth walk?
Scarce she doth the primrose head depress,
                Or tender stalk
        Of blue-veined violets
        Whereon her foot she sets.
        Virtuous she is, for we find
        In body fair, beauteous mind.

The heads of the 'private friends' among whom Shakespeare circulated his sonnets – who knows, perhaps this very 'W. H.' was one
of them – were full of charming poetic trifles of this kind, where
lovely ladies have a globe for a brow, gold for hair, ruby lips and
pearl teeth, ivory breasts, lily hands and a tread so light that they
never crush a flower. Imagine yourself expecting each new sonnet
to contain such stuff, then imagine that someone hands you this:

        My mistress' eyes are nothing like the sun,
        Coral is far more red than her lips' red,

If snow be white, why then her breasts are dun,
If hairs be wires, black wires grow on her head.
I have seen roses damasked, red and white,
But no such roses see I in her cheeks,
And in some perfumes is there more delight
Than in the breath that from my mistress reeks.
I love to hear her speak, yet well I know
That music hath a far more pleasing sound.
I grant I never saw a goddess go:
My mistress when she walks treads on the ground.
    And yet, by heaven, I think my love as rare
    As any she belied with false compare.

One of the main purposes of Shakespeare's sonnets is there in a nutshell: to express a love that is rare while also belying the 'false compare' of conventional love-poetry. As in *Love's Labour's Lost*, the intention is both to make you admire his wit and to think seriously about the realities as opposed to the fancies of love.

Ganymede

It was with the posthumous publication in 1591 of *Astrophel and Stella*, the love poetry of Sir Philip Sidney, exemplary courtier, that the Elizabethan vogue for sonneteering became a mania. Every poet who aspired to courtly preferment needed a collection of sonnets in his repertoire. Meres' list of poets who are expert in the perplexities of love reveals his knowledge of printed collections such as Samuel Daniel's *Delia* (1594), Michael Drayton's *Idea's Mirror* (1594), Nicholas Breton's *Bower of Delights* (1591) and Edmund Spenser's *Amoretti* (1595). He also refers to Sir Walter Ralegh, some of whose lyrics he would have found in an anthology of 1593 called *The Phoenix Nest*, and to a fellow Cambridge man called Samuel Page, whose sequence 'The Love of Amos and Laura' he could only have known in manuscript. We do not know how many of Shakespeare's sonnets had been written by 1598 when Meres referred to their circulation, or how he came to hear about them. We do know, however, that versions of two of them appeared in print a few months later, in a little book of twenty songs and sonnets attributed to Shakespeare and called *The Passionate Pilgrim*.

Among the poems falsely ascribed to Shakespeare in that collection were two by Richard Barnfield, whose *Cynthia* (1595) has the unique distinction among the plethora of poetry collections published in the 1590s of including a sequence of sonnets addressed not to a disdainful lady called Stella or Delia or Laura, but to a lovely boy called Ganymede. Named after a young male abducted by Jove in classical mythology, the figure was synonymous with pederastic desire, as explained in a dictionary of the period:

Ganymede: the name of a Trojan boy, whom Jupiter so loved (say the poets) as he took him up to Heaven, and made him his Cup-bearer. Hence any boy that is loved for carnal abuse, or is hired to be used contrary to nature, to commit the detestable sin of sodomy is called a Ganymede; an Ingle.

The same dictionary's definition of 'ingle' is 'a youth kept or accompanied for sodomy'.

Barnfield was writing for a male audience, Oxford and Cambridge educated, their social lives based around the Inns of Court in London. They were the readers who lapped up the dozens of volumes of love sonnets that appeared on the bookstalls outside the west door of St Paul's Cathedral throughout the 1590s, each collection with a beautiful woman as the object of desire. Barnfield's sonnets to Ganymede were startlingly different in being addressed to a 'he' instead of a 'she':

> Sometimes I wish that I his pillow were,
> So might I steal a kiss, and yet not seen,
> So might I gaze upon his sleeping eyne,
> Although I did it with a panting fear:
> But when I well consider how vain my wish is,
> Ah foolish bees, think I, that do not suck
> His lips for honey, but poor flowers do pluck

Which have no sweet in them: when his sole kisses
Are able to revive a dying soul.
Kiss him, but sting him not, for if you do,
His angry voice your flying will pursue.
But when they hear his tongue, what can control
Their back-return? For then they plain may see,
How honeycombs from his lips dropping be.

The previous legal term (Michaelmas 1594), Barnfield had published a volume called *The Affectionate Shepherd*, 'containing the complaint of Daphnis for the love of Ganymede', in which there was an explicit account of a shepherd ingling a boy: 'I came, I saw, I viewed, I slippèd in.' In an address to his 'courteous Gentlemen Readers' prefacing his second collection, he added a defensive note with regard to his first. *The Affectionate Shepherd* was not really advocating sodomy, he explains. Rather, to 'unshadow' his 'conceit', what he was offering was 'nothing else but an imitation of Virgil, in his second Eclogue, of Alexis'.

Virgil's pastoral eclogues were a schoolroom text, among the most admired and widely read poems of the ancient world. The second eclogue, itself an imitation of Theocritus, the Greek originator of the pastoral genre, is written in the voice of Corydon, a shepherd who is aflame with unrequited desire for Alexis, a 'lovely boy' ('*O formose puer*'). Claiming that one was merely imitating the most admired poet in the history of the world was a good way of deflecting the wrath of moralists out to condemn filthy sodomitical perversions.

In Barnfield's case, the disclaimer was also necessary because the dedicatee of his first book, Lady Penelope Rich (Sir Philip Sidney's 'Stella') and her lover, Charles Blunt (who as Baron Mountjoy would later become Lord Deputy of Ireland), had accused him of using them as models for Ganymede and another figure invoked in the first eclogue, Guendolena Queen of Beauty. The question of whether the dedicatee of a collection of love sonnets was or was not the subject of the poems themselves was much debated at the time. Given the association between courtship and courtiership, the plea for a lady's mercy in love was easily readable as a plea for the gift of patronage. That certainly seems to be the 'conceit' in one of the most accomplished of the collections published in the 1590s, Samuel Daniel's *Delia*, dedicated to the Lady Mary, Countess of Pembroke.

Sonnet-writing was a sophisticated game, as Barnfield suggests with that phrase about unshadowing his conceit. From the Earl of Surrey's profession of love for a certain 'Geraldine' through the identification of Sidney's 'Stella' as Lady Penelope, readers were tantalized with the question of whether love-poetry was an exercise in witty invention – in imitation of Virgil or Petrarch or Sidney – or whether there was a real-life story behind a sonnet sequence and, if there was, what was the identity of the players. Some poets positively relished leaving all possibilities open. Giles Fletcher tried to have it both ways in the title of his collection of 1593: *Licia, or Poems of love in honour of the admirable and singular virtues of his lady, to the imitation of the best Latin poets.* Imitations of the best classical examples, but also addressed to a specific lady. And was he really in love? A prefatory address to the reader explains that

for this kind of poetry wherein I wrote, I did it only to try my humour: and for the matter of love, it may be I am so devoted to some one, into whose hands these may light by chance, that she may say which thou now sayest (that surely he is in love), which if she do, then have I the full recompense of my labour, and the poems have dealt sufficiently for the discharge of their own duty.

So Giles Fletcher may just be 'trying his humour', persuading you by his art that he is in love when actually he is not. Or he may really be in love, though if he is in love, it may only be a matter of chance if the poems fall into the hands of the person he loves. His pose is that he does not care whether they do or not. What he really wants to do is show you, the reader, how clever he is.

And the identity of his beloved?

If thou muse what my LICIA is, take her to be some Diana, at the least chaste, or some Minerva, no Venus, fairer far; it may be she is Learning's image, or some heavenly wonder, which the precisest may not mislike: perhaps under that name I have shadowed Discipline. It may be, I mean that kind courtesy which

I found at the Patroness of these Poems; it may be some College; it may be my conceit, and portend nothing.

Fletcher's watchwords are 'if' and 'may be'. His refusal to explain himself is a key element of his self-conscious art. Who is Licia, what is she? Perhaps a goddess, perhaps a mortal, perhaps an allegory of Learning or intellectual Discipline, perhaps a patroness, perhaps a college, perhaps nothing.

Fletcher's refusal to unshadow Licia's identity should be remembered by everyone who tries to decode Shakespeare's sonnets. It may be granted that we would be on fairly safe ground in assuming that Shakespeare's Dark Lady is not an allegorical representation of King's College Cambridge, but we cannot rule out the possibility that she is not so much a real person as an embodiment of Venus. Or that she is Shakespeare's conceit and portends nothing beyond her reality in the text itself. So too with the 'fair youth' who seems to be the addressee of most of Shakespeare's sonnets. He does not *have* to be a real person. He may be a figuration of a patron, ideal or real. Or he may be an earthly shadowing of Adonis or an imitation of Virgil's Alexis. The climactic sonnet in Shakespeare's sequence to his beautiful young 'friend' begins 'O thou lovely boy', which is a translation of Virgil's 'O formose puer'.

Breaking the rules

The *Passionate Pilgrim* collection attributed to Shakespeare in 1599 contained a trio of sonnets and poems from *Love's Labour's Lost*, various lyrics not by Shakespeare (and some of uncertain authorship), and variant versions of two of the sonnets that appeared in the volume published exactly a decade later with the austere title page *Shake-speare's Sonnets. Never before Imprinted.* The question of when Shakespeare wrote the other 152 sonnets in that collection is hotly disputed, but we can say with certainty that versions of those numbered 138 and 144 were circulating in the 1590s, at the height of the vogue for sonneteering. They are highly likely to have been among the sugared Shakespearean sonnets that Meres had seen or heard about. They are both, however, highly unusual for the time.

Convention dictates that the love is true, the lady is pure, the poet is young and full of desire, and sex does not take place. Shakespeare begins by breaking every one of these rules:

> When my love swears that she is made of truth,
> I do believe her, though I know she lies,
> That she might think me some untutored youth,
> Unskilful in the world's false forgeries.
> Thus vainly thinking that she thinks me young,
> Although I know my years be past the best,
> I, smiling, credit her false-speaking tongue,
> Outfacing faults in love with love's ill rest.
> But wherefore says my love that she is young?
> And wherefore say not I that I am old?
> O, love's best habit's in a soothing tongue,
> And age in love loves not to have years told.
> > Therefore I'll lie with love and love with me,
> > Since that our faults in love thus smothered be.

This version, the opening poem in *The Passionate Pilgrim*, is slightly different (and slightly less tightly written) from that published as number 138 in *Shakespeare's Sonnets*. Improvements in the latter include 'seeming trust' for 'soothing tongue' in line eleven, and in the couplet 'I lie with her' rather than 'I'll lie with love' and 'flattered' for 'smothered'. But even in the early version (which may have been corrupted by scribal copying), the love is insecure, the lady is false, the poet is not 'some untutored youth' and sex does take place. The core thought behind the poem is 'I know she is lying about her fidelity, but still I lie in bed with her.' The truth, troth or sooth of the courtly lover, on which depends the whole sonnet tradition dating back to Petrarch, is undone in an instant. Conventional praise is replaced by a thinking about love that is tougher and truer to the perplexity of real life. It is a radical reinvention of love poetry in a manner achieved by no other contemporary save John Donne, whose equally innovative and tough-minded *Songs and Sonnets* circulated only in manuscript among his private friends until after his death. They were almost certainly unknown to Shakespeare.

The second sonnet in *The Passionate Pilgrim* breaks another cardinal rule. The Petrarchan lover must focus on one object of desire alone, his lovely lady (or, in the case of Barnfield, his lovely boy). Not Shakespeare:

> Two loves I have, of comfort and despair,
> That like two spirits do suggest me still:
> My better angel is a man right fair,
> My worser spirit a woman coloured ill.
> To win me soon to hell, my female evil
> Tempteth my better angel from my side,
> And would corrupt my saint to be a devil,
> Wooing his purity with her fair pride.
> And whether that my angel be turned fiend,
> Suspect I may, yet not directly tell:
> For being both to me, both to each, friend,
> I guess one angel in another's hell.
> >   The truth I shall not know, but live in doubt,
> >   Till my bad angel fire my good one out.

Wyatt and his successors moved between comfort and despair in the icy fire of their longing for one fair and unobtainable beloved. Shakespeare introduces something more dramatic: a love triangle, a version of the morality play scenario in which an 'everyman' character – or a restless spirit such as Marlowe's Dr Faustus – has a good and a bad angel hovering over him. The Petrarchan lady is traditionally an angel or goddess, whereas Shakespeare's female spirit is 'a woman coloured ill', a 'female evil' who tempts the 'better angel', 'a man right fair', into infidelity. She is sex incarnate. The angelic, pure figure is the male beloved. A man's lover sleeping with his best friend, the male bond broken by rivalry over a woman: Shakespeare had explored the theme in his early comedy *The Two Gentlemen of Verona* and would return to it in his late plays

The Winter's Tale and *The Two Noble Kinsmen*. Here he turns it into a sonnet unlike any that had gone before. For good measure, he ends with sexual disgust: 'firing out' alludes not only to a fox being smoked from a hole, but also to the sexual temptress infecting the pure man with syphilis.

This second *Passionate Pilgrim* poem, which became (with minor variants) number 144 in the 1609 volume, reads like a template for Shakespeare's entire output of sonnets. It is as if, having found himself a unique structure, Shakespeare then set about illustrating his dialectic in as many ways as possible. There is, however, no intrinsic reason to assume that the friend described in this poem as 'a man right fair' is synonymous with the 'lovely boy' to whom some of the other sonnets are addressed. Though it is perfectly possible that Shakespeare was addressing the same figure, admiring both his youth and his manliness, it is equally possible that the 'man right fair' seduced by the 'woman coloured ill' is a different character from the 'lovely boy'.

When did a boy become a man in Elizabethan England? 'Cesario', the page in *Twelfth Night* (who is really, of course, Viola in disguise) is described as 'Not yet old enough for a man, nor young enough for a boy . . . in standing water between boy and man.' The latter phrase may be a memory of Arthur Golding's translation of Ovid's *Metamorphoses*, in which Narcissus at the age of sixteen is said 'to stand between the state of man and lad', with the effect that 'The hearts of divers trim young men his beauty 'gan to love, / And many a lady fresh and fair was taken in his love.' These lines are perfectly apt for Cesario, with whom both Orsino and Olivia fall in love.

The figure of Narcissus is also apt for the youth of the sonnets who is narcissistically 'contracted to thine own bright eyes' (sonnet 1). Given that Shakespeare had already written a poetry bestseller about a very similar lovely boy, Adonis, one can almost imagine him making this analogy the starting-point for his sonnets. 'I am so fed up with all these unyielding Stellas and Delias and Licias that I will follow up the success of my *Venus and Adonis* by impressing my private friends with a sequence of sonnets about a Narcissus who refuses to reproduce himself.'

The sonnet that became number 2 in the 1609 collection exists in thirteen different early manuscripts. This wide circulation and the fact that several of the manuscripts reproduce a version different in many particulars from the one in the published collection suggest that, like the two poems which first surfaced in *The Passionate Pilgrim*, this might have been one of Shakespeare's original 'sugared sonnets'. The following version, in a manuscript now in the library of Westminster Abbey, appears to be the closest to the sonnet's original form:

> When forty winters shall besiege thy brow
> And trench deep furrows in that lovely field,
> Thy youth's fair livery so accounted now
> Shall be like rotten weeds of no worth held.
> Then being asked where all thy beauty lies,
> Where all the lustre of thy youthful days,
> To say 'within these hollow sunken eyes'
> Were an all-eaten truth and worthless praise.
> O how much better were thy beauty's use
> If thou couldst say 'this pretty child of mine
> Saves my account and makes my old excuse',
> Making his beauty by succession thine.
>   This were to be new born when thou art old
>   And see thy blood warm when thou feel'st it cold.

Like Tottel in his collection of songs and sonnets by Surrey and Wyatt, the compilers of some of the manuscripts in which this poem appeared gave it a title. In four collections, it is called 'Spes Altera', 'another hope' – the phrase is a quotation from Virgil's *Aeneid*, where Aeneas' son Ascanius is described as 'another hope for Rome'. In five other collections, it is called 'To one that would die a maid'. In another, it is 'A lover to his mistress', and another, 'The Benefit of Marriage'. Since we read the poem in the context of *Shakespeare's Sonnets*, as published in 1609, we assume that it is to a man, but some early readers clearly assumed that it was addressed to a woman.

This mistake – if mistake it is – is highly revealing: it shows that the meaning of the sonnet is different for different readers. Besides, we are perhaps over-confident in assuming that the entire sequence of the sonnets from 1–126 is addressed to a man. The 'thou' whom the speaker of the sonnets addresses is not explicitly gendered as 'him' until number 19 and, taken in isolation, many of the subsequent poems could equally well be addressed to either a man or a woman. When Shakespeare's purpose is to write about the power of art to defeat the ravages of time or the feeling of loss or rejection or disillusionment in love, the identity of the addressee is immaterial.

Meaning derives not from the poem's point of origin, but from its point of interpretation. The sonnet means what it means to the reader as he or she *imagines* the point of origin or *applies* the sentiment to his or her own situation. The same poem, furthermore, can mean different things according to the context in which it appears. Since sonnet 144 was almost certainly written several years before sonnet 126, it is quite probable that the 'man right fair' of the former does not refer to the same original (if there were originals) as the 'lovely boy' of the latter. But once the poems are collected in a single book and read as a single sequence, a narrative suggests itself and the two figures become one. As Shakespeare stitched together multiple sources to make his plays, so the collection called *Shakespeare's Sonnets* stitches together multiple poems with very different origins and styles to make a single narrative. But this narrative should no more be read back literally into Shakespeare's life than should the narrative of that other lovely boy, Viola/Cesario.

Your master's mistress

Twelfth Night is highly relevant here. Of all Shakespeare's plays, it is closest to the sonnets in its anatomy of what Meres called 'the perplexities of love'.

The play begins with what sounds very like a fifteen-line unrhymed sonnet, spoken in the voice of an archetypal Petrarchan lover who thrives on unrequitedness and uses imagery of music, the sea, food, rise and fall, all of which are typical of Elizabethan sonneteering. Like the conventional sonneteers, Orsino alludes to figures from classical mythology (Actaeon hunted down by the dogs of his own desire for lovely but chaste Diana). When Olivia appears, he says that 'heaven walks on earth', which is just what an orthodox sonneteer would say. He revels in the 'sovereign cruelty' of his stony lady, as all Petrarchan lovers do. But he is then thrown by the beauty of a lovely boy. The audience, however, knows that Cesario is really Viola, a girl in disguise, and that the body parts so lovingly blazoned by Orsino really are the 'woman's part' – except they are not, since (at least the majority of) the audience also knows that Viola is a part written for a boy actor:

> Dear lad, believe it;
> For they shall yet belie thy happy years,
> That say thou art a man: Diana's lip
> Is not more smooth and rubious, thy small pipe
> Is as the maiden's organ, shrill and sound,
> And all is semblative a woman's part.

'Thou dost speak masterly' says Orsino, allowing himself to become the master mastered by the man. Or rather the boy. Or is that the girl? Or the boy actor? Orsino claims that a woman's love is of less value than a man's because it is driven solely by 'appetite', which may be sated, whereas his capacity for desire is infinite:

> There is no woman's sides
> Can bide the beating of so strong a passion
> As love doth give my heart, no woman's heart
> So big, to hold so much. They lack retention.
> Alas, their love may be called appetite,
> No motion of the liver, but the palate,
> That suffer surfeit, cloyment and revolt.
> But mine is all as hungry as the sea,
> And can digest as much.

Here he again resembles a sonneteer, whose love is limitless because it is defined by being unrequited. And when he reappears at the end of the play, Orsino duly speaks another of his fifteen-line sonnets, this one ending with the most hackneyed rhyme in the sonneteer's repertoire:

> Why should I not, had I the heart to do it,
> Like to th'Egyptian thief at point of death,
> Kill what I love? – a savage jealousy
> That sometimes savours nobly. But hear me this:
> Since you to non-regardance cast my faith,
> And that I partly know the instrument
> That screws me from my true place in your favour,
> Live you the marble-breasted tyrant still.
> But this your minion, whom I know you love,
> And whom, by heaven I swear, I tender dearly,
> Him will I tear out of that cruel eye,
> Where he sits crownèd in his master's spite.
> Come, boy, with me. My thoughts are ripe in mischief:
> I'll sacrifice the lamb that I do love,
> To spite a raven's heart within a dove.

But then he discovers that Cesario is really Viola and he is able to resolve the tension – which is also the tension of the sonnets – between love for a lovely boy and desire for a woman:

> Your master quits you. And for your service done him,
> So much against the mettle of your sex,
> So far beneath your soft and tender breeding,
> And since you called me master for so long,
> Here is my hand. You shall from this time be
> Your master's mistress.

If Orsino is the conventional Elizabethan sonneteer, Olivia is a parodist of the genre. The sonneteer customarily enumerates his lady's beautiful body-parts, one by one in that device known as the 'blazon'. Olivia enumerates her own: 'I will give out divers schedules of my beauty. It shall be inventoried, and every particle and utensil labelled to my will: as, *item*, two lips, indifferent red:

item, two grey eyes, with lids to them: *item*, one neck, one chin and so forth.' But then love – for Cesario – catches up on her and she finds herself deploying the blazon in all seriousness: 'Thy tongue, thy face, thy limbs, actions and spirit, / Do give thee five-fold blazon.' She begins to wish that 'the master were the man' – or the man her master. Viola, meanwhile, gains a voice by becoming Cesario. In the sonnet form, the object of desire is just that, an object. In *Twelfth Night*, Viola, desired by both man and woman, is a feeling subject. Vulnerable, and thus forced to become an actor ('I am not that I play'), she soon finds herself in the situation of desiring the man she has been sent to persuade to love someone else – an analogous twist to that of *Shakespeare's Sonnets*, which begin with the speaker persuading the fair youth to marry, then dissolve into the speaker's own love for the youth.

Sonnet 20 startlingly begins 'A woman's face with Nature's own hand painted / Hast thou, the master-mistress of my passion.' The coinage 'master-mistress' is unique in the literature of the age, but it is also reminiscent of Orsino's 'Your master's mistress'. Perhaps as good an answer as any to the question of the identity of the lovely youth to whom the bulk of the sonnets are addressed is 'a figure who resembles Cesario'.

Where did Shakespeare find that phrase which he gave to Orsino, 'Your master's mistress'? The answer seems to be: in a play performed by his rivals, the boy actors of St Paul's. Published in 1600, it was called *The Maid's Metamorphosis*. Its authorship is disputed, but it may have been a late work by John Lyly, pioneer of the witty comedy of love. A duke charges two of his courtiers to kill Eurymine, a maid 'of mean descent', because his son is in love with her. She escapes to the woods, where both a forester and a shepherd fall in love with her, the former giving her a cottage and the latter a flock. Then the god Apollo falls in love with her, taking her for a shepherdess. She challenges him to prove his divinity by turning her into a man. He does. A hermit informs the duke's son that his beloved is now a man. But when they meet, he recognizes her, despite her male attire. The three Graces intercede with Apollo and Eurymine is retransformed into a girl. The hermit turns out to be not only an exiled prince but also her long-lost father, meaning that she is really a princess and thus a suitable bride for the duke's son. Comic relief is provided by some shepherd lads called Mopso, Frisco and Joculo, who indulge in bawdy banter of the following kind: 'By God, Priapus I mean.' 'Priapus, quotha? What in a god might that be?' 'A plain god, with a good peg to hang a shepherdess' bottle upon.' It is Mopso who asks, with reference to the disguised Eurymine, 'hast not found the fair shepherdess, thy master's mistress?'

The Maid's Metamorphosis was performed by the Children of St Paul's around the time that Shakespeare's *As You Like It* was played by the Chamberlain's Men. It was published before the writing of *Twelfth Night*. The coincidence of phrasing, along with the shared themes out of pastoral romance – the cross-dressing especially – suggest that the adult and boy companies showed considerable rivalry in their comedies of gender-bending desire. On both the public stage of the Globe and the private stage of the Blackfriars, nothing seems to have given audiences more pleasure than the image of a boy actor dressed as a girl dressed as a boy.

Twelfth Night is an extraordinary exploration of the permutations of desire or, in Francis Meres' term, the perplexities of love. Both Orsino and Olivia love Viola in her disguise as Cesario. Viola loves, and wins, Orsino, while Olivia has to settle for Sebastian. Orsino insists on continuing to call Viola Cesario even after he knows that she is a woman. Sebastian is puzzled, though grateful, to find himself whisked to the altar by the wealthy and beautiful Olivia, but he cannot have had time to fall in love with her. The person who really loves him is Antonio, who reminds him that for three months, 'No interim, not a minute's vacancy, / Both day and night did we keep company.' He follows his beloved despite the risk to his own life: 'But, come what may, I do adore thee so, / That danger shall seem sport, and I will go.' Like a sonneteer, he speaks of being spurred on by his 'desire, / More sharp than filèd steel' and, again, of paying 'devotion' to 'his image, which methought did promise / Most venerable worth'. He is rewarded for his devotion by being left alone and melancholy, again in the exact manner of a sonnet-writer turned away by his frosty mistress. It is very easy to imagine Antonio going away at the end of *Twelfth*

Night and writing something on the following lines, addressed to Sebastian:

> They that have power to hurt and will do none,
> That do not do the thing they most do show,
> Who, moving others, are themselves as stone,
> Unmovèd, cold, and to temptation slow:
> They rightly do inherit heaven's graces
> And husband nature's riches from expense.
> They are the lords and owners of their faces,
> Others but stewards of their excellence.

This is actually the speaker of Shakespeare's sonnets as he finds himself rejected by the fair youth or the lovely boy. Shakespeare's women are never like this. They do do the things they most do show. They move others but they are never stone themselves, unless men turn them to coldness (Leontes freezing Hermione out of his life, forcing her to become a statue of stone; Angelo's sexual ardour requiring novice Isabella's cool response). His women give – of their selves, their wit and courage. It is Shakespeare's chilly, self-controlled young men – Prince Hal, Angelo, Bertram – who take, who are the lords and owners of their faces.

To read the sonnets alongside *Twelfth Night* in this way is to see that Shakespeare's poems are more than anything else a drama of love's perplexity. We do not usually look for biographical originals for Viola/Cesario, Sebastian, Orsino, Olivia and Antonio, so we should not necessarily do so for the 'lovely boy' and the 'dark lady'. To recall Giles Fletcher again: a man may write of love without being in love, and the beloved of a sonnet sequence may be a conceit and portend nothing. For all their talk of immortalizing the beloved through the poetry of praise, *Shakespeare's Sonnets* do not immortalize anybody apart from Shakespeare. If his intention had been to share his admiration for a particular person, one would have expected him to get around to naming him (and/or her) at some point in the sequence. The very lack of names – even of a mythological-allegorical kind – suggests that attempting to 'unshadow' the origin of the sonnets is to read them against the grain. Shakespeare's original intention was to circulate them among his private friends, so perhaps we should be content to let them remain private.

The mystery of Master W. H.

Given the vogue for printed sonnets, it would have been perfectly possible for Shakespeare to have gone along to his old school-friend Richard Field, who had done such a good job with his printing of *Venus and Adonis* and *The Rape of Lucrece*, and asked him to print the sonnets. But he did not.

In 1609, long after many of them were first written, they fell instead into the hands of a publisher named Thomas Thorpe, who had a track record of bringing to press a mixture of authorized and unauthorized works. Scholars argue over the category to which *Shakespeare's Sonnets* belong. Unauthorized seems more likely. Authorized works tended to have prefatory addresses and dedications signed by their authors. Shakespeare's sonnets have no apparatus of authorial voice, only an enigmatic dedication signed with the initials of the publisher. In other instances when Thomas Thorpe took it upon himself to sign the prefatory material, it was because the author was dead or otherwise unavailable for comment. By dedicating the volume to a mysterious 'Master W. H.' and calling him 'the only begetter of these ensuing sonnets', Thorpe the publisher seems to have implied that the entire sequence was inspired by love for one person (the *only* begetter), though it obviously wasn't, since the 'dark lady' plays her part. And he tantalized the reader into finding names to fit to the initials.

Recent computer-assisted stylometric analysis has called into question Thorpe's illusion of an only begetter by revealing that it is highly probable that the sonnets were written or revised over the course of a decade or more. A variety of 'stylistic matching' experiments, especially in relation to words which Shakespeare used only very rarely, have strongly suggested that the poems in the first half of the sequence, which are mostly addressed to a man, belong to the first half of Shakespeare's career, as do the 'dark lady' sonnets. The 'man right fair' and the 'woman coloured ill' as characters in a series of poems written in the 1590s: this is consistent with their appearance in 'Two loves I have', the second sonnet of *The Passionate Pilgrim*, in print by early 1599. It suggests that the 'sugared sonnets' known to Meres are somewhere among, say, numbers 1 to 60 and 127 to 152 in the 1609 collection. But the sonnets numbered 104 to 126 in the 1609 collection show very strong marks of belonging to the middle or later period of Shakespeare's career, as do the group concerning a rival poet or poets (78 to 86). This accords with the hypothesis that the one sonnet that seems to allude to its own moment of composition, and thus to be datable with some firmness, is number 107, in which the line 'The mortal moon hath her eclipse endured' is best interpreted as a reference to Queen Elizabeth's death in 1603, and 'peace proclaims olives of endless age' to the Somerset House peace conference of 1604 or, more generally, to the new king's attempt to end the long years of war with Spain.

There are two traditional candidates for the male addressee of the sonnets. Scholars who believe they were written in the 1590s usually argue for Henry Wriothesley, third Earl of Southampton, dedicatee of *Venus and Adonis* and *Lucrece*. Scholars who believe they were written in the early 1600s usually argue for William Herbert, third Earl of Pembroke. The new evidence concerning the probable lengthy time-frame embraced by the collection raises the possibility that both groups of scholars are right: that Southampton is the 'man right fair' of the 1590s sonnets and Pembroke the 'lovely boy' of the later group (only sonnets 108 and 126 call their addressee a 'boy'). It may be we need to look for the 'dark lady' – if she had an original – in the Southampton circle and the 'rival poet' (or poets) in the Pembroke circle. This, though, is probably not the whole solution to the mystery. Sonnet 135 seems to imagine the man right fair bedding the poet's mistress. It apparently belongs to the earlier chronological grouping and yet the young man in it is called Will, which fits Pembroke rather than Southampton.

Disambiguating the 'man right fair' and the 'lovely boy' into Southampton and Pembroke does not get rid of the two fundamental problems of identifying the beloved friend of the sonnets with either of them. First, how likely is it that so great a figure as an earl would have allowed a player and play-maker of lower middle-class origins, however talented and successful he may have been, sufficient access to achieve the kind of intense intimacy that the sonnets purport to describe? Pembroke was one of the greatest literary patrons of the age, but patronage is not on a par with private passion. Secondly, is it really likely that an earl would be addressed in a dedication as a mere gentleman, as *Master* W. H.? The argument goes that the downgrading of rank was a conscious disguise on the part of the publisher (or the poet), in order to avoid naming Southampton or Pembroke and shaming him with the dark and illicit sexual matter of the poems. If so, why then *Master* W. H., not the initials alone or, for that matter, complete anonymity? *Master* was the term of address for a gentleman, not a nobleman. It is perverse to assume that W. H. was an earl before considering the possibility that he was a gentleman. The trouble is, we have no idea who he was. And, for that matter, we cannot be sure that the initials W. H. in the dedication to the *Sonnets* are not a misprint for W. S. or W. Sh., in which case Thorpe was dedicating the volume to its true begetter: Master William Shakespeare.

The Jacobean moment and the rival poet

Given the elusiveness of the Shakespearean voice, the lack of any solid evidence to link the poems to a single 'fair friend', and the uncertainty over the authorization, ordering and dedication of Thorpe's 1609 volume, the best move may be to stop trying to link the sonnets to a particular W. H. (or H. W.), and instead to link those that can be dated with a degree of assurance to a particular historical moment. Trying to unmask Master W. H. is a fool's game, but there are rewards in placing sonnets 77–86 and 104–126 in the early Jacobean moment that is suggested by both the stylistic analysis and the apparent allusion to Queen Elizabeth's death.

At this point, William Herbert, third Earl of Pembroke, does become a key player in the story, perhaps in company with his brother – at least as potential patrons, if not as lovely boys in person.

We do not know exactly what William Herbert, Earl of Pembroke, and his brother Philip Herbert, later Earl of Montgomery, looked like when they caught the eye of King James – and perhaps Shakespeare – in 1603–04. The closest we can get is this detail in Van Dyck's portrait of Philip Herbert's family: these two 'lovely boys' are his sons (and thus Pembroke's nephews).

In terms of Shakespeare's career, the year 1603 was remarkably like the year 1593. On each occasion, he was on a roll with his plays, but then suddenly found the theatres closed for a lengthy period due to plague. Back in 1593, he had begun to plan the alternative career – the road taken by his contemporaries George Chapman and Michael Drayton – of concentrating primarily on the pursuit of patronage through non-dramatic poetry (though Chapman and Drayton also wrote plays as a second string to their bows). It was during that first year of plague closure that Shakespeare dedicated *Venus and Adonis* and *The Rape of Lucrece* to the Earl of Southampton. This time around, he was much more established, due to the position of the Lord Chamberlain's Men as the acting company most favoured by the court. Reward came in the form of the royal warrant of May 1603, whereby they became His King's Majesty's Players, entitled to call themselves Grooms of the Chamber, and known familiarly as the King's Men. The task in the coming years would be to write some major new plays for court performance in front of a king who was interested in unifying the kingdoms of Britain, establishing world peace and searching out witchcraft, all themes to which Shakespeare duly turned in his next few plays.

But the most that could be hoped for was about twenty court performances per year. At £10 per performance, shared among the nine men named on the royal licence, less expenses (new costumes, payments to the hired men and script writers of other new plays, bed and board for the apprentices), that was hardly sufficient. If the theatres remained closed for too long, there would be serious penury. Shakespeare was keeping one eye on his property portfolio back in Stratford, planning his massive investment in tithes, but with the other eye he may well have been casting around for some new form of preferment or patronage.

In May 1603 his company became the King's Men. In March 1604 he and his fellow-actors were each given four yards of red cloth to wear 'against his Majesty's royal proceeding through the city of London'. In August 1604, the players waited by royal command in attendance on the Constable of Castile, special envoy from the King of Spain, on the occasion of the Somerset House peace conference. This evidence suggests that for a period of around eighteen months after the old queen's death Shakespeare was closer to the court than he had ever been. This was also a period when the public theatres were closed due to plague. It seems an obvious time for Shakespeare to have attempted to win some favours through his poetry, and the timing fits with the stylistic evidence regarding the date of composition of the later sonnets, especially the 'rival poet' (78–86) and 'lovely boy' (104–126) sequences.

Interestingly, although the vogue for sonneteering had been at its height back in the 1590s, 1603 to 1605 was a period of renewed interest in the form. Several sequences written at this time were more cynical and harder-edged than most of those of the 1590s, with their gilded pastoral flummery. The late 1590s and early 1600s had witnessed a flowering of 'snarling satire' in poetry, associated with clever, no-nonsense young men about the Inns of Court. John Donne and John Marston were in the forefront of this new movement. Something of their tone rubbed off on the later sonneteers, as well as on Shakespeare himself. *Troilus and Cressida* and *Timon of Athens*, which belong to this period, are his most bitterly satirical plays. A sonnet such as number 121, which talks of being 'vile esteemed', of 'false adulterate eyes', 'rank thoughts' and 'general evil', partakes of the mood of the time.

The style of an age is set from the top. One of the reasons why sonnet sequences about unobtainable, virginal, goddess-like women were so popular in the 1590s was that Queen Elizabeth promoted an image of herself as just such a muse to her courtiers. When King James arrived, he brought with him a very different style of court. For one thing, he was married with children. For another, paradoxical as it may seem, he encouraged a kind of eroticism around the royal body that would have shocked the late Virgin Queen.

The Herbert brothers, William and Philip, were among the most prominent courtiers under the new regime. William Herbert, Earl of Pembroke, in his twenty-third year at the time of the new king's accession, son of the great patroness of letters Mary Countess of Pembroke, and nephew of the immortal Sir Philip Sidney, had scandalized the court of the late queen. Having proved himself serially resistant to marriage proposals arranged by his family, he fell for one of the queen's maids of honour, Mary Fitton, when he saw her dancing in the court masque at his cousin's wedding. She became pregnant by him, to the fury of the queen, for whom the virginity of her maids of honour was supposed to be a mirror of her own. Pembroke was thrown in the Fleet prison, then exiled to the family's country estate, Wilton in Wiltshire. But with the death of the queen, Pembroke won his way back into royal favour. King James cared not a whit for a maid of honour's pregnancy outside of marriage. He was soon visiting Wilton, giving Pembroke the status of gentleman of the privy chamber and keeper of one of the royal forests. Knowing that Pembroke detested frogs, he put one down his neck. Pembroke responded by sneaking a live pig into His Majesty's close-stool, the kind of jape that would have been beyond conception in the age of Elizabeth. The Venetian ambassador noted the scene at James's coronation: 'The earl of Pembroke, a handsome youth, who is always with the king and always joking with him, actually kissed His Majesty's face, where-upon the king laughed and gave him a little cuff.'

Notwithstanding such intimacies, the earl was equally popular with James's wife, Queen Anne. He was clearly the coming man, and thus found himself the target of writers seeking patronage. In 1603 Ben Jonson dedicated the printed version of his play *Sejanus* to him, beginning a long association, which saw the earl granting his poet twenty pounds a year for the purchase of books and bailing him out of prison when he made the mistake of being rude about the Scots in the comedy *Eastward Ho!* Other poets receiving Pembroke's favours included George Chapman, John Davies of Hereford, Samuel Daniel and Francis Davison, the son of one of Queen Elizabeth's secretaries of state. Among the latter's works is a little epigram, 'On Painted Ladies', which turns on a pun on the name of a cosmetic called *fucus*, which is exactly the sort of joke that Pembroke loved.

There seems to have been considerable rivalry among the writers in Pembroke's coterie. Davies of Hereford wrote three very rude poems about a money-grubbing poet to whom he gives the name Fucus. The object of his particular scorn in one of these epigrams, entitled 'Of the staid furious poet Fucus', is his rival's involvement with the theatre:

> *Fucus* the furious Poet writes but Plays;
> So, playing, writes: that's, idly writeth all:

Yet, idle Plays, and Players are his Stays;
Which stay him that he can no lower fall:
For, he is fall'n into the deep'st decay,
Where Plays and Players keep him at a stay.

Perish the thought that Fucus might be Shakespeare: the epithet 'furious Poet' reveals that Davies's target was actually John Marston, who was satirized elsewhere as the bombastic braggart 'Furor Poeticus'. We will meet snarling Master Marston again later.

Though more a hunting and hawking man than a reader, Pembroke's younger brother Philip, a lovely boy of nineteen when he rode north to meet the new king, was also a patron of letters as well as a royal favourite. He was 'the first who drew the King's eyes towards him with affection'. Within months of the accession, James had made him a gentleman of the privy chamber and a Knight of the Bath. By 1605, he had received upgrades to gentleman of the bedchamber and Earl of Montgomery. Several literary works were dedicated to him.

So, for example, the poet John Davies of Hereford, having dedicated his first poetry collection, *Microcosmos*, to the elder Herbert brother in 1603, dedicated his second to the younger brother in 1605. The latter volume was called *Wit's Pilgrimage (by poetical essays) through a World of Amorous Sonnets, Soul-passions and other Passages, Divine, Philosophical, Moral, Poetical and Political* – a title in comparison to which *Shakespeare's Sonnets never before Imprinted* is spare, to say the least. One of the dedicatory poems in the front of *Wit's Pilgrimage* is addressed jointly 'to the same truly-noble Earl [i.e. Philip Herbert] and his most honourable other half, Sir James Hay, knight'. Hay was another lovely youth whom King James liked to have around and on whom he showered titles and honour. The notion of two male friends being each other's other half, like the mythological Gemini or heavenly twins, was a poetic commonplace in the period, but Davies introduces references to 'minions' and 'sweet affects' that give a certain erotic charge to the conjunction, suggestive of the heated 'homosocial' atmosphere of James's court. Stylistically, Davies's sonnets, very much like Shakespeare's, are a long way from the pastoral ease and

Petrarchan idealization that characterized most of the sequences of
the 1590s. He describes the bitter end of a sexual affair, closing a
sonnet with the line 'I am in hate with thee, and thou with me.'

Davies's *Microcosmos* collection includes a pair of sonnets to the
Earl of Pembroke which adapt the techniques of love poetry to an
aspiring writer's bid for his master's patronage. One of them focuses
on the idea of immortalizing the earl through the sonnet itself:

> Dear *Lord*, if so I could, I would make known
> How much I long to keep *thee* still alive;
> These *Lines* (though short) so long shall be thine own
> As they have pow'r *Vitality* to give:
> I consecrate this *Mite* of my devotion
> To the rich *Treasury* of thy dear fame;
> Which shall serve (though nought else worth) as a *Notion*
> For *Time* to sever thy *fame* from thy *name*:
> WILLIAM, Son's Son of *William*, dreaded *Earl*
> Of *Pembroke* . . .

The second turns on the idea of kindling Pembroke's love. It ends
with a play on the initial of his Christian name:

> I am thine *own* by double interest
> Sith once I vow'd my self to *thee* and *thine*,
> O then had I but single love of *you*,
> I should be double bound to *W*.

The pun is typographical as well as personal. In the Jacobean
printing-house 'u' was printed as 'v' and a capital 'W' was made
out of two Vs (the last word of the sonnet is thus two letters, VV).
'W' is thus at the same time 'W' for William and two 'v's, which
is to say two 'u's or '*double you*'. It is as clever a piece of multiple
word-play as that on the word 'Will' in Shakespeare's sonnets 135
and 136.

Davies's *Wit's Pilgrimage* combines a sequence of sonnets
addressed to a highly sexualized woman with a series of fawning
apostrophes in praise of the beauty, virtue and fame of various

young male aristocrats about the court: a structure not dissimilar
to that of *Shakespeare's Sonnets*. And, like Shakespeare, Davies is
much more sexually explicit than most practitioners of the form
had been in the previous decade. One sonnet speaks of 'putting
hot seed of active love . . . Into thy mouth', and another has the
lady, assuming it is a lady, handling the poet with tantalizing skill,
sustaining him at painful length on the verge of his little death:

> Enough (fell Fair!) for, thou hast done the deed
> That thou hast long been doing, which doth make
> Thy mercy less, for that, to kill with speed
> Shows more remorse than they that leisure take.
> How? and how long hast thou been martyring me
> To make my death beyond my death to stand?
> Who hath been so anatomized by thee
> That every nerve hath felt thy rigor's hand!
> Out of my heart and brains that hand hath squeezed
> The spirits that either life or sense maintain:
> For, I am all as dead, as unadvised:
> Only, for thee, I life in show retain:
> And if thou wilt have that, sith that's for thee
> Then take thou all and leave the rest for me.

To put it more bluntly, she appears to have been masturbating him
very slowly. Though Shakespeare's sonnets are never quite so
erotically explicit, the later ones especially are steeped in sexual
puns. They surely belong in the very male and homoerotic world
of the early Jacobean court, where Davies was insinuating himself,
not in the more rarefied atmosphere that surrounded the virgin
queen.

The Herbert brothers seem to have liked dirty poems. Indeed,
the Earl of Pembroke wrote a slew of erotic songs and sonnets
himself, circulating them among his private friends. One is in praise
of a dark lady ('On black hair and eyes'), others are explicit about
sexual encounters, several echo phrases out of Shakespeare's
sonnets. Could it then be that Shakespeare was competing with
Davies and others for the patronage of one or both of the Herbert

brothers in the years from 1603 to 1605? Davies seems to have had some success, to judge from the way he signs one of his dedications to Pembroke 'Your Honour's peculiar John Davies', the word 'peculiar' meaning 'especially devoted to you, belonging to you' (though it was also, alarmingly, a slang term for a wife, mistress, an exclusive sexual partner or, as in the line in *Measure for Measure* about 'groping for trouts in a peculiar river', a vagina).

After Shakespeare's death, his fellow-actors dedicated the First Folio of his collected works to the Herbert brothers. By then, the Earl of Pembroke had become Lord Chamberlain and thus patron of the acting profession in general and Shakespeare's royal company in particular. Pembroke knew Burbage personally and deeply mourned his death. In the dedication to the Folio, John Hemings and Henry Condell note that both brothers thought Shakespeare plays 'something' and 'prosecuted both them and their author, living, with so much favour'. Though the reference is primarily to favour given to Shakespeare's plays, it may also suggest that the Herbert brothers also rewarded him for his sonnets.

John Davies of Hereford knew Shakespeare and mentioned him several times in his own poems. In *Microcosmos*, he expresses his admiration for 'players' and praises Shakespeare ('W. S.') for his 'poesy' and Burbage ('R. B.') for his 'painting' – Burbage was indeed a painter as well as an actor. But he also speaks of fortune refusing the players 'better uses'. The reason seems to have been that acting was still regarded as a vulgar profession: 'And though the stage doth stain pure gentle blood, / Yet generous ye [i.e. Shakespeare and Burbage] are in mind and mood.' In another poem of the same period, *The Civil Wars of Death and Fortune* (1605), Davies wrote about the players again, noting again that fortune has been cruel to them: 'Yet some she guerdoned not to their deserts.' As in *Microcosmos*, a marginal note helpfully identifies the players who have not been raised to the status they merit by their art: 'W. S.' and 'R. B.'

Some years later, Davies wrote an epigram addressed to Mr Will Shakespeare, calling him 'our English Terence', which is as much as to say the greatest comic dramatist of the nation, as Terence was the greatest Roman comic dramatist:

Some say (good *Will*) which I, in sport, do sing,
Had'st thou not played some Kingly parts in sport,
Thou hadst been a companion for a *King*;
And been a King among the meaner sort.
Some others rail; but, rail as they think fit,
Thou hast no railing, but, a reigning Wit:
    And honesty *thou sow'st, which they do reap*;
    So, to increase their stock *which they do keep.*

The only plausible explanation of this poem is that Davies believed that had Shakespeare not been an actor he would have become 'a companion for a king', in other words received an elevated title or a senior post at court or both. Apparently, Shakespeare took this failure to gain preferment in good part. Unlike others who did not make it to the top table, he refused to 'rail', but continued as the 'reigning wit' of the public stage.

The critic Katherine Duncan-Jones has noted these references and placed them beside some other passing allusions from texts of the early Jacobean period which collectively suggest that Shakespeare and Burbage may well have believed that – thanks, no doubt to the support of the Herbert brothers – they were on the brink of knighthoods and more formal positions at court. Duncan-Jones believes that Shakespeare was about to have greatness thrust upon him. As it was, though, something went wrong. It turned out that no mere actor would be knighted in England for nearly three centuries, when Henry Irving achieved what even the great eighteenth-century master David Garrick had not.

The sonnets that may with most assurance be dated to the period 1603–05 persistently harp on a sense of the poet's shame. He admits to making himself 'a motley to the view' (an allusion to acting), to having 'sold cheap what is most dear'. He writes of his 'harmful deeds' and his name receiving a 'brand', of his 'strong infection'. But, as Davies acknowledged, he expresses 'No bitterness that I will bitter think, / Nor double penance to correct correction.' 'Vulgar scandal stamped upon my brow', 'To know my shames', 'my neglect', 'my adder's sense / To critic and to flatterer stoppèd are', ' 'Tis better to be vile than vile esteemed', 'my frailties', 'I am

that I am and they that level / At my abuses reckon up their own.'
All these phrases – from sonnets 110, 111, 112 and 121 – strongly
suggest some aura of scandal around Shakespeare's name that
adversely affected his bid for court preferment. It may simply have
been the stigma of being a public player, but the particular allusion
in sonnet 121 to how 'others' false adulterate eyes / Give salutation
to my sportive blood' has the whiff of some sexual misdemeanour
which may have sullied Shakespeare in the eyes of the Herbert
brothers.

If there is any bitterness in the sonnets of this period, it comes
in the group concerning the rival poet – or poets, since number
82 seems to say that several writers have been dedicating their
works to the fair youth. As we have seen, poets were indeed
buzzing around the Herbert brothers like wasps over a honey-pot.
George Chapman was among them, and he has been plausibly
identified as the rival of sonnet 85: 'the proud full sail of his great
verse' might allude to the inflated 'fourteener' metre of his Homer
translation, the idea of being 'by spirits taught to write, / Above a
mortal pitch' to Chapman's claim in his poem *Euthymiae raptus*
that he was inspired by Homer's very spirit, 'his compeers by night'
to his mysterious earlier poem *The Shadow of Night*, and 'that affable
familiar ghost / Which nightly gulls him with intelligence' to
Marlowe the intelligencer, whose *Hero and Leander* Chapman had
completed for publication. But, assuming that there is more than
one rival, the best candidate besides Chapman is – though biographers have largely ignored the possibility – the very man who has
been shadowing us throughout this discussion.

'In polished form of well-refinèd pen'

John Davies was a contemporary of Shakespeare and another non-
university man. He always signed his work 'of Hereford' to distinguish himself from Sir John Davies, a much better connected poet.
He came to London from the west midlands and dedicated his
career to the pursuit of poetic patronage, targeting the Percy family
as well as the Herberts. He failed to make much money from his

John Davies of Hereford: poet, penman, writing master

poetry, but achieved enormous success in a related vocation. A German visitor referred to him as 'the most famous writer of his time'. That did not, however, mean the most famous poet. It meant the most famous penman, or calligrapher. John Davies of Hereford was London's writing master par excellence, tutor in penmanship to Prince Henry and many of the young aristocrats around the court.

If one looks closely at the 'rival poet' sequence of Shakespeare's sonnets, they have a very strong focus on the *pen* of the rival. Sonnet 79 could be saying something to the effect of 'initially I praised you without the aid of anyone else, but now I'm sick, so I've enlisted the assistance of "a worthier pen" to articulate my love in beautiful form'. Sonnet 80 might say that the rival writes with 'tall building', strokes of the pen that flow like a proud sail, 83 that the rival paints the beloved with 'a modern quill'; 84 again mentions a pen; 85 is especially striking, referring to the rival's 'golden quill / And precious phrase by all the Muses filed':

> I think good thoughts whilst other write good words,
> And like unlettered clerk still cry 'Amen'
> To every hymn that able spirit affords
> In polished form of well-refinèd pen.

Which seems to say: 'I have the good poetic thoughts but I rely
on someone else to write them down in polished form with his
well-refined pen.'

And finally, an alternative explanation for the allusions in sonnet
86 is that it asks 'was it his overblown verse that attracted you (first
stanza, perhaps alluding to the bombast of *Microcosmos*) or was it
his quasi-supernatural skill in the art of handwriting ("by spirits
taught to write / Above a mortal pitch")?' Could it be that everyone has assumed that the 'rival poet' sequence is about the *poetic*
gifts of a rival, but it is actually about the gift of *penmanship* of a
rival?

But Davies was also a poet, of course, so the implication in
sonnets 82 and 83 that the rival has *published* work dedicated to the
fair youth, which Shakespeare claims he has been reluctant to do
himself, is compatible with this reading. As has been seen, Davies
published collections dedicated to both the Herbert brothers.

A story suggests itself. Shakespeare writes in praise of, say, Pembroke – though it could have been his brother (or them both). He
wants to give his potential patron a presentation copy in manuscript. It is not going to be in his own scratchy secretary hand,
which we know from the one surviving literary manuscript in
Shakespeare's own handwriting, the scene he wrote for the collaborative play of *Sir Thomas More*. So what does he do? He goes
to the greatest penman in London. Davies. But Pembroke (or
Montgomery) misses the point: he is flattered not by Shakespeare's
thoughts but by Davies's hand.

There may be a further twist. In copying a selection of Shakespeare's sonnets, Davies takes the opportunity of slipping in a
narrative poem of his own for the delectation of his patron: when
Shakespeare's Sonnets came to be published in 1609, they were
accompanied by 'A Lover's Complaint', ascribed to Shakespeare
but, according to the recent stylistic analysis of Brian Vickers,
plausibly attributable to Davies. This story might explain how it
got there.

Whether or not that last twist is fanciful, once one has spotted
all the allusions to pen, quill and writing in sonnets 78–86, Davies
inevitably becomes a leading contender for the honour of being

Shakespeare's rival. This possible solution to one of the enigmas of the sonnets does not solve all the others, but it greatly helps the case for fixing the later group of them in an early Jacobean environment. That setting in turn suggests that Shakespeare's project in these later sonnets to the 'lovely boy' may have been not so much to express some urgent personal homosexual desire as to explore the perplexities of love and service in what might be described as a newly *bisexualized* court.

Soldier

Then a soldier,
Full of strange oaths and bearded like the pard,
Jealous in honour, sudden and quick in quarrel,
Seeking the bubble reputation
Even in the cannon's mouth.

Robert Devereux, second Earl of Essex

13. The Famous Victory of Queen Elizabeth

Food for powder. Slings and arrows. Sword and buckler. Frightened with false fire. In both plot and metaphor, Shakespeare's plays are stuffed with what Othello calls the 'pride, pomp and circumstance of glorious war'. He began his career in the wake of the Spanish Armada. As he wrote through the last decade of the old queen's reign, England was overshadowed by military campaigns in the Netherlands and Ireland. He knew the art of the pre-battle pep talk. But he also knew the irony of history: King Harry says that 'We few, we happy few, we band of brothers' will be remembered on the feast day of Saints Crispin and Crispian 'From this day to the ending of the world', but as a result of the Elizabethan Protestant reform of the liturgical calendar St Crispin's Day was not celebrated in Shakespeare's England.

He also thought deeply about the cost of war. Among the most famous of Erasmus' adages was '*Dulce bellum inexpertis*', 'war is sweet to those who have not experienced it'. As far as we know, Shakespeare never did experience war at first hand, but in London and even Stratford he would have seen former soldiers who had. *Henry V* is the play not only of the stirring poetry of 'Once more unto the breach' and the Crispin oration, but also of the penetrating prose of the common soldier, Michael Williams, telling his disguised king some home truths in the spirit of Erasmus: 'I am afeard there are few die well that die in a battle, for how can they charitably dispose of anything, when blood is their argument?'

The soldier of Jaques' fourth age is 'Jealous in honour'. Falstaff on the battlefield of Shrewsbury is as hard-headed about that word as Michael Williams is about the idea that it is possible to 'die well' – making charitable donations to the poor and spiritual peace with God – in battle. The code of chivalric 'honour' had very particular political connotations in the 1590s, associations that drew Shakespeare and his acting company close to catastrophe.

Jaques' references to jealousy, honour, quickness in quarrel and a concern with 'the bubble reputation' also bring to mind a soldier who has come home from the wars, Othello – though a big part of his problem is that Venice is not really his home. And that is a

Title page of Thomas Heywood's Armada play

reminder that the theatre of war in Shakespeare's time was positively global. The unshaven, swearing soldier could have found himself in the cannon's mouth in an extraordinary variety of locations: on the plains of Flanders or the streets of London, but also aboard a man of war on the Spanish main or up against the Turk in the eastern Mediterranean.

Royal captain

National identity is shaped by defining moments, usually involving violence. The French republic is defined by a moment in January 1793 when a guillotine came down on the head of a king, the American republic by musket shot that rang out on Lexington Green one morning in April 1775.

Shakespeare's England was no different. It was defined by a royal divorce and a series of religiously motivated executions: Sir Thomas More, beheaded in 1535 for his resistance to King Henry VIII's break with the Roman Catholic church; Thomas Cranmer, burnt at the stake in 1556 for his resistance to Queen Mary's restoration of the English nation to the Roman Catholic church; Mary Queen of Scots, beheaded in 1587 for alleged involvement in the Romish Babington Plot to assassinate Queen Elizabeth. The year after Mary went to the block, there came threat in the guise of 'Armada'. The enduring myth of the courageous English underdog was shaped for the future in response to that threat. Rhetoric, history and drama each played their part in the process.

The small but proud island nation is in peril. Europe has been taken over by a ruthless empire with ambitions of global domination, a state-of-the-art military machine, an uncompromising ideology and a brutally effective internal security service. The invasion force has gathered. Now England can only wait, watch the Channel and pray. At such a time, the morale of the nation will be made or broken by the words of the leader. The power of rhetoric comes without financial cost. It might just be able to compensate for the adverse military odds. If the words prove memorable enough, they will outlive the moment and future generations will remember that 'this was their finest hour'. Thus the year 1940. But also 1588, when the threat came from Roman Catholic Spain, which held great swathes not only of Europe but also of the New World under its command. The words of defiance were those of Queen Elizabeth I.

The troops were gathered at Tilbury, on the Thames estuary, not far from the spot where the M25 motorway now crosses the

river and cars queue to enter the Thurrock Lakeside shopping
mall. On an August morning the queen rode through all the
squadrons of her army, dressed as Pallas Athene, the warrior
goddess who embodied the spirit of ancient Greece. Classical
Athens was a city famed for everything that the English nation held
dear: democracy, debate, learning, sport, poetry, theatre, empire.
Escorting the Virgin Queen were loyal courtiers: the Earl of Leicester (her former favourite), the Earl of Essex (her future favourite),
Norris the Lord Marshall and others.

Dr Lionel Sharp was chaplain to Leicester. He was a witness of
Her Majesty's 'excellent oration to her army'. He was commanded
to copy it down and 'utter it to the whole army the next day' –
that is to say, to ensure that it was heard by the many troops who
would have been out of earshot when Elizabeth spoke. Thanks to
the technology of radio, Winston Churchill in 1940 could address
the entire nation from a secure studio. At Tilbury, only a token
group of men would have heard the queen in person. In order to
address them at all, she had to take the risk of going into the field.
She began her speech by turning that risk to advantage:

My loving people, I have been persuaded by some that are careful of my
safety to take heed how I committed myself to armed multitudes, for
fear of treachery. But I tell you that I would not desire to live to distrust
my faithful and loving people. Let tyrants fear: I have so behaved myself
that under God I have placed my chiefest strength and safeguard in the
loyal hearts and goodwill of my subjects.

Only 'tyrants' such as Philip II of Spain need fear assassination. A
queen who governs by love and Christian duty can be assured of
her people's loyalty. So long as she assuages any doubts they might
have about being led by a representative of what the Scottish
Puritan John Knox had damningly called the 'monstrous regiment
of women'. This question of her womanhood is confronted boldly,
not brushed aside:

Wherefore I am come among you at this time but for my recreation and
pleasure, being resolved in the midst and heat of the battle to live and

die amongst you all, to lay down for my God and for my kingdom and for my people mine honour and my blood even in the dust. I know I have the body of a weak and feeble woman, but I have the heart and stomach of a king and of a king of England too . . . Not doubting but by your concord in the camp and valour in the field and your obedience to myself and my general, we shall shortly have a famous victory over these enemies of my God and of my kingdom.

Like Churchill over three centuries later, Queen Elizabeth was schooled in the classics. For all their differences, the two leaders shared at least one memory: each of them had spent a high proportion of their childhood hours being drilled in the Latin of Cicero. They accordingly knew that rhetorical force relies on symmetry and repetition: 'mine honour and my blood', 'my God and my kingdom', 'concord in the camp and valour in the field', and above all 'of a king' repeated and intensified as 'of a king of England too'.

A good speech also needs a soundbite: Churchill's 'finest hour', Elizabeth's 'famous victory'. The queen's speech has a highly theatrical quality, so perhaps it is not so surprising that her climactic phrase seems to have been borrowed from the stage. The leading theatre company of the 1580s was a group under the patronage of Elizabeth herself: the Queen's Men. One of their most popular plays was entitled *The Famous Victories of Henry the Fifth*. Possibly the earliest history play in the professional stage repertoire, it tells the story of King Harry's growth from rebellious youth in the company of 'Ned' and 'Sir John Oldcastle' to triumphant victor against the odds in the battle of Agincourt. The material was so good that a decade later William Shakespeare would develop it into three whole plays – the last of which, *Henry the Fifth*, includes that epitome of the pre-battle oration which so greatly inspired Churchill:

> And Crispin Crispian shall ne'er go by
> From this day to the ending of the world
> But we in it shall be remembered,
> We few, we happy few, we band of brothers.

Shakespeare's emphasis on brotherhood between monarch and common soldier replicates Elizabeth's device of stressing her love for her people more than her dominion over them. Though the language of the anonymous *Famous Victories* never rises to these heights, the play had the effect of immortalizing Agincourt as the archetypal triumph of the English underdog. By using the phrase 'famous victory', the queen was implying that the defeat of the Armada would be another Agincourt, another of England's finest hours.

Soon after Elizabeth's death, the prolific dramatist Thomas Heywood wrote a two-part play in honour of her memory, entitled *If you know not me, you know nobody*. The second part was subtitled *With the building of the Royal Exchange and the Famous Victory of Queen Elizabeth: Anno 1588*. The defeat of the Armada is the climax of the play. There the stage Elizabeth, played by a young male actor, delivers a version of the real-life queen's oration:

> Now noble soldiers, rouse your hearts like me,
> To noble resolution: if any here
> There be that love us not or harbour fear,
> We give him liberty to leave our camp
> Without displeasure.
> Our armies royal so be equal our hearts,
> For with the meanest here I'll spend my blood,
> And so to lose it count my only good.
> A march, lead on: we'll meet the worst can fall,
> A maiden Queen will be your General.

Heywood's language owes more to Shakespeare's dramatization of Henry V's pre-Agincourt speech than it does to the actual words spoken at Tilbury. In particular, the offer for any 'that love us not or harbour fear' to leave the camp 'without displeasure' is derived from Shakespeare's

> Rather proclaim it, Westmorland, through my host
> That he which hath no stomach to this fight,
> Let him depart. His passport shall be made

And crowns for convoy put into his purse:
We would not die in that man's company
That fears his fellowship to die with us.

The path from *The Famous Victories of Henry the Fifth* in the repertoire of the Queen's Men to the 'famous victory' speech at Tilbury
to Shakespeare's *Henry V* to a dramatization of the queen's speech
in Heywood's play beautifully reveals the symbiotic relationship
between the theatre and history in the late Elizabethan era.

Heywood follows the speech with a stage direction: '*They march
one way out, at the other door enter Sir Francis Drake with Colours and
Ensigns taken from the Spaniards.*' In modern film parlance, this is a
jump cut. If we were making a Hollywood blockbuster called
Armada, we would use exactly the same device, cutting at this
point from the army to the navy, swinging westward from the
camp at Tilbury to the fleet gathered at Plymouth. Above the
harbour there is a greensward known as Plymouth Hoe, from
which there is a good view of the ships below – among them, the
galleons *Ark Royal* and *Revenge*, the pinnace *Disdain* and an array
of armed merchantmen, waiting on the wind, waiting on the news.
When word comes that the Armada has been sighted, the captains
are playing a game of bowls on the Hoe. Sir Francis Drake, the
man who has circumnavigated the globe, does not rush in panic
down to the *Revenge*. There is time, he says, to finish the game
and then finish the Spaniards. English understatement, English
stoical resolve captured in an instant.

But we know by now never to trust the Hollywood version.
One of the many things the ancient Greeks and Romans taught
the Elizabethans was that the first historian, Herodotus, was the
father of lies. Dramatized history, in particular, requires the heroes
to be larger than life and the pace of events to be quickened,
'Turning the accomplishment of many years / Into an hourglass'.
Though it is widely assumed that 'This was their finest hour' came
at the climax of Churchill's 'we shall fight on the beaches' speech
of 4 June 1940, it actually belonged to another speech, delivered
two weeks later. Television documentaries frequently edit the two
together. By the same account, it was on 19 July 1588 that the

Spanish fleet was spotted off the Lizard, the southernmost tip of
Cornwall, and the news conveyed to Drake at Plymouth, whereas
Elizabeth delivered her oration at Tilbury on 9 August 1588, after
the main body of the Armada had been harried the full length of
the Channel and diverted towards Dunkirk. The real fear she was
addressing was that the Duke of Parma, Spanish regent in the
Netherlands, intended to send an invasion force of 30,000 men
across the straits of Dover in shallow-bottomed barges. The second
half of the most famous sentence in the oration makes this clear,
though it is not usually quoted: 'I know I have the body of a weak
and feeble woman, but I have the heart and stomach of a king and
of a king of England too – and take foul scorn that Parma or any
prince of Europe should dare to invade the borders of my realm.'

We need two kinds of historical knowledge in order to understand Elizabeth's full meaning: not only a knowledge of events,
but also an attunement to habits of thought and figures of speech.
At the level of events, we need to know that the Spanish and their
regent the Duke of Parma were on one (Catholic) side in the
Netherlands (which included Belgium as well as Holland), with
the English fighting in support of the Protestant freedom fighters
of the 'United Provinces' on the other.

At the more intellectual sub-stratum, we need to know that the
queen is combining two traditional ideas. First, there is the notion
that a monarch has two bodies, their own 'body natural' and the
'body politic' of the state that he or she (as if literally) embodies.
From the monarch's two bodies flows the idea of the royal 'we',
the distinctive custom of one apparent person speaking about him
or herself in the plural. Simply in terms of the progression of his
pronouns, Shakespeare's Richard II is an extraordinary study in
what happens to a king after he has abdicated one of his bodies.
From the idea of the continuity of the body politic flows the
moment of acclaim in the coronation service: 'The king is dead,
long live the king.' The considerable problems created when a new
king is proclaimed while the old king is not dead are dramatized by
Shakespeare in both *Richard II* and *Henry VI Part 3*.

Part of the brilliance of the Tilbury oration is Elizabeth's decision
to use the first person singular throughout. One would have

expected her to use the first person singular for her body natural ('I know I have the body of a weak and feeble woman'), but then to shift to the royal 'we' when referring to her body politic. But she does not use the customary 'our realm': she says 'my realm'. This is an informal, personal touch, designed to create intimacy between her and her men. When she says 'we shall shortly have a famous victory over these enemies of my God and of my kingdom', the 'my' allows the 'we' to refer to the soldiers who will fight on her behalf. She binds herself to her people by virtue of a rhetorical device.

Elizabeth's sustaining of the first person singular also allows her to combine the figure of the monarch's two bodies with a second traditional idea, that of the analogy between the body and the state. She moves seamlessly from her heart and her stomach to 'the borders of my realm', so creating a momentary image of her body as a map of England, like the frontispiece to Drayton's *Poly-olbion*.

The image of the state as a body had been used by numerous classical and neo-classical authors. Shakespeare deploys the figure for Menenius' encounter with the plebeians in the opening scene of *Coriolanus*: 'The kingly crownèd head, the vigilant eye, / The counsellor heart, the arm our soldier, / Our steed the leg, the tongue our trumpeter', and so forth. The fable of the belly is in his source, Plutarch's 'Life of Caius Martius', but the wording of the exchange also seems to echo other sources (which is exceptional in this play: of all Shakespeare's works, *Coriolanus* is the one where he stuck most closely to a single source). Scholars have accordingly proposed that he looked at, or remembered, Camden's *Remains* and an English translation of Livy's *Roman History* as well as Plutarch, but it is equally likely that he absorbed various versions of the body/state analogy by osmosis: it had taken on the force of a commonplace. That is why Elizabeth did not need to spell out her point explicitly. She expects her soldiers to understand that they are the *arms* of her realm, while she is providing them with the *heart* and the *stomach* to fight.

As a rule, Elizabeth did not rely on speech-writers. A highly educated woman, an accomplished translator of the classics, a capable lyric poet, a superb rhetorician and a witty letter-writer, she had a positively Shakespearean gift for turning language to the purpose of a moment. The Tilbury oration is stylistically consistent with other speeches of hers. It should, however, be noted that it was not published until many years after the event, so its authenticity has been called into question. Strikingly, the first edition of Heywood's play does not set the pre-Armada scene specifically at Tilbury. The queen's oration began to circulate widely in 1623, at a time of renewed anti-Spanish feeling. It was only after this that Heywood revised *If you know not me, you know nobody, part 2* and added an extra scene, specifically set at Tilbury and with additional lines for the queen. Throughout the period from the Armada to the closure of the playhouses by the Puritans in 1642, theatre played a major role in shaping the heroic image of England's warrior queen. And also of the warrior general who served her in the 1590s, the man referred to in *Henry V* as 'the general of our gracious empress': Robert Devereux, second Earl of Essex.

14. Essex Man? A Political Tragedy in Five Acts

Act one

Sir Gelly Meyrick, steward to the Earl of Essex, had a busy day on Saturday, 7 February 1601. We do not know his exact movements in the morning, though he gave a man named Bucke forty shillings, part of a former debt, for scouring and oiling muskets. About a hundred of these weapons were being prepared at Essex House, the Earl's London home, on the north side of the Thames in the legal district along what is now the Strand, centrally positioned with the court at Whitehall and Westminster to its west, the city and the Tower to the east and the Globe Theatre directly across the river.

Dinner, the main meal, was taken in the middle of the day. Sir Gelly went the short distance from Essex House to the much humbler dwelling of a friend named Gunter, who lived by the Temple Gate. His companions at table were Sir William Constable, Lord Mounteagle, Sir Christopher Blunt, Sir Charles Percy, Henry Cuffe, Edward Bushell, Ellis Jones and perhaps Sir John Davies and Sir Joscelyn Percy. It must have been a fairly early – and quick – dinner, because some time prior to two o'clock most of them were ensconced in the theatre. They had been rowed over the water to the Globe. By this time, they had been joined by Captain Thomas Lee, a key figure in the Earl of Essex's ill-fated Irish military campaign of 1599.

Between dinner and the play, Sir Gelly seems to have returned briefly to Essex House, presumably to check on business and tell his men where he could be found if required urgently in the course of the afternoon. He accordingly arrived some time after the performance had begun. 'The play', he later told his interrogators, 'was of King Harry the fourth and of the killing of King Richard the second, played by the Lord Chamberlain's players.' Performances at the theatres in Southwark, together with the jig that rounded them off, were allowed to run until five o'clock, but on a wintry February afternoon such as this it would have been dark well before then, so it is possible that the Chamberlain's Men played a shortened script.

The group dispersed after the show, some going to their homes and others to Essex House. Meyrick returned to Gunter's place for supper. Suddenly, though, in the middle of the meal, he left for Essex House, where he learned that his master had been summoned to the court – an alarming development to have occurred after dark on a Saturday. The Earl had received an official demand for his immediate attendance before the Privy Council, but also a private message warning him not to go because there was a plot to entice him to the Lord Treasurer's house, where he would be murdered. There was also a rumour that Sir Walter Ralegh and Henry Brooke, Lord Cobham, were on their way to assassinate him in his bed. Essex accordingly refused to go, even when a second summons arrived, delivered in person by Dr John Herbert, secretary to the Council. At a frenzied meeting in the withdrawing room, Essex and his followers considered their possibilities. An immediate nocturnal assault upon the court? A retreat to Wales and thence out of the country? For the Earl, running away was not an option, but he did not want to make his move without the support of the city of London. Best wait until the morning.

Through the night, his men were busy leaving messages with supporters, telling them to assemble at Essex House in the morning. As steward in charge of the household, Sir Gelly hurried between the courtyard and the gallery in a fever pitch of conferences, instructions to servants, preparation and speculation. Between one and two in the morning, his man was seen carrying a bag of pellets and a leather bag of gunpowder into the garden.

It would have been very late when Meyrick retired to his chamber, where he lay for the rest of the night with Sir John Davies, one of his master's most loyal followers, a military hard man of humble origins. A rival once described Davies as 'a shepster's son, hatched in Gutter Lane', a shepster being a woman who cuts up cloth for dressmaking. Sharing a bed was customary – it did not necessarily entail having sex. But one cannot imagine that Sir Gelly and Sir John slept much. They must have talked: about the events that had led to this sorry pass, about their expectations for the morrow. We might expect them also to have talked about the play, but there is fairly strong evidence that they did not: one member of the theatregoing party said that he thought Davies was with them, but was not sure, whereas Sir Gelly later told his interrogators that he could not remember whether or not Sir John was there, though he had said that he would attend if he could. Unless Sir Gelly was covering up for his friend, his inability to remember whether Davies attended suggests that they cannot have seen each other at the Globe and are unlikely to have debated in their bed upon the merits, or the relevance, of the performance. Having seemed for a moment to be the centre of the day, an event of great importance, the play of the killing of King Richard II drifts into seeming insignificance. This is a pattern that we will see repeated. Paradoxically, though, this fading into the background, like the invisibility of Shakespeare's name in the investigations into the events of that fateful weekend, leads us to the real interest of the story.

Essex's followers began arriving soon after daybreak. Bustle in the courtyard, spectators at the gate. At ten o'clock a small delegation arrived from court, led by the Lord Keeper of the Great Seal and the Lord Chief Justice. After some hostile exchanges in the yard, Essex led them to his study, where he left them under the protection of hard man Davies, with another of his captains guarding the door in company with three musketeers and a soldier with a caliver, matches for powder at the ready.

Once a man, even if he ranks as an earl, has taken it upon himself to detain such senior officers of state, he has no way to go but forward. Some in the yard cried 'To the court' but Essex headed east into the city in order to muster the support of the Lord Mayor and the sheriff. Between a hundred and two hundred lords, gentlemen and gallants followed behind as he headed down Fleet Street and under Ludgate. They were not fully armed: the whole adventure was unpremeditated, positively shambolic. The earl's cries that he was acting for the protection of the queen and the city, that his enemies had betrayed the country to Spain, seem to have been met with bemusement. There was no spontaneous uprising of the citizens in his support, only a light skirmish with the forces of the court at Ludgate in mid-afternoon, an ignominious retreat by water back to the stairs of Essex House, some half-hearted attempts to secure the building and destroy evidence of conspiracy. Then at dusk, surrender to a small but well-organized force under the authority of the Lord Admiral and Baron Burghley, half-brother of Essex's great adversary Robert Cecil. Over the previous weeks, Essex and his closest allies had hatched a half-baked plan to march on the court, protect the queen's person, arrest his enemies and commit them to trial. They never got near the court. Queen Elizabeth serenely continued with her Sunday routine as if nothing had happened. The rebellion was over almost before it had begun.

Arrests, investigations and interrogations began immediately. Eleven days later, Robert Devereux, second Earl of Essex, and his most senior lieutenant, Henry Wriothesley, third Earl of Southampton, were tried for high treason at Westminster and found guilty. Essex had sported a bright red waistcoat for his trial but he went to the scaffold dressed in a gown of wrought velvet, a satin suit and felt hat, all black. Southampton was reprieved and confined to the Tower.

Five others were tried for high treason at the beginning of March: Sir Christopher Blunt, Sir Charles Danvers, Sir John Davies, Sir Gelly Meyrick and Henry Cuffe. All were found guilty. The nobly descended Blunt and Danvers were given the privilege of being beheaded on Tower Hill, while Meyrick and Cuffe were hung, drawn and quartered at Tyburn. Davies 'saved his life by telling first who was in with the deepest'. Blunt, Meyrick and Cuff had seen King Richard killed in theatrical play on 7 February. Just over a month later, they were themselves killed in ritual earnest.

The case against Meyrick had three parts. First, his leading role at Essex House on the day: he had been 'captain or commander over the house', had fortified it as a place of retreat for those who had gone out into the city, and had been 'a busy, forward and noted actor in that defence and resistance, which was made against the Queen's Forces brought against it by her Majesty's Lieutenant'.

A witness had seen him up on the leads over the hall porch, with a musket laid over the wall ready to shoot towards the street gate when Burghley was approaching. Secondly, he had thrown certain gentlemen out of their lodgings near Essex House some days before, in order to accommodate divers of Essex's followers and accomplices. This was taken as evidence of his part in the pre-meditation of the rebellion. So, by implication, was his third treasonable act.

It was also proved that the afternoon before the rebellion, Meyrick with a great company of others, who were all afterwards in the action, had procured to be played before them the play of deposing King Richard the Second; neither was it casual, but a play bespoke by Meyrick, and when it was told him by one of the players that the play was old, and they should have loss in playing it, because few would come to it, there were forty shillings extraordinary given for it, and so it was played.

The first published account of the trials of Essex and his associates, written in their immediate wake by Francis Bacon, is explicit about Meyrick's purported motive in procuring the performance: 'So earnest he was to satisfy his eyes with the sight of that Tragedy, which he thought soon after his Lord should bring from the Stage to the State, but that God turned it upon their own heads.'

The case of Sir Gelly Meyrick is the first instance on record of a person being executed for commissioning the performance of a Shakespeare play. It was also a minor injustice, though one that has gone unnoticed by most commentators. Meyrick was not the man who 'procured' or 'bespoke' the revival of the old play of *Richard II*. So who did bespeak it and with what intention and why did the prosecutors – Mr Secretary Sir Robert Cecil, Attorney-General Sir Edward Coke and his junior counsel Francis Bacon – wish to pin the commission on Meyrick? Why, for that matter, did they consider something so frivolous as a stage-play worth invoking in a treason trial?

Historians sometimes find it valuable to play the game of counter-factuals, of 'what if?' What if, like Henry Bullingbrook in the play, the Earl of Essex had garnered support in the city? If he had then marched on the court and provoked a blood-bath in which the queen's person had been threatened? Because the rebellion proved so farcically ineffective, Elizabeth and her counsellors were able to show wide clemency. A handful of ringleaders were executed as an example, but most of Essex's followers got away with, at worst, brief imprisonment and a fine. Had the threat been more serious, the response would have been more draconian. The performance of the play would then have been pursued further. One can imagine the line of questioning. Were not a majority of the ringleaders present? Blunt, Meyrick, Cuffe, Davies? Did the tragedy enacted at the Globe not bear striking resemblances to a treasonous book dedicated to Essex that had already provoked extreme measures, Sir John Hayward's *History of King Henry IV*? At this point, the author of the play would surely have been interrogated. It would have been discovered that though he was now the servant of the unimpeachably loyal Lord Chamberlain, Lord Hunsdon, his printed poems had been dedicated to none other than Essex's right-hand man, the Earl of Southampton. Henry Brooke, Lord Cobham, a leading figure in the anti-Essex faction, might have chipped in with the information that this same filthy play-maker had written a so-called stage-history full of gross insult towards his revered ancestor, the Lollard martyr Sir John Oldcastle. Shakespeare had been forced to change the name to Falstaff.

A few years before Essex's act of rash rebellion, the theatres had been closed down and the playwright Ben Jonson imprisoned on the far lesser provocation of some few seditious lines in a play called *The Isle of Dogs*. Surely in this case, Cecil would have argued, the Globe must be closed, the acting company disbanded and Master Shakespeare, tarred with the Southampton brush, thrown in the Tower.

Imagine this: Shakespeare's career coming to an ignominious end in February 1601. Not only would *Measure for Measure*, *Othello*, *Lear*, *Macbeth*, *Antony and Cleopatra*, *The Tempest* and the other later plays never have been written, but John Hemings and Henry Condell would not have hung around to create a collected Folio of the plays that had been. The only survivals would have been a few quarto editions: the narrative poems, half a dozen history plays (some in garbled texts), four comedies and two tragedies. No *Hamlet* or *Twelfth Night*, no *Julius Caesar* or *As You Like It*. The whole course of English literature, indeed of western culture, would have been different.

The performance of *Richard II* at the behest of Essex's men forms a brief set-piece in every biography of Shakespeare and most accounts of theatre and politics in the Elizabethan age. But it has been persistently, damagingly, misreported. The standard account assumes that 'the strategy, it seems, was to plant the idea of a successful rebellion in the minds of the London crowd'. Thus Stephen Greenblatt in his biography *Will in the World*, repeating the view of dozens of previous commentators. 'This at least', he continues, 'is how, in the wake of the arrests, the authorities regarded the special performance, and this is how the queen herself seems to have understood it. "I am Richard II," she fumed. "Know ye not that?"' But how can the strategy of those who commissioned the performance have been to plant the idea of a successful rebellion in the minds of the London crowd when they had not themselves planned a rebellion? The trigger for Essex's march into the streets came only *after* the show, with the evening summons from the Council. Nowhere in the subsequent investigations was it explicitly claimed by Cecil and his team that this was how they regarded the performance. As for the queen's comparison of herself to Richard II, which is usually quoted together with her subsequent purported remark 'this tragedy was played forty times in open streets and houses', the authenticity of this episode seems highly suspect. Even if she really did say something of the sort, the meaning of the latter phrase has probably been misinterpreted. And it is crucial to remember that, in so far as Essex was plotting action, it was to remove from court those who had caused his downfall and exile from court following the failure of the Irish expedition, not to overthrow the queen. It was, however, the strategy of his enemies – the Cecil faction – to create the impression that he had been plotting to overthrow the queen. Before examining this bigger picture, let us go back to the bespoke performance.

Act two

It seems to have been Sir Charles Percy's idea. Towards the end of the first week of February 1601, together with his brother Sir Joscelyn Percy, Lord Monteagle and about three others, he went to find the players at the Globe. It is not known exactly which members of the acting company were present at the meeting: the surviving documentation says only 'some of the players'. But it is a reasonable assumption that several of the leading shareholders were there, perhaps those who are named as representatives of the Lord Chamberlain's Men in court documents of the period: John Hemings, Thomas Pope, Richard Cowley. Perhaps also leading actor Richard Burbage and in-house writer William Shakespeare, but that is by no means certain.

The only one of whom we can be sure is the player who doubled as company manager, Augustine Phillips. He testified that Sir Charles and his friends asked 'to have the play of the deposing and killing of King Richard the Second to be played the Saturday next, promising to get them forty shillings more than their ordinary to play it'. There are two possible senses of the word 'ordinary' here. It might mean 'forty shillings more than their normal takings'. But 'ordinary' was also the term for a fixed price for an item or a service, typically a meal at a tavern (the Elizabethan equivalent of the set menu). So it might mean 'forty shillings more than the standard fee for a command performance' – perhaps £12, instead of the £10 that was the going rate for a show at court. Phillips and his colleagues initially resisted, 'holding that play of King Richard to be so old and so long out of use as that they should have small or no company at it'. But the gentlemen were insistent and the players eventually yielded. They seem to have been given the 'forty shillings more than their ordinary' up front.

The request came on either the Thursday or the Friday, so the Lord Chamberlain's Men had a maximum of forty-eight hours in which to relearn their parts, dust off the appropriate costumes and props, and advertise the show. The repertory system was such that this was not unusual. There are other recorded instances of the players having to cope with last-minute changes in the choice of play for a performance.

The Chamberlain's Men 'play of the deposing and killing of King Richard the Second', as Phillips calls it, was by their house dramatist, William Shakespeare. Written and first performed in 1595 or 1596, it had been published in quarto format in 1597 and reprinted twice in 1598. The printed text excluded a sequence of about 160 lines in which King Richard formally hands over his throne, inverting the sacred language of the coronation ceremony and smashing a mirror. Scholars usually assume that this omission was because the scene was too politically sensitive for print, but there is no evidence of active censorship. The idea that it must have been censored is an enduring misapprehension even among some distinguished Shakespeareans. The scene appeared as a 'new addition' in the 1608 reprinting of the quarto and again, in a better-quality text, deriving from the theatre promptbook, in the 1623 Folio version of the play. Arguably, the sequence in which King Richard says 'With mine own tears I wash away my balm, / With mine own hands I give away my crown . . .', makes the play *less* subversive, turning a deposition into an abdication.

This raises the possibility, generally neglected by scholars, that Shakespeare may have written it as an addition after the real-life drama of February 1601, in order to give the impression of a formal, stately handing over of power, as opposed to the presumption and hugger-mugger of the original version that was now tarred by association with the trial of Essex and his accomplices. Nor can we wholly rule out the possibility that, to freshen up the play and as a little treat for Sir Charles Percy and his friends in return for their forty shillings above the ordinary, Shakespeare dashed off the addition on the Friday, gave it to his actors to learn overnight, allowing them to rehearse it in the morning run-through before including it in the afternoon performance. The status of the abdication sequence remains an open question, of great interest but not ultimately making any difference to our interpretation of the events of February 1601.

There was fast turnover in the highly competitive theatrical repertoire of the 1590s, save for the most successful plays that stayed in the repertoire season after season. This explains the initial reluctance of Phillips and his colleagues to revive *Richard II* for Percy and friends: as a five-year-old play, it was 'long out of use'. Shakespeare had moved on to *Henry IV Part 1*, which may have been his most commercially successful play. Then he had written *Henry IV Part 2* and *Henry V*. By early 1601, with *Julius Caesar*, *Hamlet* and *As You Like It* also completed, he was drifting away from the subject of English history. Unlike the Royal Shakespeare Company today, the Chamberlain's Men do not seem to have had the idea of reviving *Richard II* in order to play the sequence through to *Henry V* as a 'tetralogy'.

Returning now to the man with whom we began: though Sir Gelly Meyrick was executed for, among other things, procuring the play, he was not mentioned in Phillips' testimony on behalf of the actors. Under interrogation, Meyrick himself confirmed that the performance was commissioned by Percy. His tentativeness in doing so supports the view that he was not of the commissioning party: 'He cannot tell who procured that play to be played at that time except it were Sir Charles Percy, but, as he thinketh, it was Sir Charles Percy.'

So who was Sir Charles Percy? He was a younger son of Henry Percy, eighth Earl of Northumberland. His older brother, also Henry, had succeeded to the title as ninth earl in 1585 and became known as the 'wizard earl' on account of his interest in alchemy and astronomy. The family had a complicated relationship with Essex. Henry was married to Essex's sister, Dorothy Devereux, but politically close to his rival, Sir Walter Ralegh. Charles, however, was pure Essex man. He fought under the earl and was knighted by him in 1591, before Rouen, where Englishmen led by Essex had joined the Duke of Biron and Henry of Navarre in besieging the city. Sir Charles then joined the army against the rebels in Ireland, acting as colonel in command of the vanguard at the battle of the Yellow Ford on the river Blackwater in 1598. The encounter was disastrous for the English, resulting in the death of the Earl Marshal of Ireland and 1,500 of his men. To judge from his monument in Dumbleton church, Charles Percy was short and stout. But he was a fine soldier: at Blackwater, he used a skilled manoeuvre to check the enemy and protect the retreat. When Essex took over the Irish war the following year, he gave Percy command for the assault on Cahir Castle.

After the campaign collapsed, like many of Essex's most loyal followers, Percy found himself back in England, kicking his heels. It seems to have been at this time that he took a house at Dumbleton near Broadway in the heart of the Gloucestershire Cotswolds. In a surviving letter, which according to the Victorian scholar Richard Simpson was found on his person after he was arrested following the Essex rising, he complained

I am so pestered with country business, that I cannot come to London. If I stay here long, you will find me so dull that I shall be taken for Justice Silence or Justice Shallow; therefore take pity of me, and send me news from time to time, the knowledge of which, though perhaps it will not exempt me from the opinion of a Justice Shallow at London, yet will make me pass for a very sufficient gentleman in Gloucestershire.

The date of this letter is a matter for conjecture – Simpson's claim is uncorroborated and clearly Sir Charles *had* come to London early in 1601 – but it provides firm evidence of his interest in Shakespeare's history plays. The references to Justice Shallow, Justice Silence and Gloucestershire are those of a spectator (or reader) who has greatly enjoyed *Henry IV Part 2*. His pleasure in these plays is hardly surprising, given the central role they give to his own family, the Percies. A real-life soldiering Percy would have every reason to count his ancestor Harry Hotspur as his favourite dramatic character. It makes complete sense that he was the one to lead a group of Essex men to the Globe and ask for a special Shakespeare performance. We will turn in a moment to the question of why he requested *Richard II*, as opposed to one of the *Henry IV* plays, in which he would have had a more personal interest.

For his part in the Essex affair, Sir Charles spent several months in the Tower and eventually paid a fine of £500. His younger brother, Sir Joscelyn Percy, was also with the group that commissioned the play, though is not specifically mentioned as being there on the Saturday. He too marched with Essex on the Sunday and was imprisoned till the summer, then released with a fine of £500.

The third individual named by Phillips the player as being of the commissioning party was William Parker, Lord Monteagle. Raised a Catholic and not averse to the idea of a Spanish intervention in support of his co-religionists, he too had fought in Ireland. A young hothead in his mid-twenties, he was knighted by Essex at Dublin in the summer of 1599. He was adjudged to be a more significant conspirator than the Percy brothers and accordingly fined the much larger sum of £8,000. His part in the procurement of the play appears not to have been mentioned when he was examined before the Privy Council. A few years later, he executed a 180° turn in his politics: he was the man who led the authorities to go down to the vaults of parliament in November 1605, where they found Guy Fawkes and his gunpowder.

These, then, were the commissioners. Now to the particular commission: why 'the play of the deposing and killing of King Richard the Second'?

Act three

Here is an account of a historical narrative, as summarized in the summer of 1600 by Attorney General Coke. The author, it is claimed,

selected a story 200 years old, and published it last year, intending the application of it to this time, the plot being that of a King who is taxed for misgovernment, and his council for corrupt and covetous dealings for private ends; the King is censured for conferring benefits on hated favourites, the nobles become discontented, and the commons groan under continual taxation, whereupon the King is deposed, and in the end murdered.

Reading this in isolation, one would have every reason to suppose that it was a summary of Shakespeare's *Richard II*.

Except that the play was printed in 1597. 'Published it last year' is the clue that Coke is referring to a different work, Sir John Hayward's prose history, *The First Part of the Life and Reign of King Henry IV*, published to great controversy in 1599. As Coke's summary reveals, though titled *King Henry IV*, Hayward's book is really about the reign of Richard II. It covers exactly the same ground as Shakespeare's play. It is *The First Part* of the life of Henry IV, concentrating on the period when, as Henry Bullingbrook, he rose up against Richard and took the throne. The implication is that there will be a second part, continuing through Henry's actual reign. But Hayward was not given the opportunity to write that. His book was suppressed because of its association with the Earl of Essex and he was eventually thrown in the Tower. The circumstances surrounding the publication were examined in great detail during the year 1600, as Essex's enemies at court sought to build a case against him following the debacle of his Irish campaign and the dramatic breach of protocol whereby on his return he burst into Queen Elizabeth's private chamber early in the morning before she was dressed.

Lord Chief Justice Popham had some tough questions for Sir John, among them, 'What moved him to maintain, with arguments never mentioned in the history, that it might be lawful for the subject to depose the King, and to add many persuadings in allowance thereof?' and 'Might he think that this history would not be very dangerous to come amongst the common people?' Hayward was practising a new form of historical writing – or rather a revived old method, which may be traced back to the Roman historian Tacitus – whereby the chronicler's procession of events was less important than the opportunity for debate about the political theory underlying the actions of great ones. The centrepiece of his book was a pair of orations about the limits of monarchical power. Were there ever justifiable circumstances, in the interest of the state and the law, for the removal of an anointed monarch from office? As in the chronicle accounts of Richard's reign – and Shakespeare's play – the Bishop of Carlisle argues that there are not, since the king is God's sacred deputy upon earth. But Hayward also put into the mouth of the Archbishop of Canterbury a speech, for which there was no precedent in the chronicles, arguing that there might be circumstances in which men truly loyal to the state would be justified in taking action against a bad king surrounded by bad counsellors.

Hayward's intention was in no way seditious: he was interested in the academic debate, the rhetorical art of arguing first one and then the other side of the argument ('*in utramque parte*'). Francis Bacon, a prominent figure in the prosecution of Essex, recognized this. When Queen Elizabeth asked him whether he thought that Hayward was promulgating seditious ideas, he replied with a joke: 'for treason surely I found not, but for felony very many'. The queen asked him what he meant and Bacon replied that Hayward had stolen all his ideas from Tacitus. Should he be tortured on the rack for sedition? 'Nay Madam,' said Bacon, 'He is a Doctor, never rack his person, but rack his style.' An exercise in Tacitean debate, then, not a call of the people to arms against their ruler.

Taken out of context, however, Canterbury's speech had highly subversive potential. Hayward admitted that 'The stories mentioned in the Archbishop's oration, tending to prove that deposers of kings and princes have had good success, were not taken out of any other chronicle, but inserted by himself.' This probably would not have mattered if the book had remained a quasi-academic text. But Hayward and his publisher, John Wolfe, made a fatal mistake. When the manuscript was delivered to Wolfe for printing in February 1600, it had no epistle dedicatory or preface to the reader. Wolfe and Hayward agreed that it would be a neat idea to dedicate it to Essex, 'he being a martial man, and going to Ireland, and the book treating of Irish causes'. They would also have known that Essex was the most notable sponsor of Tacitean history: he had been the dedicatee of the first English translation of Tacitus, by Henry Savile (for whom he obtained the post of Provost of Eton).

Hayward was ill, so Wolfe took a copy of the book to the Earl. He called back three or four times over the next couple of weeks to see what Essex thought of it, but didn't get to speak to him, being told by his men that his lordship was too busy getting ready for his Irish expedition. Meanwhile, the book was selling exceptionally well, shifting more stock than any of Wolfe's other titles. Five or six hundred copies, half the print run of 1,000–1,200, were gone within three weeks. By that time, the wording of the dedication to Essex had come to the attention of his enemies: it was written in Latin, but translated into English it reads 'great thou art in hope, greater in the expectation of future time', a phrase easily (mis)interpreted as implying that Essex would one day be king.

Wolfe received an order from the real Archbishop of Canterbury, apparently prompted by Essex himself, to cut out the epistle dedicatory. The remaining 500–600 copies in the print run were quickly sold without it. Around Easter-time, there was more popular demand for the book, so a new edition with revisions was produced in a run of 1,500 copies. Printing was almost finished by the Whitsun holidays and Hayward prepared an apologetic epistle making clear that the book had no seditious intent. But this whole edition was taken by the wardens of the Stationers' Company to the Bishop of London, who had every copy burnt. Wolfe got fourteen days in prison as well as bearing without remuneration the heavy cost of the paper and other production expenses of both editions.

The official in the Bishop of London's licensing office who had allowed the first edition to be published was Samuel Harsnett, who would later write the *Declaration of Egregious Popish Impostures* that Shakespeare read when he was writing *King Lear*. Harsnett testified that he had been led to believe that Hayward's history was 'a mere rhetorical exornation of a part of our English history, to show the foil of the author's wit'. He approved the text before the epistle to Essex was inserted and said that he would never have allowed it had he seen that.

All this evidence from Hayward, Wolfe and Harsnett was being gathered as part of an attempt to put together a treason case against Essex in the summer of 1600. The key document in that process was a summary 'Analytical abstract of the evidence in support of the charge of treason against the Earl of Essex'. It included some incendiary claims: that one Alabaster (that is William Alabaster, poet, former chaplain to Essex, now turned Catholic) 'was sent from the Pope and King of Spain for the Earl of Essex's establishment to the Crown'. What could have been more treasonable than that? Further, the indictment claims, 'it appears that Essex was generally esteemed by the rebels in Ireland as their special friend; that secret letters and intelligences had passed between him and Tyrone, and that they had combined together that the Earl should be King of England, and Tyrone Viceroy of Ireland'.

There was no ground for either accusation, but Essex's enemies had good reason to circulate such highly damaging rumours in order to blacken his name. One wonders in passing whether the striking image of Essex and Tyrone as king and viceroy came to Shakespeare's attention. A decade later, he set *The Tempest* on an imaginary island and used the word 'plantation', which was as evocative of Ireland as it was of Virginia. In that play, a rebellion is plotted with the ambition that 'I will be king . . . and Trinculo and thyself shall be viceroys.' Stephano the drunken butler as a debased version of Essex, whose most lucrative source of income had been the Customs duties on imports of sweet wines, and Caliban 'the savage and deformed slave' as the Irishman Tyrone? A speculative fancy only.

The key accusation in the 'Analytical abstract of the evidence in support of the charge of treason against the Earl of Essex' comes after the wild claims about his league with the Pope, the King of Spain and Irish rebel leader Tyrone. Point five of the abstract concerns the publication of Hayward's *History of Henry IV*. It was to this that the examinations of Hayward, Wolfe the printer, Harsnett the licenser and others were all leading. But the accusation adds a further detail that had not been mentioned in any of the surviving depositions and confessions:

Essex's own actions confirm the intent of this treason. His permitting underhand that treasonable book of Henry IV to be printed and published; it being plainly deciphered, not only by the matter, and by the epistle itself, for what end and for whose behalf it was made, but also the Earl himself being so often present at the playing thereof, and with great applause giving countenance to it.

The accusation that Essex himself was 'so often present at the playing' of Dr Hayward's history has led some scholars to the erroneous conclusion that this controversial book might have been dramatized on the public or private stage. But the true meaning of Attorney-General Coke's claim is almost certainly that the Earl of Essex was often present at *a play that told the same story as Hayward*. The fascinating inference would then be that Robert Devereux, Earl of Essex, more than once witnessed Shakespeare's *Richard II* and made a point of loudly applauding it. He may have made himself prominent in the audience watching it at the public play-house, or he may have made a show of applause at one or more private performances.

Act four

Courtiers and gentlemen were interested in plays as the mirrors of contemporary politics. They attended the public theatres and commissioned the players to give private performances. The two leading figures in the Essex circle, the Earls of Rutland and South-ampton, were not in the audience on 7 February 1601, but they were known as frequent attenders at the public playhouses. In October 1599 they were said to be passing the time merely in going to plays every day. Shakespeare had associations with them both: he dedicated his narrative poems to Southampton and, much later, seems to have designed the motto for a tilting *impresa* for Rutland's brother, who succeeded him in the earldom.

Early in 1598, Sir Gelly Meyrick arranged an evening at Essex House for the earl and his friends. 'They had two plays, which kept them up till one o'clock after midnight.' One of the two could easily have been *Richard II*. A fortnight before, the Earl of Southampton had a play at a private feast in honour of Robert Cecil, before he left on French business. Given Essex's closeness to Southampton, he may well have been there. Given Southampton's patronage of Shakespeare, the players may well have been the Lord Chamberlain's Men. This could have been the occasion on which Cecil witnessed Essex loudly applauding a performance of *Richard II*.

What kind of plays would Essex have liked? He associated

himself with a very particular ideology. As the historian Mervyn James has shown, the Essex rising existed at a crossroads of political culture: it was the last backward-looking, aristocratic, baronial rebellion against the monarchy. The next generation would see something very different: discontent coming from the House of Commons rather than the earls, talk of the sovereignty of the law as opposed to that of the king.

In medieval times, the monarchy had strictly limited powers. The great barons, especially in the north, closely guarded their autonomy. They effectively had private armies and legal control over their domains. The so-called Tudor revolution in government was a concerted attempt to put an end to all this. Increasing central control, as much as Catholicism, provided the impulse for the rebellion of the northern earls against Queen Elizabeth in 1569, in which the Percy family was most prominent. Legal theorists and all those educators who inculcated a Ciceronian idea of civic humanism shared the new ideology of the Tudor monarchy. Private revenge, for instance, was frowned upon. In the old chivalric code, if you insulted my honour, I would throw down my gage and we would resolve our differences in hand-to-hand combat. By contrast, Attorney-General Coke and his right-hand man Francis Bacon would tell us to submit to the common law of the land and allow the queen's law courts to sort out our problem.

The ancient aristocratic families accordingly found themselves needing an alternative outlet for their sense of honour and militaristic pride. They found it in ceremonies such as the Accession Day tilts, as well as on the battlefields of the Netherlands in the 1580s and Ireland in the 1590s. Sir Philip Sidney embodied their values: author of the epic chivalric romance *Arcadia*, cut off in his prime as he rode to the rescue of a brother-officer during the battle of Zutphen, where (allegedly) he selflessly handed his water-bottle to a dying foot-soldier, telling the poor fellow that 'thy necessity is yet greater than mine'. Men of this disposition despised the new pragmatic politics of the Cecils. In the post-Sidney generation, there was no doubt as to the identity of their standard-bearer: it was Essex.

He bestrode the tiltyard and the battlefield. He gave patronage to books on war and honour. In the dedication to George Chapman's translation of Homer's *Iliad*, he is described as a modern Achilles. The poet Samuel Daniel imagined him as the man destined to lead the chivalry of all Europe in a new crusade against the infidel. Henry Cuffe, a former Oxford professor who was one of his secretaries and who was at the dinner on the day of the *Richard II* performance, dreamed in his scaffold speech of a society of 'scholars and martialists' in which 'learning and valour would have the pre-eminence'. That could have been the manifesto headline of the Essex faction.

Most provocatively of all, in spite of the queen's protests, Essex again and again used his military prerogative to confer the honour of knighthood on those who served him well in battle. This was such a powerful device for creating a chivalric 'band of brothers' that he even dubbed followers such as the earls of Southampton and Rutland, who hardly had need of the lesser rank of knight. Looking again at the list of attendees at the performance of *Richard II*, a striking fact becomes apparent. What did Sir Gelly Meyrick, the Lord Monteagle, Sir William Constable, Sir Charles Percy, Sir Joscelyn Percy and Sir John Davies have in common? All had been knighted on the battlefield by Essex.

Given that Essex and his inner circle were synonymous with this backward-looking code of chivalry, it is hardly surprising that they took pleasure in Shakespeare's great sequence of history plays concerning the pre-Tudor era. Here was the enactment of chivalry and honour in abundance, a harking back to the age when the barons were their own men. I have already suggested that Sir Charles Percy rejoiced in the sight of his ancestors Northumberland and Harry Percy, known as Hotspur, on stage. By the same account, another member of the theatregoing group was Sir Christopher Blunt, Essex's stepfather. He had been knighted on the battlefield in the Low Countries, back in the days of the Earl of Leicester's campaigns. He would have smiled to see loyal Sir Walter Blunt dying heroically on the battlefield at Shrewsbury in *Henry IV Part 1*. As for Essex himself, he claimed descent from the Earls of Hereford – Bullingbrook's title – and from Thomas of

Woodstock, Duke of Gloucester, for whose murder Richard II is held responsible in the opening scenes of the play. That murder is indeed the initial trigger for the action.

Furthermore, the play begins with a dispute going to 'chivalrous design of knightly trial'. Bullingbrook and Mowbray throw down their gages and meet in the lists at Coventry. Their man-to-man trial by lance is then interrupted by the king, who asserts his own authority by banishing them. Chivalric combat is reduced to a game, a ritual, as it was in the Accession Day tilts of Queen Elizabeth. Honour is a leitmotif throughout the play, from Mowbray's early reference to the equivalence of his honour and his life ('Mine honour is my life; both grow in one: / Take honour from me, and my life is done') to King Bullingbrook showing mercy towards the Bishop of Carlisle late in the play because 'High sparks of honour in thee have I seen.'

Again and again, Shakespeare's history plays enact the progress from the old code of honour to the new politics of pragmatic statecraft. Looked at from one point of view, the ruinous civil war that makes England bleed through the whole sequence of plays, only to be brought to an end with the marriage of red rose and white as Henry VII emerges as saviour at the end of *Richard III*, suggests that the plays fall in with the 'Tudor myth' of the emergence of a modern, unified nation. This was very much the reading of the Wars of the Roses in Shakespeare's sources, the chronicles of Halle and Holinshed. It explains why Henry VIII's servant Sir Thomas More, in his life of Richard III – reprinted in Halle, so Shakespeare's main source for that play – should have painted Henry VII's adversary as the monstrous child-killing machiavel Crookback Richard.

But looked at from another point of view, there was plenty to applaud in these plays if you were Essex or one of his men with a nostalgic taste for the martial code. There could be no more chivalric exemplar than Henry V at Agincourt. (Or could there? The killing of the French prisoners is not exactly honourable.) And then there is Talbot in *Henry VI Part 1*, fighting gallantly to take Orléans, Rouen and Bordeaux (where his son is killed). He was a sensationally successful dramatic character. Thomas Nashe described how 10,000 spectators wept to see the death of 'brave Talbot, the terror of the French': the tragedian who represented him (probably Richard Burbage) was so effective that the audience imagined they were witnessing the real Talbot lying bleeding on the battlefield 200 years before. That was in 1592. The previous summer, the Earl of Essex and his followers, as if tracing the footsteps of Talbot, had landed at Dieppe, fought at Rouen (where Essex's younger brother was killed), and then captured Gournai with the support of Marshal Biron. Ignominious retreat ensued over the winter. A relishing of Talbot's heroism in the theatre would have been one way of providing a little compensation once back home.

Shakespeare brilliantly kept both sides happy, offering a Talbot and a Hotspur for those of an Essexian disposition, but Falstaff's great deconstruction of the code of honour for those who were pragmatic Cecilites: 'Can honour set to a leg? No. Or an arm? No. Or take away the grief of a wound? No. Honour hath no skill in surgery, then? No. What is honour? A word. What is that word "honour"? Air. A trim reckoning! Who hath it? He that died o'Wednesday.' Sir Walter Blunt lying dead on the field: 'There's honour for you!'

Of all the histories, *Richard II* played best to the Essex code. The initial tiltyard business; the centrality of an Irish military campaign; Bushy, Bagot and Green as self-interested flatterers bending the ear of a vacillating and effeminate monarch in the manner of Cecil and his coterie. It all fitted like a gage. It makes complete sense that Essex would have made a point of appearing prominently in the audience at performances, whether public or private, and offering great applause.

There is evidence that he liked to use the 'conceit' of reading present affairs in the light of the past history of Richard II. What is more, his enemy Cecil knew this, from a report of Sir Walter Ralegh in 1597:

I acquainted my Lord General [Essex] with your letter to me and your kind acceptance of your entertainment; he was also wonderful merry at your conceit of Richard the 2. I hope it shall never alter, and whereof I shall be most glad of, as the true way to all our good, quiet and advancement, and most of all for her sake whose affairs shall thereby find better progression.

The allusion is cryptic, but it belongs to a phase of tentative truce between the rivals. Ralegh's implication seems to be that on this occasion Essex was willing to treat a comparison between the queen and Richard II in light-hearted fashion, and that he, Ralegh, hopes for all their sakes that it will stay that way.

But Essex could easily be perceived more seriously as a Henry Bullingbrook figure, a no-nonsense military man greeted with acclaim whenever he rode through the streets of London, as he did before heading off on his French campaign in 1591. Shakespeare may well have been aware of this identification. At the climax of *Richard II*, he describes Bullingbrook in London:

> the duke, great Bullingbrook,
> Mounted upon a hot and fiery steed
> Which his aspiring rider seemed to know,
> With slow but stately pace kept on his course,
> While all tongues cried 'God save thee, Bullingbrook!'
> You would have thought the very windows spake,
> So many greedy looks of young and old
> Through casements darted their desiring eyes
> Upon his visage, and that all the walls
> With painted imagery had said at once
> 'Jesu preserve thee! Welcome, Bullingbrook!'
> Whilst he, from one side to the other turning,
> Bareheaded, lower than his proud steed's neck,
> Bespake them thus: 'I thank you, countrymen',
> And thus still doing, thus he passed along.

There is no precedent in Shakespeare's chronicle source for this striking image of Bullingbrook's popularity. It has been invented in order to establish a contrast with the deposed Richard, who follows in after with no man crying 'God save him', and dust and rubbish being thrown out of the windows on his head. Shakespeare thus illustrates the process of the two cousins being like two buckets, one descending down a well as the other rises up. He also highlights the fickleness of the populace. At the same time, the close concentration on Bullingbrook's management of his proud horse makes a point about his strong statecraft: good horsemanship was a traditional image of effective government.

In the *Henry IV* plays, however, Shakespeare conspicuously drops the image of Bullingbrook, now king, as a popular figure. Far from showing himself among his people and exemplifying strong government, Henry IV skulks in his palace as his kingdom disintegrates around him, the penalty for his usurpation of the throne. The horseman and populist is his son Hal, who goes on to become Henry V, leading his men to triumph in battle. His return to London after the victory at Agincourt is described by the fifth act Chorus of his play in language that echoes that of the speech about his father at the corresponding moment in *Richard II*. As so often in Shakespeare, the wheel of history comes full circle. For our purposes, though, what is so interesting is that it is here, in a play performed in the summer of 1599 as Londoners waited to hear news from Ireland, that Shakespeare chose to make the boldest, most specific topical allusion in his entire work:

> But now behold,
> In the quick forge and working-house of thought,
> How London doth pour out her citizens.
> The mayor and all his brethren in best sort,
> Like to the senators of th'antique Rome,
> With the plebeians swarming at their heels,
> Go forth and fetch their conqu'ring Caesar in:
> As by a lower but by loving likelihood,
> Were now the general of our gracious empress,
> As in good time he may, from Ireland coming,
> Bringing rebellion broachèd on his sword,.
> How many would the peaceful city quit,
> To welcome him? Much more, and much more cause,
> Did they this Harry.

Shakespeare does not let go of his habitual political caution. It is a 'likelihood', not a certainty, that Essex will bring rebellion broached on his sword and it is an open question how many people will turn out to cheer him. But there is still a boldness in the comparison. When 'conquering Caesar' crossed the Rubicon and returned to Rome, there was talk of him seizing an imperial crown and Brutus and his friends had to take drastic action to save the republic. Conversely, there were moments in late-Elizabethan court politics when exasperation with the old childless queen's refusal to name an heir led some to wonder whether there might not be a future for England in some form of Roman-style republican government, with the Privy Council serving as its Senate and a strong man such as Essex in the role of consul.

Regardless of Shakespeare's semi-concealed political intentions in making the allusion – one gets the sense that he is only somewhere a little over halfway to being an Essex man – it is easy to see how the two remarkably similar passages in *Richard II* and *Henry V* could have been perceived as pro-Essex. If I am right that Bullingbrook on his noble steed being cheered through the city at the end of *Richard II* was one of the images that led Essex to give 'great applause' whenever he saw the play, it is possible that Shakespeare did influence the events of 8 February 1601.

Why did Essex turn right into the city instead of left for the court? Because he wanted people to come to their windows and cry out in his support, as they had for Bullingbrook. Subliminally, or even overtly, he was re-enacting the play in reality. But the whole thing was a shambles. It was only at dinner-time that his followers managed to rustle up a horse for him. The march began not on Bullingbrook's proud steed named 'roan Barbary', but on Shanks's pony. And sadly for Essex the good citizens of London did not live by the old chivalric code. Many of them were Puritans. They either ignored him or were busy in church. Some actively complained of his blasphemy in marching on a Sunday. He wanted to be acclaimed like Bullingbrook, but ironically the popular reaction was like that which greeted Richard: 'No man cried "God save him", / No joyful tongue gave him his welcome home.'

When Cecil and Coke's summer 1600 'Analytical Abstract of

the evidence in support of the charge of treason against the Earl of Essex' accused him of 'being so often present at the playing thereof', they meant the playing of the *story* of the rise of Bullingbrook and the deposition and murder of Richard II, not the playing of a dramatization of Hayward's book. To reiterate: if one did not know the date and context, Coke's account of Hayward's history could be taken as an account of Shakespeare's play. The play and the history narrated the same thing: the prosecution elided them.

The attempt to bring Essex to trial for treason in the summer of 1600 was not carried through. But when it was taken forward after the February 1601 rebellion, the elision remained in force in the minds of the prosecutors. Augustine Phillips the player, who knew what he was talking about, calls the show by its correct name, 'Richard the Second', his colleague Shakespeare's play. But the prosecutors, and, interestingly, the Essex men in the audience, keep calling it 'The play of King Harry IV and of the Killing of King Richard the second', consciously or unconsciously making the connection with Hayward's book. In his *Annals* of the reign of Queen Elizabeth, the contemporary historian William Camden described the exact analogy between the play and the history, which allowed Coke and Cecil to perform the elision:

Meyrick was accused that he had procured an old outworn play of the tragical deposing of King Richard the Second, to be acted upon the public stage before the conspirators, which the lawyers interpreted to be done by him as they would now behold that acted upon the stage which was the next day to be acted in deposing the Queen. *And the like censure given upon a book of the same argument*, set forth a little before by Hayward, a learned man, and dedicated to the Earl of Essex, as if it had been written as an example and incitement to the deposing of the Queen.

Neither the play nor the history was written as an incitement to the deposing of the queen, but the lawyers made them look as if they had been, because of the involvement of the Essex faction in their production, the one in 1599 and the other in 1601.

The theatre historian Leeds Barroll goes so far as to suppose the possibility that 'Shakespeare's play was thought [by Coke and his fellow-prosecutors] to be a *dramatization* of Hayward's book.' It is not necessary to assume this: as Camden discerned, it was sufficient that the two works covered the same ground. For the purposes of the prosecution case in a major treason trial, they could usefully be treated as one.

Act five

Why did Sir Charles Percy and his friends commission the special performance? They knew that something was afoot. Weapons were being prepared at Essex House, though with the emphasis on defence. On Tuesday 3 February, an inner circle of Essex men, led by Southampton, had met at Drury House. Strong-arm man Davies had produced a list of contingency plans in Essex's handwriting. The queen had to be wrested away from the earl's enemies, the Cecil faction. There were a number of options: to seize the court, the Tower or the city. Or maybe the court and the Tower simultaneously, or one and then the other. There was debate about the best strategy and the degree of violence that should or should not be used. Davies also had a list of over a hundred nobles and gentlemen, whose support could be relied upon. But there were also cautionary voices, that of Sir Ferdinando Gorges in particular. His opposition led Southampton to exclaim 'Then we shall resolve upon nothing, and it is now three months or more since we first undertook this.' The only resolution of the meeting was that each man should give his opinion in writing and leave the decision to Essex himself.

It was in this context that the Percies, Monteagle and some three others went to the Globe two or three days later. A confrontation was imminent, but nothing had been decided: a bonding exercise was needed, a steeling of the will, a visible show of solidarity. Dinner and a show for as many of the group as cared for it. The deposition of the queen was the last thing on their minds: the project was to rescue the queen from bad advisers. The notion, parroted by Shakespearean biographers and critics (including, it has to be confessed, me), that there was a conscious attempt to prepare the London public for a deposition is wildly implausible.

Why, then, *Richard II*, not any other play with a combination of politics and sword-fighting to stir the spirits? *Henry V*, for instance? The answer must be: because *Richard II* can legitimately be described as the 'signature play' of the Essex faction. A play, moreover, that had taken on extra force after Essex, like his hero and ancestor Bullingbrook, was exiled from the royal court. A trivial modern comparison for the idea of a signature play would be the tendency of modern political parties to choose a theme song for an election campaign and play it at all their rallies.

The signature play for the Essex code. A play applauded by the earl himself. Could it then have been that Sir John Hayward knew this back in 1599 and that his reason for dedicating the history to Essex was that Essex liked the play? Perhaps he and Wolfe went with their book to Essex House in February 1599 for the same reason that Sir Charles Percy and the Lord Monteagle went with their particular request for a performance to the Globe in February 1601.

Attorney-General Coke may have had even better reason than he knew for his elision of the play and the prose history. I suspect that Hayward not only made the dedication to Essex because he knew that Essex liked the play, but that he actually used the printed text of the play in the composition of the history. For a history book, Hayward's *Henry IV* is exceptionally dramatic. Much of it consists of dialogue, speeches putting forward particular viewpoints. This is a technique learned in part from the drama. The very fact that he called the book *The First Part of the Life and Reign of King Henry IV* suggests that he may have been aware of the tendency of play-makers to write two-part dramas.

In late January 1601, Coke and Cecil were again busy preparing a treason case against Essex. It would be in relation to this investigation that they would summon him to appear before the Council on the night of 7 February, sparking the next day's showdown. Hayward, who had been placed in the Tower in July 1600 and would remain there until after Elizabeth's death, was again questioned about his book. He defended his material on the

grounds that it was nearly all taken from the authoritative chronicles of Edward Halle and others. Coke pressed him on various
details that were not in the sources:

As for the words spoken by King Richard II, that princes must not rule
by limitation etc., affirms that to be a true opinion if rightly understood;
did not intend it to be taken generally, but that princes were to be
limited by the law Divine and the law of nature only; had this from a
book written three years since, but cannot remember the author.

And again:

For benevolence, he found the matter, but does not defend the word;
being asked where he found the description of the Earl [Henry Bulling-
brook], as not negligent to uncover the head, bow the body, stretch
forth the neck, arms etc., says he found in Hall and others that he was
of popular behaviour, but for the particulars, he took the liberty of the
best writers.

Clearly, then, in composing his history, Hayward collated as many
sources as he could find. Among them was 'a book written three
years since, but cannot remember the author'. So why could he
not have also consulted a book – a slender quarto playbook –
published two years since, of which he would not have known
the name of the author, since 'by William Shakespeare' does not
appear on the title page of *The Tragedy of King Richard the Second.*
*As it hath been publicly acted by the right Honourable the Lord Chamber-
lain his Servants. London: printed by Valentine Simms for Andrew Wise,
and to be sold at his shop in Paul's Churchyard at the sign of the Angel.
1597*? Since Hayward's defence was his deferral to the scholarly
authority of chronicles and precedents, he would not have admitted
under interrogation that his sources included something so vulgar
and fictive as a playbook. But if they didn't, then how do we
explain the following coincidences?

Since Shakespeare and Hayward both based their works on the
chronicles, strong parallels are to be expected. But the chronicles
make clear that 'benevolences', a particular form of taxation that

might better have been called malevolences, and that were much criticized in the 1590s, dated only from the reign of Edward IV, a century after Richard's. Hayward, however, writes of the reign of Richard II: 'Under the favourite term of benevolence, he wiped away from the people such heaps of money as were little answerable to that free and friendly name.' In Shakespeare's play Lord Willoughby, of the Percy faction, complains that 'daily new exactions are devised, / As blanks, benevolences, and I wot not what.' Shakespeare and Hayward both took their 'exactions' and 'blank charters' from Holinshed, but is it a coincidence that they both backdated the introduction of 'benevolences' to Richard's reign? In the play, Willoughby is adding to the complaint of Ross, another of the Earl of Northumberland's allies, who has just said 'The commons hath he pilled with grievous taxes.' Hayward correspondingly reports the complaint 'Great sums of money are pulled and pilled from good subjects to be thrown away among unprofitable unthrifts.' Those 'unprofitable unthrifts' are also a close echo of the play: Bullingbrook's 'upstart unthrifts', spoken with reference to Richard's cronies.

Early in the play, John of Gaunt delivers his memorable deathbed oration on how 'This England' is 'now leased out – I die pronouncing it – / Like to a tenement or pelting farm'. The king then enters and Gaunt accuses him in the same mode: 'Landlord of England art thou and not king.' There is no precedent for the metaphor of the 'landlord' in any of the chronicles, and yet Hayward, too, writes 'The profits and revenues of the crown were said to be let to farm, the King making himself Landlord of his realm.' The scene in the play is so memorable that it seems much more likely that Hayward is recalling, even quoting, it rather than that he came up with his own landlord metaphor independently.

Consider, too, the passage specifically cited in the interrogation of Hayward, concerning the way in which Bullingbrook was 'not negligent to uncover the head, bow the body, stretch forth the neck' (actually he had written 'stretch forth the hand') 'to every mean person', thus drawing 'the common multitude' to his support. This seems to be an embroidering not of the chronicles, but of Richard's lines in the play,

> Ourself and Bushy, Bagot here, and Green
> Observed his courtship to the common people.
> How he did seem to dive into their hearts
> With humble and familiar courtesy,
> With reverence he did throw away on slaves,
> Wooing poor craftsman with the craft of smiles . . .
> Off goes his bonnet to an oyster-wench.
> A brace of draymen bid God speed him well
> And had the tribute of his supple knee.

Shakespeare and Hayward deploy the exact same image of the bending of the aristocratic body towards the common multitude. This is unlikely to be a coincidence.

There is more, and this seems to me the absolute clinching evidence for the connection of Shakespeare's *Richard II* with Essex: even before the publication of Hayward's book, *this passage in the play was applied to the Earl of Essex*. Everard Guilpin's 1598 satire *Skialetheia* attacked Essex as 'great Felix', who

> passing through the street
> Veileth his cap to each one he doth meet,
> And when no broom-man that will pray for him,
> Shall have less truage than his bonnet's brim,
> Who would not think him perfect courtesy,
> Or the honeysuckle of humility?

Here the Bullingbrook comparison is used to satirize Essex, but it was also used to praise him. A slightly later anonymous poem attacking his rival Sir Walter Ralegh contrasted the latter's disdain for the common multitude with Essex's populism by again quoting the speech about Bullingbrook from *Richard II*:

> Renowned Essex, as he past the streets,
> Would veil his bonnet to an oyster-wife,
> And with a kind of humble conge [bow] greet
> The vulgar sort that did admire his life.

Other details in Hayward are also close to Shakespeare but without precedent in the chronicles: withered bay-trees as signs of the evil times, Carlisle's potent line 'What subject can give sentence on his king?' and his scornful 'My lord of Hereford here, whom you call king' (compare Hayward at the same moment: 'What subject can attempt or assist or counsel of violence against his prince and not incur the high and heinous crime of treason? . . . the Duke whom you call king'), the reaction to the usurpation of the throne that it is a particular horror in a 'Christian climate', and, most notably, Henry's disavowal of Richard's murderer, Piers of Exton.

The case for Hayward's use of Shakespeare is extremely powerful, and what is striking about it is that the details shared by them but absent from the chronicles are exactly the emphases that attracted Essex to the story and established parallels with the present: favourites perverting the monarch, unjust taxation, costly and mistaken Irish policies, Bullingbrook as a popular hero, Henry IV detaching himself from Exton and thus by implication from the actual murder of Richard. Given all this, you can hardly blame the Secretary of State and Attorney-General for regarding history and play as more or less synonymous with one another.

Cecil, addressing the Star Chamber on 13 February 1601, accused Essex of 'Making this time seem like that of Richard II, to be reframed by him as by Henry IV . . . He would have removed Her Majesty's servants, stepped into her chair, and perhaps had her treated like Richard II.' And again, in his directions for preachers throughout the land to deliver sermons on the Sunday after the uprising: from every pulpit, the people heard that in the greatest act of treason in English history the Earl of Essex, now safely confined in the Tower, had planned to set the crown of England on his own head, that he was 'plotting to become another Henry IV' and 'If he had not been prevented, there had never been a rebellion in England since Richard II more desperate or dangerous.' It is worth wondering in passing what went through Shakespeare's head as he heard that sermon (assuming that he didn't recuse himself from church that day).

Again and again, Cecil, Coke and Bacon harked back to the Hayward affair. The Shakespeare performance commissioned by

Percy played into their hands. By making the play and the history synonymous, they could link the old Hayward controversy into the events of the fateful February weekend.

It thus became necessary for them to pin the commissioning of the performance as closely as possible to Essex himself. That is why they claimed falsely that it was procured by Meyrick, Essex's own steward, who had been in charge of the weaponry and who was seen in intimate conversation with his master at various times through the weekend. For Meyrick himself, the game was up – and he could not deny that he had been at the theatre – so there was no point in reiterating in court what he had said under interrogation, namely that the play was not his but Sir Charles Percy's idea.

One of the reasons why no further summons was issued to the players may well have been that Phillips had not given the investigators the names that they wanted: if he had said that Meyrick had come to them, they could have said that the steward was acting on behalf of the master, that Essex was commissioning the performance, thus doing again what they claimed he had done with Hayward's book. But since Phillips only fingered the outer circle, they let the matter drop.

Camden saw what Coke was up to: fusing the play with the prose history. He duly noted the consequences for Hayward of the association with Essex: 'an unfortunate thing to the author, who was punished by long imprisonment for his untimely setting forth thereof'. But there was a more fortunate consequence to the elision. Had Coke summoned the author of the play, Shakespeare could have said that he had nothing to do with Hayward's seditious book – how could he have done when his play was written years before Hayward set pen to paper? The implicit linkage of the 7 February performance to the furore over the book and its dedication to Essex would have collapsed. It suited the prosecutors not to create a distinction between the book and the play. In short, Sir Charles Percy's commission for the Lord Chamberlain's Men in all probability lengthened Hayward's term in the Tower. He effectively took the rap on Shakespeare's behalf, leaving the dramatist free to write more plays. For that, much thanks.

Was Shakespeare an Essex man? *Richard II* was probably not written as an Essex play, but it was certainly read as one. Then, though, the elision with Hayward's history put the heat on to him, and Shakespeare was able to slip away into the background, his hands clean. On the very eve of Essex's execution, the Lord Chamberlain's Men were back performing a play before the queen and the court at Whitehall.

Epilogue

This story, as complicated as it is dramatic, would not be complete without its famous epilogue.

August 1601. The learned antiquary William Lambarde, Her Majesty's Keeper of the Rolls and Records within the Tower, enters the presence of the queen in her privy chamber at East Greenwich and presents her a copy of his *Pandecta Rotulorum*, a digest of rolls, bundles, membranes and parcels of historical documentation. 'You shall see that I can read,' she says. The queen then reads aloud the epistle, the title page and sixty-four pages of text, extending from the reign of King John to that of Richard III, pausing only to demand the meaning of certain Latin terms such as *oblata* and *literae clausae*.

When she falls upon the reign of Richard II, she says to Lambarde, 'I am Richard II. Know ye not that?' He gets the point: an allusion to the Earl of Essex. 'Such a wicked imagination was determined and attempted by a most unkind Gent, the most adorned creature that ever your Majesty made.' To which Her Majesty replies, 'He that will forget God will also forget his benefactors; this tragedy was played forty times in open streets and houses.' After further discussion of a painting of Richard II held by Thomas Knyvet, keeper of the royal picture gallery at Westminster, and of other antiquarian matters, the queen tucks the book into her bosom and departs for prayers with the words 'Farewell, good and honest Lambarde.' He dies a couple of weeks later.

It is a touching story and one much cited by ideologically

minded scholars of Shakespearean drama who perceive an intimate link between theatre and power politics in the period. Many commentators unquestioningly assume that Lambarde and Queen Elizabeth must have been referring to the Essex faction's commissioning of the performance of *Richard II* on the eve of his rebellion, even though that took place in a paying theatre, not an open street or house.

The trouble is, we do not know for sure that the encounter ever took place. And even if it did, there are good grounds for doubting the veracity of the dialogue. And even if the dialogue is correctly recorded, it may not have been correctly interpreted. Though most literary scholars take the story at face value, it does not have a pedigree from the period. An account of the meeting first surfaced in print in the 1780s in the antiquarian John Nichols' *Bibliotheca Topographica Britannica*. It became widely known when Nichols reprinted it in his *Progresses and Public Processions of Queen Elizabeth*.

The manuscript from which Nichols printed the story was annotated with a provenance: 'This was given me by Mr Thomas Godfrey 20 November 1650. He married Mr Lambard daughter or grandchild. Richard Berwick brought it.' And on the back there was a note signed by Thomas Lambard of Sevenoaks, an eighteenth-century descendant of the Elizabethan antiquary: 'Queen Eliza: and Mr Lambard. Given me by Sir Thos: T[w]ysden who found it amongst his grandfathers Sir Roger's papers, with Sir Roger's remarks. Mr Tho: Godfrey married ye daughter of Wm Lambard.'

At first sight, this is encouraging. Though out of the family for about a hundred years after 1650, the original manuscript is traced back to Lambarde's son-in-law. Thomas Godfrey, a sewer of the chamber of King James I, did indeed marry Margaret, Lambarde's only daughter by his second marriage, in 1609. She died two years later, but he survived until 1664, so there is no reason to doubt that in 1650, via a servant or friend named Richard Berwick, he passed it to his fellow Kentish gentleman, Sir Roger Twysden, who annotated it with the note at the end and kept it among his papers, where it was found by his grandson, who returned it to the Lambarde family. The original manuscript is lost, but the family connections seem sufficient to rule out the possibility of complete

fabrication in the eighteenth century. Queen Elizabeth *was* at
Greenwich on 4 August 1601 and, according to Lambarde's monument, now in Sevenoaks parish church, he was indeed the cus-
todian of the rolls and records in the Tower. Everything seems to
be in order.

But who recorded the conversation, and when? It is not written
in the first person. Or, to be exact, it moves suspiciously from the
third-person form to a single first-person usage towards the end.
No one claims that the original was in Lambarde's hand. He was
complaining of failing eyesight by 1587 and wrote his will in 1597.
His correspondence dries up well before 1603, though there is one
late letter dictated to an amanuensis. He died just two weeks after
the date attached to the meeting. So we cannot be at all confident
that he was the author. Godfrey is recorded as the original owner
of the manuscript, so he is a candidate for its authorship, but he
did not marry Margaret Lambarde until 1609. Perhaps he was
writing up a brief note of Lambarde's or even recording an oral
memory of his wife's. By the time of his marriage into the family,
the note or the memory would have been at least eight years old.
Furthermore, it belonged to a moment when Margaret was fifteen
and her father on his deathbed. At this point, the precision and the
technical detail in the account begin to raise suspicion. The queen
recites aloud precisely sixty-four pages of Lambarde's book. She
asks the definition of terms such as *rotulus cambii* and inquires as to
the legality of *rediseisnes*. Is this the sort of thing to have stuck in
the memory of a teenage girl for eight years or more, or to have
been meticulously recorded by a dying man who by this time
relied on an amanuensis to write his letters?

There is an obvious way of checking up on all these details. Get
down Lambarde's *Pandecta Rotulorum* and find the technical terms.
Make sure that the records from the beginning of the reign of
King John to the end of that of Richard III do run to exactly
sixty-four pages. The trouble is, despite the presence of the title
Pandecta Rotulorum (with the date 1600) on Lambarde's monument
and among lists of his works in an array of bibliographies and
biographies published after Nichols, there isn't a copy in the British
Library. There isn't a copy in any of the libraries whose holdings

are recorded in the comprehensive *Short Title Catalogue* of early English printed books. There is no record of anyone ever having read or seen a copy. We have to assume therefore that it was not a printed but a manuscript book, a unique presentation copy, complete with epistle and title page. But if the queen left the interview clutching the volume to her bosom, surely she would have kept it carefully and it would have turned up in a depository or catalogue of royally owned manuscripts? The closest we can get to the *Pandecta Rotolurum*, if it ever existed, is a manuscript copy that covers its ground, written on watermarked paper dating from the reign of King George II, well over a century after the event.

And what of Sir Roger Twysden's role in all this? He was an antiquarian, perfectly capable of describing or even inventing a volume along the lines of *Pandecta Rotulorum* and of bandying around all those Latin terms and references to 'the Rolls *Romae, Vascon, Aquitaniae, Franciae, Scotiae, Walliae et Hiberniae*'. What is more, he was an ardent royalist, a leading contributor to the Kentish petition in 1642, as a result of which he was imprisoned by parliament and then forced to sequester himself in the country. The date 1650, when he received the manuscript and appended 'remarks' to it, thus takes on considerable significance: the document suddenly seems to belong to a different historical moment. A deposed and murdered king. A rebellion. A royal tragedy played out in the open street. In 1650, this surely has more to do with a comparison between Richard II and Charles I, Henry Bullingbrook and Oliver Cromwell, than the connection between Shakespeare's play, the Earl of Essex and Queen Elizabeth. A combination of nostalgia for the 'golden age' of the queen and abhorrence at the wickedness of Cromwell and his crew could easily have led Twysden to embroider and reshape a much more rudimentary manuscript account.

So many details just do not ring true. The queen was a highly accomplished Latinist. Would she really have asked Lambarde the meaning of such easy words as 'oblata' and 'literae clausae'? Have said to him, like a proud child, 'You shall see that I can read'? Have taken the time to read sixty-four pages of antiquarian *arcana* out loud?

There is a further problem. The note on the back of the original (lost) manuscript was purportedly signed T. L., for Thomas Lambard. The reprint of the account of the interview in *Progresses and Public Processions of Queen Elizabeth* is reported as having been 'Communicated from the original by Thomas Lambard, of Sevenoaks, Esquire.' But Thomas died in 1770. It was actually his son Multon Lambard who passed the family papers to Nichols. There are so many intervening agencies between William Lambarde and the printed account – his daughter Margaret, his son-in-law Godfrey, Richard Berwick who 'brought it' to Sir Roger Twysden, Sir Roger himself and his grandson Sir Thomas Twysden, then Thomas Lambard, Multon Lambard and finally John Nichols – that we cannot say with confidence that the queen really compared herself to Richard II on this occasion and said that 'this tragedy was played forty times in open streets and houses'.

Besides, even if she did, there is no particular reason to link 'this tragedy' to Shakespeare's play. The normal usage of the word 'tragedy' in the period – not least in the dialogue in Shakespeare's own plays – was in reference to dire and lamentable events in general, not stage-plays in particular. 'He that will forget God will also forget his benefactors,' Elizabeth says, 'this tragedy was played forty times in open streets and houses.' Could this not mean, even with Essex in mind: 'Ingratitude and disloyalty are sins against both God and benefactors, but such wickedness is common enough, played out every day in both private homes and the public arena?' It seems to me that she is more likely to be talking about the fickleness of everyday life – court life especially, given the Essex connection – than alluding to some otherwise unrecorded series of forty or more extra-theatrical performances of Shakespeare or Hayward.

But, as was seen with the cross-currents between *The Famous Victories of Henry V*, the reports of the queen's speech at Tilbury, Shakespeare's *Henry V* and Heywood's dramatization of the queen's speech at Tilbury, the language of the theatre did mingle with that of the court. Ingratitude to benefactors was a common theme of both.

It happens that there are a couple of much earlier occasions on which Elizabeth glancingly compared herself to Richard II. And the Essex/Bullingbrook connection has been coming at us from all sides. The queen would have been intimately acquainted with the final legal proceedings against her former favourite. She had discussed the Hayward book with Bacon. So if we do decide to trust the Lambarde account, then it may well be that Queen Elizabeth interpreted the events of the fateful weekend as I interpret them: could the 'tragedy' played in the 'open street' have been a reference to Essex's march through the city on Sunday 8 February 1601? And could it have been made with the implication that Essex was engaged in a piece of real-life street theatre? That he was self-consciously acting out Bullingbrook's ride into London on his hot and fiery steed in the play? The opening Chorus of *Henry V* asks the audience to let the players work upon their 'imaginary forces': the force of *Richard II*'s influence on what Lambarde called the 'wicked imagination' of Essex – and we should add Sir Charles Percy and company to that – did perhaps after all translate theatrical fiction into political life, spill over 'from the Stage to the State'.

15. The Clash of Civilizations

The Moorish ambassador

In the summer of 1600, as Cecil and Coke attempted to gather evidence to bring the Earl of Essex to trial for high treason, a group of exotic strangers appeared on the streets of London. Muley Hamet was King of Barbary, a vast domain in northern Africa, covering modern-day Morocco and beyond. He dreamed of

1600: Abdulguahid (Abd-el-Oahed ben Massaood), aged 42, ambassador of the King of Barbary, in England

reoccupying Spain, from where, following the fall of Granada in 1492, his Moorish people had been expelled after centuries of coexistence with the Christians. He sent an ambassador, with a party of sixteen men, to Queen Elizabeth for exploratory talks on the possibility of forming an alliance whereby Spain would be conquered by the combined forces of the English navy and African troops. The diplomatic party landed at Dover early in August 1600 and was escorted by water to Gravesend.

A few days later, they had their first audience with the queen at Nonsuch. The interview was conducted in Spanish, with Lewis Lewkenor serving as interpreter. At the end of the meeting, the Barbary interpreter had some additional private words with Queen Elizabeth in Italian. Further meetings followed in September. There was talk of an encounter in Aleppo and of an alliance to seize both the East and West Indies from the Spaniards, dividing the spoils. But nothing definite was concluded, and the delegation planned to depart at the end of October. Then there was a delay because of the sudden death (from natural causes) of 'the eldest of them, which was a kind of priest or prophet'. So the strangers were still in London to witness the triumphal festivities on the anniversary of the queen's coronation on 17 November. A special viewing enclosure was built for them in Whitehall. It is not known when they finally departed. Muley Hamet wrote to tell Elizabeth of their safe return on 27 February 1601, the month of the Essex affair. Since the sea voyage would have taken six or seven weeks, they probably left in mid-January, which means that they would have been present during the Christmas festivities at court when the Lord Chamberlain's Men played before the queen.

Whether or not the Barbary delegation witnessed a Shakespeare play, they formed such a spectacle in London that Shakespeare would have known of their presence and, in all probability, seen them in the flesh. John Stow wrote of the interest – and hostility – that they aroused during the 'six months' space' of their stay in London. He objected to their refusal to give alms to the English poor and noted their custom of killing all their own meat in their house and turning to the east when they killed anything. The ambassador himself, Abd-el-Oahed ben Massaood, sat – or rather stood – for his portrait. The very image of a noble Moor, berobed and wearing a magnificent sword: as many critics have recognized, the figure of ben Massaood must have been in the hinterland of Shakespeare's imagining of Othello a few years later. An ambassador in London transformed into a general in Venice.

The Mediterranean theatre

The twentieth-century French historian Fernand Braudel writes in his sweeping study of *The Mediterranean and the Mediterranean World in the Age of Philip II*:

What a marvellous geopolitical map one could draw of the western half of the Mediterranean between the middle of the fifteenth and the middle of the sixteenth century, with arrows showing the old and new directions of Spanish imperialism, the positions it seized and exploited in order to gain control of the western sea . . . The Ionian Sea, the 'Sea of Crete', was by contrast the Ottoman sea . . . These two different Mediterraneans were vehicles, one almost might say they were responsible for the twin empires . . . Politics merely followed the outline of an underlying reality. These two Mediterraneans, commanded by warring rulers, were physically, economically and culturally different from each other. Each was a separate historical zone.

William Shakespeare lived on a small island of minor international influence far to the north of the great geopolitical theatre where the Cold – and sometimes Hot – War of his age was played out between two rival superpowers, sometimes on land but mostly at sea.

Politically, the Mediterranean was divided at its narrow midpoint between Sicily and Tunis: the western half is the Spanish sea, the eastern half the Ottoman. The northern shore of the western half, from Cadiz to Naples to Messina, was under the influence of Spain. The southern shore, from Alcazar to Algiers to Tunis, was a place of uncertainty, ruled by a wild mix of client regimes and wayward corsairs. A successful privateer could make his fortune there; a captured one could lose not just his life but his immortal soul. A Spanish dispatch in the year of Shakespeare's birth announced that it was raining Christians in Algiers.

Sixteenth-century navigational technique was a matter of hugging the shorelines. 'More precisely, according to the galley accounts of a Ragusan vessel, it was a matter of buying one's butter at Villefranche, vinegar at Nice, oil and bacon at Toulon. Or, as a Portuguese chronicler puts it, travelling from one seaside inn to another, dining in one and supping in the next.' On the rare occasions when ships ventured beyond the sight of land, it was to follow one of a handful of time-honoured routes: from Spain to Italy by the Balearics and the south of Sardinia, which was often called 'sailing by the islands'; from Sicily to Tunis; from Rhodes to Alexandria; or from the straits of Messina or Malta to Aleppo in Syria via the coasts of Crete and Cyprus. The islands were the essential pressure points. As Cuba and the Philippines were of inestimable strategic importance in a later era of superpower rivalry, so in this one much depended on control of Sicily, of Cyprus, of Rhodes.

Shakespeare was more aware of this fact than we have sometimes given him credit for. I suspect that he was interested in islands because they constitute a special enclosed space within the larger environment of geopolitics, perhaps a little like the enclosed space of the theatre within the larger environment of the city. An island is an experimental place where opposing forces are brought together in dramatic confrontation.

As in so many facets of the drama, Christopher Marlowe established the model. High Elizabethan tragedy was born with Tamburlaine's westward sweep from Scythia through Persia to the Ottoman empire and beyond. Part One of Marlowe's *Tamburlaine the Great* turns the old medieval 'fall of princes' motif on its head, offering a fantasy of a nobody from the distant East overthrowing the mighty Turkish Bajazeth. Part Two begins with a bewildering ethnic mix as King Sigismund brings from Christendom 'his camp of stout Hungarians, / Slavonians, Almains, Rutters, Muffs, and Danes', while the opposing Ottomans muster 'revolted Grecians, Albanese, / Sicilians, Jews, Arabians, Turks, and Moors, / Natolians,

Sorians, black Egyptians, / Illyrians, Thracians, and Bithynians'. The Ottoman army defeats first the Christians and then Tamburlaine's third force drawn from 'Afric's frontier towns', the Barbary lands of Morocco, Fez and Algiers. The two-part drama charts the rise and fall of the atheistic Tamburlaine, the fall and re-rise of the Ottoman empire. It is Mohammed, not the Christian God, who finally strikes down Tamburlaine. Marlowe recognizes that in the eastern Mediterranean and all along the Afric shore, the Christians constitute a weak, embattled and marginal minority.

Tamburlaine was a land play. It name-checked the whole of known Asia and Africa, but ignored the islands of the Mediterranean. Marlowe filled that gap in *The Jew of Malta*. Recognizing that *Tamburlaine*'s dramatic weakness was its episodic structure, the inevitable consequence of the Scythian shepherd's long-distance marches, he invented a story that focused the contest between Christianity and Islam on a single pressure point, the island of Malta. As befitted a writer who had a second career as a spy, he turned his gaze from invasion to subversion. The third force in the gap between Christianity and Islam is no longer the Scythian outsider but rather the alien within: the combination of Jew (Barabas) and hybrid Muslim. The hybrid is Barabas' villainous sidekick Ithamore, whose name suggests 'Moor', yet who is described as a 'Turk' and, since a specific point is made of his having been born in 'Thrace', may have originated as a Christian child abducted from the Balkans and forcibly converted to Islam. To complicate matters still further, his name seems to derive from the Jewish 'Ithamar', one of the sons of Aaron in the Bible.

This allusion explains the joke whereby Shakespeare gave the name Aaron to the Moor in his *Titus Andronicus*, whose relish in his own villainy is clearly influenced by that of Ithamore. The character is, so to speak, 'son of Ithamore', so Shakespeare wittily calls him after Ithamar's father!

To the Elizabethans, the name Malta would instantly have suggested the Knights of St John, defenders of Christian pilgrims against the Muslim. Jew and Malta would therefore have been perceived as an oxymoronic pairing. The play may reveal the Christian Friars as avaricious lustful hypocrites, but it is hardly a surprise that the Jew is represented as a double-crosser who betrays the island. *The Jew of Malta* fulfilled the expectation set up by its title. It was an enormously popular and influential play. An audience-member going along to a new play called *The Moor of Venice* would therefore have had a similar expectation: that this Moor too will be a Barabas or Aaron, a barbarian who puts Venice in peril.

Othello and the Ottomites

Othello is a drama rich in allusion to the southern shoreline of the Mediterranean: a maid called Barbary, the Arabian tree, an encounter in Aleppo once. And yet the play's source, Giovanni Battista Giraldi Cinthio's story in his Boccaccio-like collection of tales *Gli Hecatommithi*, concerning a Venetian lady, a Moorish Captain and his Ensign, is very unspecific in its atmosphere. The narrative is confined entirely to plotting and dialogue. There is no realization of historical setting beyond the broad context that all the stories in the collection are narrated by a group of aristocrats who have escaped to Marseilles from the war, famine and plague attendant upon the sack of Rome in 1527. It was Shakespeare who gave the story local texture – Venetian, Cypriot and Moorish – perhaps courtesy of such recently published books as Lewis Lewkenor's 1599 translation of Contarini's *The Commonwealth and Government of Venice*, John Pory's 1600 translation of *A Geographical History of Africa* by 'Leo Africanus', and Richard Knolles' 1603 *General History of the Turks*. We have already met Lewkenor in his capacity as interpreter in the negotiations with the Moorish ambassador. Pory's book was published during Abd-el-Oahed ben Massaood's time in London; its preface alludes to his presence and was dated to the very day of that coronation anniversary triumph watched by the Moors from their 'special place' in Whitehall.

In Cinthio's story of the Moor and the lady, the Venetian lords merely decide to change the guard in Cyprus, choosing the Moor as commandant of the new group of soldiers sent there. Disdemona insists on going with him and they arrive safely in Cyprus. There is no storm and there are no Turks. Whereas Cinthio's story was set, and indeed written, before the Turkish assault on Cyprus, Shakespeare updates the narrative and offers an invented variation on more recent history. The Turkish context is his most far-reaching addition to Cinthio. The representation of Cyprus as an island embattled in the Ottoman sea was surely inspired by Marlowe's treatment of Malta.

'Valiant Othello, we must straight employ you / Against the general enemy Ottoman,' says the Duke of Venice. The audience hears a consonance, heightened by the rhetorical device of *epana-lepsis*, the echoing of a sound at the beginning and the end of a sentence, between the names of the captain-general 'Othello' and the general enemy 'Ottoman'. This would have been especially apparent if, as is likely, the original pronunciation of the hero's name was Otello. Othman was the founder of the Turkish empire. Ottoman-ness is thus suggested by Othello's name, but he is turned against the origin implied by that name.

To Shakespeare and his contemporaries, Turk, Arab and Moor all represented the Islamic 'other', but they were not necessarily homogenized into a single image of generic 'barbarianism'. Arabic culture was frequently associated with learning and civilization, in contrast to the prevailing images of Turk and Saracen. A Barbar could be 'brave' rather than 'barbarous': George Peele's *Battle of Alcazar in Barbary*, a play based on real recent historical events, has both 'a barbarous Moor, / The negro Muly Hamet' and a 'brave Barbarian Lord Muly Molocco'. A Moor could help you out in your war against the Turk – or, for that matter, the Spaniard. How you judged the Islamic 'other' depended not only on ideological stereotype but also on the particularities of diplomatic liaison and changing allegiance in a world of superpower rivalry. At the end of *Alcazar*, the evil Moor Muly Mahamet is defeated (just before the end we see him on the battlefield crying 'A horse, a horse, villain a horse' – this in a play written well before *Richard III*). The throne of Barbary goes to Abdelmelec's virtuous brother, who is also called Muly Mahamet and who was the real historical figure whose ambassador Abd-el-Oahed ben Massaood visited the Elizabethan court in 1600.

Peele's play mingles historical matter with a more general sense of the barbarian, the other, the devilish – bad Muly Mahamet surrounds himself with devilish and underworld associations. Audiences would have come to *Moor of Venice* with the expectation of something similar, but witnessed a remarkable inversion in that here it is a sophisticated Venetian who is associated with the devil and damnable actions.

The primary usage of the term 'Moor' in early modern English was as a religious, not a racial, identification: Moor meant 'Mohamedan', that is to say Muslim. The word was frequently used as a general term for 'not one of us', non-Christian. To the play's original audience, one of the most striking things about the figure of Othello would have been that he is a committed Christian. The 'ground' of the play is laid out in the first scene, when Iago trumpets his own military virtues, in contrast to Cassio's 'theoretical' knowledge of the art of war (Cassio comes from Florence, home of such *theorists* of war as Machiavelli):

> And I – of whom his eyes had seen the proof
> At Rhodes, at Cyprus and on others' grounds
> Christened and heathen.

These lines give an immediate sense of confrontation between Christian and heathen dominions, with Rhodes and Cyprus as pressure points. Startlingly, though, the Moor is fighting for the Christians, not the heathen.

Again, consider Othello's response to the drunken brawl in Cyprus:

> Are we turned Turks, and to ourselves do that
> Which heaven hath forbid the Ottomites?
> For Christian shame, put by this barbarous brawl.

Such Christian language in the mouth of a Moor, a Muslim, is inherently a paradox. It suggests that Othello would have been assumed to be a convert. The 'baptism' that Iago says he will cause Othello to renounce would have taken place not at birth but at conversion. The action of the play re-converts Othello from Christianity, through the machinations of Iago. In this sense, it is fitting that Iago appeals to a 'Divinity of hell' and that Othello acknowledges at the end of the play that he himself is bound for damnation.

The notion of conversion was crucial in the Elizabethan perception of the relationship between European Christianity and the Ottoman empire. The phrase to 'turn Turk' entered the common lexicon. And the 'renegade' became a dramatic type. In *The Tragedy of Solyman and Perseda* (1588, probably by Thomas Kyd), a character called Basilisco turns Turk because the Turks, unlike the Christians, recognize his value and excellence as a soldier. There is a hit here at the poor pay of English soldiers, but Basilisco is also mocked as a braggart knight. Fun is had at his expense over the lopping of a collop of his flesh when he turns Turk, that is to say when he is circumcised.

Islam was as powerful an alien force to Europeans in the sixteenth century as Communism was to Americans in the twentieth. To turn Turk was to go over to the other side. It could happen in a number of different ways: some travellers converted by a process of cultural assimilation, others who had been captured and enslaved did so in the belief that they would then be released. It is easy to forget how many English privateers became Ottoman slaves – on one occasion, 2,000 wives petitioned King James and Parliament for help in ransoming their husbands from Muslim captivity.

If Shakespeare read all the way through Knolles' *General History of the Turks* he would have learned that once every three years the Turks levied a tax on the Christians living in the Balkans: it took the form of 10,000–12,000 children. They were deported and converted (circumcised), then trained up to become soldiers. They formed a highly feared cadre in the Turkish army known as the janizaries – there is an elite guard of them in *The Battle of Alcazar*, while Bajazeth's army in *Tamburlaine* combines 'circumcisèd Turks / And warlike bands of Christians renegade'. Othello is a janizary in reverse, not a Christian turned Muslim fighting against Christians, but a Muslim turned Christian fighting against Muslims. Although Lewkenor reports that the captain-general of the

Venetian army was always a 'stranger', historically speaking, conversion in Othello's direction, from Muslim to Christian, was much rarer than the opposite turn.

The second Elizabethan sense of the word 'Moor' was specifically racial and geographical: it referred to a native or inhabitant of Mauretania, a region of North Africa corresponding to parts of present-day Morocco and Algeria. This association is invoked when Iago falsely tells Roderigo towards the end of the play that Othello 'goes into Mauretania, and takes away with him the fair Desdemona'. Ethnic Moors were members of a Muslim people of mixed Berber and Arab descent. In the eighth century they had conquered Spain. It may be in memory of this that Othello's second weapon is a sword of Spain.

Given that the Spanish empire was England's great enemy, there would have been a certain ambivalence about the Moors – they may have overthrown Christianity, but at least it was Spanish Catholic Christianity. Philip II's worst fear was an uprising of the remaining Moors in Granada synchronized with a Turkish invasion, just as Elizabeth I's worst fear was an uprising of the Irish synchronized with a Spanish invasion. As it was, the Turks took a different turn: in 1570, shortly after the end of the Morisco uprising and Philip's ethnic cleansing of Granada, they attacked Cyprus.

The alliance of European Christians against the Ottomans was uneasy because of the post-Reformation disintegration of Europe itself. The battles between the Protestant north of Europe and the Catholic south were more prolonged, direct and intense than those between the Christian western Mediterranean and the Islamic eastern half. Independent lesser powers such as Venice and England found themselves negotiating for footholds in the Mediterranean theatre. Hence the diplomatic manoeuvring that brought the Barbary ambassadors to London – and hence also the blow to Venice caused by the loss of Cyprus in 1571.

In the travel book *Purchas his Pilgrimage*, Algiers is referred to as 'the whip of the Christian World, the wall of the Barbarian, terror of Europe, the bridle of both Hesperias (Italy and Spain), scourge of the Islands'. North Africa – where Othello and Caliban are conceived – is a demonic 'alien' territory. But at the same time, the Turks and their satellite states were vital trading partners for the English. Algiers had a golden age of commercial prosperity around the turn of the century, while at the other end of the sea Aleppo was a key trading-post on the silk route to China.

In *Othello*, it is not the Turk but Iago who 'turns' Othello back to barbarity. If we want to read the play for a contemporary political 'message', the newly anointed King's Men might be saying to the new king, 'It's not the stranger, the alien power, the Turk, who is now the threat – they have been defeated, as you reminded us in your poem on the battle of Lepanto – no, the danger is the cunning, self-serving politicker, the enemy within.' One might even go so far as to identify that enemy with Catholicism and Spanish sympathy. Why does the Venetian Iago have a Spanish name, reminiscent of St Iago of Compostella, who was known as Matamoros, the Moor killer?

Should we consider it part of the hinterland of the play that in the late sixteenth century there was a fair bit of snuggling up between the English and the Turks because their common enemy was Catholic Spain? In the 1580s we find Elizabeth's diplomats in Istanbul pointing out that English Protestantism shared with Islam a rejection of that veneration of idolatrous images which characterized Spanish and papal power. The queen actually sent some fragments of broken images to the Sultan as a token of her good intent.

There is deep irony in Iago's 'Nay, it is true, or else I am a Turk', for it *is* Iago who does the Turkish work of destroying the Christian community. All three major characters invert audience expectation: Othello is a counter-janizary, Desdemona is – contrary to ethnic stereotyping – a Venetian lady who is not lascivious, and Christian Iago is a functional Turk.

This said, the play is unlikely to have been intended as a direct intervention into contemporary diplomatic manoeuvring in the way that Pory's translation of Leo Africanus was in 1600 and Knolles' *History of the Turks*, with its dedication to King James, was in 1603. Shakespeare's plays use history but they subsume geopolitics into interpersonal encounters. They are not overtly polemical: they present questions and debates, not propaganda and positions. That is why they are so amenable to reinflection in new cultural circumstances.

There is, however, good evidence that Shakespeare became acquainted with Knolles' *History of the Turks* shortly before writing *Othello*. One link seems decisive: where did Shakespeare get the business in act one scene three about the uncertainty as to whether the Turks are heading for Rhodes or for Cyprus? It is most likely to have been from a passage in Knolles that describes the events of April 1571. The previous year Selimus Emperor of the Turks had made plans to invade Cyprus. He gave a commission to one Piall Bassa, a base-born Hungarian who had 'turn[ed] Turk and giv[en] himself to arms'. Piall fought against the Christians and was raised to high rank. He was sent by Selimus to keep the Venetians from sending reinforcements for their garrison in Cyprus. He departed from Constantinople and, says Knolles, cut through Propontis and Hellespont (a juxtaposition of names that might have stuck in Shakespeare's mind – remember the Pontic sea which keeps due on to the Propontic and the Hellespont). But Piall then heard that there was plague at Venice, so the Venetians would be unlikely to launch a counter-offensive in the short term. He therefore diverted and attacked the island of Tenos in the Cyclades, which had been in Venetian possession. Piall desisted when his superior general, Mustapha, summoned him to Rhodes with the intention of joining their two armies together and sailing against Cyprus. Compare this twist to the history with the Messenger's announcement in the play that the Turks,

> Steering with due course toward the Isle of Rhodes
> Have there injointed them with an after fleet . . .
> Of thirty sail, and now they do restem
> Their backward course, bearing with frank appearance
> Their purposes toward Cyprus.

Even more specifically, Knolles tells of how one Angelus Sorianus was sent with his galley to meet the Venetian ambassador who bore the Turkish ultimatum demanding possession of Cyprus: this is surely the source of the messenger from the galleys saying 'So was I bid report here to the state / By Signor Angelo.'

Knolles has been accepted as a source for Othello by most scholars for some time, but the significance of Piall Bassa the renegade has been neglected. A Christian Hungarian who turned Turk and led the attack on Venetian-controlled Cyprus: I suspect that it was the story of Piall that furnished Shakespeare with the idea of giving depth and historical specificity to Cinthio's tale of the Venetian Moor sent to defend Cyprus. Like Piall, Othello has risen from an obscure background to become a great general and in so doing changed his religion. But he is a reverse renegade.

There is another suggestive passage in Knolles. How come the Venetians were in control of Cyprus in the first place? In the early fifteenth century it had been an independent kingdom, but in 1523 the throne passed to one King John, who lacked courage and gave himself to pleasure – Knolles writes that 'according to the manner of his effeminate education, [he] showed himself in all things more like a woman than a man'. His wife took over the running of Cyprus while he devoted himself to vain pleasures. The wife was in turn ruled by the counsel of her nurse. And the nurse was ruled by her daughter. 'So that the people commonly said the daughter ruled the nurse, the nurse the queen and the queen the king.' The result of this was a disordered kingdom, usurpation, civil war, and an eventual league that brought in the Venetians to restore order. They paid off the Egyptians, who had a longstanding claim upon the island, and ruled it peaceably for over a century. But Selimus I conquered Egypt and in 1570 Selimus II, reviving the Egyptian claim, but now on behalf of the Ottoman empire, attacked Cyprus, taking the capital Nicosia and – the following year, through the fleet of Mustapha and Piall Bassa – the fortified port of Famagusta.

Shakespeare changes history. He sees off the Turk and implies instead that the real danger to the isle comes from the internal collapse of civil society. The story of how the Cypriots originally lost control of their own island due to emasculation serves as a model for this. Think of Othello's harsh reaction to Cassio's drunkenness, the idea that having been saved from the Turks the Venetians are now destroying themselves and 'fright[ing] the isle /

From her propriety'. Think, too, of how central it is to Iago's scheme that he should persuade Cassio that Othello is ruled by his wife – that Desdemona has become our captain's captain in the manner of old King John of Cyprus' wife (though, fortunately, she is not ruled by her nurse). Venice regarded Cyprus as a key Christian outpost against the Turk, but what happens in the play is that it is 'heathenized' from within rather than without.

Montano, the governor of Cyprus, is an interesting figure in this respect. Despite his name, he seems to be a Cypriot, not a Venetian regent. He is addressed as one of the 'men of Cyprus' and later as a 'gallant of Cyprus'. His welcome of Othello and the Venetians is thus like the old history of Venice helping to restore order after the reign of the effeminate King John. But the falling-out between Cassio and Montano becomes symbolic of Venice losing Cyprus. The divine intervention of the storm means that the island is not lost to the Turk, but destabilized through internal division. 'For even out of that will I cause these of Cyprus to mutiny,' says Iago: Cyprus being an occupied state, the danger of mutiny within and of civil war is greater than the threat from without.

A lesson for early Jacobean Ireland perhaps? Like the imaginary Turkish fleet in the play, the real Spanish armadas that had made for Ireland in 1596 and 1597 were dispersed by storms – but this did not make life any easier for the occupying English military garrison. Shakespeare was a typical post-Armada Englishman: as he had shown in his history plays, the true threat to the polity was rebellion rather than invasion.

Othello dies on a kiss, an embrace of black and white, perhaps a symbolic reconciliation of the virtues of west and east, Europe and orient. But the public image by which he wants to be remembered in the letter back to Venice is of confrontation between Christian and Turk, with himself as the defender of Christianity in Aleppo, that point of eastern extremity in Syria. In smiting himself, he recognizes that he has now become the Turk. By killing Desdemona he has renounced his Christian civility and damned himself. He symbolically takes back upon himself the insignia of Islam – turban, circumcision – that he had renounced when he turned

Christian. He has beaten a Venetian wife and traduced the state. He has been turned Turk. Not, however, by the general Ottoman but by the super-subtle Venetian, the 'honest' Iago.

16. Shakespeare and Jacobean Geopolitics

The Bohemian connection

Robert Greene's popular romance *Pandosto* told the story of a King of Bohemia who mistakenly believed that his wife was pregnant by his old friend the King of Sicilia. Shakespeare's most celebrated alteration of this story when he dramatized it into *The Winter's Tale* was the resurrection of the wronged queen, but his most puzzling change to his source was the inversion of the kingdoms. The jealous fit falls upon Sicilia instead of Bohemia.

The winter weather in Prague is somewhat colder than that in Palermo. Would it not therefore have been better to follow the original by locating the chilly court of Leontes in snowy middle Europe and the summer shepherding in sunny Sicily, which was, besides, the reputed birthplace of Theocritus, father of the pastoral genre? If Hermione is to be made the daughter of the emperor of Russia, would it not – from both a geographical and a dynastic point of view – have been more plausible to marry her to the king of nearby Bohemia rather than that of a distant Mediterranean island?

Various explanations have been proffered. Perhaps Shakespeare made the reversal so that Perdita would become a daughter of Sicily, thus furthering her resemblance to Proserpina, her mythic prototype and fellow transformer of winter to spring. Or perhaps it was because 'Sicily was well known for crimes of jealousy and revenge, while Bohemia with its fabled sea-coast was currently a frequent centre for romantic adventure.' The play's best editor, Stephen Orgel, argues that the location of the shipwreck and Antigonus' death on the coast of Bohemia, which was in reality landlocked, as opposed to Sicilia, which is in reality an island, should be regarded, like the title of the play, as something that purposefully 'removes the action from the world of literal geographical space as it is removed from historical time'.

These explanations are genre-dependent. They grow from a perception of the play as romance, myth, pastoral, tale. They ask us to detach Bohemia and Sicilia from their counterparts in the real world of early modern European geopolitics. Similar explanations would not have been forthcoming if Shakespeare had swapped England and Scotland in a history play. But are we to suppose that Shakespearean romance is wholly divorced from history and geopolitics? *The Tempest* is very interested in statecraft and dynastic liaison, while *Cymbeline* is one of Shakespeare's two extended meditations on what political historians call the British Question. *The Winter's Tale* opens, in the exchange between Camillo and Archidamus, with the language of courtiership, not that of fairy. Even to invoke that latter word is to be given an instant reminder by way of the title of Edmund Spenser's vast nationalistic romance, *The Faerie Queene*, that for the Elizabethans the poesy of romance and pastoral could also be a powerful medium for the exploration of courtiership and the expression of royal compliment.

Shakespeare wrote all his later plays in the knowledge that the King's Men were required to give more command performances at court than any other theatre company. Would he not have paused for a moment to consider the diplomatic resonances of such names as Bohemia and Sicilia in *The Winter's Tale*, Milan and Naples in *The Tempest*? After all, he knew from his run-in with the descendants of Sir John Oldcastle a decade earlier that to attach the wrong associations to a particular name could easily offend. However removed from historical reality the action may be, to invoke the kingdoms of Bohemia and Sicilia, especially in front of court audiences that might include visiting diplomats, would inevitably create a penumbra of geopolitical associations.

In the time of Shakespeare's father, the difference between the two realms in terms of political association would have been nugatory. As Holy Roman Emperor, Charles V ruled the greater part of Europe, including both Sicily and Bohemia. But Shakespeare himself lived after the division of the House of Habsburg into distinct Spanish and Austrian branches. In his time, the two kingdoms fell under separate spheres of influence. Sicilia – or more exactly the kingdom of the two Sicilies, one consisting of the island

and the other of southern Italy (otherwise known as the kingdom of Naples) – was at the heart of the Mediterranean empire of Philip II of Spain, while Bohemia (the western two-thirds of what is now the Czech Republic) became the core of the Holy Roman Empire. When Rudolf II became emperor in 1576, he moved the seat of his government from Vienna to Prague. In Shakespeare's time, the title King of Sicilia belonged to Spain, while the King of Bohemia was the senior secular elector of the Habsburg empery.

The other crucial difference was religious: Sicily was Catholic, whereas for 200 years the Bohemians had been divided from Rome – the Hussite rising of 1419–20 was in effect the first Reformation in Europe. In the words of Rudolf II's modern biographer, 'If to be Protestant is to be anti-papal, anti-clerical, and fiercely fundamentalist on matters of morality, then the majority of Czechs became Protestants *avant la lettre.*'

Fictional and fanciful as *The Winter's Tale* may be, the fact is that when the play was written the King of Sicilia was Philip III of Spain and the King of Bohemia was the Emperor Rudolf II. There were strong links between the courts of James in London and Rudolf in Prague. Rudolf's court was famously hospitable to English intellectuals, ranging from John Dee the magician to the young woman who became one of the most famous poets in all Europe, Elizabeth Jane Weston. There were also striking resemblances between the two monarchs, especially their interest in magic and their desire for European peacemaking through interdenominational match-making. These two preoccupations were closely related: Rudolf's obsession with alchemy, natural magic and Rosicrucianism was not some eccentric aberration of his melancholy personality, but rather – as was also the case with the magical interests of King James – a way to a deeper religious vision and unity beyond the confessional divisions that racked his empire. Magic and royal match-making were also, of course, distinctly late Shakespearean subjects.

Conversely, despite the Catholicism of James's queen and the king's various attempts to match his children to clients of Spain, the residual English hostility to all things Spanish, dating back to the Armada and beyond, had not gone away. In these circumstances, it seems eminently plausible that on deciding to dramatize a story about the kings of Sicilia and Bohemia, and knowing that the play would at some point go into the court repertoire, Shakespeare thought it would be politic to make the monarch with Spanish as opposed to Rudolfine associations the one who is irrational, cruel and blasphemous. I am not proposing that Leontes is in any sense a representation of Philip or Polixenes of Rudolf, but rather that tact was required in the invocation of the names of European kingdoms.

Shakespeare's tact towards Bohemia, a synecdoche for the Austro-Germanic Habsburg territories, was indeed such that *The Winter's Tale* could be played at court without embarrassment during the 1612–13 festivities in celebration of the wedding of King James's daughter Elizabeth to the Habsburg princeling Frederick the Elector Palatine – who, as it happens, would later become King of Bohemia.

Stephen Orgel's admirable Oxford edition of *The Winter's Tale* touches on the Bohemian connection, but says nothing about the status of Sicily in Shakespeare's time. There is, however, firm evidence that Shakespeare knew it was controlled by Spain. The principal source for his other Sicilian play, *Much Ado about Nothing*, is a story in Matteo Bandello set at the precise moment when Spain assumed power over Sicily. Shakespeare substitutes an army for Bandello's navy, but the Messina of Don Pedro is manifestly in Spanish hands.

Whether or not geopolitical sensitivity lay behind Shakespeare's transposition of Sicilia and Bohemia, *The Winter's Tale* can still be thought of as a play that works on a north–south axis, as opposed to the east–west one of *Othello*. The weird temporal syncretism of the play enacts the early modern rebirth of classical civilization: Apollo thunders and Ovid's Pygmalion is reborn as Giulio Romano; the setting moves between the temple of the Delphic oracle on a balmy Greek island, a very English-seeming sheep-shearing feast, and a private chapel reached via a picture-gallery and housing a Madonna-like statue. The essential geographical structure, meanwhile, is an opposition between a hot-blooded, court-dominated – hence Catholic? – south and a more relaxed, temperate north in which ordinary people (shepherd and clown) have a voice, as they do in the Protestant world where the Bible is available in the vernacular.

The Algerian Tempest

About a hundred and fifty years after the house of Aragon seized Sicily, Alfonso V took the kingdom of Naples. Both Sicily and the southern half of Italy were under Spanish control throughout the sixteenth and seventeenth centuries. The Spanish crown also held considerable territories in the northern half of Italy, including the garrison city of Milan. Which brings us back to *The Tempest*. We tend to think of Milan in that play as an autonomous dukedom and of Naples as a sovereign kingdom. In so far as we think about it at all, we assume that the dynastic liaison established by the marriage of Miranda and Ferdinand represents some kind of north–south unification of Italian statelets intended to counterbalance the papal power of Rome. In the imaginary afterlife of the play's plot, Ferdinand, son of Alonso, will one day be both King of Naples and Duke of Milan. In the historical reality of early modern Italy, both Milan and Naples were under the dominion of the Spanish crown.

Editors of *The Tempest* have noted how profoundly the name Ferdinand – perhaps also Alonso, if we hear in it an echo of Alfonso – was associated with Spanish dominion over Naples. Alfonso V, the first Iberian King of Naples, was succeeded by his illegitimate son Ferdinand, who struggled to maintain his kingdom against Turkish inroads, baronial revolts and Venetian hostilities. He was succeeded by his son, another Alfonso, who after a brief and unpopular reign made a Prospero-like retreat: he 'renounced his state unto his son Ferdinand . . . and sailed into Sicily, where he gave himself to study, solitariness and religion'. This Ferdinand lost Naples to the French, withdrew to Sicily, recovered Naples with the assistance of the Spaniards and the Venetians, then died suddenly, bringing the line of the illegitimate Ferdinand to an end, after which the kingdom of Naples was ruled by the Spanish crown through a viceroy. It has been suggested that Shakespeare knew

William Thomas's *History of Italy*, where this sequence of four generations of Alfonsos and Ferdinands is outlined, but regardless of the question of specific sources, the names carry the aura of Spanish power.

William Warner in *Albion's England* refers casually to 'The free-*Italian* States, of which the *Spaniards* part have won: / As *Naples*, Milan, royal That, and Duchy This'. Our thinking about the play in relation to imperialism receives a jolt from the idea that Milan was a colonized city-state and the kingdom of Naples a dominion of Spain. To a Jacobean audience – especially a court audience in the historical and diplomatic know – Prospero is more likely to have been regarded as the victim of intrigue which had Spanish villainy somewhere behind it than as any sort of imperial adventurer. Perhaps we should think of him as a displaced Marshal Pétain rather than a prototypical Cecil Rhodes. But then again perhaps we should think of him as neither, for what is striking about *The Tempest* is its pointed absence of allusion to Spanish matter, its lack of referential anchorage. This is not the Spanish Italy of *Much Ado about Nothing*.

The Tempest begins on a ship bound from Tunis to Naples. The exchange in act two about Carthage and 'widow Dido' has led critics to read this voyage in relation to Virgil's *Aeneid* and the legendary foundation of Rome. The characters' reflection on the legacy of Rome has a similar effect to that of the imaginary alliance between Milan and Naples: it makes the audience think about nation and *imperium* in Italian terms. But the reality of sixteenth- and early seventeenth-century Tunis was that it was a flashpoint between Spain and the Ottomans. Just as he is quiet about Spanish Naples and Milan, so Shakespeare is intriguingly silent about the allegiance of Claribel's 'African' husband. We are not told where in historical time the marriage should be imagined. When Tunis was a Spanish puppet state? When it was under the autonomous control of Euldj Ali the corsair King of Algiers? Or after Ali had enlisted the support of the Turks?

Similarly with Algiers. The supposed coupling of Sycorax and the devil suggests that Caliban is the product of some form of miscegenation, of hybrid union. Around the time *The Tempest* was written, Algiers had what Braudel calls 'a fabric of many colours'. It housed some 20,000 prisoners, about half of them Christian (Portuguese, Flemish, English, Scottish, Hungarian, Danish, Irish, Slav, French, Spanish and Italian), the other half 'heretic and idolaters' (Syrians, Egyptians, Japanese, Chinese, Ethiopians, inhabitants of New Spain) – 'and every nation of course provided its crop of renegades'. Samuel Purchas reckoned that there were 200,000 Christians resident in Algiers, most of them renegades. But instead of making Caliban the product of some specific union between a Christian and a Muslim, Shakespeare suggests various more abstract kinds of hybrid encounter, between the human and the devilish, the human and the animal, the land and the sea ('A strange fish!'). This process of abstraction from the particularities of Mediterranean setting that had characterized *Othello* has been crucial to the afterlife of the play, allowing it to be transposed to numerous new worlds.

In *The Tempest* Shakespeare is careful to remove precise references to historical time and geographic place. Most obviously, he does not name or locate the island. The dialogue about Tunis and Carthage draws pointed attention to the dangers of making historical equations, of arguing by the sort of parallelisms beloved of Plutarch and Fluellen:

GONZALO: This Tunis, sir, was Carthage.

ADRIAN: Carthage?

GONZALO: I assure you, Carthage.

ANTONIO: His word is more than the miraculous harp.

SEBASTIAN: He hath raised the wall and houses too.

ANTONIO: What impossible matter will he make easy next?

SEBASTIAN: I think he will carry this island home in his pocket, and give it his son for an apple.

ANTONIO: And, sowing the kernels of it in the sea, bring forth more islands.

Gonzalo is wrong. Tunis is not on the exact site of Carthage. Neither physically nor politically is the modern city a replication of the ancient one. To suppose that ancient history can be brought back to life, Antonio implies, is like imagining it is possible to outdo the music of Amphion's harp, which magically rebuilt the walls of Thebes.

Similarly, the realities of the island do not conform to the 'Golden Age' image conjured up by Gonzalo. It follows that we must be wary of parallelisms that propose *The Tempest* as a modern *Aeneid* and the island as an allegory of either Mediterranean or new world empires. At the same time, the very placelessness of the island – its U-topian quality – encourages the spectator to pick it up like Gonzalo's apple and scatter the seeds so that other islands – Caribbean, Irish and so forth – grow magically from it.

The art of *The Tempest* makes impossible matter easy. By veiling the real history of the sixteenth-century Mediterranean, Shakespeare takes his play out of contemporaneous geopolitics and gives it the potential to live in later history. There was really no such thing as an English empire – beyond Ireland – during Shakespeare's lifetime. The great continental shift of geopolitics from the Mediterranean to the Atlantic was in its earliest infancy. The evacuation of historical specificity from *The Tempest* is a conjuring trick that creates the illusion that Shakespeare prophesied the subsequent history of British imperialism. This made possible the manner in which the play was most frequently read in the post-Vietnam, post-colonial portion of the twentieth-century Cold War.

Othello is located on the east–west frontier between Christianity and Islam, with Othello himself functioning as the *tertium quid* that veers between the world's two dominant religions. *The Winter's Tale* plays off the Catholic south and the Protestant north. *The Tempest* returns to Marlowe's strategy in *The Jew of Malta* of compressing all the world on to the stage of a single island. But with a difference. Shakespeare *could* have grounded his play in the Balearics, made Caliban a renegade, Prospero an exile from Spanish power, Stephano and Trinculo English privateers. He did not. He replaced Malta with a darkened version of Utopia, rendering the island a pure conceptual space – or rather a purely theatrical space, for it is here that our sense of the resemblance between an island and a theatre is strongest. The play thus becomes readable as a drama of north, south, east and west.

FIFTH AGE

Justice

And then the justice,
In fair round belly with good capon lined,
With eyes severe and beard of formal cut,
Full of wise saws and modern instances.
And so he plays his part.

A wooden trencher of about 1600, showing 'The Lawyer', one of a set
illustrating some of the different ages and professions of man

17. At Clement's Inn

Most biographies of Shakespeare will tell you that he disappears from view for a seven-year period between the christening of his twins Hamnet and Judith in February 1585 and the first definite allusion to him in the London theatre world, Robert Greene's 'Shake-scene' jibe, in autumn 1592. These so-called 'lost years' have been the subject of reams of speculation: was Will a schoolmaster in the country or a tutor in a recusant household in Lancashire? Did he fight in the Dutch wars or travel to Italy? Might he have trained as a 'noverint', a lawyer's clerk, which was how his fellow-dramatist Thomas Kyd started out? Or did he simply help out with the family business in Stratford, then leave to seek his fortune in London some time around 1587, either of his own volition or to escape prosecution for poaching from Sir Thomas Lucy's deer park at Charlecote?

All of the theories rely on hearsay and circumstantial evidence. They go in and out of favour among scholars: the purported Lancashire connection was popular in the 1930s and the 1990s, but discredited in the early twenty-first century, while the poaching theory – which has a long pedigree, but was derided in the twentieth century because Lucy did not have a deer-park at Charlecote – came back into favour in the early twenty-first century when it was noted that Charlecote did have a warren, where there would have been rabbits, hare, pheasant and roe deer.

Schoolmasters like the 'Shakespeare was a schoolmaster' theory. It has good provenance, going back to the son of one of his fellow-actors, so he may well have been one, though probably in the midlands or the Welsh borders rather than Lancashire. But the plays' deep knowledge of the ways of schoolmasters and the practices of the Elizabethan classroom could perfectly well have been derived from his experience as a pupil.

Lawyers like the 'Shakespeare was a lawyer' theory. A plausible circumstantial case can indeed be constructed, but the plays' deep knowledge of lawyers and the practices of the Elizabethan court-room could perfectly well have been derived from his experience as a litigant.

The one thing we can say for sure about the 'lost years' is that all the biographers and scholars who say that Shakespeare disappears from the archival record between 1585 and 1592 are wrong. In Michaelmas term 1588, the name of William Shakespeare of Strat-ford appears in a complainant bill drawn up in preparation for a case that was brought before the Queen's Bench at Westminster a year later on 9 October 1589. On two occasions in this document William, son of John Shakespeare, is named as a party to the suit. The case might just be the missing link between Shakespeare and London.

The origins of Justice Shallow

SHALLOW: Come on, come on, come on. Give me your hand, sir; give me your hand, sir. An early stirrer, by the rood! And how doth my good cousin Silence?

SILENCE: Good morrow, good cousin Shallow.

SHALLOW: And how doth my cousin, your bedfellow? And your fairest daughter and mine, my goddaughter Ellen?

SILENCE: Alas, a black ouzel, cousin Shallow!

SHALLOW: By yea and nay, sir. I dare say my cousin William is become a good scholar: he is at Oxford still, is he not?

SILENCE: Indeed, sir, to my cost.

SHALLOW: He must then to the Inns of Court shortly. I was once of Clement's Inn, where I think they will talk of mad Shallow yet.

SILENCE: You were called 'lusty Shallow' then, cousin.

SHALLOW: I was called anything, and I would have done anything indeed too, and roundly too. There was I, and little John Doit of Staffordshire, and black George Bare, and Francis Pickbone, and Will Squele, a Cotswold man. You had not four such swinge-bucklers in all the Inns of Court again. And I may say to you, we knew where the bona-robas were and had the best of them all at commandment.

Then was Jack Falstaff, now Sir John, a boy, and page to Thomas
Mowbray, Duke of Norfolk.

SILENCE: This Sir John, cousin, that comes hither anon about soldiers?

SHALLOW: The same Sir John, the very same. I saw him break Scoggin's
head at the court-gate, when he was a crack not thus high. And the
very same day did I fight with one Sampson Stockfish, a fruiterer,
behind Gray's Inn. O, the mad days that I have spent! And to see
how many of mine old acquaintance are dead!

Some of Shakespeare's plays rely on a very small number of large
parts and others are ensemble pieces where several parts are equally
large. So, for instance, *Henry IV Part 1* is very much a three-hander.
Two-thirds of the dialogue is spoken by just three characters:
Falstaff, Hal and Hotspur. Only seven characters speak more than
about forty lines. In *Henry IV Part 2*, on the other hand, nineteen
characters speak more than forty lines and that trio of Falstaff, Hal
and Hotspur is replaced by a much larger spread of major roles.
Dramatically, we feel the loss of Hotspur, but what the difference
highlights is the fact that whereas *Part 1* focuses on the code of
honour and the development of Prince Hal's military and chivalric
virtues, *Part 2* concentrates much more on the civic virtues and
accordingly offers a wider panorama of society, including rural
society. The next two biggest parts after Falstaff and the royal
family are Justice Shallow and the Lord Chief Justice: a local
representative of justice and the head of the legal system. It is the
local man who has the slightly larger part.

The Lord Chief Justice in Shakespeare's time presided over the
Courts of Common Law, namely the Queen's Bench, the Court
of Common Pleas and the Exchequer. There was a division within
the law, and often an unseemly turf war, between the jurisdictions of the Lord Chief Justice and the so-called Court of Equity
under the Lord Chancellor. Indeed, the two courts sat on the
opposite sides of Westminster Hall. Sir John Popham, who was
the Lord Chief Justice at the time of the play, was famous for a
riotous youth. There were even stories that he had been stolen
by gypsies or become a highwayman, rumours suggestive of the
archetype of the prodigal son, which was also of course the pattern

for the story of the life of Prince Hal and his development into Henry V.

In *Henry IV Part 2*, Shakespeare reveals his deep interest in the conjunction of the local and the national. Early in the play Mistress Quickly brings an action for debt against Falstaff. She happens to bump into the Lord Chief Justice in the street and he sets about resolving it. The notion of a small claim in the debtor's court reaching the Lord Chief Justice is deliberately ludicrous: the point of the encounter between two characters from such different social strata is to yoke together the big people and the little, implicitly binding the people of England under one law.

Shallow and Silence, the Justices of the Peace in the Gloucestershire scenes, are embodiments of the process whereby the Tudor regime sought to unify the administration of the nation through a network of local officials. Among the grounds for the grant of arms to John Shakespeare, which made Will Shakespeare a gentleman, was his status as Justice of the Peace and Bailiff, Queen's Officer and Chief of the town of Stratford-upon-Avon. When the herald Sir William Dethick objected to the granting of the coat of arms to the Shakespeare family on the grounds that people such as 'Shakespeare the player' were not gentlemen, the reply came again that the man John Shakespeare was a magistrate in Stratford-upon-Avon, a Justice of the Peace.

Though much reinforced in the Tudor era, the office of Justice of the Peace went back to the twelfth-century reign of Richard the Lionheart. Justices of the Peace were typically men of good standing in the community who did not necessarily have an advanced legal training themselves. Among their main powers was the right to bind unruly persons over to 'keep the peace' (be of good behaviour), a fate that befell Shakespeare in a dispute with one Francis Langley regarding the rent on a theatre. They also regulated the use of weapons, supervised the poor law and kept the muster role, which is to say took the count of healthy men who, if required, could be enlisted for military service – this is the circumstance that brings Justice Shallow and Justice Silence into the action of *Henry IV Part 2*.

A feel for the life of a provincial Justice of the Peace is to be found in the diary of William Lambarde, whom we last met in the aftermath of the Essex rebellion. Here he is on his first day in office as a JP in his native Kent: 'I have been put in commission of the peace and likewise that day I assisted the Justices of the three divisions of the lathe of Aylesford in taking their musters at Malling, Tonbridge and Borough Green.' Lambarde quickly found that he had to spend a lot of time controlling the alehouses, 'I sent Thomas Chambers, William Coisin and Thomas Norham of Tonbridge to the gaol for keeping alehouses obstinately and against the commandment of sundry justices which had put them down.' It was his duty to deal with any potential for violence in the local community, but there were also times when his jurisdiction overlapped with that of the church courts. Towards the end of his first year in office Lambarde noted,

I took order for the punishment of Joan Pitchford of Seal, widow, and Alice Hylles from the same town, for the bearing of two bastards, and for the punishment of Thomas Byrd of the said town, turner, and Thomas Pigeon, late of the same town, turner, the reputed fathers of the said bastards, and according to that order the said Thomas and Alice were set in a cart at Sevenoaks the next day and the said Joan scourged at the same cart's tail there; as for Pigeon he was fled long before.

It is a world of petty officialdom of this kind that is conjured up in the figures of Shallow and Silence, mildly corrupt officials who are all too often over-sentimentalized on the stage.

There is a very old tradition of scholars trying to identify Justice Shallow with particular people known to Shakespeare. Could he have been based on Thomas Lucy, the local gentleman and magistrate who supposedly ran Shakespeare out of town because of his poaching? The argument is based on the presence of lines about 'lucies' in a coat of arms discussed in the first sequence of dialogue involving Shallow at the very beginning of *The Merry Wives of Windsor*. Another candidate is William Gardiner, an ill-tempered Surrey Justice of the Peace who was involved in that court action when Shakespeare was bound over to keep the peace. But Shakespeare was not the sort of writer to base stage characters specifically on real individuals whom he knew. He was more of an Autolycus, a snapper-up of trifles of personality traits from hither and yon. There may be bits of Lucy and Gardiner in these Justices, but, if so, there could equally well be others too.

The family lawyer

'I was once of Clement's Inn,' says Justice Shallow in that opening exchange with his visiting kinsman. And again, when he is with Falstaff, talking about Jane Nightwork:

SHALLOW: Nay, she must be old. She cannot choose but be old, certain she's old, and had Robin Nightwork by old Nightwork before I came to Clement's Inn.
SILENCE: That's fifty-five years ago.

This is the sequence that ends with Falstaff's celebrated line 'We have heard the chimes at midnight, Master Shallow.' But the phrase that interests me in this context is 'before I came to Clement's Inn'. Which church chimes were heard at midnight? Surely those of St Clement Danes on the Strand, famous for its bells and located close by the royal courts of justice.

Modern spectators might assume that Clements Inn is some kind of pub or hostelry. It is not, after all, one of the four famous Inns of Court – Lincoln's Inn, Gray's Inn (where there was a riotous performance of *Comedy of Errors* in 1594), the Inner Temple and the Middle Temple (where there was a famous staging of *Twelfth Night* in 1602). Clements was in fact one of the Inns of Chancery, which are much less known, much less studied, than the Inns of Court.

They seem to have taken their name because they were the original bodies that served the needs of clerks in chancery in the Lord Chancellor's office, from which all writs had to be obtained. Gradually through the fifteenth and sixteenth centuries they became places where solicitors and attorneys would do their training. Basic legal instruction would have been provided by lawyers from the Inns of Court. Each of the Chancery Inns had a loose association with one of the main Inns – they were like feeder schools, although it was perfectly possible for a chancery man to go on to a different Inn of Court from the one with which his school had its main association. By the end of the sixteenth century, a pattern was emerging whereby that division which still exists in English law between barristers (who plead in the higher courts) and solicitors (who are the client's first port of call) was enshrined through the distinction between the Inns of Court and those of Chancery, to which attorneys were confined.

Throughout the civic scenes of *Henry IV Part 2* there is a very strong sense of contemporaneity. The setting may be medieval but the reality is Elizabethan. The taking of the muster roll and the pomposity of the Justices would have been wholly familiar to Shakespeare and his audience. If we are being literalistic, the chimes at midnight scene, which takes place very shortly before the death of King Henry IV, must have occurred early in 1413. Justice Shallow says that he trained at Clement's Inn fifty-five years earlier. That would make 1358 – a time at which the Inns of Chancery had not even come into being. Clearly, it is a contemporary world being imagined here, in which Shallow is a Justice of the Peace in the late 1590s, having studied at Clement's Inn back in the 1540s.

Shakespeare was the only dramatist, indeed the only literary author, of the period ever to give a name check to Clement's Inn. So how did he know about it? Those Gloucestershire scenes in *Henry IV Part 2* have an unprecedented density of specification, so why was this particular Chancery Inn evoked in order to give specificity to Justice Shallow's legal training?

The answer takes us to the case of *Shakespeare* v. *Lambert* in the middle of the not-so-lost years. Joan Arden, the older sister of Mary Arden, Shakespeare's mother, had married an Edmund Lambert of Barton on the Heath, that village to the south of Stratford which is alluded to in the induction to *The Taming of the Shrew*. Joan and Edmund Lambert were probably godparents to Shakespeare's sister and brother, Joan and Edmund, suggesting a close bond. Unfortunately, though, relations between the Shakespeares and the Lamberts went into decline with John Shakespeare's finances.

When he ran into difficulties with his creditors in the late 1570s, he tried to raise fresh capital by mortgaging to the Lamberts a property called Asbies owned by Mary Arden in Wilmcote. A complicated dispute ensued regarding the mortgage's redemption, dragging on over many years.

On 26 September 1587 Edmund Lambert's son John agreed to pay the Shakespeares £20 in return for an absolute title to the Wilmcote estate. William Shakespeare, as heir, was named in this agreement. But it was only a verbal arrangement and the money was not paid. The following summer, John Shakespeare repeatedly went before the Stratford Court of Record (the small claims court) to recover money from another of his debtors, but without success. Needing money, on 1 September 1588, he went to John Lambert at Barton on the Heath and again said that in return for £20 he and his wife and son would relinquish their claim on Asbies. John Lambert refused, so, since the matter related to a large-scale property transaction beyond the purview of the local Court of Record, the Shakespeares took the case to the national court in London. According to a complainant's bill filed before the Queen's Bench at Westminster in Michaelmas Term 1588, 'Johannes Shakespeare et Maria uxor eius, simulcum Willielmo Shakespeare filio suo' – 'the said John Shakespeare and Mary his wife, together with William Shakespeare their son' – had always been ready both to confirm John Lambert's possession of the aforesaid premises and to deliver to the same John Lambert all writings and evidences concerning the said premises. All they wanted was some money in return for the assignment of the property – they now asked for £30 and damages.

In the first paragraph of the bill of complaint, we learn that John and Mary Shakespeare and their son William acted 'per Johannem Harborne, attornatus suum': through John Harborne their attorney. Harborne came from the little town of Knowle, not far from Stratford. As one often finds in the small world of Elizabethan professional and familial relations, a network of connections can quickly be established. There were Shakespeares at Knowle and ancestors of John Shakespeare at nearby Wroxall. Harbornes can be found in the Gild of the Holy Cross in Stratford just as Ardens and Shakespeares are to be found in the Gild at Knowle. Harborne was well placed to be employed by the Shakespeares as one of their attorneys.

In the Minutes of the 'parliament' of the Middle Temple for the year 1571 we find an admission record for 'John Horbourne, late of Clements Inn, son of Thomas Horbourne of Knoll, Warwickshire, in place of Balthazar Copleye, Under Butler, at the request of the Treasurers'. Over the following years, Harborne rose through the ranks of the Middle Temple butlers. He became chief waiter, at which time his servant was promoted to Puny Butler in recognition of 'his long and painful service in the Buttery'. It was not uncommon for chief butlers to become fellows of the Inns and to make the transition from service into actual legal activity. By 1588 Harborne was in possession of chambers in the Temple. As chief butler, he had considerable administrative duties. We find, for example, an entry 'Ordered, that the Butler who keeps the book of moots shall enter the names and case of such as shall moot in term times at New Inn, as other names and cases are entered of such as moot in the House and at the Inns of Chancery in reading times.' Harborne's form of upward mobility was akin to Shakespeare's own: the post as a junior butler enabled him to move from the Inns of Chancery up to the Inns of Court and, having gained a foothold there, he worked his way up to become a very successful lawyer and eventually a wealthy man. He bought a house in St Clement Danes and his son, who followed him into the Middle Temple, ended up purchasing a large estate called Tachley in Oxfordshire and marrying the niece of an earl: a fine instance of the social mobility that was possible in early seventeenth-century England.

In 1600 Harborne sponsored the admission to Middle Temple of Rowley Ward, a man from the village of Barford near Stratford, whose other sponsors included Thomas Greene of Stratford, a man who called Shakespeare cousin and who went on to become Master of the Bench and eventually Treasurer of the Middle Temple (and, before that, Town Clerk of Stratford and Shakespeare's lodger at New Place). By 1609, however, John Harborne was in arrears with his dues. He was ordered to pay on pain of forfeiting his chambers.

Harborne acted for the Shakespeare family in the case that was heard in 1588–89. The procedure would have been for him and the opposing attorney to take the case before the Queen's Bench at Westminster. The matter would have been sent to the county assizes at Warwick, where witnesses could be examined. The verdict would have been reported back to the court at Westminster for judgment. But what Hamlet calls 'the law's delay' was by no means uncommon. The initial recitation of the case was for some reason postponed for a whole year until Michaelmas Term 1589. It was set for conclusive hearing in Hilary Term (January 1590), but, frustratingly, there is no further mention of the case in the records of the Queen's Bench. Most cases were settled out of court, so this one may have been – though probably not to the satisfaction of the Shakespeare family, since a full eight years later, in 1597, they reopened the matter in the higher Court of Chancery. Once again, it is highly likely that Will Shakespeare conducted affairs, and paid the legal costs, on behalf of his family.

In 1588, when *Shakespeare* v. *Lambert* was first referred to the Queen's Bench at Westminster, attorney Harborne was busy with his work at the Middle Temple, while his wife and children lived in his house in St Clement Danes. The obvious question is: which member of the Shakespeare family went to London to instruct him? Before John Shakespeare's financial affairs collapsed, he sometimes went to London, in company with his friend Richard Quiney, in order to conduct legal business on behalf of the Stratford Corporation. But in 1580 he was fined a large sum of money for failing to turn up before the court in London when another case involving him was being heard. If he did not go to London then, it is unlikely that he would have done so seven years later. The inference must be that it was William, now twenty-four years old and a party to the dispute by virtue of his position as his father's heir, who instructed Harborne, either in the latter's chambers in the Temple or at his house on what is now the Strand one summer day prior to the start of Michaelmas Term.

This is not to say that Justice Shallow is a portrait of Harborne, who of course had a much better legal training than did most rural justices. But the fact that the family attorney in this crucial case was a Clement's Inn man, that Shakespeare is named as party to the suit, and that it was he who in all probability instructed Harborne provides as good an explanation as any as to why Clement's is repeatedly mentioned in the reminiscences of legal training in *Henry IV Part 2*. It is the kind of tiny detail that would have stuck like a burr in Shakespeare's inquisitive memory.

The engagement of Harborne to act in the Lambert case is pretty strong evidence of Shakespeare's presence in London (not Lancashire, let alone abroad) in the Armada year of 1588, when the drama was beginning to flourish, above all in the plays of Marlowe. Could this have been the moment when he decided to stay in town and try his fortunes on a larger stage than that of the small provincial town where his father was still struggling?

Shakespeare at law

It has often been observed that Shakespeare's plays are steeped in the law. As a man of property, he knew the intricacies and technical terms of property law: language from this semantic field duly appears across the plays and poems. The case of *Shylock* v. *Antonio* in *The Merchant of Venice*, with the brilliant resolution provided by the disguised Portia, is one of his great theatrical set-pieces, in which a legal nicety provides the dramatic coup: the bond is for flesh, but does not allow for the shedding of Christian blood. The gravediggers' comically learned dispute over whether or not the drowned Ophelia is entitled to a full Christian burial reveals knowledge, direct or indirect, of *Hales* v. *Petit*, a famous case concerning suicide (*felo de se*). The history plays and tragedies throw up many a legal conundrum that would have been familiar to Shakespeare's audience, but that is lost to us. Issues of 'natural law' are discussed in *Troilus and Cressida* and of the law of warfare in *Henry V*. The question of inheritance law in relation to illegitimacy is of great moment in the case of Falconbridge in *King John*, while the possibility of royal succession being granted by way of tanistry (election) as opposed to primogeniture is relevant to both *Hamlet* and *Macbeth*. Ecclesiastical law shapes not only the bawdy court cases discussed earlier, but also the thorny question of whether or not the marriage of Claudius and Gertrude in *Hamlet* is incestuous.

All this matter could easily have been picked up from the street and the tavern, from reading and the experience of litigation. Thomas Dekker, in his *Gull's Hornbook,* told of how in tavern conversation with laymen, attorneys would talk of nothing but

statutes, bonds, recognizances, fines, recoveries, audits, rents, subsidies, sureties, enclosures, liveries, indictments, outlawries, foeffments, judgements, commissions, bankrupts, amercements, and of such horrible matter that when a lieutenant dines with his punk in the next room he thinks verily the men are conjuring.

Such lawyers' tavern talk is comically aped by Hamlet in the graveyard scene:

why may not that be the skull of a lawyer? Where be his quiddities now, his quillets, his cases, his tenures, and his tricks? Why does he suffer this rude knave now to knock him about the sconce with a dirty shovel, and will not tell him of his action of battery? Hum. This fellow might be in's time a great buyer of land, with his statutes, his recognizances, his fines, his double vouchers, his recoveries: is this the fine of his fines and the recovery of his recoveries, to have his fine pate full of fine dirt? Will his vouchers vouch him no more of his purchases, and double ones too, than the length and breadth of a pair of indentures? The very conveyances of his lands will hardly lie in this box; and must the inheritor himself have no more, ha?

The knowledge of the law revealed by Shakespeare's plays rarely goes beyond commonplace jargon of this kind. It is thin in comparison with that to be found in the dramas of many of his contemporaries, such as fellow Warwickshire man John Marston, who trained at the Middle Temple and whose plays are steeped in case-law, courtroom technicalities and the Inns of Court frame of mind. But we cannot rule out the possibility that Shakespeare underwent some kind of rudimentary legal training in the 1580s.

A number of successful writers were initially Chancery men.

The prolific and much admired (though now forgotten) William Warner, for instance, was 'an attorney of the common pleas'. You were supposed to be the son of a gentleman to enter the chancery inns, but it was sometimes regarded as *a way of becoming a gentleman*.

William Combe was a little older than Shakespeare, but from a very similar Stratford background. Their families knew each other well. Combe went from Stratford to London, where he managed to get in to another of the Chancery Courts, the New Inn. He graduated to the Middle Temple, completed his training and returned to become a successful attorney in Warwickshire. His path, like Harborne's, reveals how the lower reaches of the law offered a potential route to success for men who for one reason or another had been unable to go to university at Oxford or Cambridge. Let us look just one more time at Shallow and Silence:

SILENCE: Alas, a black ouzel, cousin Shallow!

SHALLOW: By yea and nay, sir. I dare say my cousin William is become a good scholar: he is at Oxford still, is he not?

SILENCE: Indeed, sir, to my cost.

SHALLOW: He must then to the Inns of Court shortly. I was once of Clement's Inn, where I think they will talk of mad Shallow yet.

John Shakespeare's straitened financial circumstances meant that William could not go to Oxford, which would have been the obvious move for a clever Stratford boy. A boy called William, resentment about the cost of an Oxford education, the idea of the Inns of Court and in particular the Chancery Inns as an alternative route to gentility and a profession: given the network of connections between Warwickshire, Clement's and the Middle Temple, it is not beyond the bounds of possibility that this snatch of dialogue contains the trace of a plan for Shakespeare to follow the road taken by Harborne and Combe. One imagines a fleeting glance of him enrolled at Clement's Inn.

The Chancery Inns held Christmas revels, with plays often written and performed by the students themselves. Could Will have organized the theatricals, then failed to pay his dues and been thrown out, only to try his hand in the professional theatre?

Stepping back from speculation, there can be little doubt that Shakespeare's knowledge of the law would have grown immeasurably as he tried to explain to Harborne the complexities of the Lambert case. His legal language is especially rich in the area of property law. At a less immediately tangible level, it must be remembered that the Elizabethan grammar-school training in the classics was undertaken with an eye as much on the law as the church. The rhetorical art of the schoolboy is also that of the lawyer. Each was taught to develop the art of arguing either side of a case (*in utramque parte*), an art that Shakespeare translated to that of dramatic composition as he developed his capacity to inhabit opposing characters with equal sympathy.

It has sometimes been argued that a scornful allusion by Thomas Nashe to 'noverints' – attorneys or law clerks – who become playwrights without a proper university training in classical literature refers not only to Thomas Kyd, who certainly underwent this transformation, but also to William Shakespeare. Whether or not Shakespeare ever was some kind of noverint or apprentice lawyer, there is no doubt that he shared with his legally trained contemporaries the ability to manipulate language for the purposes of argument – not to mention financial gain – that is wonderfully anatomized in the comedy *Two Wise Men and all the rest Fools* (sometimes attributed to George Chapman). The following speech occurs shortly after the entrance of a character called Noverindo:

These be matters of mighty moment (as thou seest) which he hath to cast, and recast; to meditate, and ponder; to toss, and tumble; to revolve, and resolve; to put forward with *Pro*, and pull back with *contra*, to object, and confute; to throw doubts and mishaps like snow-balls, and against them erect bulwarks and defences, to admit wounds and scars, and to apply salves; to conclude, come what come will, to have cordials in store, and all little enough to save his best beloved in his purse.

This speech opens a window on to the workings of the legal mind. But also the tergiversations of the rhetorical mind. And perhaps the Shakespearean.

18. After Machiavelli

The Machevil

Shakespeare's writing career may have begun in 1589, as he waited for the Lambert case to come before the Lord Chief Justice's court at Westminster. It was probably some time early in that year – to judge from a topical allusion to the assassination of the Duke of Guise, leader of the Catholic faction in the French civil wars of religion – that Christopher Marlowe's hugely popular *Jew of Malta* had its premiere. Shakespeare was probably not in the cast, but he was certainly at some point in the audience: his Aaron in *Titus Andronicus* is a part written in response to Marlowe's Ithamore and his Shylock in *The Merchant of Venice* is his answer to Barabas the Jew, with the play's resolution achieved through a courtroom instead of a boiling cauldron and a bloodbath.

Marlowe's tragedy has an extraordinary opening. The prologue is spoken not by some anonymous chorus, as in *Henry V*, but by an actor pretending to be the Florentine political theorist Niccolò Machiavelli. His name is anglicized to 'Machevil', creating a suggestion of 'much evil'. Marlowe presents Machiavelli as a demonic figure and links him to the villainous protagonist of the play Barabas, the rich Jew of Malta. At the same time, he uses the Machiavellian presenter to put across a series of deeply subversive suggestions about the nature of sovereignty. Orthodox political theory propounded that kings and magistrates were God's representatives on earth, their authority sanctioned by divine law. Machiavelli replies that the only basis of effective government is raw power:

> I count religion but a childish toy,
> And hold there is no sin but ignorance.
> Birds of the air will tell of murders past:

I am ashamed to hear such fooleries.
Many will talk of title to a crown:
What right had Caesar to the empery?
Might first made kings, and laws were then most sure
When, like the Draco's, they were writ in blood.

Religion as an illusion; the idea that human knowledge does not require divine sanction; the notion that it is 'might' not 'right' that decides who rules; the proposition that the most effective laws are those based not on justice but on the severity exemplified by the ancient Greek lawgiver Draco (from whose name we get the word 'draconian'). French and English thinkers of Shakespeare's time demonized Machiavelli for holding these views, but for Marlowe the act of thinking the unthinkable made Machiavelli a model for his own over-reaching heroes.

Shakespeare was much more politically cautious. His choruses and 'presenters' seek to establish a bond of imaginative complicity with the audience, not to provoke them in this way. But he recognized the theatrical charisma of the Marlovian Machiavel and created a string of such characters himself – Aaron the Moor, Richard III, Iago, Edmund in *King Lear*. What attracted him to the type was not so much the subversive politics as the stage panache of the unapologetic villain. In Jaques' version of human development, the fifth age of man is staid. The Justice denotes middle-aged respectability: the Establishment figure, we would now say, with his position as a magistrate, his complacency, his pious clichés, his spreading paunch. The Machiavel is a wonderful device for pricking his bubble. He is the antitype: the Justice is supposed to speak for society, whereas the Machiavel speaks for himself.

What is it that makes *Richard III* a better play than the three parts of *Henry VI* that precede it? The answer is Richard's theatrical self-consciousness, his sheer delight in turning justice on its head. In *The First Part of Henry VI*, Talbot is a martial hero of high renown and Joan la Pucelle an intriguing semi-comic villain. In *The Second Part* there is splendid energy (Queen Margaret running amok) and variety (Jack Cade and the voice of the discontented commons). In *The Third Part* we witness a scene of superb theatricality when York is taunted with a paper crown before being stabbed to death. But it is not until Richard of Gloucester gets into his stride that we meet a figure with the compelling stage presence of a Falstaff or an Iago. At the climax of his first long soliloquy in act three of *The Third Part of Henry the Sixth* – a speech that the theatrical tradition has often imported into *Richard the Third* – Richard announces that he will 'play the orator', 'add colours to the chameleon', and 'change shapes with Proteus for advantages'. Each image is of the art of the actor, with his persuasive tongue and power of self-transformation.

Richard adds that he will 'set the murderous Machevil to school'. In *Richard the Third*, Shakespeare made a bold advance on Marlowe's device of introducing Machiavelli as presenter. He dispensed with a prologue and began the action with Richard's riveting soliloquy, 'Now is the winter of our discontent'. Where Marlowe had cast Barabas in the role of the Machiavel by means of a pointed structural device, Shakespeare's Richard casts himself. He announces that since his crookback prevents him from playing the role of a stage-lover, he will self-consciously adopt that of a stage-villain. For good measure, he goes on in the second scene to show that he can in fact play the lover – with such accomplishment that he successfully woos Lady Anne over the very corpse of her father-in-law even as she knows that Richard has been responsible for the murder of her first husband. As promised, he plays the orator to supreme effect. By the third act, he is changing shapes with Proteus and appearing in the colour of a holy man. By means of the orator's art of saying the opposite of what he means – 'I cannot nor I will not' accept the crown – he wins over the Mayor and citizens of London.

Legitimacy and ceremony

We can enjoy Richard, but we are never allowed to believe that Shakespeare believed with Marlowe's Machevil that might makes right, that there is no such thing as a legitimate monarch and that religion is a childish toy. Unlike nearly all his contemporaries, William Shakespeare never wrote plays that put him on the wrong side of the law. Indeed, he seems to have had a reputation for being able to handle potentially explosive material with equanimity. When the Master of the Revels, who licensed all stage performances, made strenuous objections to Henry Chettle's play of *Sir Thomas More*, Shakespeare was brought in to rewrite the most delicate scene, involving a rioting crowd.

In the Shakespearean addition, the rhetoric of Sir Thomas More, an embodiment of Justice if ever there was one, establishes harmony. In a characteristic balancing act, Shakespeare first animated the ordinary people in the crowd with colourful detail, so that they are not mere caricatures. Thus Doll says that More's care for the people is witnessed by his having 'made my brother, Arthur Watchins, Sergeant Safe's yeoman'. The invention of Arthur Watchins, whom we never meet, is a typical Shakespearean touch. But then More's voice takes command. His speech holds together two opposing theories of political justice. On the one hand, there is the old idea that sovereignty derives from God, that respect for the order of the state is a religious obligation:

> For to the king God hath his office lent
> Of dread, of justice, power and command,
> Hath bid him rule, and willed you to obey.

On the other hand, there is the (much more modern-sounding) idea that the maintenance of law depends on a social contract, which is best understood by means of imaginative empathy. More says something to the effect of: think yourself into the position of the poor and the dispossessed. Accord unto them the respect, the right to live their lives in peace, which you expect the law to accord to you. In this case, the people in need of protection are Huguenot immigrants – the play seems to have been written some time after an outbreak of rioting in London, led by apprentices who claimed that the 'aliens', Protestant refugees from the French religious wars, were taking their jobs. Sir Thomas More asks the on-stage crowd, and by extension the theatre audience, to imagine what it would be like to be an asylum-seeker undergoing forced repatriation:

> Grant them removed, and grant that this your noise
> Hath chid down all the majesty of England.
> Imagine that you see the wretched strangers,
> Their babies at their backs, with their poor luggage
> Plodding to the ports and coasts for transportation,
> And that you sit as kings in your desires,
> Authority quite silenced by your brawl
> And you in ruff of your opinions clothed.
> What had you got? I'll tell you: you had taught
> How insolence and strong hand should prevail,
> How order should be quelled, and by this pattern
> Not one of you should live an agèd man,
> For other ruffians, as their fancies wrought
> With selfsame hand, self reasons and self right,
> Would shark on you, and men like ravenous fishes
> Would feed on one another.

There is no evidence that Shakespeare ever read Richard Hooker's *Laws of Ecclesiastical Policy*, the definitive statement of the Elizabethan political settlement, a book written and published in the decade of the history plays. But in More's speech, Shakespeare articulates a political theory very close to Hooker's. Yes, the sovereign and the magistrate are God's lieutenants on earth, but at the same time they are obliged to enforce a natural law that can be discovered by the processes of reason, as in the chain of argument here, which proposes that if we shark on others, others will shark on us 'and men like ravenous fishes / Would feed on one another'.

In one sense, then, the law is above the monarch, not vice versa. It is this position that opened the way for debates about whether it was ever justifiable to depose a monarch. If a king was unjust, then he could be described as a 'tyrant' and the people, or at least the magistrates, had the right to remove him. Both biblical and classical precedents could be found for such a belief, and debates regarding it swirled in the political treatises of the sixteenth century, not least because John Calvin's Protestant theology had broken the chain of association between God, pope and king. Shakespeare's history plays and tragedies are full of usurpers (and there are even some in his comedies, notably Antonio in *The Tempest*). They are usually self-serving Machiavels. But this does not make Shakespeare an uncritical apologist for the divine right of kings: when a Richard II or a Henry VI fails to fulfil the responsibilities of sovereignty, the state totters.

As the son of a usurper, Henry V is acutely conscious of the fragility of his claim to the throne. Since he cannot rely on the theory of divine right – that belonged to Richard, not his father – he has to fall back on natural law and rational argument. His debate with Michael Williams and John Bates on the night before Agincourt throws up some awkward questions. 'Methinks I could not die anywhere so contented as in the king's company; his cause being just and his quarrel honourable,' says the disguised 'Harry le Roi'. 'That's more than we know,' replies Williams: only God can ultimately judge whether the cause is just. Bates says that it is enough to 'know we are the king's subjects'. This has the advantage for the commoner that 'If his cause be wrong, our obedience to the king wipes the crime of it out of us.' Williams will not let the point go:

But if the cause be not good, the king himself hath a heavy reckoning to make, when all those legs and arms and heads, chopped off in battle, shall join together at the latter day and cry all, 'We died at such a place' – some swearing, some crying for a surgeon, some upon their wives left poor behind them, some upon the debts they owe, some upon their children rawly left. I am afeard there are few die well that die in a battle, for how can they charitably dispose of anything, when blood is their argument? Now, if these men do not die well, it will be a black matter for the king that led them to it – who to disobey were against all proportion of subjection.

Henry replies with a series of analogies seeking to prove that 'Every subject's duty is the king's, but every subject's soul is his own.' He is, however, shaken by the debate, and in soliloquy after the common soldiers have left he confronts the possibility that the whole edifice of sovereignty is nothing more than a quasi-theatrical performance:

> And what have kings, that privates have not too,
> Save ceremony, save general ceremony?
> And what art thou, thou idle ceremony?
> What kind of god art thou, that suffer'st more
> Of mortal griefs than do thy worshippers?
> What are thy rents? What are thy comings in?
> O ceremony, show me but thy worth.
> What? Is thy soul of adoration?
> Art thou aught else but place, degree and form,
> Creating awe and fear in other men?
> Wherein thou art less happy being feared
> Than they in fearing.
> What drink'st thou oft, instead of homage sweet,
> But poisoned flattery? O, be sick, great greatness,
> And bid thy ceremony give thee cure!

The notion that the 'ceremony' on which kingship depends may be a device for the creation of 'awe and fear in other men' is deeply Machiavellian. Shakespeare's deep political cunning manifests itself in the decision to put this thought not into the mouth of Machiavelli, as Marlowe did, but into that of his most heroic king. It is one thing for a fully paid-up Machiavel such as Edmund in *King Lear* to say that 'legitimate' is no more than a 'fine word', quite another for Harry the king to suggest that 'ceremony' might be 'idle' and even, by way of pun, an empty 'idol'.

This complex scene on the eve of Agincourt reveals that for Shakespeare politics was a matter for serious *debate*. And debate is premised on the notion of opposing points of view each having an element of validity. Shakespeare does not impose his own political views. He leaves a space for his audience to make up their own minds, and that is inherently a way of giving the power of free thought to the people.

The dangers of open debate were all too apparent in an England fractured by religious dissension. Queen Elizabeth, her council and her magistrates were fully aware of the uncertainty of their hold upon power. They could not rely on divine right theory alone. After all, Mary Queen of Scots had been expelled by her Protestant subjects and Elizabeth had (eventually, reluctantly) countenanced her execution. In the Netherlands, meanwhile, the English had taken the side of the people as they rose against their king, Philip II of Spain.

Insurrection was always a dangerous matter. Not even the Shakespearean balancing act was enough to make the play of *Sir Thomas More* acceptable to the authorities. 'Leave out the insurrection wholly, with the cause thereof', demanded the Master of the Revels, with the result that the script languished in manuscript until the nineteenth century, when a scholar realized for the first time that here were a few precious pages in Shakespeare's fluent, barely punctuated hand. Contrary to the expectation established by Hemings and Condell's observation in the preface to the First Folio that when Shakespeare handed his manuscripts over to his acting company there was barely a crossing-out, the scene from *Sir Thomas More* reveals him in the process of having second thoughts even as he composes.

Shakespeare may have been the playwright chosen to fix up that particular scene in *Sir Thomas More* because of what he had achieved with the figure of Jack Cade in *Henry VI Part 2*. This artisan rabble-rouser from Kent is a highly attractive figure on stage because he speaks in the same language as the commoners in the audience. His clowning offers welcome respite from the high rhetoric and low cunning of the aristocrats, and such lines as his follower Dick's 'the first thing we do, let's kill all the lawyers' elicit an approving laugh in every age. But Shakespeare, who made his living by the literacy that his father may have lacked, can hardly be said to have approved of a character who orders the hanging of a village clerk for the crime of being able to read and write. And Cade's vision of England is self-contradictory to the core:

CADE: Be brave, then, for your captain is brave, and vows reformation. There shall be in England seven halfpenny loaves sold for a penny: the three-hooped pot shall have ten hoops, and I will make it felony to drink small beer. All the realm shall be in common, and in Cheapside shall my palfrey go to grass: and when I am king, as king I will be–

ALL: God save your majesty!

This is a double-edged 'reformation': cheap bread, unwatered ale and the land held in common sound Utopian, but Cade does not really want representative government. He wants to be king himself. Shakespeare plays a similar trick against the 'commonwealth' idealism of the courtier Gonzalo twenty years later in *The Tempest*: 'No sovereignty– / Yet he would be king on't.' If Shakespeare has an Eden, it is not a place anterior to class distinction on the lines of the old rhyme 'When Adam delved and Eve span / Who was then the gentleman?' but rather an English gentleman's country estate, a place of peace and retreat where Cade is an intruder: the Kentish garden of Alexander Iden.

The political chameleon

Shakespeare's political beliefs are as elusive as his religion, his sexuality and just about everything else about him that matters. Precisely because he was not an apologist for any single position, it has been possible for the plays to be effectively reinterpreted in the light of each successive age. In the four centuries since his death, he has been made the apologist for all sorts of diametrically opposed ideologies, many of them anachronistic – we should not forget that he was writing before the time when toleration and liberal democracy became totemic values.

But the political appropriation of him is true to his own practice: he too was a great trader in anachronism. He took the political structures of ancient Rome and mapped them on to his own time and state with fascinating effect – a technique used by nearly all the writers of his time. *The Rape of Lucrece* is set at the moment of transition from monarchy to republic, *Coriolanus* during the republican era, *Julius Caesar* at the pivotal moment when a crown is offered and refused but the republic collapses anyway, *Antony and Cleopatra* ends with the beginning of empire, and *Titus Andronicus* fictionalizes the Roman empire in decay, approaching the time when the great city will be sacked by 'barbarian' hordes from the north. *King Lear* and *Cymbeline* find echoes of the modern in the matter of ancient Britain. The history plays speak at once to the generations before Shakespeare and to his live audience.

Several others plays use contemporary Italy as a mirror. Humanist learning and mercantile travel meant that the eyes of the Elizabethans were open to alternative forms of government other than the hereditary monarchy they experienced at home. They had great admiration for Venice, regarding that island city-state as a model of anti-papal modernity and trading prowess. Venice had no monarch but a sophisticated oligarchic system, which was observed by English travellers and absorbed by readers such as Shakespeare by way of Lewis Lewkenor's translation of Contarini's *The Commonwealth and Republic of Venice* (an important source for *Othello*).

Not so long ago, it was commonplace for historians to assert that republican thought had no following in England until well into the seventeenth century – that the intellectual conditions which made the Cromwellian republic possible emerged only a few years before the extraordinary moment when the English chopped off their king's head. Recent scholarship has shown that this was not the case: republican discourse, if not overt republican polemic, was widespread in Shakespeare's time. So, for instance, the anti-imperial Roman historian Tacitus was read and discussed and admired as the most dispassionate of historians, whose work combined moral insight into the behaviour of political actors with an assessment of their value as governors. Several of Shakespeare's plays may by this light be described as 'Tacitean'. The flavour of Tacitus is wonderfully captured in Justus Lipsius' dedicatory epistle to his translation of the *Annals*: 'Behold a theatre of our modern life: I see a ruler rising up against the laws in one passage, subjects rising up against a ruler elsewhere. I find the devices which make the destruction of liberty possible and the unsuccessful effort to regain it. I read of tyrants overthrown in their turn, and of power, ever unfaithful to those who abuse it.' This could equally well serve as a conspectus of Shakespeare's history plays and political tragedies.

Tacitean history was closely associated with the circle of the Earl of Essex. After the events of February 1601, Shakespeare had to do some rapid back-pedalling.

Only one gentleman was killed on that fateful day, a Welshman, a close friend of Sir Gelly Meyrick, who was called Captain Owen Salusbury. He was shot by a sniper stationed on the steeple of St Clement Danes. His kinsman, John Salusbury of Llewenni in Denbighshire, meanwhile, fought prominently on the other side, against Essex. A few months later, John Salusbury was knighted by Queen Elizabeth for his loyalty. A poetry book was put together in his honour to mark the occasion. Entitled *Love's Martyr*, the main bulk of it was taken up with a rambling allegory by a retainer of Sir John called Robert Chester, in which the virgin queen is represented as the mythical phoenix and Sir John as a bird renowned for its loyalty, the turtle-dove. The dramatists Ben Jonson, George Chapman, John Marston and William Shakespeare were all asked to contribute poems on the same theme. Shakespeare, who, unlike the other three, did not usually undertake such commissions, contributed his own brilliant little vignette of the mystical marriage of the phoenix and the turtle, the virgin queen and her loyal courtier. It was a very good way of aligning himself with the loyal Salusbury rather than the disloyal one.

Chapman may have been playing a similar game, since he was even more closely associated with Essex than Shakespeare. His English translation of Homer's *Iliad* had carried a dedication describing Essex as the modern Achilles – an obvious analogy, in the light of Essex's espousal of the cult of chivalry and military honour. *Troilus and Cressida*, written soon after the dramatic events of 1601, may have been another subtle repositioning on Shakespeare's part.

The military plot of *Troilus and Cressida*, concerning Achilles, Agamemnon, Ajax, Hector and the rest, is derived primarily from Homer and his descendants, most notably George Chapman's 1598 translation of seven books of *The Iliad* into elevated English verse.

The love plot concerning Troilus and Cressida, the efforts of Pandarus to bring them together, and the infidelity of Cressida in the Greek camp, is derived primarily from Chaucer's *Troilus and Criseyde*. The handling of each plot is equally cynical. In its love plot the play is an anti-romance, while in its martial plot it is an anti-epic. In his anti-heroic representation of the exemplary heroes of the Trojan war, Shakespeare undermines both the style and the attitudes of Chapman's recent translation of Homer. The prologue speaks in high Chapmanesque style of 'princes orgulous', 'crownets regal', 'strong immures' and 'warlike fraughtage', but the action begins with Troilus saying 'I'll unarm again' and going on to describe himself as 'weaker than a woman's tear . . . Less valiant than the virgin in the night'. The admission of a 'feminine' language strips all glamour from the male code of war. But then the code of love is submitted to a similar pummelling: Pandarus compares the art of love to bread-making, with its progression from grinding to bolting to kneading to leavening to cooling. Troilus idealizes his love in courtly language, but at the same time compares his desire to a wound, speaking of 'the open ulcer of my heart'.

Scabs, pus and running sores ooze through the play, while the foul-mouthed Thersites proves to be the truest commentator on the war. In the second scene we are given a first account of Hector, traditionally the most noble of heroes. Here, however, he is reported to be wrathful, chiding his devoted wife Andromache and striking his armourer. An honourable man should respect his wife and servants: the honour of Hector is thus questioned from the start. There is a clear progression from the reported striking of the armourer to Hector's ignominious end, in which he is killed because of an act of vanity: he has unarmed himself in order to put on the alluring golden armour of a slain warrior.

Our first image of Ajax, another magnificent hero in Homer, is yet one more debunking. 'They say he is a very man *per se*, and stands alone,' says Alexander: this sounds like the glorious self-sufficiency of the epic hero. 'So do all men, unless they are drunk, sick, or have no legs,' replies Cressida: 'stands alone' is taken literally and thus reduced to ignobility. And, sure enough, Ajax does prove to be a singularly unheroic blockhead.

As for the great Achilles, he has withdrawn from the battle and is camping around in his tent with his gay lover, Patroclus, acting out parodies of the inflated mannerisms of the other Greek generals. Again and again, *Troilus and Cressida* reveals the discrepancy between the polished surface that is projected by a value-system, whether the heroic code or courtly love, and the tawdry reality beneath. At a philosophical level, the effect of this is deeply troubling: it is to question whether there can be such a thing as an absolute moral value. Nobody who saw this play could suppose that Shakespeare had any nostalgia for the martial world of the Earl of Essex.

19. The King's Man

Elizabethan to Jacobean: England to Britain

The Essex affair was Shakespeare's nearest brush with political disaster. Always wily, maybe he decided to be more cautious thereafter, to deal less with rebels and more with the rule of law. Soon after the old queen died, his acting company became the King's Men. The established players. Called to perform at court more often than any of their rivals. Given the status of Grooms of the Chamber in Ordinary without Fee. Each provided, at the charge of the Master of the Great Wardrobe, with four and a half yards of red cloth, against his Majesty's Royal Proceeding through the City of London. Required to attend upon the Constable of Castile, who came as ambassador from the King of Spain to hammer out the Somerset House peace treaty that brought to an end the long years of war.

In his history plays, written in the 1590s, Shakespeare always refers to his own country as England. Of his 143 uses of the adjective 'English', 126 occur in Elizabethan plays and only 17 in Jacobean. The Jacobean occurrences are almost exclusively confined to *Macbeth*, where England is played off against Scotland, and *Henry VIII*, a play notable for its nostalgia for the Tudor era. Similarly, of his 17 uses of 'Englishman', 16 are in Elizabethan plays and the remaining one in *Henry VIII*. His one use of 'Englishwoman' is in *Henry V*. Elizabethan Shakespeare, in short, was an English dramatist. Jacobean Shakespeare, by contrast, was a British one.

To be more specific, Jacobean Shakespeare was a dramatist who spoke openly in favour of his royal patron's project to create (or re-create) a kingdom of Britain. In *Cymbeline*, written for the court of King James, he used either 'Britain' to mean his country or 'Britains' for its people nearly fifty times. He only ever used the word 'British' four times, twice each in *Cymbeline* and *Lear*. The *Cymbeline* references are to 'a British ensign' and 'the British crown'. *Cymbeline* and *Lear* are intimately connected with the ambition of King James, which was ultimately blocked by the parliaments in both London and Edinburgh, to unify the separate kingdoms of England and Scotland into a single state.

As well as being a pastoral fantasy and a fairy story, complete with wicked stepmother and poison (which, thanks to an honest-hearted physician, turns out to be a mere sleeping-potion), *Cymbeline* is a play about the Romans in Britain, under the auspices of the god Jupiter. The title in the Folio contents list is 'Cymbeline King of Britain'. Shakespeare's other King of Britain was Lear, who made the mistake of dividing his kingdom in three. The editors of the Folio may have placed *Cymbeline* among the tragedies because it traverses the same elevated ground of national history and destiny. But whereas the disarray of the divided nation in *Lear* is a negative example, perhaps intended to make the play's original audience feel relief that King James had recently united the thrones of Scotland and England, the resolution of *Cymbeline* is altogether positive: 'Never was a war did cease, / Ere bloody hands were washed, with such a peace.'

Cymbeline was supposed to have been king of Britain in the year when Christ was born; at that time, the Roman emperor was Augustus. Shakespeare's audience would have known that Augustus was the Caesar to whom Cymbeline agrees to pay tribute money, despite the miraculous victory of the British when Belarius, Guiderius and Arviragus (otherwise known as Morgan, Polydore and Cadwal) hold the road against apparently insurmountable odds. The end of the play heralds an 'Augustan peace', in which Britain is imagined as the equal of Rome. Milford Haven in Wales is a vital location and point of reference in the play. The more historic-ally and politically literate members of Shakespeare's original audi-ence would have recalled that it was the port where Henry Tudor – the Richmond of *Richard III* and the future King Henry VII – landed in 1485, the year that brought the Wars of the Roses to an end and established the Tudor dynasty that turned the tables on modern Rome and began to establish for the British an image of their nation as the divinely chosen Christian successor-empire to that of Augustus.

Imagine King James watching the play: he would have seen himself as a composite version of Cymbeline and Augustus, both a British king and a neo-Roman emperor. From the point of view of characterization, the part of King Cymbeline is astonishingly under-written. His interior life is never opened to us, as is that of Lear or, in this play, Princess Innogen. All he seems to do in the long closing scene is ask questions, express amazement and pronounce benediction. This makes sense if he is intended to offer an oblique representation of James, King of Britain. It would not do to inquire too closely into the monarch's interior life. Instead, Cymbeline is the ideal spectator: during a court performance, the king would have been sitting at the focal point of the hall.

Murder and treason

A world in which your every move is watched. By God, by Satan and by the apparatus of the state. A world in which you have to take sides. In which there are always absolute claims about good and evil, salvation and damnation – no grey areas, no liberal consensus, no toleration or gentle English compromise. The Enlightenment dream of a rational state, of secular politics stripped of religious fanaticism and prejudice, has not yet come into being. That is the world of *Macbeth*.

With surveillance and paranoia came certain verbal triggers that would have rung alarum bells in the minds of Shakespeare's original audience: 'assassination', 'instruments of darkness', 'dire combustion and confused events', 'the equivocation of the fiend'. It cannot be a coincidence that the only occasion on which Shakespeare used the explosive word 'combustion' was in a play about treason written shortly after the state security service foiled a plot to blow up the royal family, the senior judiciary and the members of parliament all in one fell swoop.

Theatre was a dangerous art form in Shakespeare's time. In the absence of newspapers and television, there were just two places where the public gathered together to be informed, cajoled and provoked to thought on great issues of religion and politics: the church and the playhouse. Public sermons, not least those preached by John Donne at St Paul's, were a major spectator sport. But the message from the pulpit was invariably orthodox. Homilies on obedience to king and law were regularly delivered in every parish in the land. The king was God's representative on earth. Political dissent was a pact with the devil.

The message from the stage was different, less malleable by authority. Here the people of London could witness tyrants – kings who deserved to be deposed – and rebels and scheming politicians. Though there were always virtuous and obedient voices some-where in the mix, though the rebels and king-killers always came to a sticky end, and though every script had to be approved by a government censor, there was no way of preventing audiences from identifying with the voices of transgression and self-assertion. Macbeth and Lady Macbeth are indeed a 'dead butcher and his fiend-like queen', as Malcolm says they are. But what actor would prefer the role of Malcolm to that of Macbeth? What audience member would wish Lady Macbeth to be the kind of silent and obedient wife that homilists in the pulpit extolled as the condition to which all women should aspire? The theatre is dangerous because the Macbeths – and Richard III and Iago in *Othello* and Edmund in *King Lear* – are simply more dramatically engaging, more theatrical, than their virtuous counterparts.

Given the inherent political danger of public theatre, not to mention the impiety of its cross-dressed sexual impersonations (the original Lady Macbeth a teenage male apprentice actor, imagine that!), why was theatre allowed at all? There were indeed moments when a line was crossed and a show closed down. In the late 1590s, the authorities were so offended by a play called *The Isle of Dogs* that an order went out for all the theatres to be torn down. But it didn't happen because the royal court needed the players. Techni-cally speaking, every public performance at the Globe or the Rose was a rehearsal, a burnishing of the repertoire in readiness for the next summons to play at court on a festival night. A tragedy such as *Macbeth*, so much of which takes place at night or in gloomy weather, so viscous with the language of darkness, would have played much better by candlelight indoors at court than by daylight on the platform of the Globe.

The most important thing to remember about the circumstances of *Macbeth*'s composition is that it belongs to the early years of the reign of King James, the period when Shakespeare's theatre company ceased to be the Lord Chamberlain's Men and became the King's Men, with their formal status of Grooms of the Chamber. The sequence in which the Macbeths attempt to frame the grooms of the chamber for the murder of King Duncan was written by a Shakespeare who was himself a groom of the chamber.

King James was haunted by fears of conspiracy and treason. With good reason. He was the son of Mary Queen of Scots and Lord Darnley. While he was in his mother's womb, she was at supper in Holyrood House with her friend and counsellor David Riccio. They heard a noise. Darnley came into the room with armed followers. Riccio was frightened and hid behind his pregnant mistress, but they pulled him out and stabbed him. He was dragged away screaming and stabbed a further fifty-six times. A few months after James was born, Darnley's house was blown up and he was strangled. Suspicion fell on both Mary and the Earl of Bothwell, who promptly divorced his wife and married her. This unpopular liaison led to her deposition and to James becoming King of Scotland at the age of one. Given these circumstances, any play about violent deeds in the corridors of Scottish power would have been of signal interest to him.

Within months of his assumption of the English throne in 1603, a plot to depose him and replace him with his cousin Arbella was discovered. Her claim to the throne was arguably as good as his – analogously, Macbeth is Duncan's kinsman and, according to one interpretation of ancient Scottish law, he rather than Malcolm was the rightful heir. The year after the Arbella affair, the King's Men tried out a new play called *The Tragedy of Gowrie*, which dramatized an apparent assassination attempt that King James had survived (or possibly faked) in 1600. After two sell-out performances, the play was suppressed because 'it be thought unfit that Princes should be played on the Stage in their Life-time'. It is surprising they took the risk of staging it at all, given their near-run thing with the special performance of *Richard II* commissioned by Essex's men three years before. One wonders whether Shakespeare, with his instinct for caution and his track record of staying out of trouble, might have been absent in Stratford at the time. Such an error of political judgement is unlike him. Or perhaps he *was* involved in *Gowrie*, conceivably even as author, and this was the scandal that seems to have attached itself to his name at this time.

As *The Tragedy of Gowrie* created a stir in Southwark, across the river Guy Fawkes was beginning to fill a cellar beneath the House of Lords with gunpowder. The discovery of the plot on 5 November 1605 caused a national sensation. Trials and executions followed, including, most controversially, that of Father Garnet, leader of the English Jesuit community and confessor to several of the plotters (though he may have himself opposed the plot, and indeed exposed an earlier Catholic conspiracy for fear of the dire consequences it would have for his community of fellow-believers). At his trial, Garnet resorted to the device of 'equivocation', paltering with double sense so as to avoid either incriminating himself or committing the sins of lying upon oath and revealing the secrets of the confessional.

Garnet was sentenced to be hanged, but not drawn and quartered. Some thought that even with this mitigation the sentence was too severe. With a loud cry of 'hold, hold', part of the crowd prevented the hangman from cutting down the body while Garnet was still alive and others pulled his legs so as to ensure a speedy death. When the Porter in *Macbeth* speaks of 'an equivocator that could swear in both the scales against either scale, who committed treason enough for God's sake, yet could not equivocate to heaven' or when Lady Macbeth speaks of heaven peeping through the blanket of the dark to cry 'hold, hold', the inescapable conclusion is that the Gunpowder Plot and its aftermath were etched indelibly upon Shakespeare's mind as well such dire combustion and confused events might be, given that several of the leading conspirators were based in his native Warwickshire.

But he had learned the lesson of *Gowrie*'s closure. To dramatize contemporary events was too close to the bone. The way to approach the Gunpowder Plot was indirectly, by means of an historical drama. So it was that Shakespeare turned to Holinshed's *Chronicles of Scotland* and found the story of Macbeth, regicide, ambition's wading through a sea of blood and at last the tyrant's fall. Why this particular story? Probably because King James himself claimed descent from Banquo. In the chronicles, Banquo is a co-conspirator with Macbeth. Shakespeare changes history once again: he makes Banquo an innocent victim and emphasizes the survival of his son Fleance. When the play was performed at court in front of King James some time in 1606, there would have been a particular frisson as the weird sisters showed Macbeth the prophetic line of kings stretching out even to the crack of doom. The line would have been seen to extend from Banquo and Fleance to the living king who sat in the most prominent seat in the banqueting hall.

Macbeth is steeped in King James's preoccupations: the rights of royal succession, the relationship between England and Scotland, witchcraft, the sacred powers of the monarch, anxiety about gunpowder, treason and plot. A deeply learned man, the king had published a treatise explaining how monarchs were God's regents upon the earth and another arguing for the reality of witchcraft or 'demonology'. He considered himself something of an adept at distinguishing between true and false accusations of witchcraft. He took a deep interest in such customs as the tradition of the sacred power of the king's 'touch' to cure subjects afflicted with the disease of scrofula (known as 'the king's evil').

Religion and politics were joined seamlessly together. The Bible said that rebellion is as the sin of witchcraft: if the monarch was God's representative upon earth, then to conspire against him was to make a pact with the instruments of darkness – in the Gunpowder trials, Jesuits such as Father Garnet were described as male witches. Treason was regarded as more than a political act: it was, as one modern scholar puts it, 'a form of possession, an action contrary to and destructive of the very order of nature itself. The forces of the netherworld seek for their own uncreating purposes the killing of the legitimate king in order to restore the realm of tyranny and chaos.'

In this world, killing the king is the ultimate crime against nature. 'O horror, horror, horror', says Macduff, as he returns on stage having stared into the heart of darkness, seen how the gashed stabs on the king's body look like a breach in nature. 'Tongue nor heart cannot conceive nor name thee': the language here alludes to the famous passage in St Paul about the inexpressible wonders that God has prepared in the kingdom of heaven for those who love Him. Macduff, by contrast, has momentarily entered the kingdom of hell, where a drunken porter keeps the gate. 'Confusion now hath made his masterpiece', he continues. An artist's masterpiece is traditionally a replication of the order of divine creation. But the art here is that of confusion and death: 'Most sacrilegious murder hath broke ope / The Lord's anointed temple and stole thence / The life o' th' building.' The understanding of this play requires close attention to be paid to such words as 'sacrilegious', in which political violence is bound inextricably to articles of religious faith. 'Treason has done his worst', says Macbeth in one of those moments when his conscience is pricked. *His* worst, not *its*: Treason is not a concept but a living thing. The devil's disciple, He stalks the stage of politics and brings sleepless nights through which the guilty man shakes and sweats with fear and terrible dreams, while the guilty woman descends into insanity.

1606. Shakespeare was by now well and truly the King's Man, and yet, astonishingly, at the end of that year of fear and state trials it was before the King's Majesty at Whitehall on St Stephen's Night that he launched his most searing assault on the frailty and hypocrisy of justice and authority. That was the night when King James witnessed a performance of *King Lear*:

What, art mad? A man may see how this world goes with no eyes. Look with thine ears: see how yond justice rails upon yond simple thief. Hark, in thine ear: change places, and handy-dandy, which is the justice, which is the thief? Thou hast seen a farmer's dog bark at a beggar? . . . And the creature run from the cur? There thou mightst behold the great image of authority: a dog's obeyed in office.

Thou rascal beadle, hold thy bloody hand!
Why dost thou lash that whore? Strip thy own back:
Thou hotly lusts to use her in that kind
For which thou whip'st her. The usurer hangs the cozener.
Thorough tattered clothes small vices do appear:
Robes and furred gowns hide all. Plate sins with gold,
And the strong lance of justice hurtless breaks:
Arm it in rags, a pigmy's straw does pierce it.
None does offend, none, I say, none: I'll able 'em.
Take that of me, my friend, who have the power
To seal th'accuser's lips. Get thee glass eyes,
And like a scurvy politician seem
To see the things thou dost not.

Pantaloon

The sixth age shifts
Into the lean and slippered pantaloon,
With spectacles on nose and pouch on side,
His youthful hose, well saved, a world too wide
For his shrunk shank, and his big manly voice,
Turning again toward childish treble, pipes
And whistles in his sound.

'Pantalone' from the commedia dell'arte: *he is the old man in the centre, with the fingers behind, giving him a cuckold's horns*

20. The Myth of Shakespeare's Retirement

Pantalone the player

The lean and slippered pantaloon? Is the sixth age named after a pair of trousers? No, alas. 'Pantaloon' was originally a theatrical term, a character type from the Italian *commedia dell'arte*. The sixth age is the one that reminds us most explicitly that we go through life playing a succession of roles. Pantaloon represents authority and the older generation. In the *commedia*, he was a lean, foolish old man in a red costume, with skullcap and Turkish slippers, close-fitting jacket and baggy trousers – pantaloons.

Age is supposed to bring wisdom as well as authority. It is supposed to be worthy of respect – the 'policy and reverence of age' that, according to the letter forged by Edmund in order to frame his brother Edgar in *King Lear*, keeps the ambitious young from their fortunes 'till our oldness cannot relish them'. The reality of Shakespeare's stage-world is rather different. As Cleopatra puts it, 'age from folly could not give me freedom'. The ageing lovers Antony and Cleopatra are in their way more foolish than the young ones, Romeo and Juliet. Shakespeare's plays are full of fathers who demand the reverence and obedience due to their age and status, but who do not receive respect and do not always deserve it. From Baptista Minola in *The Taming of the Shrew* and Egeus in *A Midsummer Night's Dream* to Juliet's father to Shylock to Polonius in *Hamlet* and on to King Lear himself, Shakespeare again and again portrays fathers who show folly, not wisdom, in their attempts to make or break marital arrangements for their daughters.

So it is that the fifth age slides inexorably into the sixth. Old Polonius, giving paternal advice to Laertes before his departure for Paris, voices 'wise saws and modern instances' in the manner of the Justice, but he soon veers into pantaloonish pomposity. What is more, he is in truth a scurvy politician, who does not practise the integrity that he preaches. In the *commedia dell'arte* Pantaloon was often the father, guardian or elderly suitor of the heroine, and the frequent butt of the Clown's jokes. Hamlet's baiting of Polonius is one of the many signs that he has taken over the role of the dead court jester Yorick: he is at once both hero and clown.

At the heart of comedy is the triumph of the young over the old, of the forces of life over those of killjoy Puritanism. Pantaloon is *lean*: a sign of his parsimony. Shakespeare has more time for the unashamedly fat, for Sir John Falstaff and Sir Toby Belch. 'Dost thou think because thou art virtuous there shall be no more cakes and ale?' Theatre will always prefer cakes and ale to virtue. Malvolio in *Twelfth Night* is not an old man, but he is the play's Pantaloon. He has ensconsed himself in the sixth age long before it was due. The self-appointed guardian of order, he is a Puritan through and through, the only party-pooper in a country called Illyria, where everyone else remains in the youthful third age of the lover. The 'pantaloon', then, is an invitation to consider Shakespeare's representation of age and folly as fellow-travellers. The pairing reaches its apogee with King Lear and his Fool, to whom we will come in due course.

Though he could not have known as much at the time of writing Jaques' seven ages speech, Shakespeare himself never became an old man. Lear in his eighty-first year is an act of imagination and observation, not a transmutation of personal experience. When playing at court, Shakespeare saw a tetchy queen approaching her seventieth year, but his own fate would be to die just as he turned fifty-two. Jaques' figure of the pantaloon may remind the modern spectator of an old-age pensioner with slippers, spectacles and tobacco pouch. The temptation in linking the image to the life of its creator is to start talking about Shakespeare's retirement. To suppose that, like Prospero, he renounced his art and drowned his books. Ever since the Romantic period of the early nineteenth century, Prospero has been seen as a Shakespeare figure. His epilogue has accordingly been read as Shakespeare's farewell to the stage. Popular biographies still sometimes suppose that after writing *The Tempest* in 1611, the dramatist 'retired' to Stratford, settled down to property dealing, minor litigation and the life of the complacent country gentleman. This is a myth.

The contours of Shakespeare's career

A gentleman retiring to the country would have been likely to play a part in local civic affairs, to become a Justice of the Peace and so forth. Shakespeare showed no interest in trying to redeem his father's fall by becoming a town councillor or magistrate. He was reluctant to be drawn into the local dispute over the enclosure of some fields on the Welcombe Hills just outside Stratford. Shakespeare's 'cousin' (kinsman?) Thomas Greene, who with his wife Lettice lived for some time with Anne Hathaway in New Place, Shakespeare's big house on the corner of Chapel Street and Dead Lane, made a note in his memorandum book, dated 17 November 1614:

At my cousin Shakespeare coming yesterday to town, I went to see him how he did. He told me that they assured him they meant to enclose no further than to Gospel Bush and so up straight (leaving out part of the dingles to the field) to the gate in Clopton Hedge and take in Salisbury's piece, and that they mean in April to survey the land and then to give satisfaction and not before – and he and Mr Hall say they think there will be nothing done at all.

'Relax', Shakespeare is saying, 'we're talking about a smaller area than many people suppose and nothing is going to happen through the winter, and by the time a survey of the land is done in the spring, the whole thing will probably have blown over and nothing will be done at all.' This at a London meeting in November 1614 with Greene, who had come to town in pursuit of Thomas Combe, the man proposing the enclosure. A firm sighting in London, just eighteen months before Shakespeare's death.

The only occasion on which Shakespeare bought as opposed to rented a property in London was in March 1613, when he purchased a substantial gatehouse close to the Blackfriars theatre. Even if this was primarily an investment property, the date of its purchase reveals Shakespeare's continuing commitment to London in his final years. Greene manifestly knew where to find him in town, so presumably the address of his *pied à terre* was known back in Stratford. In mid-December 1614, Greene is back in Stratford, writing to Shakespeare – which may imply that Shakespeare was in London for a month or more at this time.

The contours of Shakespeare's career are clear, though the detail remains full of uncertainty. He began as a player, probably in the late 1580s. He then revealed a talent for improving the scripts of plays in the repertoire of his company. In 1592 he is clearly identified as an actor turned playwright in *Greene's Groatsworth of Wit*. Early that year, Lord Strange's Men played 'Harry the Sixth' – almost certainly the chronicle drama we now call *Henry VI Part 1* – to great acclaim at the Rose. Just as his career was taking off at this point, the theatres were closed for an extended period, initially because of anxiety about public disorder and subsequently because of plague. During the long closure, Shakespeare tried his hand as a non-dramatic poet, dedicating his *Venus and Adonis* and then his *Rape of Lucrece* to the Earl of Southampton. When the theatres reopened in the summer of 1594, a new company was formed under the patronage of Henry Carey, Lord Hunsdon, who was Queen Elizabeth's Lord Chamberlain, in charge of court festivities. The Lord Chamberlain's Men constituted themselves as a joint stock company, with Shakespeare as one of the shareholders. Since several of the other shareholders had previously been with Strange's Men, it is likely that Shakespeare had been too. The fragmentary surviving evidence suggests that his own acting parts with the new company were limited. His main role was to be their in-house dramatist, producing about three new plays a year. There must be a strong likelihood that he also oversaw, and perhaps polished up, scripts submitted by other dramatists, but this is an aspect of his work that it is almost impossible to recover.

The second great turning-point of Shakespeare's career came in the early years of the new king's reign. The theatres were closed because of plague from May 1603 to April 1604, again from May to September 1604, October to December 1605, and then for most of the time from July 1606 to February 1610, apart from a brief reopening between April and July 1608. Shakespeare was at the height of his powers and his productivity when old Queen Elizabeth died. James had given Shakespeare and his fellows the ultimate accolade of patronage in the form of the title King's Men. But during the first six and a half years of James's English reign, the public theatres were closed for over four years, open for under two.

This fact had huge consequences for Shakespeare, not always fully perceived by biographers. He had already made enough money from his shareholding in the company to purchase a large house, together with farmland and other properties back in Stratford. He no longer needed to endure the discomfort of touring. In all probability, he spent the greater proportion of these long plague years at home. Only one foot remained in London. The other was planted ever more firmly back in Stratford, despite that lack of a desire to play a part in local government or the civic life of the community.

Several fragments of evidence suggest that Shakespeare gave up acting at this time. He is in the cast lists of Ben Jonson's plays *Every Man in his Humour* (1598) and *Sejanus* (1603), but, unlike Richard Burbage, John Hemings, Henry Condell and the rest of his fellows in the King's Men, not those of *Volpone* (1605), *The Alchemist* (1610) and *Catiline* (1611). The inference must be that he stopped acting around the time of the 1603–04 plague outbreak. Perhaps the sense of shame that he alludes to in sonnets 110–112, written around this time, had something to do with his decision.

The First Folio includes a list of 'The names of the principal actors' in Shakespeare's plays. An early owner of a copy of the great book scribbled marginal notes beside several of these names. Richard Burbage: 'by report'. John Lowin: 'by eyewittnesse'. Joseph Taylor: 'know'. William Ostler: 'hearsay'. He is recording his knowledge of the actors. Against Shakespeare he wrote 'ceast' or 'least' or possibly 'best' (the initial letters are hard to decipher) 'for making'. The words 'dramatist' and 'playwright' were not in common currency at this time: the author of a play was known as the 'maker'. So, for instance, in a book called *The Thunderbolt of*

God's Wrath against hard-hearted and stiff-necked Sinners, Christopher Marlowe was referred to as 'a poet and a filthy play-maker'. The enigmatic comment of the Folio reader may therefore suggest that Shakespeare was 'best' for writing, not acting. Or that, as 'maker' of the plays, he did the 'least' acting – unsubstantiated theatrical tradition associates him with small parts, such as the ghost of old Hamlet and the aged servant Adam, borne on Orlando's back in *As You Like It*. If Shakespeare was a kind of stage director, in the manner of Peter Quince organizing the rehearsal of 'Pyramus and Thisbe' in *A Midsummer Night's Dream*, it would make sense for him to have been only a bit-part player himself. If, however, the word is 'ceast for making', the implication would be that Shakespeare began as an actor, then doubled as actor and maker, but eventually ceased acting and became just a maker. Whatever the reading, the suggestion is that this early reader who knew something about the King's Men associated Shakespeare with play-making rather than acting.

Less ambiguous than the Folio annotation is a recently discovered list of 'Players of Interludes' in the records of the royal household, dated 1607. This document lists Burbage the lead actor, Hemings the actor and company manager, Armin the company clown and others of the King's Men – but not Shakespeare. If he was still acting, he would unquestionably have acted at court. This is the strongest piece of evidence that during the Jacobean plague years Shakespeare was no longer sharing in the grind of being a working, touring actor.

The productivity rate of his writing greatly slowed at this time. What would have been the point of turning out a plethora of new comedies if they could not be showcased at the Globe? With the London theatres closed so much of the time and a large repertoire on the stocks, Shakespeare seems to have focused his energies on writing a few long and complex tragedies that could have been played on demand at court. *Othello*, *King Lear*, *Antony and Cleopatra*, *Coriolanus* and *Cymbeline* are among his longest and poetically grandest plays. *Macbeth*, his other major Jacobean tragedy, survives only in a shorter text, which shows signs of adaptation after his death, while *Timon of Athens* seems to have been a not wholly successful collaboration with another dramatist, Thomas Middleton. Each of these plays moves conspicuously between two worlds: Venice and Cyprus in *Othello*, court and open country in *Lear*, Rome and Egypt in *Antony and Cleopatra*, Rome and 'a world elsewhere' in *Coriolanus*, royal court and wild Wales in *Cymbeline*, Scotland and England in *Macbeth*, Athens and a wood in *Timon*. The general tendency is to drift away from Rome or Athens or the court, from *negotium* to *otium*. This was Shakespeare's own plague-fleeing progress at the time of writing. So then: there is a Stratford Shakespeare before 1611, but by the same account there is a London Shakespeare after 1611, albeit on a part-time basis.

Gossip usually begins from a grain of truth. John Ward, vicar of Stratford-upon-Avon after the Restoration of the monarchy in 1660, accurately recorded that Shakespeare had just two surviving daughters and one living grand-daughter. He also made the following note in his diary:

I have heard that Mr Shakespeare was a natural wit, without any art at all; he frequented the plays all his younger time, but in his elder days lived at Stratford and supplied the stage with 2 plays every year, and for that had an allowance so large that he spent at the rate of a thousand pounds a year, as I have heard.

The implausibly vast annual expenditure witnesses to gossip's exaggerations, but there is no particular reason to doubt the main contention, namely that Shakespeare immersed himself in the life of the theatre in the early part of his career, but later lived back home in Stratford. What is striking about Ward's memorandum is the implication that in his elder days Shakespeare actually lived and wrote in Stratford, supplying his later plays to the actors but, by implication, not being involved in actually putting them on.

There is evidence – principally on the basis of tax arrears – of Shakespeare being resident in Bishopsgate and then moving to the liberty of the Clink in Southwark, close to the Globe, in the late 1590s. He lodged with the Mountjoys in Silver Street in the early 1600s. But, remarkably, there are no firm sightings of him in London between autumn 1604, when he presided over the hand-fasting of Mary Mountjoy and Stephen Belott, and May 1612 when he was sworn in at the Westminster Court of Requests under the denomination 'William Shakespeare of Stratford upon Avon in the county of Warwick, gentleman of the age of 48 years or thereabouts'. That absence from the archives is consistent with his absence from the casts of Jonson's later plays and the 1607 list of players at court.

There is, by contrast, no doubt about his presence in Stratford during these years: in 1605 he made a massive investment in a lease of 'tithes of corn, grain, blade and hay' in three neighbouring villages, together with small tithes of the entire parish of Stratford. This cost him £440, the equivalent of nearly £100,000 in early twenty-first-century terms. He would, one suspects, have been more interested in staying around to monitor the performance of an investment of this size than in returning to London to watch performances of his own plays. He was also busy litigating in the Stratford courts, one particular case dragging on from August 1608 to June 1609.

Most biographers prefer to ignore the fact that we cannot formally prove that Shakespeare was in London between autumn 1604 and early summer 1612. We tacitly assume that he was present to hand over his works and for script meetings regarding his collaborative plays, but this is no more than an assumption. Given that for so much of this period, plague closed the public theatres and put all Londoners in fear for their lives, he was sensible to stay away as much as possible. The only times when he would really have wanted to be in London would have been when his plays were put on at court. But his absence from the 1607 list of players requires us to countenance the possibility that he was not present at such occasions as the performance of *King Lear* before the King's Majesty at Whitehall on the night after Christmas, 1606.

If he were absent, one would have to ask why. Having achieved so much – the admiration of monarchs and earls, the status of gentleman and the title of His Majesty's Groom of the Chamber – it would have been galling to miss the plaudits at court. Ill health is a possible explanation. A darker one is that some scandal kept him away. Are there hints in that group of sonnets about the 'stain' on his name? Any courtier with the marks of disease had to stay well away from the king until cured. If Shakespeare had contracted or, more to the point, had been perceived to have contracted syphilis, he would effectively have been forced into Timon-like exile.

To put all this another way: *Shakespeare may never have fully retired, but he may well have semi-retired much earlier than we suppose.* Consider the pattern of his writing partnerships. He began as the fixer-up of old plays. Some of his earliest original works were collaborative – perhaps a scene or more for the domestic tragedy of *Arden of Faversham*, almost certainly the Countess of Salisbury scenes in the history play of *Edward III*. There is a fierce scholarly debate about when he wrote the great crowd scene for *Sir Thomas More*, but its composition represents a task of the kind that was typical for him in these early years. There are signs of George Peele's hand in *Titus Andronicus* and Thomas Nashe's in *Henry VI Part 1*, though in neither case is it entirely clear whether Shakespeare was revising their earlier work independently or actively co-writing with them. Pre-Chamberlain's Shakespeare is in considerable measure a collaborative author.

After 1594, however, with the establishment of the Lord Chamberlain's Men and Shakespeare's new status as company playmaker, he wrote alone until at least 1603. Scholars argue about the degree of collaborative authorship in pre-Chamberlain's plays such as the *Henry VI* cycle, but every play that can be dated with security to the Chamberlain's period is solo-authored: *The Comedy of Errors, Love's Labour's Lost, A Midsummer Night's Dream, Romeo and Juliet, Richard II, The Merchant of Venice, Henry IV Parts 1 & 2, Much Ado about Nothing, Henry V, As You Like It, Julius Caesar, Hamlet, The Merry Wives of Windsor, Twelfth Night, Troilus and Cressida.* To this rich list we can probably also add *Richard III, King John* and *Love's Labour's Won*, though there is not a consensus about the dates of the first two, and the last is lost. The earliest Jacobean plays are also solo-authored: *Othello, Measure for Measure, All's Well that Ends Well. Macbeth, King Lear* and perhaps *Antony and Cleopatra* were big court showpieces for the year 1606.

But during the years of extended plague closure, Shakespeare countenanced collaborative work for the first time since his early career. An almost watertight case has been made for the hand of Thomas Middleton in *Timon of Athens* and an absolutely secure one for that of George Wilkins in *Pericles*. Around this time Shakespeare may also have worked with Middleton on a lost play – or rather series of short plays – called *Four Plays in One*. Only one of the four survives, the darkly compelling *Yorkshire Tragedy*. Most scholars attribute it to Middleton, but it was published in 1608 under the title *A Yorkshire Tragedy written by W. Shakespeare*. It certainly has marks of his style, if not his hand, in at least the first scene.

In *Pericles*, there is a firm division of labour. Wilkins writes the first half and Shakespeare the second. That was not the usual pattern of collaborative authorship. It suggests that Wilkins began and then gave up (or was, as we now say, 'taken off the project'), so Shakespeare finished off the play. But in the case of *Timon* there is an intricate parcelling out of scenes of a kind more characteristic of active collaboration. Middleton was a London man through and through, willing to endure life in the city through years of plague. The *Timon* and possibly *Four Plays in One* collaborations may have constituted Shakespeare's first semi-retirement, his flirtation with the possibility of handing over more of the day-to-day writing duties to a Londoner – though with the proviso that he would continue to work alone on big new plays that could be readied for performance before the king, especially during the Christmas season. *Coriolanus*, *Cymbeline*, *The Winter's Tale* and *The Tempest* come into this latter category.

For some reason the Middleton collaboration did not work out. There is no record of *Timon* ever having made it to the stage – certainly not of it sustaining its place in the repertoire. Shakespeare turned his attention to an alternative prospective successor, John Fletcher. The latter had a proven track record of successful collaborative work: 'Beaumont and Fletcher' were, indeed, becoming synonymous with the very idea of a writing partnership. They were allegedly so close to each other that they shared a bed in their lodgings, a wardrobe of clothes and a wench. Fletcher may have sparked Shakespeare's interest with *The Woman's Prize; or, The*

Tamer Tamed, one of his solo-authored works, which was a self-conscious riposte to *The Taming of the Shrew*, in which Petruchio gets his come-uppance from a second wife (like Lysistrata in the ancient comedy of Aristophanes, she leads a rebellion of the wives in which they refuse to sleep with their husbands until they get their way). Shakespeare was also impressed with the new style of tragi-comic romance that Beaumont and Fletcher pioneered in a play called *Philaster; or, Love Lies a-Bleeding*. He borrowed liberally from its techniques when he came to write *Cymbeline*.

So it was that by 1612, Fletcher was identified as the man who would succeed Shakespeare as in-house dramatist for the King's Men. Plague had abated, so the repertoire needed refreshing. Fletcher was eased into the role by means of three collaborative plays. The court chamber accounts show that in May 1613 John Hemings, company manager, was paid for performances by the King's Men of a number of plays, some old and some new, including 'Cardenno'. This play was obviously a particular success because it was chosen to be performed again in a special presentation for the benefit of the Duke of Savoy's ambassador on 8 June 1613. Based on a story taken from the 1612 English translation of Cervantes' *Don Quixote*, the play survives indirectly via a heavily altered eighteenth-century adaptation. Back in the seventeenth century, the original text had been registered for publication as 'The History of Cardennio, by Mr Fletcher and Shakespeare', but it never appeared in print.

Its success at court may have been what prompted Shakespeare and Fletcher to work closely together on another new play, *All is True, representing some Principal Pieces of the Reign of Henry VIII*. Sir Henry Wotton records the misadventure that befell it at one of its first performances, on 29 June 1613:

Now, to let matters of state sleep, I will entertain you at the present with what has happened this week at the Bank's side. The King's players had a new play, called *All is True, representing some Principal Pieces of the Reign of Henry VIII*, which was set forth with many extraordinary circumstances of pomp and majesty, even to the matting of the stage; the Knights of the Order with their Georges and garters, the Guards with their embroidered

coats, and the like: sufficient in truth within a while to make greatness
very familiar, if not ridiculous. Now, King Henry making a masque at
the Cardinal Wolsey's house, and certain chambers being shot off at his
entry, some of the paper, or other stuff, wherewith one of them was
stopped, did light on the thatch, where being thought at first but an idle
smoke, and their eyes more attentive to the show, it kindled inwardly,
and ran round like a train, consuming within less than an hour the whole
house to the very grounds. This was the fatal period of that virtuous
fabric, wherein yet nothing did perish but wood and straw, and a few
forsaken cloaks; only one man had his breeches set on fire, that would
perhaps have broiled him, if he had not by the benefit of a provident
wit put it out with bottle ale.

Wotton's account reveals how much care the King's Men took in
their efforts to represent 'pomp and majesty' on stage: from the
matting on the floor to the garters and crosses of St George on the
costumes, everything is contrived 'to make greatness very familiar'.
Intriguingly, though, the effect of transforming royal processions
through Whitehall and Westminster into passages of a play on the
matted stage of a thatched theatre in the margins of Southwark is
also to make greatness seem just a little 'ridiculous'.

The players owned the Globe Theatre, which they had built
themselves back in 1599, so freeing themselves from the disputes
with landlords that had previously dogged them. The fire that
destroyed it in the high summer of 1613 was a disaster for the
King's Men. In order to generate income, they were forced to
head off on tour again – in the autumn, they are found at Oxford,
Stafford and Shrewsbury – but they also needed to maintain the
repertory in their winter house at Blackfriars and to be ready to
play before the court at the drop of a hat (they did so, twice in
November, once in January and several times in February 1614).
Amazingly – and one suspects that the business *nous* of Hemings
drove the project – they rebuilt the theatre, bigger and better than
before, by the summer of 1614.

A spectacular new play was necessary for its opening and, to
judge from a prologue allusion to 'our losses', this may have been
the occasion in which *The Two Noble Kinsmen* was given its first

outing in the public playhouse. When that play was published in 1634, the title page announced that it had been presented with great applause at the Blackfriars and that it was 'written by Mr John Fletcher and Mr William Shakespeare, Gentlemen'. Other nuggets of evidence combine to suggest that Fletcher and Shakespeare wrote this play – which reveals a pattern of close collaboration – some time between the burning and the reopening of the Globe. It was probably played at Whitehall for the court and Blackfriars for the gallants during the winter of 1613–14, before being staged at the new Globe the following summer. So here is Shakespeare still at work in late 1613, maybe even some time into 1614. That he was still active at this time accords with the purchase of the Blackfriars gatehouse in 1613 and the meeting with Greene in London in the autumn of 1614. What kind of retreat to rural retirement is this?

21. The Principal Comedians

'And the rest of his fellows'

The Chamberlain's Men were highly regarded and took the lead annually at court. One of the earliest references to Shakespeare in their company is as joint payee, together with Richard Burbage and William Kempe, for performances given at court in the Christmas season of 1594. That same season, the Chamberlain's Men also played *The Comedy of Errors*, probably a new play at the time, during an evening's festivities at one of the Inns of Court. They were in demand, the new team on a roll. Burbage was the company's leading serious actor, their answer to Edward Alleyn of the Admiral's Men, who had made his name with Christopher Marlowe's mighty tragic parts. Kempe was the company clown. The image of the tragedian, the clown and the play-maker going together to receive the company's payment for their Christmas performances before the queen is a very striking one. It binds Shakespeare intimately to his fellows, reminds us that he wrote his leading tragic parts for Burbage and his clown's roles for Kempe (then, after Kempe left the company in 1599, for his successor, Robert Armin).

No other Elizabethan dramatist prior to Shakespeare was a company insider as he was. Acting companies nearly always form a close-knit body. In Shakespeare's middle years, his key relationships were his friendships with the rest of the Chamberlain's Men. No document gives a more touching sense of their intimacy than the will of Augustine Phillips, actor and company manager, the man who spoke on behalf of them all during the investigation into the links between their *Richard II* and the Earl of Essex's rebellion. Phillips died early in the summer of 1605. He remembered the whole company: the hired men, who played the smaller parts and were paid on a piecework basis; his 'fellows', the shareholders who played the leading roles and shared the profits; and the apprentices, who played the women's and children's parts:

Item, I give and bequeath unto and amongst the hired men of the Company which I am of, which shall be at the time of my decease, the sum of five pounds of lawful money of England to be equally distributed amongst them. Item, I give and bequeath to my fellow William Shakespeare a thirty shillings piece in gold, to my fellow Henry Condell one other thirty shilling piece in gold, to my servant Christopher Beeston thirty shillings in gold, to my fellow Lawrence Fletcher twenty shillings in gold, to my fellow Robert Armin twenty shillings in gold, to my fellow Richard Cowley twenty shillings in gold, to my fellow Alexander Cook twenty shillings in gold, to my fellow Nicholas Tooley twenty shillings in gold . . . Item, I give to Samuel Gilborne, my late apprentice, the sum of forty shillings and my mouse-coloured velvet hose, and a white taffety doublet, a black taffety suit, my purple cloak, sword and dagger, and my bass viol. Item, I give to James Sands my apprentice the sum of forty shillings and a cittern, a bandore and a lute, to be paid and delivered unto him at the expiration of his term of years in his indenture of apprenticeship.

Burbage and Hemings are named as executors of the will. They are each given a silver bowl worth £5.

There is a whole world of company life in this document. The versatility of the player: he must handle a sword and dagger one moment, play a bass viol, cittern, bandore or lute the next. (A bandore was a guitar-like instrument, used as bass to the cittern.) The importance of clothes: costumes were always more of a drain on the company budget than scripts. The bond between a master actor and his apprentices, past and present: a bond that was strengthened by the custom of the apprentice living with his master, giving them the opportunity to practise their lines together late at night and early in the morning. The possibility of progression through the ranks: Cook and Tooley had started out as apprentices – they are the likeliest candidates for the original casting of Juliet, Beatrice, Portia, Rosalind, Viola, all the great female parts of Shakespeare's Elizabethan years – but by 1605 they are full shareholders. The generosity of the senior company man towards his juniors: Condell, Fletcher, Armin and Cowley had all become shareholders relatively recently, while Beeston was only a 'servant'. Above all, the pride of place given to 'my fellow, William Shakespeare': the first name in the list, one of the largest bequests. We may detect a special bond between the two men, leading us to suspect that they constituted the business brains of the company, the organizers who day in and day out knocked actors and productions into shape.

That Shakespeare was an actor himself, that he worked daily with his fellow-actors and that he wrote all his plays from 1594 to the end of his career for the same ensemble are among the reasons why he returned so persistently to the image of the world as a stage and man's life as the enacting of a series of parts. Hamlet welcomes to Elsinore a company of players who in several key particulars, such as their rivalry with a new group of boy actors, hold up a mirror to Shakespeare's own company. 'He that plays the king shall be welcome,' says the Prince,

his majesty shall have tribute of me: the adventurous knight shall use his foil and target: the lover shall not sigh *gratis*: the humorous man shall end his part in peace: the clown shall make those laugh whose lungs are tickled o'th'sear: and the lady shall say her mind freely, or the blank verse shall halt for't.

The King, the Adventurous Knight, the Lover, the Humorous Man, the Clown, the Lady: Hamlet's knowledge of the players suggests that a degree of typecasting was customary in Shakespeare's theatre, a practice borne out by the occasional tendency of his scripts to use generic speech headings such as King, Clown, Bastard and Braggart. This way of thinking is what lies behind the identification of the old man of the sixth age as the Pantaloon.

One is inevitably tempted to ask for which actors Shakespeare was writing when he conjured up a new king, a lover, humorous man or pantaloon. The evidence is maddeningly elusive. We have a list of the 'principal Comedians' who played in Ben Jonson's comedy *Every Man in his Humour*, premiered by the Chamberlain's Men in 1598. It is printed in two columns: William Shakespeare is at the top of one, Richard Burbage at the top of the other. Beneath them are Augustine Phillips and John Hemings, then Henry Condell and Thomas Pope, Will Sly and Christopher Beeston, Will Kempe and John Duke. Beeston and Duke were minor figures, who soon moved on to other companies (though it is from Beeston – a good source – that we get the story of Shakespeare spending some time in his youth as a schoolmaster in the country). The key players beside Shakespeare – 'the rest of his fellows', as the shareholders of the acting company were usually described when their business manager received payment for performances at court – were Burbage, Phillips, Hemings, Condell, Pope, Sly and Kempe. Four of them died before Shakespeare, the three others he remembered in his will.

Unfortunately, the Jonson list is not linked to the names of the characters in the play. In helping to cast Shakespeare's kings, adventurous knights, lovers, humorous men, ladies and clowns, another list of actors' names, though of questionable date, is rather more helpful than the one attached to *Every Man in his Humour*. It is the 'plot' or backstage storyboard of an old play called *The Seven Deadly Sins Part 2*. The play itself is lost, but there is enough in the plot to make a few suggestions. Richard Burbage played a tyrannical king and Augustine Phillips an effete one. George Bryan, who left the company shortly before *Every Man in his Humour* went into production, played a lord or counsellor. Thomas Pope had a comic part. John Hemings seems to have had a 'choric' role and Henry Condell played a young lord. Kempe was the clown. Cooke and Tooley were there, with several other apprentices, including one 'Ned', who just might have been Edmund Shakespeare, apprenticed to (so presumably lodging with) his big brother. Little is known about the characteristics of the leading apprentices, who seem to have been Tooley and Cooke. It may perhaps be inferred that one was a lot taller than the other, since Shakespeare often wrote for a pair of female friends, one tall and fair, the other short and dark (Helena and Hermia, Rosalind and Celia, Beatrice and Hero). Tooley and Cooke were born the same year, 1583, so we cannot say that one or the other was taller because he was older.

Put Hamlet's list of types together with the plot of *The Seven Deadly Sins* and we may begin to suppose that we could reconstruct the original casts of Shakespeare's plays. Did 'stuttering' Hemings, as he became known, play Polonius in *Hamlet* and Lafew in *All's Well that Ends Well*? When Condell graduated to the status of full sharer, did he become Edgar in *Lear* and Malcolm in *Macbeth*? But one quickly discovers that – save for Burbage's lead roles and the generic part of the clown – all this is mere speculation. We do not even know for sure whether the original Falstaff was Kempe or Pope.

Still, we can sketch out the careers of the actors, and ask whether or not there is a similar pattern in their lives to that of Shakespeare, with its movement towards provincial property holding and away from the stage (without altogether renouncing it). Did any of the 'principal comedians' become lean and slippered pantaloons in real life?

Augustine Phillips is first glimpsed travelling with the company Strange's Men in the plague summer of 1593. He must have become one of the original Lord Chamberlain's Men the following year. In May 1595, 'Phillips his Jig of the Slippers' was registered for publication. Not a slippered pantaloon himself, then, but perhaps the author of a jig featuring one? Jigs were comic afterpieces performed after the main play. A mix of song, dance, slapstick and bawdy, they were very popular – some audience members turned up towards the end of the afternoon for the jig alone. The bass viol, cittern, bandore and lute that Phillips left to his apprentices in his will suggest he was a talented instrumentalist and thus a key player in the jigs. But he also played serious parts and acted as business manager. His role as company spokesman in the Essex affair bespeaks his importance. In 1599, he was one of the five actors who each bought a 10 per cent share in their new theatre building, the Globe (this was their way of getting out of the clutches of their troublesome landlord at their old theatre called The Theatre). The other four 10 per cent sharers in the new theatre building were Shakespeare, Pope, Hemings and Kempe, with the remaining 50 per cent in the hands of the Burbage family.

Like Shakespeare, Phillips was upwardly mobile. Famously, one of the officials in the College of Heralds complained about the dishing out of coats of arms and 'gentlemanly' status to such dubious figures as 'Shakespeare the Player'. Less well known is a precisely analogous complaint from a junior pursuivant in the College that 'Phillips the player had graven in a gold ring arms of Sir William Phillipp, Lord Bardolph, with the said Lord Bardolph's coat [of arms] quartered.' This suggests that, either fraudulently or authentically but certainly presumptuously, Phillips claimed kinship with Lord Bardolph. It is very tempting to suppose that as an in-house joke, Shakespeare named one of Falstaff's companions Bardolph and cast Phillips in the role, also giving him a cameo as 'Lord Bardolph'. Thus the Porter at the very beginning of *Henry IV Part 2*: 'What shall I say you are?' Phillips as Lord Bardolph: 'Tell thou the earl / That the Lord Bardolph doth attend him here.' Knowing the sense of humour that actors have, this would have cracked them up backstage. Just a few lines later Lord Bardolph speaks of 'A gentleman well bred and of good name'. A palpable hit: Phillips was indeed of the first generation of actors to claim social status for the profession. By 1604, he could afford a country house in the village of Mortlake, just as Shakespeare afforded New Place back in Stratford. Unlike Shakespeare, though, he did not live to enjoy a semi-retirement. Just over a week after making that will in May 1605, 'sick and weak in body, but of good and perfect mind and remembrance', he died, leaving a widow and five children.

Richard Burbage, four years younger than Shakespeare, came from a theatre family. His father James had built The Theatre in Shoreditch, the first enduring purpose-built playhouse in the land. In this sense, he was the father of the profession. James had two boys. Cuthbert, Shakespeare's contemporary, continued the entrepreneurial tradition of his father. He invested in the Chamberlain's Men and their theatre buildings, leaving his younger brother Dick to tread the boards. Burbage the tragedian was supposedly like the shape-changing god of classical myth, Proteus: 'so wholly transforming himself into his part, and putting off himself with his clothes, as he never (not so much as in the tiring-house) assumed himself again until the play was ended'. The original Richard III, Romeo, Hamlet, Othello and Lear, he seems to be the model for the exemplary actor described by John Webster: 'By a full and significant action of body, he charms our attention: sit in a full theatre, and you will think you see so many lines drawn from the circumference of so many ears, whiles the actor is the centre.' Thus the defining charisma of the great actor: to hold the whole house under his command, drawing imaginary lines of attention from their ears. This in a bustling open-air daylight theatre. Burbage played until his death in 1619, upon which he was mourned by an array of epitaphs. Some were expansive, one of them lamenting that Hamlet, Lear and Othello had died with him. Another was pithy in the extreme: 'Exit Burbage'. Yet another, by the dramatist Thomas Middleton, suggested that his death was like a total eclipse over the world of the theatre:

> Astronomers and star-gazers this year
> Write but of four eclipses; five appear,
> Death interposing Burbage – and their staying
> Hath made a visible eclipse of playing.

John Hemings was two years younger than Shakespeare, also from the shires of the west midlands. He was sent to London and apprenticed into the grocery business at the age of eleven. After nine years' graft, he became a freeman shortly before his twenty-first birthday and – exactly how, when and why, we do not know – made the unlikely shift from grocery to acting. Very shortly after finishing his apprenticeship he married a young widow with a theatre background: Rebecca Knell, just seventeen, had been married to an actor called William Knell, who was killed in a fight with a fellow-actor when the Queen's Men were on tour at Thame in Oxfordshire in 1587. Hemings and Rebecca had fourteen children, one of whom grew up to become a playwright, author of a lost comedy called *The Coursing of a Hare; or, the Madcap* and an extant *Jew's Tragedy* that is stuffed with Shakespearean quotation and imitation.

Like Phillips, Hemings was with Strange's Men in '93 and an original sharer in the Chamberlain's Men in '94. He retained his links with the grocers, apprenticing his own 'boys' into their livery company as a way of creating a legal bond between master and trainee. In the royal patent that turned the Chamberlain's Men into the King's Men, Hemings' name comes directly after those of Shakespeare, Burbage and Phillips. When the company was re-licensed in 1619, he was at the head of the list. After Phillips' death, it was Hemings who collected the money for command performances. Court records speak of him as the man responsible for 'presenting' the plays of the King's Men before the court, suggesting that he spent many hours in liaison with the Revels office, undertaking a variety of tasks that would now be divided between a producer, a stage manager and a house manager. Freemen of the Grocers' Company often became extremely prosperous businessmen: Hemings had the training to take over the role of company manager and steer his colleagues through the difficult years of plague and fire. Probably the prime mover behind the publication of the First Folio of Shakespeare's collected plays in 1623, Hemings died a wealthy man in 1630. Called 'stuttering Hemings' in a poem on the Globe fire, he might just have been the man who both played the pantaloon on stage and became one in life.

Because of the co-signed prefatory material to the Folio, John Hemings' name is yoked for ever to that of Henry Condell. They are bound together into history even more immovably than Beaumont and Fletcher. Condell was the younger partner. It is probable that he was initially a 'hired man' with the Chamberlain's Men and that he moved up to the status of shareholder when George Bryan became the first of the original group to part company with his fellows in 1597. For a long time, Condell and his wife lived as near neighbours to Hemings and Rebecca, in the parish of St Mary Aldermanbury in the city of London, close to where Shakespeare lodged with the tire-making Mountjoys. Condell ended his life as a gentleman with an out-of-town home (in Fulham, which was then a village).

Thomas Pope, another of the original sharers, was renowned

for comic roles. He died in 1603. Little is known about him, except that he had been an actor for many years before the formation of the Chamberlain's Men. Back in 1586, together with George Bryan and Will Kempe, he was among a group of English 'instrumentalists and tumblers' in the entourage of the Danish ambassador, Henrik Ramel. They accompanied Ramel when he went home to the Danish court at Elsinore, where they worked as entertainers for several months. It is pleasing to suppose Pope as the lead Player in *Hamlet*, arriving at the court in Elsinore and putting on an entertainment there, just as he had done in real life over ten years before. And it is more than likely that he provided Shakespeare with some local colour, perhaps describing the gun platforms that can still be seen on the terrace at Kronborg Castle above the port that is now called Helsingor. At risk of sounding like a scene from the film *Shakespeare in Love*, there must also have been a conversation along the following lines. Shakespeare: 'I want to include some former schoolfellows who spy on Hamlet and who always act together as a pair – you've been to Elsinore, Tom, give me Danish names for them.' Pope: 'Well, when I was there with George and Will, we worked for the Master of the Palace, name of George Rosenkrantz, and then there was the Marshal of Denmark, Peter Guildenstern.' Shakespeare: 'Rosencrantz and Guildenstern? Good names. Thank you kindly, Tom.'

Pope, Bryan and Kempe were together again back in England in the early 1590s with Lord Strange's Men. Will Kempe became one of the stars of the Chamberlain's Men, leading the jigs, with their songs and rhymes, dances and bawdry, while also playing clown parts in the main play. A number of his jigs survive, directly or indirectly. In one of them, the Clown (who is always the leading character) is cheated out of his mistress by a sexton. He gets her back by lying in a grave dug by the sexton and leaping out, as if he were a ghost returning to life. Could Shakespeare have clocked this comic business and turned something similar to darker purpose in the graveyard scene of *Hamlet*? Another Kempe jig, *Singing Simpkin*, perhaps provides a hint for *The Merry Wives of Windsor*. The luscious young wife of an aged miser seduces a soldier called Bluster, who goes to hide in a chest in order not to be found out by the returning husband, only to discover that Simpkin is already there, having already cuckolded the old man. The jig offers a simplified version of the stock parts of both 'the seven ages' and Hamlet's list of actor-types. In *Singing Simpkin* we have, in Hamlet's nomenclature, the Braggart Knight, the Humorous Man, the Clown and the Lady, or, in that of Jaques, a Lover, a Soldier and a Pantaloon. The structure of Shakespearean comedy often involves working with these archetypes, but complicating and individualizing them. Thus in *The Merry Wives*, the husband with the 'humour' of obsessive jealousy is a relatively young man, Ford, not the traditional aged miser husband of cuckold comedy. The aged character is Falstaff, the Braggart Knight.

Though the question remains open as to whether the part of Falstaff was written for Pope or Kempe, the latter was undoubtedly Costard in *Love's Labour's Lost*, Peter (the Nurse's servant) in *Romeo and Juliet*, Bottom in *A Midsummer Night's Dream*, Lancelet Gobbo in *The Merchant of Venice* and Dogberry in *Much Ado about Nothing*. He would have left a great hole in the company when he left in 1599 and danced off all the way to Norwich. Tradition has it that he and Shakespeare fell out over the question of the Clown's ad-libbing, but that tradition is based on no firmer evidence than Hamlet's strictures to the players: 'let those that play your clowns speak no more than is set down for them'.

Kempe was replaced by Robert Armin, who relied more on cerebral wit than physical comedy. As many critics have noticed, this accounts for the change of style in Shakespeare's later fools: Touchstone in *As You Like It* (perhaps so named because Armin had been apprenticed as a goldsmith), Feste in *Twelfth Night*, Thersites in *Troilus and Cressida*, Lavatch in *All's Well that Ends Well*, Autolycus in *The Winter's Tale* and above all Lear's Fool are all to varying degrees wise, witty and cynical, written for a vein of verbal humour very different from Kempe's more innocent folly. Though all these fools like to expose the hypocrisy of the great, that did not stop Armin sharing Shakespeare's upward mobility. He too obtained himself a coat of arms and the status of gentleman.

Great theatre is made not only by the quality of a script and the

brilliance of individual performances – and there is ample evidence
that Shakespeare and his peers provided the former, Burbage,
Kempe, Armin and their fellows the latter – but also by the
chemistry *between* the actors. The closest we get to a glimpse of
their interplay is John Webster's induction to the version of
John Marston's *The Malcontent* performed by the King's Men in
1604. In a bravura piece of self-conscious theatricality, on come
Richard Burbage and Henry Condell, together with John Lowin
(a recent acquisition, who went on to become one of the company's lead actors) and John Sinklo (a skinny man for whom
Shakespeare wrote such minor parts as the First Beadle in *Henry IV
Part 2* – he could also have been the original Andrew Aguecheek).
They warm the audience up for the main action by . . . playing
themselves.

Enter Will Sly with a low stool, followed by an agitated 'tire-
man' (dresser or property man from backstage). Sly pretends to be
a young gallant from the audience, claiming his privilege of sitting
on his stool on the edge of the stage. The tire-man is not happy:
that may be the custom in the exclusive 'private' theatres, but it is
not acceptable at the Globe. 'I'll hold my life thou tookest me for
one of the players', says Sly. 'No, sir', says the tire-man, knowing
full well that this *is* one of the players. Sly then explains that he
has seen the show before and has most of the jokes written down
in his table-book, so, stationed prominently on his stool, he can
advise the actors on their performances. He asks to speak with
'Harry Condell, Dick Burbage and Will Sly'. Sinklo then enters,
and he and Sly engage in some very rude banter concerning
the previous evening's supper at a citizen's house, involving the
measuring of the size of the 'cut' belonging to the lady of the
house. Burbage, Condell and Lowin then enter.

There is some business between Burbage and Sly concerning
the feather in the latter's hat, complete with a direct quotation
from the dialogue between Hamlet and Osric on the same subject,
strongly suggesting that the Osric scene (a late addition to *Hamlet*)
was a popular cameo, in all probability played by Burbage and
Sly. The actors then discuss the play they are about to perform,
and in particular the fact that it was originally written for one of

the boys' companies but has now mysteriously found itself ('with additions') in their own adult repertoire. Sly provides an insight into the 'excellent memory' of an actor: he offers to lay a bet of a hundred pounds that, despite not having studied the formal 'art of memory', he could walk just once down the row of goldsmiths on Cheapside, take notice of the signs and repeat them back instantaneously.

Some further banter concerns the Trojan war, with special reference to the sodomitical tendencies of Achilles. Burbage has to go off in order to get ready for his appearance in the main play and Sly concludes the induction with an extempore prologue, which sounds very like a (mildly obscene) parody of the epilogue of *As You Like It*: 'Gentlemen, I could wish for the women's sakes you had all soft cushions; and, gentlewomen, I could wish that for the men's sakes you had all more easy standings.' For regular playgoers who could pick up the allusions and in-jokes, but above all for the actors themselves, it is a lovely little scene. There would have been added wit if the actor whose real name was Will Sly and who is pretending to be an audience member had once played the Shakespearean part of Christopher Sly, the 'audience member' in the induction to *The Taming of the Shrew*.

Sweet William's purge

A couple of years before Burbage and friends appeared as themselves in the induction to *The Malcontent*, Burbage and Kempe had been represented on stage by some student actors in Cambridge, during a specially written Christmas show called *The Return from Parnassus Part 2*.

'Burbage' and 'Kempe' audition some students (played by students) for the parts of Shakespeare's Richard III and Hieronimo in Thomas Kyd's *Spanish Tragedy*. The audition speeches chosen by the students are 'Now is the winter of our discontent' and 'Who calls Hieronimo from his naked bed?' (in the *Spanish Tragedy*'s most famous scene, the hero appears in his night-shirt, summoned at night to discover that his son has been murdered and must be revenged). *The Return from Parnassus* is full of jokes about callow students imagining that they can court girls by quoting *Romeo and Juliet* and *Venus and Adonis* at them: 'We shall have nothing but pure Shakespeare and shreds of poetry that he hath gathered at the theatres!'

The author and some of the cast of *The Return from Parnassus* probably saw *Hamlet* when it was played before the university around this time, but the drama clearly reveals intimate knowledge of the London theatre world. One particular speech is highly intriguing. 'Burbage' suggests that with a little teaching the students might be able to pen some parts of their own. 'Kempe' replies,

Few of the university pen plays well, they smell too much of that writer *Ovid*, and that writer *Metamorphosis*, and talk too much of *Proserpina and Jupiter*. Why, here's our fellow *Shakespeare* puts them all down, ay, and *Ben Jonson* too. O, that *Ben Jonson* is a pestilent fellow, he brought up *Horace* giving the poets a pill, but our fellow *Shakespeare* hath given him a purge that made him beray [beshit] his credit.

This is a joke at the expense of the common players – Kempe reveals his ignorance by thinking that *Metamorphosis* is the name of a writer rather than a work by Ovid – but it is also an allusion to the so-called *poetomachia*, or 'poets' war' that was shaking the theatrical profession at the time.

'Faith, there has been much to-do on both sides,' says Rosencrantz to Hamlet, 'and the nation holds it no sin to tar them to controversy. There was for a while no money bid for argument unless the poet and the player went to cuffs in the question.' The controversy in question began as an argument between Ben Jonson and rival dramatist John Marston about poetic style and methods of characterization, played out on the 'private' stage of the boy actors, but then in 1601 spilled over on to the public (or 'common') stage of the Globe and drew in Shakespeare's acting company. Rosencrantz's 'much to do on both sides' is probably an allusion to the intimate relationship between Jonson's *Poetaster*, performed by the Children of the Chapel Royal in spring 1601, and *The Untrussing of the Humorous Poet*, performed by the Lord Chamberlain's Men that autumn, and then published the next year under the title *Satiromastix* ('the whipping of the satirist'), with attribution to Thomas Dekker.

A flood of scholarly ink has been spilt over the nature of Shakespeare's involvement in what Dekker called 'that terrible *Poetomachia*, lately commenced between *Horace the Second* [Jonson], and a band of lean-witted *Poetasters*'. The main piece of evidence that Shakespeare became involved is the passage in *The Return from Parnassus Part 2*, which was produced at St John's College during the Christmas vacation of 1601–02, shortly after the London staging of *Satiromastix*. What exactly is being alluded to in the claim 'Why, here's our fellow *Shakespeare* puts them all down, ay, and *Ben Jonson* too. O, that *Ben Jonson* is a pestilent fellow, he brought up *Horace* giving the poets a pill, but our fellow *Shakespeare* hath given him a purge that made him beray his credit'?

At the climax of *Poetaster*, the Roman poet Horace (Jonson's self-representation) feeds emetic 'pills' to Crispinus (his representation of Marston), who vomits up fragments of Marston's outlandish poetic diction. The specificity of the first part of the allusion in *The Return from Parnassus* is incontrovertible. What of the second? *Satiromastix* was the explicit reply to *Poetaster*. It contains a scene in which Crispinus (Marston) and Demetrius (Dekker) come to Horace (Jonson) 'like your physicians, to purge / Your sick and dangerous mind of her disease'. After failing in their attempt to reason him out of his satirical mode, they embarrass him when he stages a court entertainment in the form of a masque involving 'strange fashions of apparel' evocative of the animal transformations in 'Ovid's Morter-Morphesis'. The obvious interpretation of the second part of the *Parnassus* allusion is that it is a reference to this recently performed play, especially given the conjunction with a reference to Ovid's *Metamorphoses*. The *Satiromastix* purge is the response to the *Poetaster* pill.

The published text of the play was, however, attributed to Dekker. So what was Shakespeare's involvement with *Satiromastix*? Why did the Cambridge author attribute the purge to him? The obvious explanation is that at the time of the Cambridge play (Christmas 1601) *Satiromastix* had recently been performed by

Shakespeare's acting company, but not yet published. Performances of plays were often advertised by title rather than author.
Dekker's name became associated with the play only when it
appeared in print some months later, so the Cambridge author
probably just assumed that it was by Shakespeare, whom he knew
to be the Chamberlain's company dramatist.

Since the *Parnassus* allusion pre-dates the appearance of *Satiromastix* in print, the Cambridge author – or a close acquaintance in a
position to report back to him – must have seen it on stage in
London. Could it then be that he saw Shakespeare acting in the
play, further strengthening his association with the purge of
Jonson? If so, what part did he play?

Given that almost every major playwright of the moment is
comically alluded to in one or more of the plays of the poets' war,
it is not beyond the bounds of possibility that Dekker makes a mild
joke at the expense of Shakespeare in the character who rejoices
in the name of Sir Adam Prickshaft. Shakespeare was not averse to
playing on his own name. The combination of 'shake' and phallic
'speare', especially in conjunction with the first name 'Will', has
robust bawdy possibilities. Shake-speare, Prick-shaft? Then maybe
'Sir' to tease Shakespeare for his upward mobility in getting himself
a coat of arms and the status of gentleman? Ben Jonson had already
had fun over the brash yellow of Shakespeare's new coat of arms
and the presumption of his motto, 'not without right', by introducing into his *Every Man out of his Humour* a social-climbing countryman called Sogliardo, who gets himself yellow arms and the motto
'not without mustard'. As for the Christian name: theatrical
tradition gives Shakespeare the part of old Adam, the servant in *As
You Like It*. Sir Adam Prickshaft is a bad amateur writer, a foolish
aspirational gentleman poet. It would have been very witty to
have him played by the supreme professional, Master William
Shakespeare.

Sir Adam Prickshaft's opening lines sound familiar: 'God
morrow, god morrow, go, in, in, in, to the bridegroom, taste a
cup of burnt wine this morning, 'twill make you fly the better all
the day after. You are an early stirrer, Sir Quintilian Shorthose.'
This is a clear allusion to the opening lines of one of Shakespeare's

most popular characters, Justice Shallow in *Henry IV Part 2*: 'Come on, come on, come on. Give me your hand, sir: give me your hand, sir. An early stirrer, by the rood! And how doth my good cousin Silence!' Furthermore, there is a gag about Sir Adam Prickshaft that runs throughout the play: he has 'but a remnant or parcel of hair, his crown is clipped and pared away – methinks 'tis an excellent quality to be bald.' The composition of an ode in praise of his baldness becomes part of the plot. Whatever doubts may exist about the various surviving images of Shakespeare, one thing is for sure: he was bald on top. The combination of the name, the direct allusion to *Henry IV* and the fact that Sir Adam Prickshaft is a balding poet would be an extraordinary coincidence if the part had nothing to do with Shakespeare. Prickshaft is one of the poets who participates in the humiliation of Horace/Jonson, so if Shakespeare played the part and the Cambridge author witnessed it, his 'our fellow Shakespeare hath given him a purge' may be an allusion to Shakespeare the actor as well as, or instead of, Shakespeare the writer.

Shakespeare may have been gently teased in the portrayal of Sir Adam Prickshaft, whether or not he acted the part. There is another possible role for him in *Satiromastix*, in its way a more likely one, given what we know of Shakespeare as an actor. An epigram of 1610 by John Davies of Hereford says that the dramatist was renowned for playing the part of kings. An old theatrical tradition identified the ghost of old King Hamlet as his finest performance. The ribald 'William the Conqueror' anecdote about the citizen's wife would have had an additional layer of meaning if, as is very plausible, Shakespeare had once played the part of William the Conqueror in the popular comedy *Fair Em, the Miller's Daughter*. Couple these associations with the fact that Dekker transposed the action of *Poetaster* from Jonson's ancient Rome to Norman England. There must be a strong possibility that when the Chamberlain's Men played *Satiromastix*, William Shakespeare was cast in the relatively small part of King William Rufus, son of William the Conqueror. What better compliment could Dekker pay Shakespeare than to act out the rivalry between the lesser playwrights under the auspices of the master, King William. A strong hint is provided by the way in which the king is addressed at the climax of the action: 'my Princely sweet-William'. Shakespeare was renowned for the *sweetness* of his poetry. Thus William Covell, another Cambridge don, in a note of 1595: 'All praiseworthy: *Lucrece* Sweet Shakespeare, Wanton *Adonis*'. Francies Meres in 1598 wrote of Shakespeare's *sugared* (hence sweet) sonnets and Richard Barnfield of his *honey-flowing* vein. To John Weever in 1599, he was *honey-tongued* Shakespeare. In *The Return from Parnassus Part 1*, a student called Gullio quotes a stanza from *Venus and Adonis*, and another student called Ingenioso replies 'Sweet Mr Shakespeare!' And in *Part 2*, one Judicio tells of how Shakespeare's 'sweeter verse contains heart-throbbing line'. The allusion to Shakespeare's purge in *The Return from Parnassus* must be based on a theatrical visit rather than a published play text. If the author went to the Globe and saw Shakespeare play the part of the King William who presides over the administration of the purge to Jonson, it would make sense for him to have his stage representations of Burbage and Kempe speaking of 'our Shakespeare' in the way that they do.

Shakespeare's participation in this performance is the probable explanation for some lines in the 'Apologetical Dialogue' that Jonson appended to *Poetaster* after the appearance of *Satiromastix*. Jonson says that since he had satirized the players, he does not mind that they have made money at the box-office by satirizing him in return. But he has one disappointment:

> Only amongst them, I am sorry for
> Some better natures, by the rest so drawn,
> To run in that vile line.

'The rest' must be Marston and Dekker, so who are those of 'better nature' who have allowed themselves to be drawn into the quarrel? Burbage and his fellows, perhaps, but most obviously Shakespeare, whom Jonson later praised for his honest, 'open and free nature'. Sweet William's purge was, I suspect, delivered not by way of his writing, but through his participation in Dekker's play. The failure of critics to see this — leading to the pursuit of red herrings such as Ajax in *Troilus* and Malvolio in *Twelfth Night* — stems from a forgetting that in the Elizabethan years Shakespeare was also a company man. He was not a solitary writer in his garret but one of the working 'tragedians of the city'.

Robert Armin: Touchstone, Feste, Lavatch, Lear's Fool

22. The Foolosopher

Opening the Silenus box

There are just ten occurrences of the word 'philosopher' in the Shakespeare concordance.

In *The Merchant of Venice*, one of Portia's suitors, a melancholy man, is compared to 'the weeping philosopher', Heraclitus, who wept at how people gather up treasure for themselves while neglecting to take care to bring up their children well. The philosopher is someone who anatomizes human folly and hypocrisy. Jaques in *As You Like It* answers well to the description.

But *As You Like It* plays the melancholy man off against the Fool. Where Jaques weeps, the Fool anatomizes folly through laughter. Paradoxically, it is the man of folly who perhaps has the true wisdom. The word 'philosopher' is used twice in *As You Like It*. Touchstone describes Corin as 'a natural philosopher', in response to Corin's down-to-earth wisdom ('the property of rain is to wet and fire to burn' – a very philosophical statement). Here the word 'natural' has a double sense: from Touchstone's point of view it means foolish (a village idiot was known as a 'natural'), but to the audience it also suggests that Corin speaks the truth of nature – which is the opposite to that of the court. The truth of nature, as opposed to the flattery of the court, is exactly what King Lear has to learn: the structural movement of his play is strikingly similar to that of *As You Like It*. Lear goes to the country with his Fool, who serves as his touchstone, but he is also exposed to the plain wisdom and virtue of the low-born, such as the Old Man who follows Gloucester.

The second reference in *As You Like It* is to 'the heathen philosopher'. It occurs immediately after the saying 'The fool doth think he is wise, but the wise man knows himself to be a fool.' This is the most famous saying of Socrates. In the sixteenth century, it had become proverbial; it was quoted in the widely known *Adagia* of Erasmus. The longest of the adages concerns the 'Sileni of Alcibiades': a Silenus was a kind of box that was hideous on the outside, but revealed a deity when opened. Socrates, Erasmus said, was like a Silenus box, with his snuffly nose and peasant face. On the surface, he was a blockhead bumpkin who used simple language and had no care for appearance, but within there was deep wisdom, his wisest insight being that he knew nothing. Christ was also seen as a Silenus, because of his humble exterior, his poverty, his rejection by the elite, his time in the wilderness. According to Erasmus, the real truth of things is the most profoundly concealed, not easily detected by the many, certainly not by those with wealth and rank – these are just externals. Socrates' paradoxical wisdom, Christ's ethos of love which proposes turning the other cheek instead of the superficially reasonable requital of an eye for an eye – these are inversions of expected values. Erasmus' word for this is 'praeposterum', a rhetorical figure of reversal. The English translation of this adage aptly uses the word 'topsy-turvy'. King Lear in his madness which is his time of greatest sanity: 'What, art mad? A man may see how this world goes with no eyes. Look with thine ears: see how yon justice rails upon yon simple thief. Hark, in thine ear: change places, and handy-dandy, which is the justice, which is the thief?'

Sight only gives you the superficial appearance: the robes of the justice and the rags of the thief mark out their allotted roles. But close your eyes and listen, and the railing voice of the justice is as much an affront to the law of love and forgiveness as any act of theft could be. Robes and furred gowns hide all. *The Tragedy of King Lear* is about the deceptiveness of appearance and dress; it does not respect those who have power. When Lear takes off his finery, he opens the Silenus box of wisdom.

Touchstone's adage about knowledge and ignorance is an indication that Shakespeare's plays are sceptical of the claims made by conventional rationalizing philosophy. They are more interested in the paradoxes of 'wise folly'. That scepticism is apparent from the fourth use of 'philosopher' in the comedies. In *Much Ado about Nothing*, Leonato is distraught that the honour of his daughter and his family name have been besmirched by Claudio's accusation of sexual infidelity. He refuses to listen to the 'counsel' of his brother: passion overrides rational advice. People always advise 'patience' to those who are in sorrow, but they're not able to apply the advice to themselves when suffering. Leonato says:

> I will be flesh and blood,
> For there was never yet philosopher
> That could endure the toothache patiently,
> However they have writ the style of gods,
> And made a push at chance and sufferance.

The irony here is specifically directed against Stoicism, the philosophy which preaches 'patience' in the face of adversity and recommends that we aspire to be like the gods who are above suffering, that we try not to be influenced by fortune. A testing of the limits of Stoicism is one of the principal motifs of the Roman plays.

Of Shakespeare's ten uses of the word 'philosopher', four occur in the comedies and none in the histories. The other six are confined to two tragedies, written in close proximity to each other. They are two tragedies which follow a similar pattern of a man going from high to low estate, out from city or court to forest or stormy place where there's scarce a bush. In this 'outside' space, the protagonist is filled with fury at his fellow-humans.

One of these two plays is *Timon of Athens*. Jaques may fancy himself as a philosopher, but this play includes the only professional philosopher in Shakespeare: Apemantus. He is an extreme embodiment of the philosophy embraced by Jaques: Cynicism. A Cynic takes the Stoic rejection of worldliness to an extreme. A Cynic, the saying had it, was a Stoic without a tunic. The paradigm was Diogenes, who rejected 'civilization', returned to the 'natural' life, became a vagabond, was outspoken and without shame. Apemantus is 'the philosopher' in Shakespeare. Yet for Apemantus, as for Jaques, Cynicism is a pose, a performance – they both actually rather enjoy company and food. It is Timon himself who becomes the real Cynic. In act two of *Timon*, the Fool goes off with

Apemantus: 'I do not always follow lover, elder brother, and woman: sometime the philosopher.' As on many occasions in Shakespeare, a line spoken by the Fool is at a deeper level applicable to the main character. Timon is the one who follows the way of the philosopher instead of the lover. He becomes a Diogenes, rejecting all worldliness, dying in his cave by the seashore.

And so to *King Lear* itself. The three occurrences of the word 'philosopher' are clustered together in the hovel. 'First let me talk with this philosopher. / What is the cause of thunder?' 'Noble philosopher, your company.' 'I will keep still with my philosopher.' To these we should add, in the same passage, 'I'll talk a word with this same learnèd Theban.' Since philosophy began in ancient Greece, 'Theban' is a synonym for 'philosopher'. The allusion may even be specifically to a Diogenes-like philosopher from Thebes, Crates the Cynic.

So who is Lear's philosopher? He is poor Tom o'Bedlam. Why does Lear call an apparent madman his philosopher? What other kinds of 'philosopher' are there in the play? To what is Tom an alternative?

Gloucester blames it all on the stars: 'These late eclipses in the sun and moon portend no good to us.' Edmund disputes this: 'An admirable evasion of whoremaster man, to lay his goatish disposition on the charge of a star.' He argues that things often regarded as the 'natural order' are in fact 'custom' − for him, primogeniture and the stigmatism of bastardy would come into this category. The position articulated here is close to that of Michel de Montaigne in the closing section of his longest essay, 'An Apology of Raymond Sebond': any custom abhorred or outlawed by one nation is sure to be praised or practised by another. But if you have nothing save custom, no divinely sanctioned hierarchy, then where does your value-system come from? Edmund commits himself to 'nature' as a principle of survival and self-seeking. In this, he has been seen as a proto-Hobbesian philosopher, espousing a doctrine of raw competition. Montaigne argues instead for Christian love and humility. Perhaps this is what Edmund moves towards at the end of the play, with his last attempt to do some good and his discovery that he was beloved.

Gloucester's philosophical orientation, meanwhile, turns towards the Stoic idea of finding the right timing for death. After his mock suicide he says: 'Henceforth I'll bear / Affliction till it do cry out itself / "Enough, enough" and die.' But he can't sustain this position: in act five scene two, when Lear and Cordelia lose the battle, Gloucester is in 'ill thoughts again', wanting to rot. Edgar responds with Stoic advice: 'Men must endure / Their going hence even as their coming hither. / Ripeness is all.' But this idea of good timing doesn't work out: by mistiming the revelation of his own identity to Gloucester, Edgar precipitates his father's death.

The pattern, then, is of Stoic comfort not working: in act four scene one Edgar reflects on his own condition and cheers himself up with thoughts about the worst, then his father comes on blinded and he's instantly confounded – things are worse than before. If the case of Edgar reveals the deficiency of Stoic comfort, that of Albany demonstrates the inadequacy of belief in divine justice. His credo is that the good shall taste 'the wages of their virtue' and the bad drink from the poisoned 'cup of their deservings'. This scheme works for the bad, but not for the good. In the closing scene, Albany tries to orchestrate events, to make order out of chaos, but each of his resolutions is followed by new disaster. He greets the restored Edgar, then immediately hears the news of Gloucester's death, then the news of the two queens' deaths; then Kent comes on, dying; then in response to the news that Cordelia is to be hanged, Albany says 'The gods defend her', only for Lear to enter with her in his arms already hanged – the gods haven't defended her. Then Albany tries to give power back to Lear – and he promptly dies. Then he tries to persuade Kent and Edgar to divide the kingdom, provoking Kent to go off to die. The final speech of the play suggests a final realization that Stoic comfort won't do, that it's better to speak what we feel than what we ought to say.

So the Stoic philosophy fails. One aspect of Poor Tom as philosopher is to offer an alternative, extreme position. The idea is similar to that in *Timon*: the truest philosopher is the most Cynical. Timon and Tom – is there purpose in the resemblance of names? – take to an extreme the philosophical idea of rejecting worldly goods, possessions, even clothes. They are Cynics, Stoics without tunics.

Diogenes' most famous saying was mediated to Shakespeare through Montaigne's 'Apology of Raymond Sebond', in the translation of John Florio:

Truly, when I consider man all naked (yea be it in that sex, which seemeth to have and challenge the greatest share of eye-pleasing beauty) and view his defects, his natural subjection, and manifold imperfections; I find we have had much more reason to hide and cover our nakedness, than any creature else. We may be excused for borrowing those which nature had therein favoured more than us, with their beauties to adorn us, and under their spoils of wool, of hair, of feathers, and of silk to shroud us.

Compare Lear: 'Is man no more than this? Consider him well. Thou ow'st the worm no silk, the beast no hide, the sheep no wool, the cat no perfume. Ha? Here's three on's are sophisticated; thou art the thing itself. Unaccommodated man is no more but such a poor, bare, forked animal as thou art.' Montaigne's point is that it is arrogant and illogical to suppose that humans are 'naturally' superior to animals, chosen by God as the supreme beings, since in our natural state of nakedness our bodies have defects, vulnerability and 'manifold imperfections' in comparison with those of animals, adorned as they are with wool, hair or feathers that we borrow in order to clothe ourselves. Lear sees 'Poor Tom' in his state of primary nakedness, without the silk of the worm, the hide of the beast or the wool of the sheep (let alone the perfume that is taken from the cat) and starts to take off his clothes so that he too can return to the state of nature.

The influence of Montaigne's essay is the key to the play's critique of Stoicism. 'What is man like?' asks Montaigne.

Let us now but consider man alone, without other help, armed but with his own weapons, and unprovided of the grace and knowledge of God, which is all his honour, all his strength, and all the ground of his being. Let us see what hold-fast or free-hold he hath in this gorgeous and goodly equipage . . . Is it possible to imagine any thing so ridiculous, as this miserable and wretched creature, which is not so much as master of himself, exposed and subject to the offences of all things, and yet dareth call himself Master and Emperor of this Universe? In whose power it is not to know the least part of it, much less to command the same.

Lear's mistake is that he tries to command that which he does not know. The weather, the 'admirable moving of heaven's vault' in time of storm, is not controlled by man, not for his benefit. Montaigne's essay is an attack on those who argue that reason is our highest faculty and a sign of the power of the human subject: 'Presumption is our natural and original infirmity. *Of all creatures man is the most miserable and frail, and therewithal the proudest and disdainfulest* ... When I am playing with my cat, who knows whether she hath more sport in dallying with me, than I have in gaming with her?' Man is the only animal whom God has left 'naked on the bare earth', 'having nothing to cover and arm himself withal but the spoil of others' – other animals have their shells, hair, wool, hide and feathers. Furthermore, 'Generation is the chiefest natural action: we have a certain disposition of some members, fittest for that purpose' – yet we're the one animal disgusted by the sight of genitals. The disgust cited by Montaigne is expressed by Lear in his infamous disquisition on the sulphurous pit. Lear's words may not, after all, come from some personal disgust at women on Shakespeare's part: they are in an historically identifiable philosophical, or rather *anti*-philosophical, tradition.

Montaigne's work is a perpetual critique of abstract wisdom in the name of experience. As the passage about the philosopher and the toothache in *Much Ado about Nothing* suggests, Shakespeare had been engaging in a similar critique throughout his career. He always finds theory wanting in the face of action. He is more interested in how people perform than in what they profess. He was, after all, a performer himself. His reading of Montaigne in Florio's translation some time before the writing of *Lear* gave him a more philosophically articulated basis for his longstanding practice.

'What do I know?' asks Montaigne. I know experience, he replies to himself in his final essay. At the end of the *Sebond* essay, he suggests that all we can do is fall back on divine grace, on God:

'Whatsoever we attempt without his assistance, whatever we see without the lamp of his grace, is but vanity and folly.' Again, the attack is specifically upon Stoicism. We will be saved by 'our Christian faith', not 'Stoic virtue'. Raymond Sebond had argued that you could infer God from the order of created nature and from the reason. The 'apology' in Montaigne's title is ironically meant: the essay comprehensively refutes Sebond's natural religion and says that what you need instead is blind, irrational faith.

King Lear comes to a similar conclusion, but it does so not through thinking, in the manner of Montaigne, but through enactment – through performance. It moves from a theoretical and philosophical inquiry into deep causes to a practical faith in the surface truth of human actions and a trust in the wisdom to be gained from immediate experience.

Albany says (in the original Quarto version of the play, where his role is fuller than in the Folio revision):

> If that the heavens do not their visible spirits
> Send quickly down to tame the vile offences, it will come,
> Humanity must perforce prey on itself,
> Like monsters of the deep.

He is instantly mocked by the news that Gloucester has been blinded and Cornwall slain. Albany regards the servant who kills Cornwall as an agent of divine justice, but he can't make sense of Gloucester's blinding. Edgar, though, tries to do so in the final scene, in a notably cruel 'eye for an eye' judgement: 'The dark and vicious place where thee he got / Cost him his eyes.' But this notion of divine justice certainly can't account for Cordelia's death. We should recall here Shakespeare's two major alterations to his source, the old anonymous play of *King Leir*: its happy ending was removed, Cordelia being wantonly killed, and the whole of the action was displaced from a Christian to a pagan setting. Albany's lines quoted above are close to the source:

> Oh just *Jehova*, whose almighty power
> Doth govern all things in this spacious world,

How canst thou suffer such outrageous acts
To be committed without just revenge?

This sentiment is voiced by the play's Kent-figure as he and Leir
are about to be killed by a murderer sent by Gonorill and Ragan.
But then there is a benign divine intervention: it thunders, the
murderer quakes and drops his knife. By the end of *Leir*, justice
does come: Gonorill and Ragan are defeated, Leir and Cordella
restored.

Remove the Christian values and structure: what do you then
have? You have humanity as monsters, preying on each other. You
have no value structure or sure knowledge. You have something
very much like the 'Apology of Raymond Sebond' without its
Christian ending. But in Shakespeare's strand of 'wise fooling',
a kind of divinity is smuggled back into the raw natural world
of *Lear*.

In praise of folly

Shakespeare's key additions to the old *Leir* play that he was reworking are the characters of the Fool and Poor Tom. They force us to
turn from the 'Apology of Raymond Sebond' to another 'counter-
Renaissance' work. Socrates' saying that he is the wisest of men
because he knows he is the most ignorant was quoted by Erasmus
not only in his *Adagia*, but also in his *Praise of Folly*.

Erasmus' Folly's first claim is that only she brings joy. Proof:
your face lights up when she comes forward to speak; you were
gloomy before, you perk up when she comes on stage. Isn't this
what happens with the Fool in a play? Don't you feel good the
very moment Lear's Fool appears? Orators attempt to clear the
mind of troubles and sorrows by means of elaborate speeches. Folly
achieves this in a flash simply by making an appearance. The Fool's
one-liners make more sense of Lear's predicament than do the
Stoic rationalizations of Gloucester and Edgar.

This is the attraction of the court fool: he is fun and he speaks
the truth, whereas purportedly wise rhetoricians invert the truth.

Only the fool is allowed to speak the truth without incurring displeasure. With Folly, no art is needed to find the mind's construction in the face: 'For in me (ye must think) is no place for setting of colours, as I cannot say one thing, and think another: but on all sides I do resemble myself.' People who disguise themselves always unwittingly reveal their true identity. In the play's opening scene we are invited to contrast the plain-speakers with those who say one thing and think another: Cordelia and Kent are pitted against Goneril and Regan. The tragedy of the court is that you can only gain advancement there through false speaking. Plain-speaking Kent is forced into disguise as servant Caius.

Biology is an affront to rationalizing philosophy. Everybody, even the Stoic philosopher, has to do the same undignified thing in order to make a baby. Life itself does not come from the respectable parts of the body, but from the part so foolish that it can't be mentioned without a snigger. So says Erasmus' Folly, in the same (anti-)intellectual tradition as Lear's 'Let copulation thrive.' Folly notes, too, that we love babies, who lack wisdom. Growing old is a return to childishness. Lear is happiest on the heath and in the reunion scene when he's lost his grip on reality.

The Stoic philosopher tries to be ruled by reason rather than passion. But for Erasmus the notion that to be wise you must suppress the emotions is inhuman. The most important thing is to 'feel' – as Gloucester has to learn, to see the world not rationally but 'feelingly'. Folly points out that friendship is among the highest human values, and it depends on emotion. The people who show friendship to Lear (Fool, Kent as Caius, Edgar as Poor Tom and then as Peasant) and to Gloucester (Servants, Old Man) are not the wise or the rich.

We are ruled by our passions and our bodies. We go through life performing a series of different roles of which we are by no means in control. In Folly's eyes, 'All this life of mortal men, what is it else, but a certain kind of stage play?' Historical consciousness and political posturing are so much mere breath; they are no more than part of the brief and often risible performance that is human life. 'When we are born we cry that we are come / To this great stage of fools.' 'What sport and pastime the Gods themselves have

at such Folly of these silly mortal men.' In the great theatre of the
world, with the gods as audience, we are the fools on stage. Under
the aspect of Folly, we see that a king is no different from any
other man. The trappings of monarchy are but a costume: this is
both Folly's and Lear's discovery.

Folly tells us that there are two kinds of madness – one is the
thirst for gold, sex and power. That is the madness of Regan,
Cornwall, Edmund and company. Their madness is what Lear and
Timon reject. The second madness is the desirable one, the state
of folly in which 'a certain pleasant raving, or error of the mind,
delivereth the heart of that man whom it possesseth from all
wonted carefulness, and rendreth it divers ways much recreated
with new delectation'. This 'error of the mind' is a special gift of
the goddess Folly. Thus Lear is happy when his mind is free, when
he's running around in his madness like a child on a country
holiday. 'Look, look, a mouse: peace, peace, this piece of toasted
cheese will do't.' That brings a smile to our faces, not least because
the mouse isn't really there. In the Folio text of the play, Lear
repeats his demand to 'look, look' at the end of his life. Cordelia
is dead, but he deceives himself into the belief that she lives – that
the feather moves, that her breath mists the looking-glass. His final
words are spoken in the delusion that her lips are moving – 'Look
on her, look, her lips, / Look there, look there!' Her lips aren't
moving, just as there isn't a mouse, but it's better for Lear that he
should not know this. Philosophers say that it is miserable to be
deceived. Folly replies that it is most miserable 'not to be deceived',
for nothing could be further from the truth than the notion that
man's happiness resides in things as they actually are.

We are far from the pursuit of conventional wisdom now, from
the pantaloonish clichés of Polonius with his 'To thine own self
be true, / And it must follow, as the night the day, / Thou canst
not then be false to any man.' Deception may conceivably be a
good thing, says this darker, more paradoxical play. As the wise
Fool puts it, 'I would fain learn to lie.' Lying is destructive in the
mouths of Goneril, Regan and Edmund at the beginning of
the play, but Cordelia – the Fool's double – has to learn to lie. At
the beginning, she can only tell the truth (hence her banishment),

but later she lies beautifully and generously when Lear says that she has cause to do him wrong, and she replies 'No cause, no cause'.

The closing section of Erasmus' *Praise of Folly* undertakes a serious praise of Christian 'madness'. Christ says that the mystery of salvation is hidden from the wise and given to the simple. He delighted in common people, surrounded himself not with the rich and the powerful, but with working fishermen and humble women. He chose to ride an ass when he could have mounted a lion. The language of his parables is steeped in simple, natural things – lilies, mustardseed, sparrows. We might compare Lear's language of wren, dog and garden waterpots in act four of the play. The fundamental folly of Christianity is its demand that you throw away your possessions. Lear pretends to do this in act one, but actually he wants to keep 'The name, and all th'addition to a king'. Only when he loses his knights, his clothes and his sanity does he find happiness.

But he also becomes kind. Little things show us this: in act one, he's still always giving orders. Even in the storm he continues to make demands: 'come, unbutton here'. In the end, though, he learns to say *please* and *thank you*: 'Pray you undo this button. Thank you, sir.' He has begun to learn true manners not at court, but through the love he shows for Poor Tom, the image of unaccommodated man, the image of himself: 'Didst thou give all to thy daughters? And art thou come to this?' True wisdom comes not in Gloucester's and Edgar's words of Stoic comfort or Albany's hapless faith in divine providence, but in moments of folly and love, as in this exchange:

EDGAR: Bless thy five wits!
KENT: O pity! Sir, where is the patience now
That you so oft have boasted to retain?

Patience is the boast of the Stoic. It's a retainer like the hundred knights. To achieve true wisdom, you must let it go. You must let even the wits, the sanity, go. What you must keep are the *pity* and the *blessing*. Pity and blessing are at the very heart of *King Lear*.

Pity means the performance of certain deeds, such as showing kindness to strangers. Blessing is a performative, in the sense of the philosopher J. L. Austin: a performative is an utterance that effects an action by being spoken or by means of which the speaker performs a particular act. Typically blessing is accompanied by a small but forceful *gesture*, a kind of action that is of vital importance on the bare boards of the Shakespearean theatre.

For all the inventiveness of their language, both Montaigne and Shakespeare were fascinated by an aspect of humanity that is anterior to language. In the 'Apology of Raymond Sebond', Montaigne notes that animals can express emotions: a dog will bark in one way and a horse will know that he is angry, he will bark in another way and it will be clear that he is not perturbed. We don't actually need educated speech in order to articulate our emotions and to communicate with others. There is an expressive language even of the eyebrows and the shoulders. And as for the hands:

What do we with our hands? Do we not sue and entreat, promise and perform, call men unto us, and discharge them, bid them farewell and be gone, threaten, pray, beseech, deny, refuse, demand, admire, number, confess, repent, fear, be ashamed, doubt, instruct, command, incite, encourage, swear, witness, accuse, condemn, absolve, injure, despise, defy, despite, flatter, applaud, bless, humble, mock, reconcile, recommend, exalt, show gladness, rejoice, complain, wail, sorrow, discomfort, despair, cry out, forbid, declare silence and astonishment?

Montaigne's list of emotions, actions and desires that may be performed by the hands is like a litany of the processes through which Lear has to go in the course of his play. The actor, with the gestures of his hands and the other parts of his body, is able in the most literal sense to *perform* the full gamut of human being.

The progression from command to questioning to entreaty is one of Shakespeare's most striking developments of the character of the King in the old *Leir* play. In *King Lear* the exterior trappings of Christianity that characterize the source-play are emptied out and replaced by a processual, performative approach to being. But despite the pagan setting, those essentials of the Erasmian and

Montaignian – that is to say the counter-Renaissance – Christian vision, are still there: folly and love.

Fool and Tom teach us to split apart the idea of *philo-sophy*. The word is derived from Greek *philos*, love, and *sophos*, wisdom. The natural history of *King Lear* rejects the law of *sophos* in the name of *philos*. Erasmus' great mock-encomium had a neat word for the folly of those who pursue wisdom. But by the end of the *Praise*, with its discovery that true wisdom is paradoxically to be found in folly, the word is no longer to be mocked. It is one of the Greek coinages that Erasmus slips into his Latin text, partly in homage to his friend, Sir Thomas More: 'Morosophos'. 'Moros' is Greek not only for the name 'More', but also for 'foolish' (hence our 'moron'). The compound word may be attached most aptly to the Shakespeare of *King Lear*. In writing this play, he was not a historian. Nor was he a philosopher. He was a FOOLOSOPHER.

SEVENTH AGE

Oblivion

Last scene of all,
That ends this strange eventful history,
Is second childishness and mere oblivion,
Sans teeth, sans eyes, sans taste, sans everything.

Mortui divitiae ('a dead man's wealth'): from Geffrey Whitney's
A Choice of Emblemes: *the only possession taken to the grave by both
rich man and poor is 'a shrouding sheet of twine'. Or, as Hamlet observes,
Caesar, Alexander the Great and Yorick the clown come to the same dust.*

23. The Readiness is All

It is possible to go through life without being a schoolboy, a lover, a soldier, a justice or (if you die young) a pantaloon. Only the first and last ages are inevitable. Jaques' final scenes seamlessly join old age to death. You never know when the comfortable retirement of the lean and slippered pantaloon will give way to the 'second childishness' of extreme old age. As Falstaff reminds us, an old man's bald head and round belly make him seem like a baby all over again – especially if he starts dribbling and burbling inarticulately. Old people lose their teeth and find themselves munching as gummily as infants. The word *infans* was applied not only to young ones who had not yet developed the arts of rational thought and speech, but also to old ones who had lost it. As Jaques' speech comes to an end with 'Sans teeth, sans eyes, sans taste, sans everything', the skill of Shakespeare's writing is such that it is not clear at which moment we move from the 'second childishness' of senility to the 'oblivion' of death. Teeth fall out, eyesight fades and taste-buds are dulled, but it is the skull in the grave that rests in silence 'sans everything'.

All life histories, whether strange and eventful like those in the plays, or dull and respectable like Shakespeare's own, end in death. Even the comedies, the traditional form for celebrating the energies of life, smell of mortality. From the entrance of Monsieur Marcadé (whose name suggests Mercury, messenger of death) to announce the French king's demise, halting the festivities of *Love's Labour's Lost*, to the brother for whom Olivia mourns, to the Mamillius who will not be resurrected alongside his mother in *The Winter's Tale*, Shakespeare refuses to deny death. His history plays are littered with corpses and, formally speaking, though Hemings and Condell set them apart from the tragedies in the First Folio, so as to unify the parade of the national past, many of them are tragedies. Though the Henrys offer more of a generic mix, all three Richard plays were explicitly titled as tragedies when first published in quarto or octavo format: *The Tragedy of King Richard the Second*, *The Tragedy of King Richard III*, *The True Tragedy of Richard Duke of York* (the original title of *Henry VI Part 3*). From Homer's *Iliad* and Greek tragedy, through Seneca's Latin re-workings of Euripides to the famous Marlowe plays in which Edward Alleyn bestrode the stage when Shakespeare's career began, high poetic imagination, in drama especially, was dominated by tragedy: the genre of humankind's confrontation with the oblivion that we call death.

English Seneca by candlelight

The term 'Tragedy' as a generic description entered English usage with the Elizabethan translation of the Roman dramatist Seneca. In 1559 there was published *The sixth Tragedy of the most grave and prudent author Lucius Anneus Seneca entitled Troas, with divers and sundry Additions to the same, newly set forth in English by Jasper Heywood*. A year later, *The second Tragedy of Seneca entitled Thyestes* was 'faithfully Englished', again by Jasper Heywood. The Stationers' Register entry referred to *Troas* as a 'treate' (treatise) rather than a tragedy. Again, when *The lamentable Tragedy of Oedipus . . . out of Seneca* was published in 1563, it was entered in the Register as a 'lamentable history'. This suggests that the word 'tragedy' was not yet familiar descriptive shorthand for a kind of play. But by the end of the century, that was precisely what it was, as may be seen from Polonius' disquisition on the dramatic genres, in which Seneca is synonymous with a 'heavy' play.

What is a Senecan tragedy like? It is structured in five acts, divided by a Chorus. The action is a reaction to a terrible event that has taken place in the past, of which we may be reminded by a ghost. The central character cannot easily be labelled either a hero or a villain. Usually he or she is called to revenge. But the drama takes place in his head, not on the stage. We hear a lot about blood and cruelty and sensational violence, but always at second-hand. This is a drama to be heard or read more than to be seen. The principal interest is verbal – the rhetoric, the verbal figures, the *sententiae*, the set-piece descriptions of the 'Nuntius' (messenger). The play consists of a series of monologues of self-definition, in which the problem of evil is inextricable from the problem of knowledge. Once self-discovery is achieved, death is the only course. Seneca's philosophical essays are meditations on the art of quelling the passions through the power of reason. His tragedies show what happens when passion runs out of control.

The Elizabethan translations of the *Ten Tragedies* of Seneca were collected in a single volume in 1581. In the preface to that volume, Thomas Newton weighed the philosophizing against the passion: 'gravity of philosophical sentences, weightiness of sappy words, authority of sound matter beateth down sin, loose life, dissolute dealings and unbridled sensuality'. But this is a response to tragedy read, not tragedy seen. In the preface to Greene's *Menaphon*, Tom Nashe noted that 'English Seneca read by candlelight yields many good sentences . . . whole Hamlets, I should say handfuls, of tragical speeches', but he went on to suggest that having bled Seneca dry for his language, playwrights working for the popular stage would need to look elsewhere – to lurid Italian novellas, for instance – for their dramatic action.

Seneca provided the professional dramatists with both structures and *sententiae*. Thomas Kyd's *Spanish Tragedy* begins with a Ghost and a personification of Revenge, as *Thyestes* begins with a Ghost and a Fury advocating revenge. Shakespeare quotes a famous appeal to the gods from the *Hippolytus* in its original Latin, '*Tam lentus audis scelera, tam lentus vides?*' ('Are you so slow to hear crimes, so slow to see?'). The rhetoric of self-examination in the Elizabethan tragic soliloquy is learned in part from Senecan man – but only in part, for its flexibility has more in common with the epistolary self-expression of Ovidian woman (the *Heroides*). At its core, popular tragedy was not Senecan. How could it be, when what was required for popularity was not philosophizing but action, replete with spectacle and leavened by comedy?

The classically educated Sir Philip Sidney considered that there was 'neither decency nor discretion', neither 'the admiration and commiseration' proper to tragedy nor the 'right sportfulness'

proper to comedy, in the 'mongrel tragi-comedy' of the Elizabethan theatre. He looked down on the contemporary drama: 'all
their plays be neither right tragedies, nor right comedies, mingling
kings and clowns'. Sidney was writing in the early 1580s, perhaps
thinking of works like *A Lamentable Tragedy mixed full of Pleasant
Mirth, containing the Life of Cambises King of Persia*, a hoary old
piece also mocked by Shakespeare (Falstaff's 'I will do it in King
Cambyses' vein'). But there is no reason to suppose that Sidney
would have thought any better of Kyd, Marlowe and Shakespeare,
all notable minglers of king and clown. For Sidney, there was a
single exception to the sorry norm. He had seen one play which
was 'full of stately speeches and well-sounding phrases, climbing
to the height of Seneca's style, and as full of notable morality,
which it doth most delightfully teach, and so obtain the every end
of Poesy'– though his praise was then qualified by the complaint
that the play in question did not obey the classical unities of place
and time.

The play was *The Tragedy of Gorboduc*, first performed on
6 January 1562 at the Inner Temple and repeated later the same
month by royal command before the queen's own presence at
Whitehall. Its proximity to the era of Jasper Heywood's English
Seneca is noteworthy. The joint authors, both students of the Inner
Temple, were Thomas Norton and Thomas Sackville, both from
well-to-do backgrounds (Sackville's father was a first cousin of
Anne Boleyn). *Gorboduc* is often described as the first English
tragedy. It is certainly the earliest surviving play for performance
in the vernacular that resembles a classical tragedy, and the first to
be written in the iambic pentameter blank verse that became the
medium of the great tragedies of the 1590s and early 1600s. It was
frequently revived at the Inner Temple, and was published in 1565,
so was available for imitation. But it had little influence on the
public stage.

English Senecan tragedy was written by elite amateur authors
for elite courtly or academic audiences. It was something to be
read in the closet or heard in a hall (often on the occasion of a
banquet), as one would hear a lecture or attend a debate. It was
above all concerned with wise policy. In his *Life of Sir Philip Sidney*,

Fulke Greville wrote that the purpose of ancient tragedy was to 'exemplify the disastrous miseries of man's life, where order, laws, doctrine and authority are unable to protect innocency from the exorbitant wickedness of power, and so, out of that melancholic vision, stir horror or murmur against divine providence'. The key phrase here is 'the exorbitant wickedness of power'. Greville and other learned Elizabethans saw Seneca's plays in the context of his life, which was lived very close to the exorbitancies of Roman imperial power – banished by Claudius because he was supposedly having an affair with Caligula's sister, Seneca was recalled in order to become Nero's tutor and speech-writer, eventually accused of conspiring against the emperor's life, and left with little choice but an honourable suicide in his bath. 'Elite Elizabethan Seneca', as one might call it, was in the tradition of 'advice to princes'. Sackville proceeded from writing the second half of *Gorboduc* to contributing the 'Induction' and 'Fall of Buckingham' to the *Mirror for Magistrates*: both play and tragic poem are about the workings of power, about courtly ambition and its undoing.

Gorboduc, originally played in the presence of members of the queen's privy council, stages a debate about the question of succession and the dangers of civil war, intensely topical issues early in the reign of the unmarried queen who had turned her country's religious orthodoxy back from Catholicism to Protestantism. The story is taken from the chronicles of early English history in the tradition that goes back to Geoffrey of Monmouth's twelfth-century *Historia Regum Britanniae*. Gorboduc unwisely decides to divide his kingdom; his sons, Ferrex and Porrex quarrel over the succession; Porrex kills Ferrex and in revenge his mother kills him; civil war breaks out when Fergus, Duke of Albany, raises an army and tries to seize the throne.

A generation later, very similar 'early British' subject-matter was played out on the public stage in such anonymously written dramas as *The True Chronicle History of King Leir* (*c.*1590) and *Locrine* (*c.*1594, attributed on its title page to 'W.S.', though almost certainly not by Shakespeare). But the style was very different. Whereas the public stage required action and spectacle, *Gorboduc* is for the most part a static work of Senecan debate. All the action takes place off-stage and is reported in a series of messenger speeches. The audience's attention is focused on political reflection by means of paired scenes in which a prince is advised by first a good and then a bad counsellor. The play is stuffed with moral *sententiae* on Senecan themes. Fortune's mutability:

> the price of mortal joys,
> How short they be, how fading here in earth,
> How full of change, how brittle our estate,
> Of nothing sure, save only of the death,
> To whom both man and all the world doth owe
> Their end at last —

The endurance of the stoic self:

> The heart unbroken, and the courage free
> From feeble faintness of bootless despair,
> Doth either rise to safety or renown
> By noble valour of unvanquished mind,
> Or yet doth perish in more happy sort.

Classical and neo-classical tragedy were more concerned with how people react to terrible events than with the events themselves. Revenge is the archetypal theme of tragedy because it is the most drastic re-action to an earlier action. In *Gorboduc*, which is divided into a classical five acts, bloody deeds are symbolically anticipated in a dumb show before each act, then narratorially reconstructed in messenger speeches towards the end of the acts. A moralizing Chorus then signals the act closure. The debates that form the bulk of the play are witnessings of the space between — the sowing of the dangerous seed and the reaping of the bloody whirlwind. Tragedy is what happens in the 'interim'. The various counsellors represent externalizations of the choices available to the main characters, and in this sense they are structurally analogous to the Vice and Virtue figures of the morality play tradition. The function of the characters is to convey different positions in the political debate; the human interest of dramatic interaction is merely a consequence of this. The soliloquy as a vehicle of character development is absent.

In the public drama of the 1590s, tragedy is still located in the 'interim', but both the sowing of the seed and the reaping of the whirlwind are seen before our eyes, and the choices facing the protagonist are explored more inwardly, typically through soliloquy. The psychological dimension of the political becomes as important as the political itself. Thus Brutus' tremendously powerful version of the 'interim':

> Between the acting of a dreadful thing
> And the first motion, all the interim is
> Like a phantasma, or a hideous dream:
> The genius and the mortal instruments
> Are then in council, and the state of man,
> Like to a little kingdom, suffers then
> The nature of an insurrection.

Julius Caesar is a dramatization of the most famous political assassination in history, yet at this moment insurrection is merely a metaphor for the mental turbulence of the individual on a sleepless night before a momentous day.

The most distinguished tragedies for reading, or 'closet dramas', emerged from the Pembroke circle in the 1590s. The Countess of Pembroke herself translated the *Marc Antoine* of the French neo-classical dramatist Robert Garnier. Published in 1592, Mary Sidney's *Antonius* is often described as the first English tragedy by a woman. If one adds the qualifiers 'complete' and 'published', this is true, but given that high classical tragedy was not aimed at a diverse audience the fact of publication is somewhat anomalous. Mary Sidney was not actually the first learned aristocratic lady to 'English' a tragedy: credit for that must go to one Joanna (also known as Jane) Lumley who, a full half-century earlier, undertook a partial manuscript translation of Euripides' *Iphigenia at Aulis* (probably via Erasmus' Latin version), with particular emphasis on those parts of the play that extolled the virtues of female sacrifice. In a manner characteristic of the humanism of the court of King

Henry VIII, Joanna Lumley introduced many Christian allusions into Euripides' pagan narrative.

The ultimate source of Garnier's *Marc Antoine* was Plutarch. The matter was that which Shakespeare brought to the public stage some fifteen years later. Garnier, a magistrate, dramatized his Plutarchan material in Senecan form in order to reflect on the tragedy of civil war in sixteenth-century France. Mary Sidney's Englished *Antonius* includes choruses of commoners – first Egyptians, then Roman soldiers – but its primary emphasis was not the many but the few. The play is an exploration of the damage that may be caused to the body politic if the private desires of the great are allowed to override their public duties. To become a lover is to put at risk one's judgement as a governor.

We should be wary of jumping to the conclusion that Mary Sidney's intentions in undertaking and publishing her translation were overtly topical rather than broadly exemplary, yet her theme was highly relevant to the concerns of the English court in the early 1590s. This was the period in which the Earl of Essex was beginning to gain considerable influence over the queen. The Sidney circle, with their strong commitment to Protestant virtue, were deeply committed to an image of Elizabeth as noble Roman, not sensuous Cleopatra. Samuel Daniel's *Cleopatra* (published 1594), a sequel to his patroness's play, is a further exploration of the potential of erotic passion to bring down a royal line. Fulke Greville, also a member of the Sidney circle, destroyed his own *Antony and Cleopatra* for fear that its representation of a queen and a great soldier 'forsaking empire to follow sensuality' might be 'construed or strained to a personating of vices in the present governors and government'. On 'seeing the like instance not poetically, but really, fashioned in the Earl of Essex then falling (and ever till then worthily beloved both of Queen and people)', Greville's own 'second thoughts' were 'to be careful'. We are back in the territory of the special performance of *Richard II*. The need for caution is well demonstrated by the fate of Daniel's second Senecan tragedy, *Philotas*, which concerned a notable soldier and a conspiracy against Alexander the Great: it was written for private performance some years before the fall of Essex, but then staged by the Queen's Revels after the fall, and misconstrued as an allegory of the Essex plot, causing Daniel to be called before the Privy Council to defend himself.

Greville's most celebrated lines of verse occur in one of the choruses in *Mustapha*, one of his two surviving Senecan tragedies:

> O wearisome condition of humanity!
> Born under one law, to another bound:
> Vainly begot, and yet forbidden vanity,
> Created sick, commanded to be sound:
> What meaneth Nature by these diverse laws?

The paradox compounded here offers a distinctively Protestant, even Calvinist, version of tragedy: we are begotten and born, we decay and die, under the rule of the body, yet spiritually we are bound to a law which requires the mortification of bodily desire. The sentiment belongs in a closet drama because the paradox can only be resolved through an individual act of faith that is dependent on the work of the private closet: examination of conscience, meditation upon biblical texts and disciplined prayer.

That to philosophize is to learn how to die

When the paradox of humankind's bodily and spiritual duality is explored on the public stage, it must be enacted visually rather than stated rhetorically as it is by Greville. The two most powerful examples are Marlowe's Dr Faustus and Shakespeare's Hamlet. Hamlet himself speaks of the duality:

What a piece of work is a man! How noble in reason, how infinite in faculty, in form and moving how express and admirable, in action how like an angel, in apprehension how like a god! The beauty of the world, the paragon of animals – and yet to me, what is this quintessence of dust?

Hamlet's public image is that of the versatile 'Renaissance man' who is at once soldier, scholar and courtier, the embodiment of the three mature ages of man in one. Privately, he struggles to hold together the many pieces of the jigsaw of human being: he finds it difficult to move from 'apprehension' to 'action'. Soliloquizing on what Brutus called the 'interim', and in reflecting upon his father's untimely murder and his mother's hasty remarriage he is unable to sustain his belief in humankind's beauty and admirability. It is only when he faces up to the graveyard and the skull that he is able to accept the mortification of the body, the implication of the words of the funeral service that will be evoked by the entrance of Ophelia's cortège, as Hamlet throws down the jester's decayed head:

We therefore commit [her] body to the ground, earth to earth, ashes to ashes, dust to dust, in sure and certain hope of resurrection to eternal life, through our Lord Jesus Christ, who shall change our vile body, that it may be like to his glorious body, according to the mighty working whereby he is able to subdue all things to himself.

Hamlet is obsessed by the division between words – the medium of noble reasoning, the faculty of admirable expression – and matter, the substance of the body and of action. The play begins from something insubstantial: a moral imperative, a paternal injunction from beyond the grave. The first question to be resolved is whether the ghost has substance. Hamlet's tragic dilemma is to proceed to an act of revenge without himself becoming the beast which he takes Claudius to be. The dilemma is dramatized by the duality between soliloquy (words, the self) and action (deeds, engagement with others). It is compounded by the play's restless self-consciousness: Lucianus in *The Mousetrap* has no difficulty in proceeding from words to action, but his identity as a player raises the possibility that to perform the action demanded may be to act a performance. Hamlet has an existential problem: he wishes to be himself rather than a role which one might play (the Revenger), but for much of the play he cannot reconcile his wish with the knowledge that to be human means to have a set of social relations (which are especially constrained if one is a prince) and a body that is both desiring (like his mother's) and mortal (like his father's).

Literary genre is a means of structuring experience. As the title of Dante's divine poem the *Commedia* reminds us, the structure of Christianity is essentially that of comedy: it looks forward to the day of resurrection, when, as 'The Order for the Burial of the Dead' puts it, 'our vile body' is sloughed off and we become like to the 'glorious' (eternal, pure, spiritual) body of Jesus Christ. Elizabethan tragedies usually end with piles of bodies being carted off for burial. Elizabethan audiences would be bound to ask themselves which souls among the dead persons of the drama are imagined to be saved. Hamlet and Laertes exchange forgiveness, Laertes dying on a prayer that on the day of judgement he should not be held to account for Hamlet's death nor Hamlet for his and his father's. Ophelia is not mentioned here, for hers – as we learn from the gravediggers' debate about burial rites – was a doubtful case, since suicide meant damnation whereas accidental death left open the possibility of salvation.

In his 'To be, or not to be' soliloquy, Hamlet has worried about the hereafter; in his dying speeches, he is more concerned with the manner in which his history is recorded on earth. The audience cannot know his ultimate destination, just as they cannot know their own. In the Protestant world-picture 'a noble heart' – Horatio's final judgement on his friend – does not guarantee salvation. 'Goodnight, sweet prince, / And flights of angels sing thee to thy rest!' is the expression of a hope, not the statement of a fact. Hamlet's closing emphasis on the telling of his story – his history, his posthumous fame – is a sign of the secularization of the drama during the reign of Elizabeth. The gravedigger reminds us that the pagan hero Alexander the Great and the court clown Yorick come to the same end. Only the dust is certain.

But Hamlet seems ready for that. As many critics have observed, he is a changed man on his return from the English voyage: 'If it be now, 'tis not to come: if it be not to come, it will be now: if it be not now, yet it will come: the readiness is all.' He has come to a mood that could be described as Stoic acceptance. Or, more strictly, since he combines a classically achieved 'readiness' or 'constancy' with a Christian sense of 'providence' ('there's a divinity that shapes our ends' . . . 'there's a special providence in the fall of a sparrow'), we should say neo-Stoic acceptance.

Hamlet is a great reader. In the first published version of the play, he speaks his 'To be or not to be' soliloquy as he enters 'poring upon a book'. A book and a philosophical 'question'. To an educated Elizabethan, it would almost certainly have been apparent that Hamlet is reading the *Tusculan Questions* of Marcus Tullius Cicero. A university man such as Hamlet would have been expected to read this hugely influential book in its Latin original, but it was also available in an English version of 1561 with the catchy title *Those five QUESTIONS, which Mark Tully Cicero disputed in his Manor of Tusculanum: Written afterwards by him, in as many books, to his friend and familiar Brutus, in the Latin tongue, and now out of the same translated and englished by John Dolman, Student and fellow of the Inner Temple*. The first of those 'questions' (*disputationes*), debated in dialogue form, was 'whether death be evil: yea or no?' Cicero's conclusion, ultimately derived from a famous speech by Socrates when he is condemned to death (as reported in Plato's *Apology*), is that we should not fear death. Why? Because after death, either the soul survives or it does not. If it does not, then death 'resembles sleep without any trouble of dreams'. If the soul does survive, then it will go to what Hamlet calls 'The undiscovered country from whose bourn / No traveller returns' where it will meet a just judge. A person who has lived a good life accordingly has nothing to fear in the afterlife. Hamlet's problem is that if he carries out his father's demand for revenge or if he kills himself in despair at the ills of life, then he will be a murderer or a self-murderer and will accordingly have something to fear when he meets the ultimate judge. He has to go on a long journey of his own before he reaches the state of 'readiness' for death.

If there is a single book that parallels his journey, that brings us close to the workings of the mind of Hamlet, it is Montaigne's *Essays*. Scholars debate as to whether or not Shakespeare saw Florio's translation before it was published in 1603. The balance of evidence suggests that he probably did not, but rather that his mind and Montaigne's worked in such similar ways that Hamlet seems like a reader of Montaigne even though he could not have been one.

Imagine that Hamlet could have read Montaigne. He would

have found a meditation on the pros and cons of suicide in an essay called 'A custom of the isle of Cea', but he would most characteristically have turned to the essay in the first book, strongly influenced by Cicero's *Five Questions*, called 'That to philosophize is to learn how to die'. As a university-educated reader, he would have been trained to copy the pithiest wisdom from his reading into his commonplace book, known as his 'tables'. Here are some of the sentences of Montaigne, as translated by Florio, that we can imagine the princely student of Wittenberg copying out (in that 'fair' handwriting which served him so well when devising the 'new commission' for the killing of Rosencrantz and Guildenstern):

CICERO saith, that to *Philosophize is no other thing, than for a man to prepare himself to death:* which is the reason that study and contemplation doth in some sort withdraw our soul from us and severally employ it from our body, which is a kind of apprentisage and resemblance of death; or else it is, that all the wisdom and discourse of the world doth in the end resolve upon this point, to teach us not to fear to die.

Hamlet would have relished the double sense there. The *action* of study and contemplation is a little rehearsal for death, in that it involves a withdrawal from the bustle of life. At the same time, the ultimate *content* of philosophy is the knowledge that we are all going to die, and that we should accordingly, as the Duke puts it in *Measure for Measure*, 'Be absolute for death.'

The Duke's oration to the condemned Claudio offers a typically neo-Stoic mix of classical resignation and Christian *contemptus mundi*. Montaigne and Hamlet have a subtly different emphasis. They seek to cultivate contempt not for the world, but for death. They teach themselves to be ready but not to be afraid. A fool, says Montaigne, deals with fear of death by not thinking about it. A wise man simultaneously thinks about it all the time and gets on with his life:

Now of all the benefits of virtue, the contempt of death is the chiefest, a mean that furnisheth our life with an easeful tranquillity and gives us a pure and amiable taste of it . . . The end of our career is death, it is the necessary object of our aim: if it affright us, how is it possible we should step one foot further without any ague ... Let us learn to stand and combat her with a resolute mind ... let us remove her strangeness from her, let us converse, frequent, and acquaint ourselves with her, let us have nothing so much in mind as death, let us at all times and seasons, and in the ugliest manner that may be, yea with all faces, shapen and represent the same unto our imagination. At the stumbling of a horse, at the fall of a stone, at the least prick with a pin, let us presently ruminate and say with our selves, what if it were death itself? And thereupon let us take heart of grace, and call our wits together to confront her. Amidst our banquets, feasts, and pleasures, let us ever have this restraint or object before us, that is, the remembrance of our condition, and let not pleasure so much mislead or transport us that we altogether neglect or forget how many ways our joys or our feastings be subject unto death, and by how many hold-fasts she threatens us and them ... He who hath learned to die hath unlearned to serve ... A man should ever, as much as in him lieth, be ready booted to take his journey, and above all things, look he have then nothing to do but with himself ... let death seize upon me whilst I am setting my cabbages, careless of her dart, but more of my unperfect garden.

We do not know whether Shakespeare grew cabbages in his garden at New Place, but it is a reasonable bet that he would have shared Montaigne's hope of ending his life in some such way. The readiness was all.

24. Shakespeare the Epicurean

'a Centre whereto all lines come'

There are alternatives to Stoicism. Montaigne again provides a model: though his flexible mind and sinewy, associative style led him to range freely between philosophical (and anti-philosophical) possibilities, there is a broad movement through the three books of his essays from an emphasis on Stoic resolve in the first through the radical scepticism of the second to a different kind of acceptance in the third book, an acceptance that embraces the needs of the body as well as the discipline of the mind. Stoics were always trying to repress their bodily urges, as in a more extreme way did Christians in the Pauline tradition, whereas in a long essay at the core of his last book, innocently entitled 'Upon some verses of Virgil', Montaigne wrote the sixteenth century's most honest and explicit account of sexual desire and how it does not ever go away, however old and undignified we grow. Shockingly, from the point of view of the church's teaching, he suggests that having sex is at the centre of things: 'All the world's motions bend and yield to this conjunction, it is a matter everywhere infused; and a Centre whereto all lines come, all things look.' If we are asked why nearly all Shakespeare's works – his tragedies as well as his comedies and poems – are suffused with the language of sexual desire, often expressed through unremittingly bawdy word-play, we should perhaps direct the inquirer to this sentence of Montaigne.

Add to Stoicism an acknowledgement of the needs of the body and the raw materiality of things, then what do you get? The answer is a powerful philosophy that had a largely bad press in the Renaissance, but that might actually have been the closest Shakespeare came to a belief.

The Montaigne of the third book especially thinks along the following lines. Proposition: that pleasure is the beginning and end of living happily. We naturally want pleasure or at the very least the absence of its opposite, pain. We should therefore seek to satisfy our desires. But some pleasures bring subsequent pains, so they are not to be desired. Montaigne asks: would we get drunk if we had the hangover before instead of afterwards? (Lady Macbeth: 'Was the hope drunk / Wherein you dressed yourself? . . . And wakes it now to look so green and pale?') Pleasure may require us to limit our desires. Mental pleasures are greater than physical ones because they are more enduring. Freedom from disturbance may accordingly be a particular pleasure, achieved by a withdrawal from the turmoil of public life.

Throughout his essays, Montaigne had meditated, as Shakespeare does throughout his plays, on the value and the limitation of the Stoic resolve to bear misfortune patiently. However much you are in control of your mind, Montaigne remarks in 'Of constancy', you can't stop yourself from trembling if a gun goes off in your ear or from going tense and pale if a building collapses beside you. Again, the point is that bodily sensation is an essential part of experience: this is the missing element in both the Stoic faith in the pure power of the mind to control the self and the Pauline duality that tries to split the immortal soul from the mortal or self-mortified body. The true route to happiness may require us to be more relaxed and flexible than either Seneca or St Paul would allow:

We must not cleave so fast unto our humours and dispositions. Our chiefest sufficiency is, to apply our selves to divers fashions. It is a being, but not a life, to be tied and bound by necessity to one only course. The goodliest minds are those that have most variety and pliableness in them.

Variety and pliableness: the difference between mere being and a fully lived life. If Shakespeare's copy of Florio's Montaigne were ever to be found, this is the kind of sentence that would be heavily underlined or annotated with a marginal tick or a remark such as 'true wisdom'.

This way of thinking was shaped above all by the ancient Greek philosopher Epicurus, who lived out his beliefs in a philosophical community known as the Garden, to which – scandalously – women and slaves were admitted. Most of Epicurus' voluminous original writings are lost, but they were transmitted to the Romans and thence to the Renaissance via their poetic reworking in Lucretius' *De rerum natura* ('Of the nature of things'), perhaps the greatest philosophical epic poem ever written. Shakespeare is unlikely to have known Lucretius directly, but he would have discovered many quotations from him and meditations on his Epicurean ideas when he read Montaigne.

A reader of Lucretius would have discovered an entirely different world-picture from that of Christianity or indeed Platonism. The universe consists of nothing but atoms swerving unpredictably in a void. A human being is but a conglomeration of atoms which at death are dispersed back into the universe. There is no immaterial soul, no immortality, no active god intervening in our affairs. Since death is nothingness, there is no need for superstition. The good life is accordingly to be achieved through friendship, through kindness to those around you, and through the pursuit of pleasure – with the proviso that over-indulgence of the appetites will not bring enduring happiness.

Epicureanism was regarded with great suspicion in Shakespeare's time for two reasons: because it was atheistic and because it seemed to license sensual indulgence. A marginal note in the Geneva Bible railed against the Epicures for making 'a mock and scoff at all religions'. An orthodox Elizabethan such as Sir John Davies, in his *Orchestra*, a long poem imagining the cosmos as a harmonious dance ordered by God, regarded the Lucretian-Epicurean idea of atomic *chance* as the illusion of a sickened brain:

> Or if this All which round about we see
> (As idle *Morpheus* some sick brains hath taught)
> Of undivided *motes* compacted be,
> How was this goodly Architecture wrought?
> Or by what means were they together brought?
> > They err that say they did concur by chance,
> > Love made them meet in a well-ordered dance.

And in the grotesque figure of the gluttonous sensualist Sir Epicure Mammon in *The Alchemist*, Ben Jonson gave stage life to the idea of Epicureanism as a philosophy of self-indulgence.

Shakespeare was not a proponent of Lucretian atheism or atomism. In *Julius Caesar*, Cassius espouses the Epicurean philosophy, whereas Brutus is a Stoic. But when foreboding ravens, crows and kites hover in place of mighty eagles over the army of Cassius, Cassius interprets the change as a divine sign and is therefore forced to modify his Epicurean belief that the gods do not intervene in human affairs:

> You know that I held Epicurus strong
> And his opinion: now I change my mind
> And partly credit things that do presage.

'Partly credit' is good: he has not entirely renounced the Epicurean scepticism about omens and auguries.

Shakespeare did sometimes associate Epicureanism with sensual excess. Thus Goneril condemning King Lear's hundred knights and squires:

> Men so disordered, so debauched and bold,
> That this our court, infected with their manners,
> Shows like a riotous inn: *epicurism* and lust
> Makes it more like a tavern or a brothel
> Than a graced palace.

And Master Ford condemning fat, lecherous Sir John Falstaff in *The Merry Wives of Windsor*: 'What a damned Epicurean rascal is this!' Macbeth scorning those who have turned against him: 'Then fly, false thanes, / And mingle with the English epicures.' And Roman Pompey expressing his disdain for Mark Antony's Egyptian lifestyle with Cleopatra: 'epicurean cooks / Sharpen with cloyless sauce his appetite'.

But the moment one considers the context of these utterances, Shakespeare's sympathy for the Epicureans becomes apparent. Are we supposed to agree with Goneril? To damn Falstaff? To despise

Siward and the other 'English epicures' who help Macduff and Malcolm to rescue bleeding Scotland from the clutches of the murderous Macbeth? To prefer Roman austerity to Antony and Cleopatra's gaudy nights? For gluttony, Falstaff is Sir Epicure's match, but with a key difference: he does not really care about mammon (money) and he embodies those true Epicurean virtues of kindness and friendship every bit as much as he is an eater, drinker and seeker after pleasure.

Shakespeare is often praised for sympathizing equally with all his characters. But he did not. There are some characters with whom he fell in love. Falstaff and Cleopatra are pre-eminent among them and they are true Epicureans. Like Montaigne, they refuse to pretend that there is no such thing as the body.

The Roman fool

Shakespeare was a contrarian. He took the commonplaces of his age and stood them on their heads – or, in the case of *Titus Andronicus*, sliced off their heads and baked them in a pasty. Rome was synonymous with civilization and the Goths with barbarism: so Shakespeare considers the possibility that Rome was just as barbarous as the Gothic wilderness. Roman Stoicism proposed that it was healthy to keep your emotions under tight restraint: so Shakespeare voices the need to give your feelings vent: 'Sorrow concealèd, like an oven stopped, / Doth burn the heart to cinders where it is.'

Brutus in *Julius Caesar* is a self-confessed Stoic, who believes that however bad life becomes it has to be endured by putting on the armour of 'patience'. But in the last resort he cannot maintain his position: as Cassius has to accept the power of prophecy, so Brutus commits suicide in contravention of his own principles. Shakespeare is always interested in how words are confounded by deeds, how philosophical positions collapse under the pressure of action and circumstance.

In his 'Life of Caius Martius' Plutarch gives a brief character-sketch of the Roman general who, by virtue of his heroic endeavour behind the closed gates of Corioles, gained the surname Coriolanus:

For this Martius' natural wit and great heart did marvellously stir up his courage to do and attempt noble acts. But on the other side, for lack of education he was so choleric and impatient that he would yield to no living creature, which made him churlish, uncivil, and altogether unfit for any man's conversation.

As the name Martius suggests, Coriolanus has all the martial virtues. His tragedy is that he has none of the civil ones. He devotes himself wholly to the code of valour (Latin *virtus*). He has a suitably austere Roman wife, who usually appears in company with a chaste companion (Valeria, the very opposite of Cleopatra's companion Charmian). And when his son Young Martius, a chip off the old block, is praised for tearing the wings off a butterfly with his teeth, we gain a glimpse into the kind of upbringing that Coriolanus may be imagined to have had. 'Anger's my meat', says Volumnia: perhaps in compensation for the premature disappearance of her husband, she has bred up an angry young man, ready to serve Rome on the battlefield where one senses she wishes she could go herself – as she does at the end of the play. If *Antony and Cleopatra* is about the tragic consequences of the dissolution of Romanness, *Coriolanus* is about the equally tragic result of an unyielding adherence to it. 'It is held', says Cominius,

> That valour is the chiefest virtue, and
> Most dignifies the haver: if it be,
> The man I speak of cannot in the world
> Be singly counterpoised.

'If it be': Coriolanus' own mode of speaking, by contrast, is what he calls the 'absolute shall'. To leave room for an 'if' would be to call his whole world-picture into question.

The *Tragedy of Coriolanus* brings the absolute embodiment of *virtus* into hostile dialogue with other voices. As in *Julius Caesar*, the action begins not with the hero but with the people, to whom

Plutarch (a believer in the theory that history is shaped by the deeds of great men alone) never gives a voice. In the very early period of the Roman republic, around the fifth century before Christ, Rome faced two threats: an external danger from neighbouring territories (the Volscians, based in Antium and Corioles) and the internal danger of division between the patricians and the plebeians. The martial hero is supremely successful in dealing with the external threat through force, but his attempt to handle internal affairs in the same way leads to his banishment and eventual death. The opening scene reveals that the people do have a case: the first citizen argues cogently against inequality, speaking 'in hunger for bread, not in thirst for revenge'. Diplomacy is the skill needed here; Coriolanus, who is always 'himself alone' and who trusts in the deeds of the sword rather than the blandishments of the word, will have no truck with compromise. His pride and his desire to stand alone are only allayed when he faces his mother, wife and son pleading for him to have mercy on the city. Volumnia appeals to the bond of family; after her eloquent entreaty, Coriolanus hovers for a moment in one of the most powerful silences in Shakespeare. He sets aside his code of manly strength, accepts the familial tie, and in so doing effectively signs his own death warrant. He has for the first time fully recognized the claims of other people, escaped the bond of absolute self. The knowledge of what he has done brings a kind of peace: 'But let it come,' he says of his inevitable end. He is speaking here in the voice of Stoic resignation.

Coriolanus is a study in the consequences of the lack of that 'pliableness' which Montaigne, following Epicurus, recommended as the basis of a well-lived life. *Antony and Cleopatra* takes the idea of the shifting self to an extreme of dissolution. Shakespeare's Epicurean tragedy, its action sprawls around the Mediterranean world as it gives historical form to the mythical encounter between Venus (the principle of love) and Mars (the god of war). The play is structured upon a series of oppositions: between female and male, desire and duty, the bed and the battlefield, age and youth, Stoicism and Epicureanism, above all Egypt and Rome.

Henry Cockeram's *English Dictionary*, published in the same year as Shakespeare's First Folio, has an entry for Cleopatra: 'an Egyptian

Queen, she was first beloved of Julius Caesar; after, Marcus Anthonius was by her brought into such dotage that he aspired the Empire, which caused his destruction.' The idea that a great law-giver or warrior could be destroyed by the lure of sexual desire was commonplace in the period. An earlier dictionary reminded the reader of how King Solomon in the Bible 'exceeded all men in wisdom and knowledge' but 'nevertheless was by dotage on women brought unto idolatry'. The primary definition of 'dotage' was 'to be mad or peevish, to play the fool (as old folks do)'. To dote was to go against reason; to fall too far in love was to lose one's wits. At the same time, the word was used with reference to old age: senility atrophies the powers of reason and makes an old person become a child again.

'Nay, but this dotage of our general's / O'erflows the measure' says a Roman soldier in the very opening line. From the Roman point of view it is a monstrous embarrassment that one of the three men who rule their great empire should be disporting himself like an infatuated teenager. Perhaps he is indeed entering his dotage, approaching the second childhood of the seventh age of man. From the Egyptian point of view, the power of desire is on the contrary something that transcends the petty world of tribal politics. Antony is torn between the two worlds: one moment he kisses Cleopatra and says 'The nobleness of life / Is to do thus', yet the next he says 'These strong Egyptian fetters I must break / Or lose myself in dotage.'

Romanness meant stoically controlling the passions within the restraint of reason, but in Egypt love is imagined as something that neither can nor should be controlled or measured. Its capacity is infinite. The love of Antony and Cleopatra 'find[s] out new heaven, new earth'. And love's medium is poetry: in this play Shakespeare gives his lyrical powers freer rein than ever before or after. Though the opening lines are spoken by a Roman, their style is loyal to Cleopatra: the sentence overflows the measure of the pentameter line, preparing the way for the liquid imagery of Egypt – with the fertile river Nile at its heart – that will overcome the measured rigidity of Rome.

Against the grain of the Renaissance idealization of the age of

Augustus, *Antony and Cleopatra* depicts Octavius as a mealy-mouthed pragmatist. The play is concerned less with the seismic shift from republic to empire than with the transformation of Mark Antony from military leader to slave of sexual desire: 'Take but good note, and you shall see in him / The triple pillar of the world transformed / Into a strumpet's fool.' To Roman eyes, *eros* renders Antony undignified to the point of risibility, but the sweep of the play's poetic language, down to its closing speech ('No grave upon the earth shall clip in it / A pair so famous'), celebrates the fame of the lovers, whose imagined erotic union in death is symbolic of cosmic harmony. Octavius himself has to admit that the dead Cleopatra looks as if 'she would catch another Antony / In her strong toil of grace': 'toil' is sweatily sexual, but 'grace' suggests that even the most Roman character of them all is now seeing Antony and Cleopatra as something other than self-deluding dotards. The aura of Cleopatra's last speech is still hanging in the air; the power of the poetic language has been such that a sensitive listener will half-believe that Cleopatra has left her baser elements and become all 'fire and air'. She is, as Charmian so superbly puts it, 'A lass unparalleled': just one of the girls, but also the unique queen and serpent, embodiment of the Nile's fertility and the heat of life itself.

In Plutarch's 'Life of Marcus Antonius' Antony claims descent from Anton, son of Hercules; to Shakespeare's Cleopatra he is a 'Herculean Roman'. His allegiance to the greatest of the myth-ical heroes is strengthened by the strange scene in the fourth act, when music of hautboys is heard under the stage and the second soldier offers the interpretation that 'the god Hercules, whom Antony loved, / Now leaves him'. The memorable image of Antony and Cleopatra wearing each other's clothes, the 'sword Philippan' exchanged for the woman's 'tires and mantles', thus comes to suggest the cross-dressing not only of Mars and Venus (i.e. war and love), but also of the strong-armed hero Hercules and Omphale, the Lydian queen who subdued his will and set him to work spinning among her maids. The latter tale was often moralized in the Renaissance as a warning against female wiles. But Shakespeare enjoys the staging of Cleopatra's allure.

Although the 'Life of Marcus Antonius' shows more than usual interest in the main female character, the historical structure of Plutarch's narratives is always premised on the lives of his male heroes. Shakespeare's play alters this focus to emphasize the death of the woman, not that of the warrior, as the climax of the story. The female perspective stands in opposition to the male voice that orders the march of history. In tone and language *Antony and Cleopatra* may be described as a 'feminized' classical tragedy: Egyptian cookery, luxuriant daybeds and a billiard-playing eunuch contrast with the rigours of Roman architecture and senatorial business.

At the end of the drama, young Octavius Caesar is left in sole charge of the empire. He will become Augustus, who was regarded as the embodiment of enlightened imperialism – a model for the ambitions of Shakespeare's patron, King James. But all the poetry of the play has been on the Egyptian, the Epicurean side. From Enobarbus' entranced memory of the barge at Cydnus to the final enrobing for the serpent's kiss of death, the language of Cleopatra works its magic upon the listener. Theatre's power to create illusion is of a piece with her seductive arts.

She is the consummate actress, able to change her mood on a whim, to keep all around her guessing as to whether she is in earnest or at play. Linguistically, she has a marvellous gift of combining a tone of lightness and wonderment with a sexily down-to-earth robustness: 'O happy horse, to bear the weight of Antony!' She is also the only woman in Shakespeare's tragedies to have a wit comparable to that of such comic heroines as Rosalind in *As You Like It* and Portia in *The Merchant of Venice*. 'Can Fulvia die?' she asks with feigned incredulity, playing on the *double entendre* whereby to die meant to have an orgasm. Roman wives, she implies, are frigid creatures. Cleopatra is a grown-up Juliet: utterly confident in her body, she relishes her own sexuality and is the dominant partner in the relationship.

There is, however, a darker side to her powers. She uses both her sexual allure and her regal authority not only to seduce and to charm, but also to manipulate and to emasculate. She savages the messenger who brings news she does not want to hear. Her principal courtiers are women, Charmian and Iras. Plutarch complained that the affairs of Antony's entire empire were determined by these two women of the bedchamber who frizzled Cleopatra's hair and dressed her head. The only men in her entourage are a eunuch, Mardian, and a Greek, Alexas, whose name was synonymous with homoerotic desire.

Shakespeare was a realist as well as a romantic, a skilled politician as well as a supreme poet. He was equally capable of imagining Antony's dramatic trajectory as a rise and as a fall. He was perpetually both inside and outside the action, both an emotionally involved participant in the world he created and a wryly detached commentator upon it. So he invented a new character, Enobarbus, the only major player in the story who is absent from the historical source. Enobarbus embodies the pliable self recommended by Epicurus and Montaigne, only to recognize, tragically, that pliability eventually leaves him with nothing but death. He berates himself for his abnegation of that cardinal Epicurean virtue, friendship. Intelligent, funny, at once companionable and guardedly isolated, full of understanding and admiration for women but most comfortable among men (there is a homoerotic frisson to his bond with Menas and his rivalry with Agrippa), clinically analytical in his assessment of others but full of sorrow and shame when his reason overrides his loyalty and leads him to desert his friend and master, Enobarbus might just be the closest Shakespeare came to a portrait of his own mind.

Last words

The final scene of Shakespeare's final solo-authored play, *The Tempest*, begins with Prospero, prompted by Ariel, deciding on forgiveness instead of revenge:

> Though with their high wrongs I am struck to th'quick,
> Yet with my nobler reason gainst my fury
> Do I take part: the rarer action is
> In virtue than in vengeance. They being penitent,

> The sole drift of my purpose doth extend
> Not a frown further. Go, release them, Ariel:
> My charms I'll break, their senses I'll restore,
> And they shall be themselves.

It is not only Prospero who is being prompted here. It is also Shakespeare. The book that does the prompting is the same as that for Gonzalo's speech about the ideal commonwealth much earlier in the play: the essays of Montaigne in the English translation of John Florio, published in 1603.

In the middle of Montaigne's second book, there is a run of essays that Shakespeare seems to have read exceptionally closely. 'Of the affection of fathers to their children' touches on questions of inheritance, household government and the respect due to old age: matter for *King Lear*. The following essay concerns the military tactics of the ancient Parthians, a subject to which curiously detailed attention is given in *Antony and Cleopatra*. The next is 'Of books', in which Montaigne recommends Plutarch above all other authors: the Plutarch plays of *Timon of Athens*, *Coriolanus* and *Antony and Cleopatra* preoccupied Shakespeare in his Jacobean years. The final essay in the sequence is the lengthy 'Apology of Raymond Sebond', which underwrote so much of the thinking in *King Lear*.

Between 'Of books' and the 'Apology' is an essay 'Of cruelty', which begins by arguing that true virtue reveals itself when the inclination to goodness is tested:

He that through a natural facility and genuine mildness should neglect or contemn injuries received, should no doubt perform a rare action, and worthy commendation. But he who being touched and stung to the quick with any wrong or offence received, should arm himself with reason against this furiously-blind desire of revenge, and in the end, after a great conflict, yield himself master over it, should doubtless do much more.

Montaigne's 'a rare action' prompts Shakespeare's 'the rare action', his 'stung to the quick' Shakespeare's 'struck to the quick'. But the connection goes beyond these precise verbal echoes: both passages turn on the idea of 'virtue' being achieved when 'reason' over-comes the desire for 'vengeance'. With Montaigne's characteristic contrariness, the essay 'Of cruelty' is essentially about the need for compassion, the cardinal virtue that Prospero has to learn.

Immediately after the passage quoted by Prospero, Montaigne proceeds to a defence of the philosophy of Epicurus. This is one of a number of moments scattered through the *Essays* when Montaigne shows notable sympathy for the most maligned thinker of the ancient world. Shakespeare would have been equally sympathetic when he discovered some of the following ideas of Epicurus in his reading of Montaigne. The view that true wisdom involves being content to live in the moment rather than reflect anxiously on the past and the future. The hypothesis that the seat of the self might be in the stomach. The recognition that laws are necessary for society since 'without them, men would inter-devour one another'. The acknowledgement that desire and sensuality are an essential part of what it is to be human. A questioning of the Stoical faith in the stiff upper lip: 'Epicurus doth not only pardon his wise man to cry out when he is grieved or vexed, but persuadeth him to it.' The analogy between the multiplicity of possible interpretations of a text or a human encounter and the multiplicity of possible swerves and conjunctions of the atoms in the universe: 'we open the matter, and spill it in distempering it. Of one subject we make a thousand; and in multiplying and dividing we fall again into the infinity of Epicurus his atoms.' And finally a resistance to the pursuit of public glory and posthumous fame – summed up in the Epicurean precept that would have been the perfect motto for Shakespeare: 'HIDE THY LIFE'.

We need to dispose of the old myth that Shakespeare's theatrical signing-off came with the epilogue to *The Tempest*. The final words he wrote for the theatre were probably those not of Prospero Duke of Milan, but of Theseus Duke of Athens, at the end of *The Two Noble Kinsmen*:

> O, you heavenly charmers,
> What things you make of us! For what we lack
> We laugh, for what we have are sorry, still

> Are children in some kind. Let us be thankful
> For that which is, and with you leave dispute
> That are above our question. Let's go off,
> And bear us like the time.

A wry shrug towards the gods and their way of making fools of us. A recognition that we never entirely shake off childhood and its ways of behaving. A paradox expressed by way of a rhetorically balanced pairing: 'For what we lack / We laugh, for what we have are sorry'. It really ought to be the other way round, sorrow for what we lack and laughter for what we have, but its being this contrary way is the essence of what makes us human. A tragi-comic mingling of laughter and sorrow. A thankfulness for the blessings we have, beside a refusal to engage in theological and philosophical disputes 'that are above our question'. If Shakespeare's farewell is that of Theseus, not Prospero, it places him somewhere between the Epicurean notion that what we know is experience, not divinity, and the self-denying ordinance of the philosopher Ludwig Wittgenstein centuries later: 'whereof we cannot speak thereof we must be silent'.

The final order, to 'bear us like the time', sounds at first like a reiteration of the end of *King Lear*: 'The weight of this sad time we must obey.' But it is not. The ending of *The Two Noble Kinsmen* is a time of both funeral and marriage. The funeral-baked meats will coldly furnish forth the marriage table without a bitter Hamlet to complain about the sudden change of mood. There will be sorrow but then there will be laughter. There will be eating and drinking, Falstaff's Epicurean needs. Thus Shakespeare's last stage words, binding the infinite space of his imaginative world in a nutshell.

25. Exit and Re-entrance

To the memory of Master W. Shakespeare

We wondered, Shakespeare, that thou went'st so soon
From the world's stage to the grave's tiring-room.
We thought thee dead, but this thy printed worth
Tells thy spectators that thou went'st but forth
To enter with applause. An actor's art
Can die, and live to act a second part.
That's but an exit of mortality;
This, a re-entrance to a plaudity.

James Mabbe, commendatory poem in the First Folio

According to Stratford gossip, 'Shakespeare, Drayton and Ben Jonson had a merry meeting and it seems drank too hard, for Shakespeare died of a fever there contracted.' A note to this effect is to be found in the diary of John Ward, the town's vicar in the years immediately after the Restoration of the monarchy. Ward also seems to have made a note of his intention to meet with Judith Quiney, Shakespeare's surviving daughter, but she died early in 1662, before he was able to carry out what would have been one of the most valuable interviews in literary history. In its absence, there is no way of confirming the veracity of the story about the drinking party. Biographers assume that, if it did take place, it would have been in Stratford. Though London-based for most of his literary career, Drayton was a Warwickshire man with a patroness in the village of Clifford Chambers just outside Stratford. Shakespeare's son-in-law John Hall once cured him of a tertian fever by means of an emetic infusion spiced with syrup of violets.

Shakespeare had made his will a couple of months before, which a man usually did only when he believed he was close to death, so there is a presumption that he would not have been sufficiently well to travel to London. But that is only a presumption: there is nothing to prevent the alternative possibility of a recovery, a last trip to put London affairs in order, a night at the Mermaid with Ben and Michael, a fever contracted in crowded company and exacerbated by the journey home to Stratford in a damp English April. After all, fever is not the usual aftermath of mere drunkenness.

Or the whole thing may be invention: irascible Ben Jonson did not like Michael Drayton, so it is fanciful to suppose them making their farewells to the dying Shakespeare together. The only solid facts are the record of the burial of 'Will. Shakspere, gent.' in the parish register of Holy Trinity, Stratford-upon-Avon, the gravestone in the chancel, inscribed with a rhyme cursing whomsoever may move the bones beneath, and the monument on the north wall of the chancel recording that Shakespeare died on 23 April 1616, in his fifty-third year. This same monument credits him with the wisdom of Socrates and the art of Virgil, while claiming that 'quick nature died' with him and yet 'all that he hath writ / Leaves living art, but page, to serve his wit'. Thanks to the pages of his books, Shakespeare's art lives on after the death of his body.

'An actor's art / Can die, and live to act a second part': so wrote James Mabbe in the clever, under-rated commendatory poem he contributed to the edition of Shakespeare's complete plays published seven years later in handsome folio format. An actor becomes another person for a few hours. At the end of every performance, that person dies. In a tragedy, the actor plays at death and resurrection, breathing last words one moment and rising to take a bow the next. And yet the stage actor always knows that at the end of every show a particular incarnation is gone, never to return. Macbeth's shadowy 'poor player' and Prospero's 'these our actors' who melt into air are images of the peculiar fragility and evanescence of the actorly self. As Mabbe puts it, the actor can 'live to act a second part', yet 'That's but an exit of mortality'. A play published, on the other hand, is 'a re-entrance to a plaudity'. By living in print, the writer can extend for centuries – perhaps for all time – that glorious moment of applause which for the actor lasts at most for a few minutes each day and then, on retirement, is heard no more.

Each of the commendatory poems in the First Folio ends on an image of Shakespeare achieving a second life through his book. Mabbe's poem is preceded by that of Leonard Digges, which says that the Stratford monument may be dissolved by time but the 'wit-fraught book' will ensure that Shakespeare 'canst never die, / But, crowned with laurel, live eternally'. Digges in turn is preceded by Hugh Holland, who, like Mabbe, uses the image of the grave as a 'tiring-house' to which the actor returns after the show of life. The poem contrasts the brevity of Shakespeare's mortal span to the endurance of his work: 'For though his line of life went soon about, / The life yet of his lines shall never out.' And before these three short poems, there is Ben Jonson's much longer elegy 'To the memory of my beloved, the AUTHOR Master William Shakespeare and what he hath left us' – the 'AUTHOR' capitalized as if to suggest the contrast between the endurance of the writer and the mortality of the actor. Jonson's closing image is of the 'light' of Shakespeare's book shining down in benign influence over 'the drooping stage'.

What was Shakespeare remembered for, above all else? Wherever you look, the answer is the same. Opposite the title page of the Folio, with its engraving of the author, is another poem by Jonson, in which he says that the engraver has drawn Shakespeare's face very well but that if he could have 'drawn his wit' he would then have produced a print that surpassed every engraving ever made in the whole history of art. But since it is of course impossible to create a visual reproduction of the inside of Shakespeare's head as well as the outside of it, the reader should turn the page and read the book instead of lingering over the picture. Jonson's own witty point is that the book itself is the imprint of the greatest wit the world has ever seen.

In his longer poem, Jonson suggests that Shakespeare's 'wit' is so great that Nature herself will vouchsafe no other. 'Wit' was also the climactic word on the inscription on Shakespeare's church-monument. It reappears on another gravestone in the chancel of Holy Trinity, that of Shakespeare's daughter Susanna, who died in

1649: 'witty above her sex . . . Something of Shakespeare was in that.' To all his first admirers, then, Shakespeare was great above all for his 'wit'.

To us, the word conjures up the snappy sayings of Oscar Wilde ('I have nothing to declare except my genius'). To Jonson and his contemporaries, it meant much more. Old English 'wit or 'gewit' referred to the mind as the seat of consciousness and thought – to have lost one's mind was to be out of one's wits. By the sixteenth century, the word was applied not only to the faculty of thinking and reasoning but also to a person who was particularly well endowed with that faculty. Since language is the means of expressing thought, 'wit' became especially associated with linguistic talent – and there one sees the origin of the more confined modern sense. In John Florio's English–Italian dictionary of 1598, *A World of Words*, Italian '*mente*' is defined as 'the highest and chiefest part of the soul, the mind, understanding, wit, memory, intent, will, advice, remembrance, counsel, prudence, judgement, thought, opinion, imagination, conceit, knowledge, heart, wisdom, providence or foreknowledge of man'. In praising Shakespeare's wit, Jonson is alluding not just to his linguistic facility but to a whole panoply of mental powers.

My aim throughout this book has been to explore Shakespeare's wit in the full sixteenth-century sense of the word: we have encountered his memory, counsel, prudence, opinion, providence and the rest, in addition to his 'pleasant wittiness in words, merry conceits or witty grace in speaking wit'. Shakespeare was not, as John Milton later suggested, a child of nature, 'warbling his native wood-notes wild'. He was – the term was a positive one in the sixteenth century – a magnificently *artificial* writer. He wrote with, to use more of Florio's definitions, *accorgimento* ('wariness, foresight, craft, wiliness, wit'), *acutezza* ('sharpness, policy, subtlety, vivacity of wit or sight') and *intellétto* ('understanding, wit, discretion, capacity, knowledge, skill, reason, discourse, perceiving, intelligence, sense, or judgement'). These were the qualities most admired in a writer, a thinker, a speaker. That is why in the second poem in the First Folio, Ben Jonson's elaborate epistle of praise, Shakespeare is described as '*Soul of the Age*'.

But did Shakespeare think of himself as a writer who would be read after his death? Many of the sonnets turn on images of immortality through writing and yet Shakespeare appears not to have sought to usher in that immortality by personally seeing his sonnets into print as soon as they were written. The fact that he did not supervise the publication of his own collected works in his lifetime, as Ben Jonson did his, has led to the widespread belief that Shakespeare was careless of posthumous fame. The story is, however, a little more complicated than popular myth suggests.

'And yet to times in hope my verse shall stand'

The original manuscripts of Shakespeare's works do not survive: the sole extant composition in his hand is that single scene from *Sir Thomas More*, a multi-authored play that cannot really be described as 'his'. Shakespeare survives only because his works were printed. In his lifetime there appeared some twenty works, nearly all printed in the compact and relatively low-priced format, which may be thought of as the equivalent of the modern paperback, known as quarto. The term is derived from the fact that each sheet of paper that came off the press was folded to make four leaves.

First there were the poems *Venus and Adonis* (1593) and *Lucrece* (1594). The publication history of the plays began with *The most lamentable Roman tragedy of Titus Andronicus, as it was played by the right honourable the Earl of Derby, Earl of Pembroke and Earl of Sussex their servants* and *The first part of the contention betwixt the two famous Houses of York and Lancaster, with the death of the good Duke Humphrey, and the banishment and death of the Duke of Suffolk, and the tragical end of the proud Cardinal of Winchester, with the notable rebellion of Jack Cade, and the Duke of York's first claim unto the crown*. Both were printed in 1594. The latter was a variant version of the play that in the 1623 First Folio was called *The Second Part of Henry the Sixth*. In 1595 there followed *The true tragedy of Richard Duke of York and the death of good King Henry the sixth, with the whole contention between the two houses Lancaster and York, as it was sundry times acted by the right honourable the Earl of Pembroke his servants* (in octavo as opposed to quarto format). It was a variant version of the play that in the 1623 First Folio was called *The Third Part of Henry the Sixth*.

In 1597 *The tragedy of Richard the Second, as it hath been publicly acted by the right honourable the Lord Chamberlain his servants* appeared without the deposition scene that was inserted in some later quarto printings and the Folio. The same year saw texts of *The tragedy of Richard the Third, containing his treacherous plots against his brother Clarence, the pitiful murder of his innocent nephews, his tyrannical usurpation, with the whole course of his detested life and most deserved death. As it hath been lately acted by the right honourable the Lord Chamberlain his servants* and *An excellent conceited tragedy of Romeo and Juliet, as it hath been often (with great applause) played publicly by the right honourable Lord of Hunsdon his servants*. The latter was printed in a short and often flawed text that was replaced by a new quarto of 1599 ('*Newly corrected, augmented and amended*') which sought to establish a more authoritative text.

Two more plays appeared in 1598. The first of Shakespeare's comedies to reach print was *A pleasant conceited comedy called Love's Labours Lost, as it was presented before her highness this last Christmas. Newly corrected and augmented by W. Shakespeare*. This wording on its title page '*newly corrected and augmented*' may imply that there was an earlier, less good quality text, now lost, which the new edition was intended to replace. The other play published that year, *The History of Henry the fourth, with the battle at Shrewsbury between the King and Lord Henry Percy surnamed Henry Hotspur of the north, with the humorous conceits of Sir John Falstaff*, became, to judge from the number of times it was reprinted, Shakespeare's bestselling drama.

1600 was a rich year, with the appearance in print of no fewer than five plays. Two were histories: *The Second Part of Henry the fourth, continuing to his death and coronation of Henry the fifth, with the humours of Sir John Falstaff and swaggering Pistol, as it hath been sundry times publicly acted by the right honourable the Lord Chamberlain his servants* and *The chronicle history of Henry the fifth, with his battle fought at Agincourt in France, together with Ancient Pistol, as it hath been sundry times played by the right honourable the Lord Chamberlain his servants*. The latter was another short and often flawed text, highly variant from that published in the posthumous Folio. The other three were comedies: *The most excellent history of the merchant of Venice, with the extreme cruelty of Shylock the Jew towards the said merchant, in cutting a just pound of his flesh, and the obtaining of Portia by the choice of three chests. As it hath been diverse times acted by the Lord Chamberlain his servants*; *A Midsummer Night's Dream, as it hath been sundry times publicly acted by the right honourable the Lord Chamberlain his servants*; and *Much Ado about Nothing, as it hath been sundry times publicly acted by the right honourable the Lord Chamberlain his servants*.

The last comedy to be printed in Shakespeare's lifetime was *A most pleasant and excellent conceited comedy of Sir John Falstaff and the merry wives of Windsor, intermixed with sundry variable and pleasing humours of Sir Hugh the Welsh knight, Justice Shallow and his wise cousin Master Slender, with the swaggering vein of Ancient Pistol and Corporal Nym. By William Shakespeare. As it hath been diverse times acted by the right honourable my Lord Chamberlain's servants, both before her majesty and elsewhere* (1602). Once more, this was a short and often flawed text, highly variant in comparison with that published in the posthumous Folio.

The tragical history of Hamlet Prince of Denmark by William Shakespeare, as it hath been diverse times publicly acted by his highness' servants in the city of London, as also in the two universities of Cambridge and Oxford, and elsewhere was published in 1603. It was another short and often flawed text. As with *Romeo and Juliet*, it was swiftly replaced by a new quarto: the edition of 1604/5 advertised itself as 'Newly imprinted and enlarged to almost as much again as it was, according to the true and perfect copy', and sought to establish a more authoritative text.

Three years of silence followed. Then in 1608 there appeared *Mr William Shakespeare his true chronicle history of the life and death of King Lear and his three daughters, with the unfortunate life of Edgar, son and heir to the Earl of Gloucester, and his sullen and assumed humour of Tom of Bedlam. As it was played before the King's majesty at Whitehall upon St Stephen's night in Christmas holidays, by his majesty's servants playing usually at the Globe on Bankside.*

Three works went into print in 1609. *The late and much admired play called Pericles, Prince of Tyre. With the true relation of the whole history, adventures and fortunes of the said prince, as also, the no less strange and worthy accidents in the birth and life of his daughter Mariana. As it hath been diverse and sundry times acted by his majesty's servants at the Globe on the Bankside. By William Shakespeare* appeared in a deeply flawed text that was not included in the First Folio, perhaps for licensing reasons. *Troilus and Cressida* was printed in two variant states, discussed below. And then there was *Shakespeare's Sonnets, never before imprinted* – the latter volume also included the poem 'A Lover's Complaint by William Shakespeare', though its title page makes no mention of the fact.

No new Shakespearean works went into print in the last seven years of his life.

Several of the works printed in Shakespeare's lifetime were reprinted one or more times prior to the First Folio of 1623. Several other works printed in Shakespeare's lifetime were also attributed to him, among them the short collection of sonnets and songs *The Passionate Pilgrim* (first published late 1598 or 1599, containing a mixture of poems by Shakespeare, by others and of uncertain authorship), a number of plays that were definitely not by him (e.g. *The first part of the life of Sir John Oldcastle*) and some with which he had a connection in so far as they were performed by his acting company (e.g. *The London Prodigal* and *A Yorkshire Tragedy*).

A clear pattern is discernible from the title pages of the quartos. The title pages serve as advertisements, giving tasters of the content, with particular emphasis in the histories on plotting and battle and in a range of plays on the 'humours' (verbal conceits) of certain characters (Falstaff, Pistol, Evans, Edgar as Tom o'Bedlam in *Lear*). From the late 1590s onwards, but not before, Shakespeare's name is a selling-point. Most of the title pages emphasize the success that the plays have achieved on stage, some the fact that they have been played at court. In a few cases, a later edition is intended to replace a defective earlier one (e.g. *Romeo and Juliet*, *Hamlet*, probably *Love's Labour's Lost*).

The publication pattern of the plays suggests bursts of demand and periods of slackness in the market, with clusters of newly printed works appearing in 1594–95, 1597–1600, 1602–04/5 and

1608–09. Seven histories, six comedies and five tragedies were published in Shakespeare's lifetime, revealing that he was admired in all three genres, though, to judge from numbers of reprints, it was the histories and tragedies that found more readers.

In sum, the quartos are variable in quality of printing, degree of authorization and nature of underlying copy: some of them, such as the long Second Quartos *Hamlet* and *Romeo*, are perhaps best seen as 'literary' or 'reading' texts authorized by Shakespeare and/ or his company, while others, such as the short First Quartos *Hamlet* and *Romeo*, offer fascinating approximations to the possible structure and extensive cutting of early performance but not accurate transcriptions of Shakespeare's words. The quartos are 'raw' or 'of the moment' Shakespeare as opposed to 'edited' or 'collected' Shakespeare.

In 1619, the publisher Thomas Pavier printed editions of *Henry V*, the two previously published *Henry VI* plays (with the joint title *The whole contention between the two famous houses, Lancaster and York*), *King Lear*, *The Merchant of Venice*, *The Merry Wives of Windsor*, *A Midsummer Night's Dream*, *Pericles* and two plays that had been attributed to Shakespeare (*The First Part of Sir John Oldcastle* and *A Yorkshire Tragedy*). An element of through-pagination suggests that this was intended as some kind of 'collected Shakespeare'. There was precedent for such a collection: three years earlier, in 1616, Ben Jonson had become the first English playwright to collect his works for the public stage together in a single volume, though he had also included the more elevated and respectable matter of his poems and court masques.

With the assistance of their patron, the Earl of Pembroke, the leading players of the King's Men (Richard Burbage, John Hemings and Henry Condell) obtained an order preventing Pavier, or anyone else, from going any further with such an enterprise. It was probably at this time that the actors began considering the possibility of a collected Shakespeare of their own. Burbage died later in 1619, so Hemings and Condell carried forward the project. Materials were gathered and printing began in 1621. The First Folio (so named for the large size and single fold of its paper) eventually appeared in 1623. It included thirty-six plays, but not the poems and sonnets. The plays were seventeen of the eighteen published in Shakespeare's lifetime (*Pericles* was omitted – and *Troilus and Cressida* nearly was, with licence to include it being obtained only at the last minute, after the whole book had been printed off, which accounts for the absence of the play from the contents list), *Othello* (which had appeared in an independent quarto while the Folio was under preparation), and a further eighteen plays that had never appeared in print (though a couple of them had been licensed for earlier publication that did not materialize). Were it not for the Folio, these eighteen plays would have been lost to posterity: *The Tempest*, *The Two Gentlemen of Verona*, *Measure for Measure*, *The Comedy of Errors*, *As You Like It*, *The Taming of the Shrew*, *All's Well that Ends Well*, *Twelfth Night*, *The Winter's Tale*, *King John*, *The First Part of Henry the Sixth*, *Henry the Eighth*, *Coriolanus*, *Timon of Athens*, *Julius Caesar*, *Macbeth*, *Antony and Cleopatra*, *Cymbeline*.

The conventional wisdom has it that the absence of printed editions of these latter plays in Shakespeare's lifetime means that he did not care about being read and his work enduring after his death. The poor quality and seemingly unauthorized status of some of the quartos are invoked to lend support to this argument. There is, however, a strong contrary argument that the good quality and seemingly authorized status of many of the other quartos suggest that Shakespeare did care about being read and his work enduring after his death. Save in the case of the court dramatist John Lyly, it was not usual in the 1580s and 1590s for a playwright's name to appear on the title page of a printed script, but from the late 1590s onwards Shakespeare's name was prominent on his. Comedies were generally regarded as lightweight works, intended primarily for performance and perhaps for less elevated readers. Histories and tragedies were, however, sometimes considered good reading matter for serious people. Good quality, so presumably authorized, versions of many of Shakespeare's Elizabethan history plays and tragedies duly appeared in print. With *Romeo and Juliet* and *Hamlet*, there seems to have been a conscious desire to provide a good reading text in place of a shoddy and unauthorized printing of a theatre script.

The Two Gentlemen of Verona and *The Comedy of Errors* were short, early comedies. *The Taming of the Shrew* and *King John* seem to have been reworkings of older plays that were printed in Shakespeare's lifetime, possibly with the intention of their being passed off as his. *The First Part of Henry the Sixth* was a collaborative play, not a work of sole Shakespearean authorship. *As You Like It* was registered for publication soon after it was written, though it did not appear in print. Remove these six from the list of plays that were only published posthumously and a striking fact emerges: twelve of the other thirteen were written after 1600, eleven of them after the accession of King James in 1603.

This neglected statistic chimes with the other evidence for Shakespeare's partial withdrawal from the theatrical and literary world following the long plague outbreak of 1603–04 and the possible scandal surrounding his name at that time. We might go so far as to divide his career, rather on the lines of my earlier proposition that Elizabethan Shakespeare was an English author, Jacobean Shakespeare a British one: Elizabethan Shakespeare *did* care for the publication of what he regarded as his most important works, whereas Jacobean Shakespeare did not.

Intriguingly, though, during the plague years of 1608 and 1609, there does seem to have been a conscious attempt to refashion Shakespeare as a 'literary dramatist'. The 1608 title page of *King Lear* mentions a royal command performance, but its phrase '*true chronicle history*' suggests that the purchaser will be obtaining a text worthy to be read beside other history books, not just a piece of stage illusion. The 1609 quarto of *Troilus and Cressida* is even more suggestive. The book exists in two separate states: one with the title page *The History of Troilus and Cressida. As it was acted by the King's Majesty's servants at the Globe. Written by William Shakespeare*, the other with a title page omitting reference to the stage: *The Famous History of Troilus and Cresseid. Excellently expressing the beginning of their loves, with the conceited wooing of Pandarus Prince of Licia. Written by William Shakespeare.* Furthermore, copies in this second state include a prefatory epistle that makes claims for the readerly as opposed to the theatrical text:

A never writer to an ever reader. News.

Eternal reader, you have here a new play, never staled with the Stage, never clapper-clawed with the palms of the vulgar, and yet passing full of the palm comical; for it is a birth of your brain that never undertook anything comical vainly. And were but the vain names of comedies changed for the titles of Commodities, or of Plays for Pleas, you should see all those grand censors that now style them such vanities flock to them for the main grace of their gravities: especially this author's Comedies, that are so framed to the life that they serve for the most common Commentaries of all the actions of our lives, showing such a dexterity and power of wit that the most displeased with Plays are pleased with his Comedies. And all such dull and heavy-witted worldlings as were never capable of the wit of a Comedy, coming by report of them to his representations, have found that wit there that they never found in themselves, and have parted better witted than they came: feeling an edge of wit set upon them, more than ever they dreamed they had brain to grind it on. So much and such savored salt of wit is in his Comedies that they seem (for their height of pleasure) to be born in that sea that brought forth Venus. Amongst all there is none more witty than this.

Some scholars have (understandably but in my view wrongly) inferred from certain phrases in this preface that *Troilus and Cressida* was written for private performance, perhaps to a sophisticated audience of student lawyers at the Inns of Court, who would have appreciated its vein of formal debate and rhetorical elaboration. But the language of Pandarus, with his direct addresses to 'tongue-tied maidens', 'sisters of the door-hold trade' and 'some gallèd goose of Winchester' (meaning Southwark prostitutes), implies the social and sexual mix of the Globe audience, not the male exclusivity of the Inns of Court. There is no reason to doubt that the play was, in the words of the title page of those other copies of the quarto, 'acted by the King's Majesty's Servants at the Globe'. The suggestion that *Troilus* is somehow too intellectual for the public playhouse, that it was written for elite 'private' taste, is mere condescension. Plenty of other Globe plays by Shakespeare and his contemporaries stretch the intellectual sinews while simultaneously appealing to the humour of the privy and the bedroom.

The whole point of the *Troilus* epistle is to defend the super-sized 'wit' of Shakespeare. The words 'wit', 'witty' and 'witted' could hardly have been repeated more often. The argument is that even people who disapprove of the stage can learn about 'all the actions of our lives' by *reading* Shakespeare's work. The epistle is a defence of Shakespeare as literary dramatist, as a text to be read. '*Never staled with the stage*' and so forth in the first sentence has the qualifying phrase '*for it is a birth of your brain*'. This surely means something to the effect of: *what you are holding in your hand is a book, not a stage performance; the serious reader ('ever reader') creates the play in his mind when he reads it.* A written text, animated in the brain, read in the study: that's the thing that is '*never staled with the stage, never clapper-clawed with the palms of the vulgar*'. It is a general statement, the exact opposite of Dr Johnson's remark in his 1765 preface to Shakespeare that 'a play read affects the mind like a play acted'. The *Troilus* preface writer is not saying that the play has never been staged publicly, rather that a published play is a different, and more valuable, thing than a staged one.

One might almost suppose that the two title pages were a marketing strategy. If you were a theatregoer and snapper-up of playbooks, you could buy the 'As it was acted at the Globe' version, but if you were a sophisticated reader (an '*ever reader*') who thought the theatre really rather vulgar, you could buy the version with a title page that makes it look like a history book with no mention of the stage, together with the epistle making you feel good about reading such a thing. The modern analogy would be when a movie tie-in leads to the repackaging of the cover of a classic or literary novel – the 'classic' cover is kept available for the snobbier readers who would not want to be thought to have bought the book because of the movie, but for the moviegoers there is a version with the same text but a different cover, showing the star. Whether or not the circulation of the two states of *Troilus* was deliberate, the highly sophisticated claim of the epistle to the effect that a reader can give birth to a Shakespeare play in his brain is a key moment in the history of Shakespeare's *literary* reputation.

Why, then, was there no follow-up? This would have been the perfect moment to publish such elevated plays as *Julius Caesar*, *Coriolanus* and *Antony and Cleopatra*, to make Shakespeare into the

English Plutarch not just of the stage but of the page. We simply do not know the answer. If the 1609 sonnets really were unauthorized, and if they were perceived to smack of lechery or even sodomy, Shakespeare may have shied away from the world of print. But that takes us back into the realm of wild surmise.

'Read him, therefore, and again, and again'

We can, however, find out something about *how* Shakespeare was read during and immediately after his own lifetime. The earliest references are to his poems. *Venus and Adonis* in particular was favoured reading matter among university students and other young wits. Without question it was the bestselling long poem of the age, and to judge from an array of allusions it was regarded as both funny and racy, potentially even a handbook for seduction. *Lucrece* was an exercise in graver matter and it may be that Shakespeare was happier about the publication of his tragedies and histories than his comedies because he wanted readers to regard him seriously as a writer.

Educated Renaissance readers often annotated their books. There is, for instance, a copy of Florio's 1603 translation of Montaigne's essays which reveals its owner reading for knowledge, for example by underlining historical names, and for good judgement, for example by putting the marginal comment 'a sage or wise man' against a passage in which Montaigne argues that the actions of princes are best judged after their death. This typical reader underlined bits and pieces of wisdom and information, putting marginal ticks against those with which he agreed (for example the statement that 'we shall never rail enough against the disorder and unruliness of our mind'), but sometimes also expressing his dissent – thus 'Happy they that can rejoice and gratify their senses with insensibility, and live by their death' is given a resounding marginal 'no!' Renaissance readers both drew wisdom from their books and brought opinions to them: they read to learn, but also to debate.

The process is seen at work in marginalia in some of the surviving copies of the Shakespeare First Folio. The Glasgow copy with those intriguing notes scribbled against the list of names of principal actors at the beginning of the book also has some brief annotations to the comedies: 'pretty well' for *The Tempest*, 'stark naught' for *The Two Gentlemen of Verona*, 'very good; light' for *The Merry Wives of Windsor*. There are underlinings of admired passages and the marginal annotation 'ap' (perhaps meaning *approbo*, 'I endorse this') to highlight approved sentiments. This mode of reading, with an emphasis on beauties and on points of particular moral value that might merit copying into a commonplace book, is concordant with the way in which early modern readers responded to classical texts and serious histories.

The most extensively annotated First Folio is now in the Kodama Memorial Library of Meisei University in Japan. It was owned in the early to mid seventeenth century by a man called William Johnstoune. The annotations are in secretary hand: to give a feel for their closeness to Shakespeare's own time, they are quoted here in original spelling.

Sometimes they consist of reminders of details of the action, such as 'Tamora broght to bed of a blacke moore and sends to aaron to stabbe it' (*Titus Andronicus*). But there are also broad aesthetic and moral judgements. Thus near the end of *Measure for Measure*: 'pleasant conclusions of the aduentures'. And at the climax of *The Merchant of Venice*:

Feares wittily wroght and fairlie quenched
Conceiued feares and losses happily remoued
Intricassies cleered and Ioyfullie ended

In many places, *sententiae* – gobbets of moral wisdom – are copied from the text. The notes on the opening scenes of *The Tempest* show how the annotator's mode of reading is to move from an initial summary of the action and sentiments of the play to a moral conclusion or a piece of good 'policy':

Feare and confusion in sea tempest
Scornfull contempt of danger
Signes of a man born to be hangd
Counsellors can not command the Weather

Simplicitie of princes too bookish
Compassion for the death of persons perished by shipwrak
Learning preferred to empire
Power abused by fauorits coosening prince & people
Their Ingratitude and ambition

The annotator seems to have regarded *The Tempest* as an unusually
political play among the comedies. Generally, his emphasis in the
comedies is upon women, love and marriage. He sees poetry as a
vehicle of erotic desire: 'loue made by poesie . . . powerfull effects
of poesie' (*The Two Gentlemen of Verona*). And he is aware that
parental will does not always lead to happiness: 'miserie of forced
marriage' (final note on *The Merry Wives of Windsor*).

Where there is a generalizing sentence, it is sometimes copied
into the margin: 'No philosopher could euer endure the toothake
patientlie' (*Much Ado about Nothing*). Generally speaking, the annotator shares the commonplace morals and prejudices of the age:
'Iewish opinions . . . Their hatefull vsuries . . . Scripture ill cited
and peruersedlie applied' (*The Merchant of Venice*). But at the same
time he has the sensitivity to follow Shakespeare's more flexible
mode of thinking. Thus in response to the famous 'hath not a Jew
eyes' speech, his annotations run from 'The Iewes miserie and
vindicatiue mind' to the humanistic 'One man in most things like
another in desires passions and suffrances'.

Johnstoune, if he is the annotator, is on the lookout for advice
about how to achieve the good life: 'Haters of musicke are brutish
and not to be trusted', he notes (*Merchant of Venice*), and 'Securitie
and happinesse of retired life' (*As You Like It*). He does not seem
particularly attuned to contradiction: 'Against cruell sport of killing
Innocent deere', he scribbles, failing to see that Jaques is offering
a critique of that very idea of 'security and happiness of retired life'
that the Duke has been commending. Nor does he fully understand
Shakespeare's subtle representation of Rosalind: 'a woman never
wants an excuse of her faults' is the best he can manage for her.
And there is no question of possible irony in the close of *The
Taming of the Shrew*: 'Husband commended for making her who
when she was a maide and after she was first maried wes Intolerablie

shrew and scolding to become loving and obedient . . . Duties of true obedience of a wife to her husband.'

The orthodox vision comes across from some comments on *All's Well that Ends Well*, which, like *The Tempest*, is seen as one of the more serious and politically engaged comedies:

Iust cause of warre
Subiects sould not prye in the affaires of state
A gracious mother in law
Warre is phisicke to restlesse young men surfetted with ease

Judgements on characters, meanwhile, tend to be black and white, in contrast to Shakespeare's own sense (articulated explicitly in this play) that the web of our life is of a mingled yarn and that there is always some glimmer of good in things evil (and vice versa): 'Helens merited praise . . . Diana claimes mariage of the Count and he slanders her perffidiouslie.'

Turning to the histories, one again gets a sense of an intelligent reader who understands Shakespeare's techniques – 'The auditours Imagination must supplie the strangenesse of Incredible representations of the stage' (prologue to *Henry V*) – but who wants to find certainty where modern critics prefer doubt and irony: 'The kings excellent wisdome and knowledge of all virtues politick and martial' (King Harry). 'The king', it is noted, is 'sensible of the curse god sends vpon princes who make vniust warre'. But there is no linking of this insight to the epilogue that reveals how England is cursed by King Harry's premature death and the disastrous civil wars of the following reign.

Johnstoune reads very much as a gentleman. He has little sympathy for the lower-class characters who would presumably have appealed to the groundlings: he dismisses the quarrel between Nym and Bardolph as 'foolish brawles of dastardlie rogues and whoores'.

Occasionally an annotation reveals a closer attention to the text than that of many more modern and apparently more sophisticated critical readers. 'Once more unto the breach, dear friends' is read as an 'encouragement to the cruell actions of mercilesse warre', in which King Harry voices 'Persuasions seuerall to gentlemen and yeamen'. Here the annotator perceives that different parts of the speech are addressed to different parts of the army. It is usually assumed that Harry begins by addressing his whole army as 'friends' in true comradely fashion. The annotation's careful differentiation between gentlemen and yeomen makes one see that actually the speech has a tripartite division, characteristic of classical rhetoric. First the king addresses his intimate 'friends' – the word frequently meant 'kinsmen' – which is to say the fellow-royals (Exeter, Bedford, Gloucester) who lead the army. Then he turns to the officer class and only at the end to the common soldiers. A strong sense of hierarchy pervades the speech, for all the talk of equal brotherhood.

There is very little to interest Johnstoune in *Romeo and Juliet*, but he heavily annotates *Timon of Athens*. Its themes of friendship and ingratitude, its anxieties about creditors and false friends, make it very much a play for a gentleman. For us, it is instructive to see how what subsequently became one of the Folio's most neglected plays provided this early reader with far more 'matter' for reflection than one of his most popular. Equally instructive is the discovery that what *we* regard as the central matter of some plays was almost invisible to an early reader: *Othello* is peppered with marginalia concerning the lusts of women and the miseries of jealousy, but the annotations have nothing to say about the issue of race.

Johnstoune's views might seem commonplace, but the very fact of their plainness and good sense provides an insight into why he felt it worthwhile to read Shakespeare attentively. His first note on *Antony and Cleopatra* reads 'Martiall courage turned to effeminat loue'. This may be only a paraphrase of the first speech of the play, but it cuts to the chase, summarizing the central theme in an instant and placing the drama in the tradition of classical humanism: the conflict between *negotium* and *otium*, masculine action and effeminizing desire, public duties and private passions, was at the core of humanistic understanding of the foundational texts of Greece and Rome. Cleopatra takes her place alongside Helen of Troy, the women encountered by Odysseus as distractions on his journey home, Virgil's Dido, not to mention an array of Ovidian temptresses, as an impediment to martial valour and civic service.

Modern critics agonize over King Lear's reasons for rejecting

Cordelia and Kent at the beginning of his play. Johnstoune simply notes next to Goneril and Regan's speeches that 'flatterie blinds the king'. Be wary of flatterers: again, this is classic humanist advice. And the resonance of the word 'blinds' needs no spelling out: the image structure of the play has worked upon this reader before he has had a chance to notice it.

We sometimes think of the close reading of Shakespeare as a later phenomenon, stemming from the rise of Bardolatry in the eighteenth century. We suppose that J. W. von Goethe and Samuel Taylor Coleridge pored over Hamlet's soliloquies with hitherto unknown reverence. Yet our annotator in the years immediately after the publication of the First Folio works through the 'To be or not to be' soliloquy with pen in hand, scoring a stroke under the first few words of each line to mark off that he has read and thought about them. 'Question whether we ought to ouercome our selues and our passions by extreame patience or die seeking desperat reuenge', he writes in the margin, recognizing the Montaigne-like spirit of self-interrogation that is Hamlet's hallmark.

The annotations in this copy of the First Folio reveal that Shakespeare was read in just the same way that his source materials such as North's Plutarch would have been read: he became a classical humanist text, a repository of wisdom and a pretext for debate, as soon as he was in print. But this process was already at work when the plays were first staged. The earliest incontrovertible reference we have to a specific performance of a Shakespeare play is the record of the revels at Gray's Inn on 28 December 1594: 'a Comedy of Errors (like to *Plautus* his *Menechmus*) was played by the Players'. Here the play is approached by way of its quality as an imitation of a classical source. So too with law student John Manningham's account of *Twelfth Night* at the Middle Temple Candlemas festivities on 2 February 1602:

At our feast we had a play called 'Twelve Night, or What you Will,' much like the *Comedy of Errors*, or *Menaechmi* in Plautus, but most like and near to that in Italian called *Inganni*. A good practice in it to make the Steward believe his Lady-widow was in love with him, by counterfeiting a letter as from his Lady in general terms, telling him what she liked best in him, and prescribing his gesture in smiling, his apparel, etc., and then, when he came to practise, making him believe they took him to be mad.

As he watches and reflects on the play, Manningham reads by an art of comparison with the literary tradition – 'most like and near to' – and for the purpose of discovering 'good practice'. This is a humanist mode of reading, whereby Shakespeare is treated as a classic even as his company generates an early performance. Ben Jonson's prediction in his dedicatory poem at the front of the First Folio began to become true even before it was written:

> Triumph, my Britain, thou hast one to show
> To whom all scenes of Europe homage owe.
> He was not of an age, but for all time!
> And all the muses still were in their prime
> When like Apollo he came forth to warm
> Our ears, or like a Mercury to charm!
> Nature herself was proud of his designs,
> And joyed to wear the dressing of his lines,
> Which were so richly spun, and woven so fit,
> As since she will vouchsafe no other wit.
> The merry Greek, tart Aristophanes,
> Neat Terence, witty Plautus, now not please,
> But antiquated and deserted lie
> As they were not of nature's family.

'Look / Not on his picture, but his book'

According to a tradition reported to John Aubrey in the later seventeenth century, Shakespeare made an annual visit home to Stratford. On the way, he would stop off in Oxford, where he lodged in the Crown Inn, hosted by the Davenants, whose son William, born in 1606, would grow up to be a playwright, theatre impresario, Poet Laureate, adapter of Shakespeare's plays and worshipper of his memory. William Davenant was almost certainly

Shakespeare's godson and after a few drinks he liked to claim that he was his natural son. Ownership of the so-called Chandos portrait – swarthy, Italianate, with a suitably theatrical earring – can be traced back to Davenant, making it the most plausibly authentic of the many portraits of the period that have been wishfully proposed as images of Master Shakespeare. But the only image that can be said with absolute certainty to represent Shakespeare is the dome-headed figure on the title page of the First Folio, which is accompanied by Ben Jonson's poem attesting that the engraver has 'hit / His face' to the life. The problem with the Folio engraving, which was almost certainly taken from a lost portrait rather than an actual sitting, is that it is clumsily executed and fails to realize a sense of Shakespeare's inner life.

Jonson turned this deficiency to advantage, pointing out in his poem that the essence of Shakespeare is his 'wit' rather than his 'figure'. The reader should therefore 'look / Not on his picture, but his book'. Though the search for Shakespeare's image will continue with new faces and false dawns, it is fitting that so little is known about his appearance and personal characteristics. The same goes for his handwriting. His signature survives on various legal documents, but it was not uncommon for a lawyer to sign on a client's behalf. The notion that authentication, let alone character, resides in handwriting is anachronistic. The words 'by me, William Shakspeare' at the end of his will are probably in his hand, but not even this is absolutely certain. The elusiveness of both his face and his hand is in keeping with the process whereby he made himself invisible through absorption in his works.

In the end what we have are those works, and for that we should be most thankful to John Hemings and Henry Condell, who collected the material for the First Folio. So the place to end is a touching and too-little-known poem in their praise. The author is not known, but the surviving text appears in an early seventeenth-century manuscript collection formerly belonging to the Salusbury family, for whom the volume *Love's Martyr* was prepared – that volume which includes Shakespeare's beautiful poem about the phoenix and the turtle-dove, who embody 'Beauty, truth and rarity, / Grace in all simplicity'.

To my good friends Mr John Hemings and Henry Condall
　　To you that jointly, with undaunted pains,
　　Vouchsafed to chant to us these noble strains,
　　How much you merit by it is not said,
　　But you have pleased the living, loved the dead,
　　Raised from the womb of earth a richer mine
　　Than Cortez could with all his Casteline
　　Associates: they did but dig for gold,
　　But you for treasure much more manifold.

When John Keats first opened George Chapman's Elizabethan translation of Homer's *Iliad*, he felt like Cortez standing on a mountain top looking out at a new ocean of literary glory. For the anonymous author of this poem, Hemings and Condell went one better than Cortez. He dug for gold in the new world, whereas they 'raised from the womb of earth' treasures 'more manifold' than gold: they saved the plays of Shakespeare from oblivion.

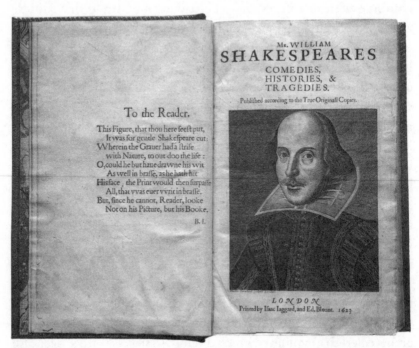

Acknowledgements

The reading for this study of Shakespeare in the cultural context of his age began more than a decade ago when I was the lucky recipient of a British Academy Research Readership and visiting fellowships at the Folger Shakespeare Library in Washington DC and the Huntington Library in San Marino, California. I am grateful to the University of Warwick for a term's study leave towards the end of the journey. The most valuable spur to the delivery of a long-gestated project was Simon Callow's request to develop the script for a one-man show about Shakespeare in his cultural 'moment'. It was this dramatic intervention that gave me the idea of structuring the story according to Jaques' seven ages: my warmest thanks, my eager anticipation.

Early versions of some sections were tried out as lectures and essays over a period of years: I am grateful for the invitations that gave me this opportunity and to audience members for reactions and suggestions (special thanks to Warren Boutcher and David Colclough of Queen Mary College). Quentin Skinner's insistence on the importance of context for the understanding of meaning in the history of ideas has been an intellectual inspiration. Draft chapters benefited from the comments of colleagues and experts. I am particularly grateful to Peter Mack for his reading of the Schoolboy, Colin Burrow for looking at my reading of the sonnets and Paul Hammer, Gabriel Egan and Cyndia Clegg for their comments on Essex Man (a much abbreviated version of the latter was delivered as my 2008 British Academy Shakespeare Lecture). Paul Raffield, Gary Watt and Sir John Baker helped with certain points in the fifth age, as did Robert Bearman at the Shakespeare Birthplace Trust, Leslie Whitelaw, archivist of the Middle Temple, and Robert D. Pepper, who (for some reason anonymously) first drew my attention to John Harborne. Stanley Wells responded with good-humoured scepticism to a number of my heretical proposals. Vicky Ironmonger helped to tidy the reference notes.

Completion of the book was delayed by my young daughter's renal failure and subsequent transplantation: my gratitude to the medical profession and her donor family belongs in another place, but here I wish to thank David Ebershoff at Random House in New York and Mary Mount at Viking Penguin in London for their forbearance, as well as their faith in the project – and, when I finally delivered, for their invaluable suggestions for improvement. Thanks also to Will Hammond and Eleo Gordon at Viking, and my copy-editor Janet Tyrrell. The incomparable Andrew Wylie secured the deal and kicked me back into action when I was flagging.

While I wrestled with Shakespeare's attitude to Renaissance neo-Stoicism, Paula, Tom and Ellie lived the reality of heroic resolve in the face of adversity – it is impossible to give adequate voice to my gratitude to them for allowing me to find the space to finish both this book and an edition of Shakespeare's complete works at such a time. Being still in the first of his seven ages Harry the dedicatee was too young to understand any of the turmoil and the industry, but his smile and his sunny disposition made every day worthwhile.

References

p. 3 **the Shakespearean moment** Patrick Cruttwell, *The Shake-spearean Moment and its Place in the Poetry of the 17th Century* (1954), especially chap. 4, 'The society of the Shakespearean moment'.

p. 3 **inconceivably wise . . . *representative* poet** Emerson, 'Shak-speare' in *Representative Men* (1850); 'Self-Reliance' in *Essays: First Series* (1841).

p. 5 **Everything we know about** Shaw, review of Frank Harris, *The Man Shakespeare* (1910), repr. in John Gross, *After Shakespeare: Writing Inspired by the World's Greatest Author* (2002), p. 10.

p. 5 **if his biography is** Everett, 'Reade him, therefore', *TLS* Commentary, 17 August 2007.

p. 9 **A sad tale's best . . . Thou met'st** *The Winter's Tale*, 2.1.33, 3.3.99. Unless otherwise stated, all Shakespearean quotations are from *The RSC Shakespeare: Complete Works*, edited by Jonathan Bate and Eric Rasmussen (2007), with occasional textual variants.

p. 10 **What an unmatchable torment** Thomas Dekker, *The Wonderful Year 1603, wherein is showed the Picture of London lying sick of the Plague* (repr. 1966), pp. 38–9. Spelling is modernized in all quotations.

p. 10 **Forsomuch as the plague** Stow, *The Chronicles of England* (1580), pp. 1121–2.

p. 11 **Forasmuch as by the** Quoted, E. K. Chambers, *The Elizabethan Stage* (4 vols, 1923), 4. 313.

p. 14 **this great stage of fools** *Lear*, 4.5.182.

p. 14 **I will attend my husband** *Comedy of Errors*, 5.1.100–103.

p. 15 **Behold, my lords . . . This brat is none of mine** *Winter's Tale*, 2.3.119–24, 113–16.

p. 16 **The empress . . . Zounds . . . broach the tadpole . . . Go to the empress** *Titus Andronicus*, 4.2.71–2, 73, 87, 146–70.

p. 16 **Renownèd Lucius** *Titus*, 5.1.20–24.

p. 16 **bare ruined choirs** *Sonnet* 73. 'Choirs' brilliantly combines musical and architectural senses. 'Birds' conceivably plays on the name of William Byrd, the age's greatest composer of church music, whose published masses of the early 1590s are in the Catholic tradition.

p. 18 **'mystery' plays**   For an excellent account of 'Shakespeare and the mystery cycles', see Rowland Wymer in *English Literary Renaissance*, 34 (2004), pp. 265–85.

p. 20 **Matters of religion**   Royal proclamation of 16 May 1559, in Chambers, *Elizabethan Stage*, 4. 263–4.

p. 23 **gorgeous Playing-place**   John Stockwood, *A Sermon preached at Paul's Cross* (1578), sig. J7v.

p. 24 **order and reform**   Patent of Commission for Edmund Tilney as Master of the Revels, 24 December 1581, in Chambers, *Elizabethan Stage*, 4. 285–7.

p. 24 **spies**   See Scott McMillin and Sally-Beth Maclean, *The Queen's Men and their Plays* (1998).

p. 25 **The argument of Tragedies ... In stage plays**   Stephen Gosson, *Plays confuted in Five Actions* (1582), sigs. C5r, E5r.

p. 26 **sandy-bottomed Severn ... smug and silver Trent**   *1 Henry IV*, 3.1.65, 101.

p. 28 **John Elder**   See Peter M. Barber, 'Mapping Britain from afar', *Mercator's World* (July/August 1998), excerpted at http://www.walkingtree.com/excerptbarber.html.

p. 30 **This Tenham**   Lambarde, *A Perambulation of Kent* (written 1570, published 1576, repr. 1826), pp. 222–3.

p. 31 **Lord, who would live turmoiled**   *2 Henry VI*, 4.10.11–14.

p. 31 **liberal, valiant, active, wealthy**   *2 Henry VI*, 4.7.45.

p. 31 **Warwickshire**   Intriguingly, the only non-Shakespearean play of the period to mention Warwickshire is the anonymous *Tragical History, Admirable Achievements and various events of Guy Earl of Warwick*. Though not published until 1661, it may date from as early as 1593. It includes a chirpy, upwardly mobile servant called Sparrow who comes from Stratford-upon-Avon: the only mention of the town in Elizabethan drama. It has sometimes been suggested that Sparrow is a jibe at Shakespeare, analogous to the 'upstart crow' insult. This fits nicely with the allusion to Guy of Warwick in *King John*, discussed below. See further, Helen Cooper, 'Guy of Warwick, upstart crows and mounting sparrows', in *Shakespeare, Marlowe, Jonson: New Directions in Biography*, ed. T. Kozuka and J. R. Mulryne (2006), pp. 119–38.

p. 31 **What a devil . . . In Warwickshire I have true-hearted friends**   *1 Henry IV*, 4.2.35; *3 Henry VI*, 4.8.9.

p. 33 **kin to Shakespeare's mother**   Mark Eccles' definitive *Shakespeare in Warwickshire* (1961) suggests that Mary Arden's grandfather Thomas Arden may have been descended from a younger son of the wealthy Park Hall Ardens, but scholars have failed to establish the precise pedigree. The grant of arms to the Shakespeare family refers to Mary's father as 'a gentleman of worship', suggesting a pedigree of good breeding.

p. 33 **a true-hearted friend**   See further, Randall Martin and John D. Cox, 'Who is "Somerville" in *3 Henry VI*?', *Shakespeare Quarterly*, 51 (2001), pp. 332–52.

p. 35 **the very heart of England bleed**   Samuel Daniel, *The Civile Wars between the Houses of Lancaster and York* (1609), Book 7, stanza 58.

p. 35 **Now *Stratford* upon *Avon***   Dedicatory poem to Dugdale's *Antiquities of Warwickshire* (1656), repr. in Cokaine, *Small Poems of Divers Sorts* (1658), p. 112.

p. 36 ***Warwickshire, Varvicensis Comitatus***   Edmund Bohun, *Geographical Dictionary* (1693), p. 432.

p. 37 **like the old Robin Hood of England**   *As You Like It*, 1.1.77–80.

p. 38 **The duke's very first speech . . . fleet the time carelessly**   *As You Like It*, 2.1.1–17, 1.1.79–80.

p. 40 **There is an upstart crow**   *Greene's Groatsworth of Wit* (1592, repr. 1966), pp. 45–6, written in the voice of Robert Greene but now usually attributed to another playwright, Henry Chettle.

p. 40 **Amazonian trull . . . tiger's heart**   *3 Henry VI*, 1.4.114, 137.

p. 40 **shake my sword . . . shake off these names**   *All's Well*, 2.5.85, *2 Henry VI*, 4.8.17, *Tempest*, 2.2.67, *Two Gentlemen*, 2.5.25, *Twelfth Night*, 5.1.59.

pp. 40–41 **divers of worship**   Chettle, prefatory epistle to *Kind-Heart's Dream* (registered for publication, December 1592).

p. 41 **apology was to Peele**   See Lukas Erne, 'Biography and mythography: rereading Chettle's alleged apology to Shakespeare', *English Studies*, 79 (1998), pp. 430–40.

p. 41 **to the celestial** *Hamlet*, 2.2.114–15.

p. 41 **Well, I'll break in** *Errors*, 3.1.88–94.

p. 42 **vile esteemed . . . vulgar scandal** *Sonnets* 121, 112. See also 110, with its apparent reference to being an actor ('made myself a motley to the view').

p. 43 **By this, poor Wat** *Venus and Adonis*, 697–708.

p. 43 **I'll pheeze you** *Taming of the Shrew*, Induction, 1.1–4.

p. 44 **Am not I Christopher Sly** *Taming of the Shrew*, Induction, 2.14–17.

p. 44 **Is thy name William?** *As You Like It*, 5.1.15–25.

p. 45 **their dialogue** Duncan-Jones, *Ungentle Shakespeare* (2001), p. 26.

p. 45 **Speak, citizens** *King John*, 2.1.369.

p. 46 **I speak for all England** See the historian Patrick Collinson's lectures, ' "This England": the consummation of English nationhood in the long sixteenth century', published in *Douglas Southall Freeman Historical Review*, Spring 1999, pp. 2–114.

p. 46 **a good blunt fellow** *King John*, 1.1.72.

p. 47 **Colbrand the Giant** *King John*, 1.1.226.

p. 47 **Richard that robbed** *King John*, 2.1.3–4.

p. 47 **This England never did** *King John*, 5.7.116–22.

p. 48 **I am I** *King John*, 1.1.176.

p. 48 **document that may be dated** See David Kathman, 'Reconsidering *The Seven Deadly Sins*', *Early Theatre*, 7.1 (2004), pp. 13–44.

p. 49 **a Gentleman** Armin, *Nest of Ninnies* (1608), p. 48.

p. 50 **Mrs *Hall* of *Stratford*** Hall, *Select Observations on English Bodies of Eminent Persons in desperate Diseases* (1679), observation 19.

p. 51 **Mr *Hunt* of *Stock-green*** Hall, observation 15.

p. 53 **I hold it ever** *Pericles*, 3.2.27–43.

p. 54 **O thou goddess** *Cymbeline*, 4.2.214–21.

p. 55 **cinque-spotted** *Cymbeline*, 2.2.40–41.

p. 55 **The marigold that goes** *The Winter's Tale*, 4.3.121–2.

p. 55 **Were such things here** *Macbeth*, 1.3.85–7.

p. 56 **sweet marjoram** *Lear*, 4.5.103.

p. 56 **Alack, 'tis he** *Lear*, 4.3.1–6.

p. 57 **Carnations and gillyflowers** Quoted in J. W. Scholl, 'The gardener's art in *The Winter's Tale*', *Modern Language Notes*, 27 (1912), pp. 176–8.

p. 57 **There be three sorts** Gerard, *Herbal* (1598), II. ii. §2. 179.

p. 58 **long purples** *Hamlet*, 4.6.153 – the roots resemble testicles, so the plant had many obscene local names.

p. 59 **saffron to colour** *Winter's Tale*, 4.3.38.

pp. 60–61 **as boldly . . . shot daily . . . an honourable and joyful peace . . . honourably and joyfully received** Stow, *Chronicles of England* (1580), pp. 1126–8.

p. 62 **I dreamt that I** A. L. Rowse, *The Case Books of Simon Forman: Sex and Society in Shakespeare's Age* (1974), p. 31.

p. 63 **When my cue comes** *A Midsummer Night's Dream*, 4.1.195–205.

p. 64 **The bottom of God's secrets** Geneva Bible (1557), *1 Corinthians*, 2.10.

p. 65 **To name the bigger light** *The Tempest*, 1.2.393–4.

p. 65 **two great lights** Genesis, 1:16, in the translation of the 'Bishops' Bible', officially prescribed for use in church during Shakespeare's childhood.

p. 65 **the seven planets** Marlowe, *Dr Faustus* (1604 text), 2.3.60.

p. 66 **harbingers preceding** *Hamlet*, 1.1 (Quarto-only passage following 1.1.117).

p. 66 **an extraordinary sign** Gloss to *Matthew* 2:2 in Geneva Bible (1560).

p. 67 **And new philosophy** Donne, *Complete English Poems*, ed. A. J. Smith (1971), p. 276.

p. 68 **The heavens themselves** *Troilus*, 1.3.86–92.

p. 69 **Take but degree . . . solid globe** *Troilus*, 1.3.110, 114.

p. 69 **Strength should be lord** *Troilus*, 1.3.115–25.

p. 70 **If celestial spheres** Hooker, *Laws of Ecclesiastical Polity* (1593), Book 1, chap. 3.

p. 70 **Take away kings** *Homilies* (first published 1547), Book 1, Homily 10, 'An exhortation to obedience'.

p. 70 **moral philosophy . . . the hot passion . . . a free determination . . . What's aught . . . particular will** *Troilus*, 2.2.172, 174, 175, 54, 55.

p. 71 **by reflection** *Troilus*, 3.3.102–105.

p. 71　**Mars his true moving**　1.2.1–2, a scene that is probably not by Shakespeare.

p. 72　**This is the excellent foppery**　*Lear*, 1.2.93–103.

p. 73　**Eamon Duffy**　See his *The Stripping of the Altars: Traditional Religion in England 1400–1580* (1994).

p. 74　**Dreaming on naught**　Jonson, *Every Man in his Humour* (1616 text), 1.1.17–19.

p. 74　**Are these the fruits**　*Poetaster*, 1.2.5–9.

p. 79　**William, how many numbers**　*Merry Wives of Windsor*, 4.1.14–52.

p. 81　**good literature**　Preamble to charter of King Edward's, Lincoln.

p. 81　**In this kind**　On 'Exercitatio and imitatio' in Erasmus, *De Copia*, quoted in T. W. Baldwin, *William Shakspere's Small Latine and Lesse Greeke* (2 vols, 1944), 2. 241.

p. 82　**And to the intent**　Statutes for Guisborough, York (1561), quoted in Baldwin, 1. 430. 'Tully' was the colloquial name for Marcus Tullius Cicero, greatest of Roman orators.

p. 84　**What's here?**　*Titus*, 4.2.18–23.

p. 85　**one auspicious . . . An understanding**　*Hamlet*, 1.2.11, 20, 29, 86, 97.

p. 85　***Ego pauper laboro***　Lily, *Brevissima*, with English translation from John Stockwood, *The Treatise of the Figures at the End of the Rules of Construction in the Latin Grammar construed* (1652), sig. A8v.

p. 86　**I had an Edward**　*Richard III*, 4.4.39–44.

p. 87　**Did the night-guarding**　*Brevissima*, with translation from Stockwood's crib 'for the help of the weaker sort in grammar schools', sig. C1r.

p. 87　**So many hours**　*3 Henry VI*, 2.5.31–4.

p. 87　**silver hairs . . . ferret eyes**　*Julius Caesar*, 2.1.150–55, 1.2.192.

p. 87　**Friends, Romans**　*Julius Caesar*, 3.2.70–96.

p. 88　**Romans, countrymen**　*Julius Caesar*, 3.2.13–20.

p. 88　**this is an art**　*Institutio Oratoria*, 2.17.26, trans. H. E. Butler (1922).

p. 89　**The truest poetry**　*As You Like It*, 3.3.12. Though it does not mention Shakespeare, Quentin Skinner's brilliant essay 'Moral ambiguity and the Renaissance art of rhetoric', which focuses on the figure of *paradiastole*, a device of extenuation whereby a vice is redescribed as a virtue, is highly relevant to this discussion (originally published in the journal *Essays in Criticism*, 1994, Skinner's article is revised and expanded as chap. 10 of his *Visions of Politics: Volume 2: Renaissance Virtues*, 2002). More recently, Skinner has begun applying his argument to Shakespeare, for example in a paper called 'Shakespeare and rhetorical redescription' and a forthcoming series of Clarendon Lectures at Oxford University.

p. 89 **the whole Ethiopian** Stockwood's translation and explanation of Lily, *Treatise of the Figures*, sig. C6r.

p. 89 **elaborate handbooks** T. W. Baldwin, in the standard work on Elizabethan grammar-school texts, *William Shakspere's Small Latine and Lesse Greeke* made extensive claims (chap. 35) for Shakespeare's knowledge of Susenbrotus' *Epitome troporum ac schematum grammaticorum et rhetoricum*, but Lawrence D. Green has powerfully refuted this view, on the basis that there simply were not enough copies of Susenbrotus available to supply the grammar schools. None of the formal rhetorical handbooks, least of all Puttenham's much discussed *Art of English Poesy*, circulated in anything like the numbers of the grammar-school textbooks of Lily and Erasmus: the full-scale rhetorical handbooks were designed for elite readers in university and around the court. See Green, '*Grammatica movet*: Renaissance grammar books and *elocutio*', in *Rhetorica Movet: Studies in Historical and Modern Rhetoric in Honour of Heinrich F. Plett*, ed. P. L. Oesterreich and T. O. Sloane (1999), pp. 73–115.

p. 89 **Uneasy lies the head** *2 Henry IV*, 3.1.31.

p. 90 **How easily the wrong** Feste in *Twelfth Night*, 3.1.9.

p. 90 **Ye white-limed** *Titus Andronicus*, 4.2.100–105.

p. 90 **Indeed, it is** *Julius Caesar*, 1.3.33–5.

p. 91 **Dost thou not** *Antony and Cleopatra*, 5.2.348–9.

pp. 91–2 **Cannot be ill ... And nothing is ... palter with us** *Macbeth*, 1.3.141, 1.3.152, 5.7.58.

p. 92 **they were taught to write it** The next section draws extensively on the invaluable work of my colleague Peter Mack: *Elizabethan Rhetoric* (2002), chap.1, and 'Rhetoric, ethics and reading in the Renaissance', *Renaissance Studies*, 19 (2005), pp. 1–21.

p. 93 **Write a letter** Erasmus, *De Copia*, quoted, Baldwin, 2. 240.

p. 94 **Paris and Troilus** *Troilus and Cressida*, 2.2.167–76.

p. 94 **a companion** *Love's Labour's Lost*, 5.1.5–18.

p. 95 *Via*, **goodman . . . Nor understood none** *Love's Labour's Lost*, 5.1.102–3.

p. 96 **Yea, from the table** *Hamlet*, 1.5.103–14.

p. 96 **I remember the players** Jonson, *Timber*, quoted in E. K. Chambers, *William Shakespeare* (2 vols, 1930), 2. 210.

p. 98 **That is, who** John Brinsley, *Ludus Literarius* (1612), pp. 123–4, as quoted, Mack, *Elizabethan Rhetoric*, pp. 18–19.

pp. 99–100 *Fauste, precor gelida* . . . **for the elegancy** *Love's Labour's Lost*, 4.2.72–98.

p. 100 **at Pentecost** *Two Gentlemen of Verona*, 4.4.142–56.

p. 102 **Latin anagram** The anagram is inexact; the particulars of the life and identity of 'Palingenius' are still disputed by scholars.

p. 103 **Wherefore if thou dost** Palingenius, *The Zodiac of Life*, trans. Googe (1565 edn), book 6, lines 1215–30.

p. 104 **Shall we their fond pageant . . . Behold, the heavens** *A Midsummer Night's Dream*, 3.2.114–15; *Coriolanus*, 5.3.195–7.

p. 104 **wretched life . . . The body fades** *Zodiac of Life*, 6. 1353–66.

p. 105 **Some have made 7 parts** *The French Academy*, trans. T. B. C. (1586), p. 563.

p. 106 **I would there were** *Winter's Tale*, 3.3.61–3.

p. 109 **The books that serve** *The Essays of Montaigne*, trans. John Florio (1603, repr. 1933), Book 2, chap. 10, p. 364.

p. 110 **I have no skill** 'To morrow is a new day', *Essays*, 2.4, p. 320.

p. 112 **Ovid's shorter works . . . A variety of Greek authors** Ovid: George Turbervile's *Heroides* (1567), Thomas Underdowne's *Ibis* (1569) and Thomas Churchyard's *Tristia* (1572). Horace: *Ars Poetica*, *Satires*, and *Epistles* by Thomas Drant (1566–7). Prose: *The Golden Ass* by Apuleius (William Adlington, 1566), some of Livy (in William Painter's *Palace of Pleasure*, 1566) and Pliny (by one J. A., 1565, from a French abridgement of the *Natural History*). Greek authors: Xenophon (*Cyropaedia* by William Barker, 1560–67) and Polybius (first book of the *History*, by Thomas Watson, 1568).

p. 112 **in their painful exercises** Dedication (dated December 1564) to *First Four Books of . . . Metamorphosis* (1565), repr. in *Shakespeare's Ovid, being Arthur Golding's Translation of the Metamorphoses*, ed. W. H. D. Rouse (1904, repr. 1961), p. iii.

p. 113 **Leicester's encouragement** See Eleanor Rosenberg, *Leicester: Patron of Letters* (1955).

p. 113 **The translators** Here I paraphrase C. H. Conley, *The First English Translators of the Classics* (1927), a detailed study of the early Elizabethan translation movement, by way of H. B. Lathrop, *Translations from the Classics into English from Caxton to Chapman 1477–1620* (1933), p. 230, the subsequent pages of which offer some cogent criticisms of the hypothesis that the translation movement was a political one, orchestrated by Leicester. Rosenberg, chap. 5, lends cautious support to Conley.

p. 114 **there is salmons** *Henry V*, 4.7.16–26.

p. 114 **My intent is not** *Shakespeare's Plutarch*, ed. T. J. B. Spencer (1964, repr. 1968), pp. 7–8.

p. 115 **Now Brutus** 'Life of Marcus Brutus', *Shakespeare's Plutarch*, pp. 116–17.

p. 116 **It must be by his death** *Julius Caesar*, 2.1.10–13.

p. 116 **Shakespeare's favourite classical poet** This section draws extensively on my *Shakespeare and Ovid* (1993) and my introduction to the 2000 reprint of J. F. Nims' edition of Golding's translation of the *Metamorphoses*.

p. 117 *auraeque . . .* **Ye Ayres** Ovid, *Metamorphoses*, 7.197–8. Golding's 1567 translation, 7.265–6. Since I am concerned with philological detail here, Golding is quoted in his original spelling.

pp. 117–18 **Ye elves of hills . . . and rifted . . . Graves . . . By my so potent** *The Tempest*, 5.1.38, 50, 53–4, 55.

p. 120 **She hath been reading** *Cymbeline*, 2.2.46–8.

p. 120 **For worse than Philomel** *Titus Andronicus*, 5.2.194–5.

p. 121 **But all the story** *Midsummer Night's Dream*, 5.1.23–7.

p. 122 **That instant** *Twelfth Night*, 1.1.22–4.

p. 123 **The gods themselves** *Winter's Tale*, 4.4.29–36.

p. 124 **She felt the kiss** Golding's 1567 translation, 10.319–20.

p. 124 **O, you are men of stones** *King Lear*, 5.3.264.

p. 125 **Does not the stone** *Winter's Tale*, 5.3.43–4.

p. 128 *politi propriis* Cicero, *On the Republic*, 1.17.28 (Loeb text).

p. 128 **education and training** Aulus Gellius, *Attic Nights*, 13.17.1 (Loeb translation).

p. 128 **that virtue must**   Quentin Skinner, *The Foundations of Modern Political Thought*, vol. 1: *The Renaissance* (1978), p. 259.

p. 128 **degrees, whereof**   *The Book named The Governor*, ed. S. E. Lehmberg (1962), p. 2.

p. 129 **What cares these roarers**   *Tempest*, 1.1.14.

p. 129 **and to him put . . . And to my state**   *Tempest*, 1.2.83–91.

p. 130 **Awaked an evil nature . . . He was indeed**   *Tempest*, 1.2. 109, 119.

p. 131 **Have I, thy schoolmaster**   *Tempest*, 1.2.201–3.

p. 131 **Fear is of no**   *De Pueris*, 503E–505A, trans. William Harrison Woodward, in his *Desiderius Erasmus concerning the Aim and Method of Education* (1904), pp. 203, 206.

p. 132 **with humane care . . . Whom stripes . . . Abhorrèd slave**   *Tempest*, 1.2. 405, 404, 411–12.

p. 132 **Where the devil**   *Tempest*, 2.2.56.

p. 133 **My foot my tutor?**   *Tempest*, 1.2.549.

p. 133 **theme of woe . . . when every . . . Look, he's**   *Tempest*, 2.1.6, 16, 13.

p. 134 **Temperance was a delicate wench**   *Tempest*, 2.1.39.

p. 134 **the fair soul herself**   *Tempest*, 2.1.113–14.

p. 134 **I should think**   *The Education of a Christian Prince*, trans. Lester K. Born (1936), p. 241.

p. 134 **By alliances**   *Christian Prince*, p. 243.

p. 135 **Had I plantation**   *Tempest*, 2.1.131.

p. 135 **that hath no kind of traffic**   Montaigne, *Essays*, trans. John Florio (1603, repr. 1933), Book 1, chap. 30, p. 164; *Tempest*, 2.1.137–43.

p. 136 **No sovereignty**   *Tempest*, 2.1.145–6.

p. 136 **Here is that which**   *Tempest*, 2.2.66–7.

p. 137 **bounteous lady . . . Scarcity and want**   *Tempest*, 4.1.66–8, 125.

p. 138 **pains, / Humanely . . . Pray you tread softly**   *Tempest*, 4.1.204–6, 210.

p. 138 **were I human**   *Tempest*, 5.1.23.

p. 139 **The devil speaks in him**   *Tempest*, 5.1.140.

p. 139 **O brave new world . . . 'Tis new to thee**   *Tempest*, 5.1.205–7.

p. 140 **Look down, you gods . . . strong imagination** *Tempest*, 5.1.228–9, 2.1.197–8.

p. 140 **Be not afeard** *Tempest*, 3.2.118–26.

p. 140 **humanist critique** Skinner, *Foundations*, pp. 255–62.

p. 141 *Alumnus* **. . . All that** Dedication to Camden in Huntington Library copy of *Cynthia's Revels* (1601); Epigram 'To William Camden'.

p. 142 **It is true** *Timber: or, Discoveries made upon Men and Matter as they have flowed out of his daily Readings* (1641, repr. 1966), p. 10.

p. 146 **As Plautus and Seneca** Meres, *Palladis Tamia: Wit's Treasury* (1598), quoted, Chambers, *Shakespeare*, 2. 184.

p. 146 **Seneca cannot** *Hamlet*, 2.2.353–4.

p. 150 **ransacked to furnish** Stephen Gosson, *Plays Confuted* (1582), quoted in Stuart Gillespie, *Shakespeare's Books: A Dictionary of Shakespeare's Sources* (2001), p. 404, a superb A–Z compendium to which, along with the still authoritative *Narrative and Dramatic Sources of Shakespeare*, ed. Geoffrey Bullough (8 vols, 1957–75), this section is much indebted. See also Robert Miola, *Shakespeare's Reading* (2000).

p. 153 **for though the camomile** *1 Henry IV*, 2.4.295–6, parodying Lyly, *Euphues*: 'though the camomile, the more it is trodden and pressed down, the more it spreadeth, yet the violet the oftener it is handled and touched, the sooner it withereth and decayeth' (1578, ed. Warwick Bond, 1902, vol. 1, p. 196).

p. 153 **my Book of Songs** *Merry Wives*, 1.1.140.

p. 156 **the first heir . . . graver labour** *Venus and Adonis*, dedication.

p. 161 **startling result** Jeanne Jones, *Family Life in Shakespeare's England: Stratford-upon-Avon 1570–1630* (1996), p. 90. I owe this reference to Stanley Wells.

p. 162 **twenty-sixth or twenty-seventh year** She was born before 1558, when the surviving local baptismal register commences; our knowledge of her age is based on her gravestone: she died in August 1623 at '67 years' (unless this is an engraver's error for '61 years').

p. 166 **a schoolmaster** John Aubrey, *Brief Lives* (1681), on the testimony of William Beeston, an actor whose father was a colleague of Shakespeare in the Chamberlain's Men.

p. 169 **that she clapped her hand** See Bernard Capp, 'The poet and the bawdy court: Michael Drayton and the lodging-house world in early Stuart London', *Seventeenth Century*, 10 (1995), pp. 27–37.

p. 170 **lewd, seditious** Privy Council order concerning *The Isle of Dogs*, E. K. Chambers, *The Elizabethan Stage* (4 vols, 1923), 3. 453.

p. 170 **Five years he had not bedded** Jonson, *Conversations with Drummond*, in *Works*, ed. C. H. Herford and P. Simpson (13 vols, 1925), 1. 448.

p. 175 **licentious life** See further, Charles Nicholl's brilliant reconstruction of the affair and Shakespeare's role in it, *The Lodger: Shakespeare on Silver Street* (2007).

p. 177 **You must be purgèd . . . Here I stand** *Love's Labour's Lost*, 5.2.816; *Romeo and Juliet*, 5.3.235–6.

p. 178 **had the running** Quoted, Chambers, *Shakespeare*, 2. 12.

p. 179 **that William Bartlett** E. R. C. Brinkworth, *Shakespeare and the Bawdy Court of Stratford* (1972), p. 166. I am much indebted to this study.

p. 179 **beckoning with . . . God's wounds** Brinkworth, pp. 122, 128.

p. 180 **According to one historian** Laura Gowing, *Domestic Dangers: Women, Words, and Sex in Early Modern London* (1996), p. 36.

p. 180 **impudent quean . . . did not think that Phoebe** Case of 1613, quoted, Gowing, p. 69.

p. 180 **maggoty whore** See Gowing, pp. 66–7.

p. 181 **thou art a whoremaster** Case of 1610, quoted, Gowing, p. 72.

p. 181 **In *Othello*** Lisa Jardine skilfully reads *Othello* in the light of defamation cases in her essay ' "Why should he call her whore?" Defamation and Desdemona's case', in her *Reading Shakespeare Historically* (1996), chap. 1.

p. 181 **she is a strumpet** Porter, *Two Angry Women* (1599), 1.2.522–7, quoted, Gowing, p. 123.

p. 182 **I did hear** Case of 1629, quoted, Gowing, p. 68.

p. 183 **there are no women** Quoted, Gowing, p. 14. See also p. 118 for a case involving Joan Hewes, a woman who took the box office money and sold fruit at the Red Bull theatre in Clerkenwell.

pp. 183–4 **great offence . . . If it appear** All quotations in this paragraph from *All's Well that Ends Well*, 5.3.

p. 186 **Upon a time** In *The Diary of John Manningham, of the Middle Temple, and of Bradbourne, Kent, Barrister-at-Law, 1602–1603*, ed. John Bruce (1868), entry dated March 1602. Manningham had the information from a 'Mr Touse'. There were many connections between Shakespeare and the Middle Temple.

p. 187 **POMPEY: You have not heard** *Measure for Measure*, 1.2.67–81.

p. 187 **traders in the flesh . . . gallèd goose** *Troilus*, 5.11.44, 52–3.

p. 188 **it openeth the body** *A brief and necessary treatise, touching the cure of the disease called morbus Gallicus, or lues venerea, by unctions and other approved ways of curing: newly corrected and augmented by William Clowes of London, master in chirurgery* (1585), fol. 25v.

p. 189 **Patients would often** Colin Milburn, 'Syphilis in faerie land: Edmund Spenser and the Syphilography of Elizabethan England', *Criticism*, 46 (2004), pp. 597–632.

p. 190 **I pardon that man's life** *King Lear*, 4.5.117–35.

p. 192 **Thomas Quiney** Brinkworth, *Shakespeare and the Bawdy Court* p. 143.

p. 194 **Let me twine** *Coriolanus*, 4.5.103–23.

p. 195 **He propounded** *The French Academy* (1586), pp. 3–4.

p. 195 **philosophy . . . purgeth pride** *French Academy*, p. 43.

p. 196 *in life* *French Academy*, Epistle Dedicatory.

pp. 196–7 **brave conquerors . . . To love . . . barren tasks** *Love's Labour's Lost*, 1.1.8–10, 31–7, 47.

p. 197 **For every man** *Love's Labour's Lost*, 1.1.151–2.

p. 197 **miracles are past** *All's Well that Ends Well*, 2.3.1.

p. 197 **It is the manner** *Love's Labour's Lost*, 1.1.201.

p. 198 **a dishclout** *Love's Labour's Lost*, 5.2.710–11.

p. 198 **women's eyes . . . the books** *Love's Labour's Lost*, 4.3.352–5.

p. 198 **Taffeta phrases** *Love's Labour's Lost*, 5.2.428–30.

p. 199 **Such is the simplicity** *Love's Labour's Lost*, 1.1.207.

p. 200 **mellifluous . . . most passionate** Meres, *Palladis Tamia: Wit's Treasury* (registered for publication 7 Sept 1598), quoted, Chambers, *Shakespeare*, 2. 194–5.

p. 200 **anguish of mind** Edward Phillips' definition of 'perplexity' in his *New World of Words* (1658).

p. 200 **I had rather** *Merry Wives*, 1.1.140.

p. 202 **I find no peace** *Songs and Sonnets, written by the right honourable Lord Henry Howard late Earl of Surrey and other* (1557, ed. E. Arber, 1903), p. 39. Tottel's texts have a not inconsiderable number of errors, because they were often edited from inferior copied manuscripts. Here I have corrected 'season' to 'seize on' and 'scrape' to 'scape' and inserted 'thus' for the sake of sense.

p. 204 **First her brow** W. H., 'Another of the same' (following a poem also signed W. H., called 'Wodenfride's Song in praise of Amargana'), in *England's Helicon* (1600), ed. Hugh Macdonald (1949), pp. 65–6.

p. 204 **My mistress' eyes** *Shakespeare's Sonnets*, no. 130.

p. 206 **Ganymede: the name** Randle Cotgrave, *A Dictionary of the French and English Tongues* (1611).

p. 206 **Sometimes I wish** Barnfield, *Cynthia, with certain Sonnets and the Legend of Cassandra* (1595), sonnet 8.

p. 207 **I came, I saw** Barnfield, *The Affectionate Shepherd* (1594), first eclogue, line 6.

p. 212 **Not yet old enough** *Twelfth Night*, 1.5.115–17.

p. 212 **to stand between** Ovid, *Metamorphoses*, 3.438, trans. Golding (1567).

p. 213 **When forty winters** Text from Westminster Abbey, MS 41, fol. 49, with spelling modernized and light punctuation introduced. See further, Mary Hobbs, 'Shakespeare's Sonnet 2: "A Sugared Sonnet"?', *Notes and Queries* (1979), pp. 112–13, and Gary Taylor, 'Some manuscripts of Shakespeare's Sonnets', *Bulletin of the John Rylands Library*, 68 (1985–6), pp. 210–46.

p. 213 **another hope for Rome** *Aeneid*, 12.168.

p. 214 **addressed to a man** Heather Dubrow in her article ' "Incertainties now crown themselves assur'd": the politics of plotting Shakespeare's Sonnets', *Shakespeare Quarterly*, 47 (1996), pp. 291–305, and Paul Edmondson and Stanley Wells in their book *Shakespeare's Sonnets* (2004) are among the few scholars to be properly sceptical of this assumption.

p. 215 **Dear lad** *Twelfth Night*, 1.4.29–34.

p. 215 **There is no woman's** *Twelfth Night*, 2.4.94–102.

p. 216 **Why should I not** *Twelfth Night*, 5.1.105–19.

p. 216 **Your master quits you**   *Twelfth Night*, 5.1.301–6.

p. 216 **I will give out**   *Twelfth Night*, 1.5.177–80.

p. 217 **Thy tongue**   *Twelfth Night* 2.1.226–8.

p. 218 **By God, Priapus . . . hast not found**   *The Maid's Metamorphosis* (1600), 3.2.

p. 218 **No interim . . . But, come what may . . . desire . . . his image**   *Twelfth Night*, 5.1.82–3, 2.1.33–4, 3.3.4–5, 3.4.283–4.

p. 219 **They that have power**   Sonnet 94.

p. 220 **In other instances**   This important point is made by Colin Burrow in 'Life and work in Shakespeare's poems', *Proceedings of the British Academy*, 97 (1998), pp.15–50.

p. 220 **computer-assisted stylometric analysis**   See MacDonald P. Jackson, 'Vocabulary and chronology: the case of Shakespeare's Sonnets', *Review of English Studies*, 52 (2001), pp. 59–75, building on A. Kent Heiatt, Charles Heiatt and Anne Lake Prescott, 'When did Shakespeare write *Sonnets* 1609?', *Studies in Philology*, 88 (1991), pp. 69–109.

p. 222 **we have no idea who he was**   For a deliberately fanciful speculation that he might have been another William Herbert, Master William Herbert, a minor Welsh poet and kinsman of the Earl of Pembroke, who published a volume of verse under the initials 'W. H. Gent.' in 1606, see my *Times Literary Supplement* Commentary on the subject (forthcoming in late 2008).

p. 226 **The earl of Pembroke**   Quoted, Michael Brennan, *Literary Patronage in the English Renaissance: the Pembroke Family* (1988), p. 105.

p. 226 **Of the staid**   *The Scourge of folly* (1611), epigram 114.

p. 227 **Furor Poeticus**   In the anonymous Cambridge play *The Return from Parnassus Part 2*.

p. 227 **the first who drew**   Edward Hyde, Earl of Clarendon, *The History of the Rebellion and Civil Wars in England* (6 vols, repr. 1992), 1.74.

p. 228 **I am in hate**   *Wit's Pilgrimage* (1605), no. 97.

p. 228 **Dear Lord**   'To the right noble and no less learned than judicious Lord, William Earl of Pembroke', in *Wit's Pilgrimage*, sig. Mm1v.

p. 228 **I am thine *own***   'To the same'.

p. 229 **Enough (fell Fair!)**   *Wit's Pilgrimage*, no. 33.

p. 229 **erotic songs and sonnets**   Printed after his death in *Poems written by the Right Honourable William Earl of Pembroke, Lord Steward of His Majesty's Household, whereof many of which are answered by way of Repartee by Sir Benjamin Ruddier, Knight* (1660). 'On black hair and eyes': p. 61. The authorship of many of these poems, which originally circulated in manuscript, is disputed.

p. 230 **And though the stage**   Davies, *Microcosmos* (1603), p. 215.

p. 231 **Some say (good *Will*)**   Davies, *The Scourge of Folly* (1610), epigram 159.

p. 231 **Katherine Duncan-Jones**   See her essay 'Shakespeare's status anxiety', *Times Literary Supplement*, 11 April 2006.

p. 234 **analysis of Brian Vickers**   *Shakespeare, A Lover's Complaint, and John Davies of Hereford* (2007), though see also the riposte by MacD. Jackson, *Review of English Studies*, 58 (2007), pp. 723–5.

p. 239 **pride, pomp**   *Othello*, 3.3.392.

p. 239 **We few . . . From this day**   *Henry V*, 4.3.62, 60.

p. 239 ***Dulce bellum inexpertis***   Erasmus, *Adagia*, 4.1.1.

p. 239 **I am afeard**   *Henry V*, 4.1.117–23.

p. 242 **My loving people . . . Wherefore I am**   'Queen Elizabeth's Armada speech to the troops at Tilbury, August 9, 1588', in *Elizabeth I: Collected Works*, ed. Leah Marcus, Janel Mueller and Mary Beth Rose (2000), pp. 325–6.

p. 243 **And Crispin Crispian**   *Henry V*, 4.3.59–62.

p. 244 **Now noble soldiers**   Heywood, *If you know not me, you know nobody, part 2* (1606), sig. K1r.

p. 244 **Rather proclaim it**   *Henry V*, 4.3.36–41.

p. 245 **Turning the accomplishment**   *Henry V*, Prologue 30–31.

p. 248 **its authenticity has been called into question**   See especially Susan Frye, 'The myth of Elizabeth at Tilbury', *Sixteenth Century Journal*, 23 (1992), pp. 95–114, but also the defence of its authenticity, largely on the basis of the survival of an early manuscript in the hand of Dr Lionel Sharp, by Janet M. Green, ' "I my self": Queen Elizabeth's oration at Tilbury camp', *Sixteenth Century Journal*, 28 (1997), pp. 421–45.

p. 252 **saved his life**   *Calendar of State Papers: Domestic Series of the Reign of Elizabeth 1601–1603*, ed. Mary Anne Everett Green (1870), p. 18.

p. 252 **captain or commander . . . It was also proved** *State Trials* (1719), vol. 1, p. 203.

p. 253 **So earnest he was** *Practices and Treasons attempted and committed by Robert, Earl of Essex, and his Complices* (1601), sig. K3r.

p. 255 **the strategy, it seems . . . This at least** Greenblatt, *Will in the World: How Shakespeare became Shakespeare* (2004), p. 309.

p. 255 **the bespoke performance** This performance, and in particular the tricky question of its relationship to Sir John Hayward's *History of Henry IV*, has been a matter of scholarly debate ever since an ill-tempered exchange of views between the American scholars Evelyn May Albright and Ray Heffner in the journal *PMLA* between 1927 and 1932. My detailed reassessment is based on a return to primary sources, but has also benefited from the following articles: Leeds Barroll, 'A new history for Shakespeare and his time', *Shakespeare Quarterly*, 39 (1988), pp. 441–64; Cyndia Clegg, 'Archival poetics and the politics of literature: Essex and Hayward revisited', *Studies in the Literary Imagination*, 32 (1999), pp. 115–32, and 'The untried treason case against Robert Devereux, the earl of Essex' (unpublished); Arthur Kinney, 'Essex and Shakespeare versus Hayward', *Shakespeare Quarterly*, 44 (1993), pp. 464–6; and Rebecca Lemon, 'The faulty verdict in "The Crown v. John Hayward"', *Studies in English Literature*, 41 (2001), pp. 109–32. On completing the chapter, I had the benefit of seeing Paul Hammer's excellent essay, 'Shakespeare's *Richard II*, the play of 7 February 1601 and the Essex Rising', in *Shakespeare Quarterly*, 59 (2008), pp. 1–35, which arrives independently at some very similar conclusions to mine.

p. 256 **to have the play of the deposing** 'The examination of Augustine Phillips', *Calendar of State Papers: Domestic Series of the Reign of Elizabeth 1598–1601*, ed. Mary Anne Everett Green (1869), p. 578. Subsequent references to this volume of the *State Papers* are given with the abbreviation *CSPD* and a page number.

p. 257 **With mine own tears** 4.1.201–2. The Q4/Folio addition runs from 4.1.157–317: the argument that it must have been in the original version, and was therefore suppressed for the first quarto, depends on the assumption that the ensuing line where the quarto picks up, 'A woeful pageant have we here beheld' (318), must be a reference back to Richard's abdication antics, but the phrase could equally well refer to York's acclaim of Henry Bullingbrook as king, the latter's ascent of the empty throne and the arrest of the Bishop of Carlisle for his protests at this treason. The awkwardness of an arrested Carlisle standing silently on stage watching the abdication, when one would have expected him to be marched straight off in the custody of the Abbott of Westminster, is an insufficiently considered piece of evidence in support of the possibility that the sequence is an addition, not a cut.

p. 258 **He cannot tell** 'Sir Gelly Meyricke 17 Feb 160[1]', quoted, Chambers, *Shakespeare*, 2. 324.

p. 259 **I am so pestered** *CSPD*, p. 502.

p. 260 **selected a story** *CSPD*, p. 449.

p. 261 **What moved him** *CSPD*, p. 404, where it is dated '? Feb 1600', but almost certainly belonging to July.

p. 262 **for treason . . . Nay Madam** *Sir Francis Bacon his Apology, in Certain Imputations concerning the late Earl of Essex* (1604, printed by Shakespeare's friend Richard Field), sig. C2r–C3r.

p. 262 **The stories mentioned** *CSPD*, p. 449, 11 July 1600.

p. 262 **he being a martial man** Examination of John Wolfe the stationer, *CSPD*, pp. 450–51, 13 July 1600.

p. 263 **great thou art** Translation from English edition of Camden's *Annals* (1630), p. 193.

p. 263 **a mere rhetorical exornation** *CSPD*, p. 452.

pp. 263–4 **was sent from the Pope . . . it appears that Essex** 'Analytical abstract', *CSPD*, pp. 454–5, tentatively dated there to 22 July 1600, but probably prepared some days later.

p. 264 **I will be king** *Tempest*, 3.2.91–2.

p. 264 **the savage and deformed slave** *The Tempest, dramatis personae*.

p. 264 **Essex's own actions** *CSPD*, p. 455.

pp. 264–5 **Hayward's history . . . might have been dramatized** This interpretation has led the distinguished historian Blair Worden to a startling new interpretation of the bespoke performance of *Richard II*. He reads Coke's statement as implying that there was a dramatization of Hayward's book, which Essex frequently attended and applauded. Having conjured up such a work, Worden proposes this play, not Shakespeare's, was the one performed at the Globe on 7 February 1601 (see his essays 'Which play was performed at the Globe Theatre on 7 February 1601?' *London Review of Books*, 10 July 2003, and 'Shakespeare in life and art: biography and *Richard II*', in *Shakespeare, Marlowe, Jonson: New Directions in Biography*, ed. Takashi Kozuka and J. R. Mulryne (2006), pp. 23–42). This argument is implausible for many reasons. Even in its own terms, it has a curious illogic. Essex's supposed presence 'at the playing' of Hayward's history leads Worden to suppose that Hayward's history was played on the afternoon of 7 February – and yet Essex wasn't present at the play that afternoon! He had nothing to do with the commissioning of the special performance from the Chamberlain's Men. It was Sir Charles Percy's idea. Besides, there is no mention of a dramatization in any of the interrogations of parties associated with Hayward's *History of Henry IV*. Nor is there any precedent for the idea of an instantly commissioned dramatization of this kind. The notion that Essex instigated a dramatization and watched it frequently, and that his followers then persuaded the Chamberlain's Men to perform it in February 1601 in no way conforms to the way in which plays were written in the period. There is no instance of the Chamberlain's Men having two different versions of the same story on the stocks at the same time. Their version of 'that play of King Richard', as manager Phillips called it, was Shakespeare's. Interestingly, much later, in 1611, the astrologer Simon Forman *did* see them (they were now the King's Men) perform a different *Richard II* play at the Globe, one that was conspicuously pro-Richard and anti-Bullingbrook. It had nothing to do with Hayward's *History*. The association of Shakespeare's play with the unfortunate events of February 1601 seems to have led his company, after the lapse of a decent period of time, to commission a new, safe *Richard II* from another dramatist. The script of this substitute Richard play does not survive, but one particular, hitherto unnoticed, detail in Forman's account of it strongly suggests that it was composed some time after 1606: 'Remember also how the Duke of Lancaster [John of Gaunt] asked a wise man whether himself should ever be king and he told him no, but his son should be a king' (Forman,

'Richard the 2 at the Globe 30 April 1611', quoted in Chambers, *Shakespeare*, 2. 339–40). The unknown author of the new Richard play has patently borrowed this detail from the weird sisters' prophecy to Banquo in *Macbeth*, which, because of its allusions to the Gunpowder Plot, can be dated with certainty to 1606. Even if we allow Worden his fancy that there was a dramatization of Hayward, in what sense could it have been 'an old play and long out of use' in February 1601 when the earliest it could have been created was after the publication of the history in February 1599? And when would Essex have found time to be 'so often present at the playing thereof'? As was seen from Wolfe's testimony, he was busy preparing his forces for Ireland: not the moment to commission a play and attend a series of performances or even semi-dramatized readings of a history book. At the end of March, he crossed the Irish Sea. After his return in September, he was placed under house arrest.

p. 265 **They had two plays** *Report on the Manuscripts of Lord de l'Isle and Dudley preserved at Penshurst Place* (6 vols, 1914–66), 2. 90.

p. 266 **historian Mervyn James** 'At a crossroads of the political culture: the Essex revolt, 1601' and 'English politics and the concept of honour, 1485–1642', in his *Society, Politics and Culture: Studies in Early Modern England* (1986), pp. 308–465.

p. 266 **thy necessity** Fulke Greville's 'Life of Sidney', in *The Prose Works of Fulke Greville, Lord Brooke*, ed. John Gouws (1986), p. 77.

p. 267 **scholars and martialists** *Calendar of State Papers Domestic 1601–1603*, p. 15.

p. 268 **chivalrous design** *Richard II*, 1.1.81.

p. 268 **Mine honour . . . High sparks** *Richard II*, 1.1.183–4, 5.6.29.

p. 269 **brave Talbot** *Pierce Penniless his Supplication to the Devil* (1592), quoted, Chambers, *Shakespeare*, 2. 188.

p. 269 **Can honour set . . . There's honour** *1 Henry IV*, 5.1.130–33, 5.2.135–6.

p. 269 **I acquainted my Lord General** Letter from Ralegh to Cecil, dated 6 July 1597.

p. 270 **the duke** *Richard II*, 5.2.8–22.

p. 271 **But now behold** *Henry V*, 5 Chorus, 22–35.

p. 272 **No man cried** *Richard II*, 5.2.29–30.

p. 273 **Meyrick was accused** Camden, *Annals*, trans. R. Norton (1630), pp. 192–3 (my italics).

p. 274 **Shakespeare's play was thought** Barroll, 'New History', p. 453.

p. 274 **Then we shall resolve** There is a good account of this meeting in G. B. Harrison's still valuable *The Life and Death of Robert Devereux Earl of Essex* (1937), pp. 280–81.

p. 276 **As for the words . . . For benevolence** 'Examination of John Hayward before Sir John Peyton and Att. Gen Coke', 22 Jan 1601, in the Tower, *CSPD*, p. 540.

p. 277 **Under the favourite term** Hayward, *The First Part of the Life and Reign of King Henry the IIII* (1599), p. 55.

p. 277 **daily new exactions** *Richard II*, 2.1.251–2.

p. 277 **The commons** *Richard II*, 2.1.248.

p. 277 **Great sums . . . upstart unthrifts** Hayward, p. 63; *Richard II*, 2.3.122.

p. 277 **This England . . . Landlord** *Richard II*, 2.1.50–60, 2.1.113.

p. 277 **The profits** Hayward, p. 55.

p. 278 **Ourself and Bushy** *Richard II*, 1.4.22–32.

p. 278 **passing through the street** Guilpin, *Skialetheia* (1598), sig. C3v.

p. 278 **Renowned Essex** Printed by J. O. Halliwell in *Poetical Miscellanies* (1845), p. 17; the poem belongs to the period of Ralegh's fall in 1603.

p. 279 **Other details in Hayward** *Richard II*, 2.4.8; 4.1.115, 128, 124; 5.6.29–44 (compare Hayward, pp. 51, 102, 109, 115, 133). The parallels were first discussed by Evelyn May Albright in her essay 'Shakespeare's *Richard II* and the Essex Conspiracy', *PMLA*, 42 (1927), pp. 686–720. She concluded from them that *Hayward influenced Shakespeare*. This argument was patently absurd, since the play was written well before the history. Albright was duly demolished by Ray Heffner, 'Shakespeare, Hayward and Essex', *PMLA*, 45 (1930), pp. 754–80. But neither Heffner nor most subsequent scholars considered the obvious counter-inference: that *Shakespeare influenced Hayward*. The obsession with Shakespeare means that scholars are nearly always more concerned with his possible sources than with his plays *as sources* – but examples of the latter are in fact exceptionally interesting as indications of the place of his plays in the culture of his time. The parallels are, however, diligently noted by *Richard II*'s Arden editors, Peter Ure (1956) and Charles Forker (2002).

p. 279 **Making this time . . . plotting to become** *CSPD*, pp. 555, 565–8.

p. 280 **an unfortunate thing** Camden, *Annals*, p. 193.

p. 281 **You shall see . . . Farewell, good** John Nichols, *The Progresses and Public Processions of Queen Elizabeth*, 3 vols (1823), 3. 552–3.

p. 282 **This was given me** *Bibliotheca Topographica Britannica* (9 vols, 1780–90), no. 42; manuscript provenance discussed in F. L. (a Lambarde?), 'Queen Elizabeth and Richard II', *Notes and Queries*, new series 7 (1913), p. 6.

p. 283 **one late letter** To a fellow Kentish Justice of the Peace, Sir John Leveson (holograph now in Staffordshire Record Office, D593/C/10/1).

p. 284 **a manuscript copy** British Library Lansdowne MS 319, ff. 47r–79v. I owe this, and a number of other valuable Lambarde references, to Carl Berkhout of the University of Arizona.

p. 288 **He sent an ambassador** The following account is indebted to Bernard Harris, 'A portrait of a Moor', in *Shakespeare and Race*, ed. Catherine M. S. Alexander and Stanley Wells (2000), pp. 23–36 (first published in *Shakespeare Survey*, 1958).

p. 288 **the eldest of them** *CSPD*, 21 Oct 1600.

p. 289 **What a marvellous** Braudel, *Le Méditerranée et le Monde Méditerranéen à l'Époque de Philippe II*, trans. Siân Reynolds, abr. Richard Ollard (1992), pp. 100–101.

p. 290 **sailing by the islands** Braudel, pp. 65–7.

p. 290 **his camp of** *2 Tamburlaine*, 1.1.21–2, 61–4, quoted from *Tamburlaine*, ed. J. W. Harper (1971).

p. 291 **an oxymoronic pairing** For the complex interplay of Christian, Muslim and Jew in the early modern Mediterranean, see Bernard Lewis, *Cultures in Conflict: Christians, Muslims and Jews in the Age of Discovery* (1995). For the process of linked demonization, A. H. and H. E. Cutler, *The Jew as Ally of the Muslim: Medieval Roots of Anti-Semitism* (1986).

p. 292 **Venice in peril** Does an oxymoronic conjunction unite opposites or highlight contradictions? See the discussions relating Othello to Leo Africanus in Emily Bartels, 'Making more of the Moor: Aaron, Othello, and Renaissance refashionings of race', *Shakespeare Quarterly*, 41 (1990), pp. 433–54, and Michael Neill, '"Mulattos", "Blacks", and "Indian Moors": *Othello* and early modern constructions of human difference', *Shakespeare Quarterly*, 49 (1998), pp. 361–74. For Bartels, a positive reading of Leo leads to a perception of Othello as an assimilated Christian: the Moor *of Venice*. But for Neill, Leo's 'amphibian' identity as both Muslim and Christian suggests a hybridity that would have been regarded as inherently monstrous: the *Moor* of Venice.

p. 293 **Valiant Othello**   *Othello*, 1.3.53–4.

p. 293 **origin implied by that name**   There may also be a more distant resonance: Othman was also an alternative spelling of Uthman, third caliph of the Islamic empire back in the seventh century. A son-in-law of the prophet Muhammad, it was under his rule that the Arabs became a naval power and extended their rule to North Africa and Cyprus. Before being assassinated, he oversaw the compilation of the authoritative version of the Koran.

p. 293 **a barbarous Moor**   *The Battle of Alcazar in Barbary*, 1594 (repr. 1907), lines 9–10, 15.

p. 293 **A horse**   *Alcazar*, line 1414.

p. 294 **And I**   *Othello*, 1.1.27–9.

p. 294 **Are we turned**   *Othello*, 2.3.152–4.

p. 295 **turn Turk**   On this, see Daniel J. Vitkus' excellent article, 'Turning Turk in *Othello*: the conversion and damnation of the Moor', *Shakespeare Quarterly*, 48 (1997), pp. 145–76, subsequently incorporated in his book, *Turning Turk: English Theater and the Multicultural Mediterranean, 1570–1630* (1999).

p. 295 **Muslim captivity**   See Nabil Matar, *Islam in Britain 1558–1685* (1998), p. 27. I am deeply indebted to this admirable study.

p. 295 **circumcisèd Turks**   *1 Tamburlaine*, 3.1.8–9.

p. 296 **goes into Mauretania**   *Othello*, 4.2.224–5.

p. 296 **Turkish invasion**   See J. H. Elliott, *Europe Divided 1559–1598* (2nd edn, 2000), pp. 122–5.

p. 296 **the whip of the Christian**   *Purchas his Pilgrimage* (1619, repr. 20 vols, 1965), 9. 278.

p. 297 **It's not the stranger**   On Lepanto and *Othello*, see Emrys Jones, '*Othello*, *Lepanto*, and the Cyprus wars', *Shakespeare Survey*, 21 (1970), pp. 47–52. For the historical context, Andrew Hess, 'The Battle of Lepanto and its place in Mediterranean history', *Past and Present*, 57 (1972), pp. 53–73. For suggestive remarks on Shakespeare's creation of 'a seemingly historical background by transforming international violence into dreamland peace', see Philip Edwards, 'Shakespeare, Ireland, Dreamland', *Irish University Review*, 28 (1998), pp. 227–39 (p. 232).

p. 297 **Matamoros**   See further, Barbara Everett, '"Spanish" Othello: the making of Shakespeare's Moor', in *Shakespeare and Race*, pp. 64–81 (first published in *Shakespeare Survey*, 1982).

p. 297 **Nay, it is true**   *Othello*, 2.1.117.

p. 298 **shortly before writing *Othello***   Since *The History of the Turks* was published in 1603, this to my mind disproves Ernst Honigmann's argument in his recent Arden edition for a 1601–02 rather than the traditional 1603–04 date for *Othello*.

p. 298 **Steering with due course**   *Othello*, 1.3.39–44.

p. 299 **So was I bid**   *Othello*, 1.3.15–16. Because Honigmann wants to argue for an early date, his Arden edition says nothing of any of this.

p. 299 **fright[ing] the isle**   *Othello*, 2.3.158–9.

p. 300 **For even out of that**   *Othello*, 2.1.262–3.

p. 302 **resemblance to Proserpina**   Ernst Honigmann, 'Secondary sources of *The Winter's Tale*', *Philological Quarterly*, 34 (1955), pp. 27–38. Cf. Jonathan Bate, *Shakespeare and Ovid* (1993), p. 232.

p. 302 **Sicily was well known**   Geoffrey Bullough, *Narrative and Dramatic Sources of Shakespeare* (8 vols, 1957–75), 8. 125.

p. 302 **removes the action**   Orgel, introduction to his edition of *The Winter's Tale* (1996), p. 37.

p. 304 **If to be Protestant**   R. J. W. Evans, *Rudolf II and his World: A Study in Intellectual History 1576–1612* (1973), p. 29.

p. 304 **interdenominational match-making**   On this, see Evans, pp. 80–83. For speculations as to Rudolf's possible influence on the figures of the Duke in *Measure for Measure* and Prospero in *The Tempest*, see Robert Grudin, 'Rudolf II of Prague and Cornelius Drebbel: Shakespearean archetypes?', *Huntington Library Quar-*

terly, 54 (1991), pp. 181–205. David Scott Kastan speculates interestingly on the Rudolfine context of *The Tempest* in his *Shakespeare after Theory* (1999), pp. 191–4.

p. 305 **story in Matteo Bandello** Possibly known to Shakespeare in the French version of Belleforest.

p. 306 **dominion of the Spanish crown** The large body of scholarship on Shakespeare's representations of Italy is highly variable in the extent to which it does or does not attach weight to the Spanish influence. For starting-points, see *Shakespeare's Italy: Functions of Italian Locations in Renaissance Drama*, ed. Michele Marrapodi et al. (1993).

p. 306 **Ferdinand – perhaps also Alonso** Though Orgel again comes closest, when he makes passing mention of the Aragonese connection in a note on how 'The search for historical figures behind the play in fact offers some possibilities that resonate tantalizingly' – *The Tempest*, ed. Stephen Orgel (1987), p. 43n.

p. 306 **renounced his state** Thus W. Thomas, *History of Italy* (1549), cited by Bullough, 8.249–50, as a book that Shakespeare probably knew.

p. 307 **The free-*Italian*** *Albion's England*, 12.75, quoted, Jeffrey Knapp, *An Empire Nowhere: England, America and Literature from 'Utopia' to 'The Tempest'* (1992), p. 334n.

p. 307 **corsair King of Algiers** For further speculation on the significance of Tunis, see Richard Wilson, 'Voyage to Tunis: new history and old world in *The Tempest*', *Journal of English Literary History*, 64 (1997), pp. 333–57. Also several valuable essays in *'The Tempest' and its Travels*, ed. Peter Hulme and William Sherman (2000).

p. 308 **a fabric of many colours** Braudel, p. 645.

p. 308 **Samuel Purchas** See Matar, *Islam in Britain*, p. 16.

p. 308 **GONZALO: This Tunis** *The Tempest*, 2.1. 68–76.

p. 309 **an English empire** On this, see e.g. Jeffrey Knapp, *An Empire Nowhere*, and especially David Armitage, 'Literature and Empire', in *The Oxford History of the British Empire Volume 1: The Origins of Empire* (1998), pp. 99–123.

p. 313 **All of the theories** Lancashire theory: see, for example, Oliver Baker, *In Shakespeare's Warwickshire and the Unknown Years* (1937) and Richard Wilson, *Times Literary Supplement*, 19 December

1997, pp. 11–13. Revival of Charlecote theory: René Weis, *Shakespeare Revealed* (2007).

p. 313 **Lawyers like**   See, for example, W. Nicholas Knight, *Shakespeare's Hidden Life: Shakespeare at the Law 1585–1595* (1973).

p. 314 **all the biographers**   Shakespeare's more thorough biographers mention this case, but few of them pursue it in any detail. The only scholars to mention the Shakespeare attorney John Harborne are, I think, Knight in *Shakespeare's Hidden Life* and Robert D. Pepper in his excellent unpublished typescript lodged in the library of the Middle Temple, 'John Shakespeare's butler: new light on the lost years'.

p. 314 **SHALLOW: Come on, come on**   *2 Henry IV*, 3.2.1–24.

p. 317 **I have been put . . . I sent Thomas . . . I took order**   *William Lambarde and Local Government*, ed. Conyers Read (1962), pp. 42–6.

p. 318 **SHALLOW: Nay, she must be old**   *2 Henry IV*, 3.2.152–4.

p. 320 **per Johannem Harborne**   The first paragraph is omitted from the transcription of the bill in Chambers, 2. 35, though printed in full in J. O. Halliwell-Phillipps, *Outlines of the Life of Shakespeare* (2 vols, 1886), 2. 11.

p. 321 **John Horbourne**   *Minutes of Parliament of the Middle Temple*, ed. C. T. Martin (4 vols, 1904), 1. 177.

p. 321 **Ordered, that the Butler**   *Minutes*, 3. 543.

p. 323 **steeped in the law**   George W. Keeton, *Shakespeare's Legal and Political Background* (1967) remains a good introduction, though stronger on the former than the latter, which is best approached via Ian Ward's excellent *Shakespeare and the Legal Imagination* (1999).

p. 324 **statutes, bonds**   Dekker, *Gull's Hornbook* (1609), pp. 26–7.

p. 324 **why may not that be**   *Hamlet*, 5.1.74–83.

p. 325 **SILENCE: Alas, a black ouzel**   *2 Henry IV*, 3.2.6–11.

p. 326 **noverints**   Nashe, preface to Robert Greene's *Menaphon* (1589).

p. 326 **These be matters**   *Two Wise Men and all the rest Fools* (1619), act one scene one, pp. 6–7.

p. 327 **I count religion**   Marlowe, *The Jew of Malta* (1633), opening of 1.1.

p. 329 **play the orator . . . add colours . . . change shapes . . . set the murderous**   *3 Henry VI*, 3.2.189–94.

p. 329 **I cannot nor I will not** *Richard III*, 3.7.206.

p. 330 **made my brother** Scene for *Sir Thomas More*, 55–6.

p. 330 **For to the king** Scene for *Sir Thomas More*, 116–18.

p. 331 **Grant them removed** Scene for *Sir Thomas More*, 87–102.

p. 332 **Methinks I could . . . If his cause . . . But if the cause** *Henry V*, 4.1.110–25.

p. 333 **And what have kings** *Henry V*, 4.1.192–206.

p. 334 **Leave out the insurrection** Manuscript annotation by Sir Edmund Tilney, on *Sir Thomas More* manuscript, now in the British Library.

p. 334 **the first thing we do** *2 Henry VI*, 4.2.57.

p. 334 **CADE: Be brave, then** *2 Henry VI*, 4.2.48–53.

p. 335 **No sovereignty** *The Tempest*, 2.1.145–6.

p. 336 **Behold a theatre** Latin preface to *Annals*, trans. Lipsius (1572). For Shakespeare and republican thought, see further Andrew Hadfield, *Shakespeare and Republicanism* (2005).

p. 337 *Love's Martyr* In their Arden edition of *Shakespeare's Poems* (2007), Katherine Duncan-Jones and Henry Woudhuysen decisively prove that Shakespeare's 'Phoenix and Turtle' poem (or poems, if the 'Threnos' at the end of it is read as an independent piece) belongs with the rest of the *Love's Martyr* volume in 1601, and was not a much earlier poem, as some scholars have supposed. They link the collection to Sir John Salusbury's political problems later in the year; I place it closer to the moment of his knighthood.

p. 338 **princes orgulous . . . I'll unarm again** *Troilus and Cressida*, prologue, 2–13; 1.1.1; 9–11.

p. 338 **the open ulcer** *Troilus and Cressida*, 1.1.48.

p. 338 **They say . . . So do** *Troilus and Cressida*, 1.2.19–20.

p. 341 **Never was a war** *Cymbeline*, 5.4.568–9.

p. 343 **dead butcher** *Macbeth*, 5.7.114.

p. 344 **it be thought unfit** See E. K. Chambers, *The Elizabethan Stage* (4 vols, 1923), 1. 328.

p. 345 **an equivocator . . . hold, hold** *Macbeth*, 2.3.6–9, 1.5.51–2.

p. 346 **a form of possession** See part 5 of Stuart Clark's magisterial *Thinking with Demons: The Idea of Witchcraft in Early Modern Europe* (1997), pp. 549–682.

p. 347 **O horror . . . Tongue nor heart** *Macbeth*, 2.3.59–60.

p. 347 **Confusion now**   *Macbeth*, 2.3.62–5.

p. 347 **Treason has done**   *Macbeth*, 3.2.26.

p. 347 **What, art mad?**   *King Lear*, 4.5.153–72.

p. 351 **policy and reverence . . . till our oldness**   *Lear*, 1.2.44–5.

p. 351 **age from folly**   *Antony and Cleopatra*, 1.3.67.

p. 352 **Dost thou think**   *Twelfth Night*, 2.3.88–9.

p. 353 **At my cousin Shakespeare**   Quoted, Chambers, *Shakespeare*, 2. 142.

p. 355 **scribbled marginal notes beside**   The copy is now in Glasgow University Library: see http://special.lib.gla.ac.uk/exhibns/month/july2001.html.

p. 356 **Players of Interludes**   Peter R. Roberts, 'The business of playing and the patronage of players at the Jacobean courts', in *James VI & I: Ideas, Authority and Government*, ed. Ralph Houlbrooke (2006), pp. 81–105.

p. 357 **I have heard**   C. Severn, *Diary of John Ward* (1939), p. 183, quoted, Chambers, *Shakespeare*, 2. 249.

p. 359 **courtier with the marks of disease**   Germaine Greer makes this point in *Shakespeare's Wife* (2007), p. 305, but – because she wants to portray Anne Shakespeare as a capable woman keeping house in Stratford alone – she does not consider the possibility of Shakespeare semi-retiring back to Warwickshire much earlier than 1611.

p. 361 **Now, to let matters**   Wotton, letter to Sir Edmund Bacon, 2 July 1613, quoted, Chambers, *Shakespeare*, 2. 343–4.

p. 365 **Item, I give**   Will of Augustine Phillips, signed 4 May, proved 16 May, 1605, in Chambers, *Shakespeare*, 2. 73–4.

p. 366 **He that plays the king**   *Hamlet*, 2.2.294–8.

p. 367 **rest of his fellows**   A typical formula reads 'To John Hemings and the rest of his fellows his Majesty's Servants the Players upon warrant for presenting before His Majesty nine several plays' (Chambers, *Shakespeare*, 2. 345).

p. 367 **of questionable date**   Dave Kathman argues powerfully for 1597–98: see his 'Reconsidering *The Seven Deadly Sins*', *Early Theatre*, 7 (2004), pp. 13–43. Andrew Gurr stands by the traditionally held much earlier date: 'The work of Elizabethan plotters and *2 The Seven Deadly Sins*', *Early Theatre*, 10 (2007), pp. 67–87. The date is immaterial to the argument about stock roles.

p. 369 **Phillips the player** E. Nungezer, *A Dictionary of Actors and other Persons associated with the Public Representation of Plays in England before 1642* (1929), p. 282.

p. 369 **What shall I say . . . A gentleman** *2 Henry IV*, 1.1.3–5, 32.

p. 369 **so wholly transforming** Richard Flecknoe, *A Short Discourse of the English Stage* (1664).

p. 370 **By a full and significant** Webster, 'The character of an excellent actor' (1615).

p. 370 **Astronomers and star-gazers** 'On the death of that great master in his art and quality, painting and playing: Richard Burbage', in Thomas Middleton, *Collected Works*, ed. Gary Taylor and John Lavagnino (2007), p. 1889.

p. 373 **let those that play** *Hamlet*, 3.2.26–7.

pp. 374–5 **I'll hold my life . . . Harry Condell . . . excellent memory . . . Gentlemen** Induction by Webster in Marston's *The Malcontent*, ed. G. K. Hunter (1975), pp. 8–16.

p. 376 **We shall have nothing . . . Few of the university** *The Second Part of the Return from Parnassus*, played at St John's College, Cambridge, Christmas 1599–1600, act 4.

p. 376 **Faith, there has been** *Hamlet*, 2.2.317–19.

p. 377 **like your physicians** Dekker, *Satiromastix, or The Untrussing of the Humorous Poet* (1602), sig. C3v.

p. 377 **The obvious interpretation** Ably argued by J. B. Leishman in the introduction to his edition of *The Three Parnassus Plays* (1949). Some scholars have rejected the obvious interpretation and proposed instead that Shakespeare's purge of Jonson came in another form. The most popular suggestions are that the character of either Malvolio in *Twelfth Night* or Ajax in *Troilus and Cressida* is intended as a jibe at Jonson, and that the 'purge' refers to the humiliation of said characters. But neither Ben Jonson nor a 'purge' is mentioned in either Shakespeare play. As far as *Twelfth Night* is concerned, it can hardly be a reply to *Poetaster* because it was written and performed before *Poetaster*: we know this for the simple reason that a character in Jonson's play says that he has seen a performance of *Twelfth Night*. The possibility that the reference is to *Troilus and Cressida* has rather more mileage (see, for example, James Bednarz, *Shakespeare and the Poets' War* (2001), pp. 35–52), but it depends on a highly inferential as opposed to a theatrically explicit identification of Ajax with Jonson. The argument in a nutshell is that the name Ajax sounds like 'a jakes', Jonson was notoriously anal, and 'beray' in *The Return from Parnassus* means 'beshit'. All this seems very tortuous in comparison with the simplicity of the *Satiromastix* explanation. We should apply the principle of Occam's razor. If a simple explanation is compatible with the evidence, there is no need to seek a complicated one. Since a purge is administered to a character representing Jonson in *Satiromastix*, there is no need to complicate our explanation of the allusion in *The Return from Parnassus*.

pp. 378–9 **God morrow . . . Come on**   *Satiromastix*, sig. B3r; *2 Henry IV*, 3.2.1–2.

p. 379 **but a remnant**   *Satiromastix*, sig. G2v.

p. 380 **my Princely sweet-William**   *Satiromastix*, sig. M2r.

p. 380 **All praiseworthy . . . sweeter verse**   Chambers, *Shakespeare*, 2. 193, 201.

p. 380 **Only amongst them**   'Apologetical Dialogue' intended for *Poetaster, or The Arraignment* (1602).

p. 380 **his participation in Dekker's play**   There is a further (outside) possibility, namely that he actually wrote the 'purge' scene for the Chamberlain's version of Dekker's play. Most of *Satiromastix* is written in prose, the medium at which Dekker excelled. Nearly all the sequences in verse are 90 per cent end-stopped. There is, however, a very curious passage of about sixty lines in the second scene, a verse interjection in an exchange that is otherwise in prose. The lines immediately before and after the passage join seamlessly together, suggesting that it may well be an interpolation. What is more, here the ratio of end-stopped to run-on lines is not 9:1, as elsewhere in the play, but 2:1. Dekker was capable of writing run-on verse, as may be seen from his best play, *The Shoemaker's Holiday*, but the sudden stylistic switch might well be a sign of a second authorial hand. The hand, perhaps, of an author who by this time in his career was composing far more run-on lines than he had in his early works. The scene in question just happens to be the one when the 'poetasters' tell Horace/Jonson that they have come as 'physicians' to 'purge' him of his satirical bile. Could it be that the anonymous author of *The Return from Parnassus* was right, and that Shakespeare helped Dekker out at this crucial point in the play? Could the sixty-line sequence, which begins with a delicious parody of Ben Jonson's lyric poetry and ends with the offer 'We come like your physicians, to purge / Your sick and dangerous mind of her disease', be a new addition to the canon of Shakespeare? The passage stands out from the rest of the play because of its conciliatory tone. Crispinus (Marston) and Demetrius Faninus (Dekker) are for once at peace with Horace (Jonson). The bargain of friendship does not, however, endure beyond this moment and at the climax of the play Jonson/Horace is brought on wearing the costume of a satyr and then publicly humiliated by being untrussed. Shakespeare was always careful to avoid giving offence. The desire to stand in the middle and not to commit himself to any cause is of a piece with his famed 'disinterestedness', his ability to see both sides of a question. It is intriguing, therefore, that the self-contained passage from *Satiromastix* reads like an attempt to mediate between the warring poets. If these lines are by any chance Shakespeare's contribution to the *poetomachia*, then it is ironic that the *Parnassus* playwright spoke of him putting Jonson down and that Jonson himself was upset by his friend's being drawn into the affair. For this is the one moment in all the 'to do', the 'controversy' and the 'cuffs in the question' when the rival poets are reconciled. As far as I am aware, the only critic to have pursued this possibility was W. Bernhardi, in an article in German published a century and a half ago – *Hamburger Litteraturblatt*, 79 (1856).

p. 382 **the weeping philosopher**   *Merchant of Venice*, 1.2.34.

p. 382 **a natural philosopher . . . the property**   *As You Like It*, 3.2. 24, 20.

p. 382 **the heathen philosopher . . . The fool doth think**   *As You Like It*, 5.1.24–6.

p. 383 **Sileni of Alcibiades**   *Adagia* (1515), 3.3.1, trans. Margaret

Mann Phillips, *Erasmus on his Times: A Shortened Version of the Adages of Erasmus* (1967), p. 77.

p. 383 **What, art mad?**   *King Lear*, 4.5.153–5.

p. 384 **I will be**   *Much Ado*, 5.1.35–9.

p. 385 **I do not always follow**   *Timon of Athens* 2.2.118–19.

p. 385 **First let me . . . Noble philosopher . . . I will keep . . . I'll talk a word**   *King Lear*, 3.4. 128–9, 148, 154, 131.

p. 385 **Crates the Cynic**   Suggested in R. A. Foakes's note to this line in his third series Arden edition of *King Lear* (1997), p. 283. The 'good Athenian' at line 176 would then be Diogenes himself.

p. 385 **These late eclipses**   *King Lear*, 1.2.83.

p. 385 **An admirable evasion**   *King Lear*, 1.2.98–9.

p. 385 **a proto-Hobbesian philosopher**   See J. F. Danby's still-valuable *Shakespeare's Doctrine of Nature* (1949).

p. 386 **Henceforth I'll bear**   *King Lear*, 4.5.88–90.

p. 386 **Men must endure**   *King Lear*, 5.2.10–12.

p. 386 **the wages of**   *King Lear*, 5.3.320–1.

p. 386 **The gods defend her**   *King Lear*, 5.3.263.

p. 386 **final speech of the play**   I regard the Folio ascription of this speech to Edgar as superior to the Quarto's to Albany, on the grounds that Edgar's stripping down in act three is an exposure to feeling, occurring in conjunction with Lear's feeling with and for the poor, which makes him the character better prepared to voice this sentiment.

p. 387 **Truly, when I consider**   'An Apology of Raymond Sebond', in *The Essays Or Moral, Politic and Millitary Discourses of Lo: Michael de Montaigne . . . First written by him in French. And now done into English*, trans. John Florio (1603), p. 280.

p. 387 **Is man no more**   *King Lear*, 3.4.86–9.

p. 387 **Let us now but consider**   'Apology of Raymond Sebond', p. 258.

p. 388 **admirable moving . . . Generation is the chiefest**   'Apology of Raymond Sebond', pp. 260, 262, 271.

p. 389 **Whatsoever we attempt**   'Apology of Raymond Sebond', p. 321.

p. 389 **If that the heavens**   *King Lear*, Quarto Passages 153–6 (*RSC Complete Works*, p. 2078).

p. 389 **The dark and vicious** *King Lear*, 5.3.184–5.

p. 389 **Oh just *Jehova*** *King Lear*, lines 1649–52, quoted from *Narrative and Dramatic Sources of Shakespeare*, ed. Bullough, 7. 377.

p. 390 **counter-Renaissance** The scholar Hiram Haydn's valuable term for the sceptical, ironical tradition of the sixteenth century: *The Counter-Renaissance* (1950).

p. 391 **For in me** Erasmus, *Moriae Encomium* (in Latin, 1509), trans. Thomas Chaloner (1549), *The Praise of Folie*, ed. Clarence H. Miller (1965), p. 10.

p. 391 **feelingly** *King Lear*, 4.5.152.

p. 391 **All this life** Chaloner, p. 38.

p. 391 **When we are born . . . What sport** *King Lear*, 4.5.181–2; Chaloner, p. 68.

p. 392 **a certain pleasant raving** Chaloner, p. 52.

p. 392 **Look, look** *King Lear*, 4.5.99–100.

p. 392 **Look on her** *King Lear*, 5.3.327–8.

p. 392 **not to be deceived** Chaloner, p. 63.

p. 392 **To thine own self** *Hamlet*, 1.3.81–3.

p. 392 **I would fain** *King Lear*, 1.4.131–2.

p. 393 **No cause** *King Lear*, 4.6.80.

p. 393 **The name** *King Lear*, 1.1.130.

p. 393 **come, unbutton here** *King Lear*, 3.4.90.

p. 393 **Pray you undo** *King Lear*, 5.3.326.

p. 393 **Didst thou give** *King Lear*, 3.4.47.

p. 393 **EDGAR: Bless thy five wits** *King Lear*, 3.7.13–15.

p. 394 **What do we** Florio's Montaigne, p. 261.

p. 395 **Morosophos** Translated by Chaloner (p. 10) as 'foolelosophers'.

p. 401 **gravity of philosophical sentences** *Seneca his Ten Tragedies* (1581), preface.

p. 401 **English Seneca** Greene's *Menaphon* (1589), preface by Nashe.

p. 401 ***Tam lentus*** *Titus Andronicus*, 4.1.84, Seneca, *Hippolytus*, 672, though probably remembered from a grammar-school extract, not the original play text. Some scholars attribute this scene to George Peele, but I am not convinced that his involvement in the play extended beyond the opening sequence.

pp. 401–2 **neither decency . . . all their plays** Sidney, *An Apology for Poetry*, ed. Geoffrey Shepherd (1973), p. 135.

p. 402 **I will do it**   *1 Henry IV*, 2.4.284.

p. 402 **full of stately speeches**   *Apology for Poetry*, p. 134.

p. 403 **exemplify the disastrous miseries**   Greville, *Life of Sidney*, chap. 14.

p. 404 **the price . . . The heart unbroken**   *Gorboduc*, in *Minor Elizabethan Tragedies*, ed. T. W. Craik (1974), 4.2.150–55, 3.1.142–6.

p. 405 **Between the acting**   *Julius Caesar*, 2.1.63–9.

p. 406 **forsaking empire**   Greville, *Life of Sidney*, chap. 14.

p. 407 **O wearisome condition**   'Chorus Sacerdotum' in *The Tragedy of Mustapha* (1609), sig. B2r.

p. 407 **What a piece of work**   *Hamlet*, 2.2.284–7.

p. 408 **We therefore commit**   'The Order for the Burial of the Dead' in *The Book of Common Prayer* (first published 1549).

p. 409 **Goodnight, sweet prince**   *Hamlet*, 5.2.308–9.

p. 409 **If it be now**   *Hamlet*, 5.2.151–2.

p. 409 **there's a divinity**   *Hamlet*, 5.2.10, 5.2.150.

p. 410 **poring upon a book**   *Hamlet* (First Quarto, 1603), sig. D4v. For the derivation of the soliloquy from Cicero, see further, T. W. Baldwin, *William Shakespere's Small Latine and Lesse Greeke*, 2. 603–7, supplemented by Ronald Knowles, 'Hamlet and counter-humanism', *Renaissance Quarterly*, 52 (1999), pp. 1046–69.

p. 410 **resembles sleep**   Cicero, trans. Dolman, *Those Five Questions* (1561), sig. G5r.

p. 410 **The undiscovered country**   *Hamlet*, 3.1.85–6.

p. 411 **CICERO saith**   Montaigne, *Essays*, trans. Florio (1603, repr. 1933), p. 48.

p. 411 **Be absolute for death . . . The Duke's oration**   *Measure for Measure*, 3.1.5–41.

p. 411 **Now of all the benefits**   *Essays*, pp. 55–6.

p. 413 **All the world's motions**   Montaigne, *Essays*, trans. Florio, p. 772.

p. 414 **Was the hope drunk**   *Macbeth*, 1.7.37–9.

p. 414 **We must not cleave**   Opening of the essay 'Of three commerces of society' (Florio trans., p. 737).

p. 415 **a mock and scoff**   Note to Acts, 17:18 (St Paul before the Areopagus), in 1599 London edition of Geneva Bible.

p. 415 **Or if this All**   Sir John Davies (not to be confused with John Davies of Hereford), *Orchestra or A Poem of Dancing* (1596), stanza 20.

p. 416 **You know that I** *Julius Caesar*, 5.1.83–5.

p. 416 **Men so disordered** *Lear*, 1.4.186–90, my italics.

p. 416 **What a damned** *Merry Wives*, 2.2.186.

p. 416 **Then fly** *Macbeth*, 5.3.7–8.

p. 416 **epicurean cooks** *Antony and Cleopatra*, 2.1.29–30.

p. 417 **Sorrow concealèd** *Titus*, 2.4.36–7.

p. 418 **For this Martius'** Plutarch, 'Life of Caius Martius Coriolanus' in *Shakespeare's Plutarch*, p. 297. The best analysis of Shakespeare's testing of the limits of Stoicism in the Roman plays is Geoffrey Miles, *Shakespeare and the Constant Romans* (1996).

p. 418 **It is held / That valour** *Coriolanus*, 2.2.75–9.

p. 419 **in hunger for bread** *Coriolanus*, 1.1.16.

p. 419 **But let it come** *Coriolanus*, 5.3.201.

pp. 419–20 **an Egyptian Queen** Cockeram, *English Dictionary* (1623), s.v. Cleopatra.

p. 420 **exceeded all men** Thomas Elyot, *Dictionary* (1538), s.v. Salomon.

p. 420 **Nay, but . . . The nobleness . . . These strong** *Antony and Cleopatra*, 1.1.1–2, 1.1.38–9, 1.2.110–11.

p. 420 **find[s] out new heaven** *Antony and Cleopatra*, 1.1.17.

p. 421 **Take but good note** *Antony and Cleopatra*, 1.1.11–13.

p. 421 **No grave . . . she would catch . . . fire and air . . . A lass** *Antony and Cleopatra*, 5.2.410–11, 396–7, 325, 356.

p. 421 **the god Hercules** *Antony and Cleopatra*, 4.3.21–2.

p. 421 **sword . . . tires** *Antony and Cleopatra*, 2.5.25–6.

p. 422 **O happy horse** *Antony and Cleopatra*, 1.5.26.

p. 422 **Can Fulvia die?** *Antony and Cleopatra*, 1.3.68.

p. 423 **Though with their high wrongs** *Tempest*, 5.1.29–36.

p. 424 **He that through a natural** Montaigne, *Essays*, trans. Florio (1603, repr. 1933), book 2, chap. 11, pp. 371–2.

p. 425 **virtue that Prospero has to learn** The importance of the essay 'Of cruelty' to *The Tempest* has been generally neglected by critics, in contrast to the much-studied links with 'Of the cannibals'. A notable exception is Arthur Kirsch, 'Virtue, vice, and compassion in Montaigne and *The Tempest*', *Studies in English Literature*, 37 (1997), pp. 337–52.

p. 425 **without them, men would inter-devour** 'Apology of Raymond Sebond', p. 503.

p. 425 **Epicurus doth not only** 'Of the resemblance between children and fathers', p. 683.

p. 425 **we open the matter** 'Of experience', p. 965.

p. 425 **HIDE THY LIFE** 'Of glory', p. 561.

p. 425 **O, you heavenly** *Two Noble Kinsmen*, 5.4.147–53.

p. 426 **The weight of this sad time** *King Lear*, 5.3.344. As noted earlier, even here there is a critique of the neo-Roman code: Stoicism demands a speaking of 'what we ought to say', whereas Edgar says 'Speak what we feel.'

p. 427 **Shakespeare, Drayton** John Ward, quoted, Chambers, *Shakespeare*, 2. 250.

pp. 428–9 **An actor's art . . . the drooping stage** See edited texts of First Folio commendatory poems in *RSC Complete Works*, pp. 61–2.

p. 430 **the highest and chiefest** Borrowed by Florio from the definition of '*mens*' in Thomas Thomas' Latin dictionary, *Dictionarium Linguae Latinae et Anglicanae* (1587).

p. 430 **pleasant wittiness in words** Florio's definition of Italian '*sale*' (salt or seasoning). Subsequent definitions also Florio's.

p. 430 **warbling his native** Milton's poem 'L'Allegro' ('The happy man', 1631).

p. 437 **a 'literary dramatist'** My account of this whole question has been much stimulated by Lukas Erne's important revisionist study, *Shakespeare as Literary Dramatist* (2003).

p. 438 **tongue-tied maidens . . . sisters . . . some gallèd goose** *Troilus and Cressida*, 3.2.179, 5.11.49, 52.

p. 440 **copy of Florio's . . . Montaigne** Huntington Library pressmark 60466.

p. 441 **Meisei University** Quotations from Akihiro Yamada, *The First Folio of Shakespeare: A Transcript of Contemporary Marginalia* (1998).

p. 445 **a Comedy of Errors** *Gesta Grayorum* (printed 1688, from a manuscript of the 1590s), quoted, Chambers, *Shakespeare*, 2. 320.

p. 445 **At our feast** Chambers, *Shakespeare*, 2. 327–8.

p. 446 **Triumph, my Britain** 'To the memory of my beloved, the author Mr William Shakespeare', *RSC Complete Works*, p. 61.

p. 448 *To my good friends* Spelling modernized; manuscript now in the National Library of Wales, Aberystwyth, first published by Sir Israel Gollancz in *Times Literary Supplement*, 26 June 1922.

Index

Note: Page numbers in *italic* refer to illustrations